The Critics of
KEYNESIAN
ECONOMICS

*Edited with an
Introduction and new Preface
by*
HENRY HAZLITT

The Foundation for Economic Education, Inc.
Irvington-on-Hudson, New York 10533

About the Editor and Publisher

Henry Hazlitt (1894–1993) began his distinguished career in 1913 at *The Wall Street Journal*. He went on to write for several newspapers, including *The New York Evening Post, The New York Evening Mail, The New York Herald*, and *The Sun*. In the early 1930s he was literary editor of *The Nation*, and succeeded H. L. Mencken as editor of the *American Mercury* in 1933. From 1934 to 1946 he served on the editorial staff of *The New York Times*. While at *The Times*, he wrote a series of courageous editorials opposing the trend toward radical intervention by all levels of government. From 1946 to 1966 he was the "Business Tides"columnist for *Newsweek*.

Mr. Hazlitt will be remembered as an eloquent writer, an incisive economic thinker, and a tireless defender of freedom. His best known book was *Economics in One Lesson*, which has sold more than one million copies since its first publication in 1946. He wrote or edited seventeen other books, including *The Failure of the "New Economics"* (1959) and *The Foundations of Morality* (1964). He was a Founding Trustee of The Foundation for Economic Education.

The Foundation for Economic Education (FEE), established in 1946 by Leonard E. Read (1898–1983), is the oldest economic research organization dedicated to the preservation of individual freedom and the private property order. Its goal is to study the moral and intellectual foundation of a free society and share its knowledge with individuals everywhere. It avoids political controversies. FEE is a purely educational organization, publishing and sponsoring seminars and lectures devoted to the limited government, private property principles it espouses. In addition to books, its principal publication is the monthly journal, *The Freeman*.

©1995 The Foundation for Economic Education, Inc.
Originally published 1960 by D. Van Nostrand Company, Inc.

ISBN 1-57246-013-X
(Previously ISBN 0-87000-401)

For further information, contact
The Foundation for Economic Education
30 South Broadway
Irvington-on-Hudson, New York 10533
Telephone (914) 591-7230
Fax (914) 591-8910

PRINTED IN THE UNITED STATES OF AMERICA

Foreword

Nearly twenty years ago, in his 1977 Preface to the Second Edition, Henry Hazlitt joyfully reported that prevailing academic opinion had changed and that Keynesian doctrines no longer went unchallenged. But he also observed that "the vast majority of politicians and governments today are persistently applying the Keynesian remedies, even though they do not know that they are Keynesians."

These words could have been written in 1995, two years after his journey's end. Although the many limitations, defects, errors, and shortcomings of the Keynesian system have become apparent, its basic principles are still with us. Most academic economists continue to use the aggregative approach and to dwell on the macro factors that influence, and which are influenced by, the whole economy. To them, national income, national growth, levels of employment, savings, consumption, and fiscal policy are more important than the pricing of goods and services. Now, though, in contrast to their colleagues of the 1950s and '60s, contemporary Keynesians no longer show any great missionary zeal for their cause. They humbly admit that they know precious little about the forces affecting economic events. After all, the mass unemployment which they meant to alleviate is still with us—and even tends to grow worse whenever they apply their Keynesian antidotes. It continues to plague most industrial countries despite the fact that their governments continue to cling to a policy of keeping expenditures at high levels and spend freely without fear of mounting deficits. Even the Keynesians now wonder how long this process can continue.

Henry Hazlitt clearly foresaw the calamity. He saw that "in the foreseeable future it [deficit spending] seems more likely to accelerate than to come to a stop." In the 1980s and '90s his fears were confirmed when, in most of the world's industrial countries, soaring budget deficits depleted national savings as never before while government debt soared from some 40 percent of GDP in 1980 to more than 70 percent in 1994. Savings and investments declined spectacularly—especially in Canada, Great Britain, Sweden, Australia, and the United States—bringing economic stagnation and falling standards of living. Throughout the world the Keynesian legacy painfully manifested itself in the form of frequent borrowing binges to finance both public and private consumption.

Mr. Hazlitt summed it all up in a few terse words which may be quoted for as long as the world remembers the Keynesian cult. "In spite of the incredible reputation of the *General Theory*, I could not find in it a single important doctrine that was both true and original. What is original in the book is not true, and what is true is not original. In fact, even most of the major errors in the book are not original, but can be found in a score of previous writers."

Having challenged every major Keynesian tenet in his 1959 volume, *The Failure of the "New Economics,"* and having thoroughly exploded its fallacies, Mr. Hazlitt added authoritative confutation by gathering some two dozen important critiques by eminent economists and publishing them in this volume. Out of isolated essays and journal articles he created an impressive and many-sided criticism of the Keynesian structure. He fashioned this companion volume which records the voices of its prominent critics.

HANS F. SENNHOLZ

PREFACE TO THE SECOND EDITION

The present anthology was first published in 1960. As I point out in the first two pages of my original Introduction, it was a sort of byproduct of my book, *The Failure of the "New Economics": An Analysis of the Keynesian Fallacies* (1959). *Critics* went through several printings, but has been out of print since 1973.

In the seventeen years since my anthology's original appearance, there has been a profound change in the academic reputation of Keynes's *General Theory*. It is no longer accepted as the new gospel. Professors of economics can openly declare themselves to be non-Keynesians and even anti-Keynesians, and still be treated with respect. In the serious press, the revolt has gone even further. Economic papers from the London *Economist* to *The Wall Street Journal* have published articles declaring that "Keynes Is Dead."

Both as cause and result of this change of thought, over these seventeen years hundreds of articles have appeared pro and con on Keynesianism. And some of the criticisms have been first-rate. One or two authors already included in my earlier compilation, like Professors F. A. Hayek and W. H. Hutt, have themselves made additional contributions. Obviously if I were to compile a non-Keynesian anthology afresh, of the same length as the original one, and including articles or excerpts published since 1960 as well as previous to it, I would have to omit several already there to make room for new ones.

But my compilation would lose as well as gain something. It is true that in 1960 critics of the Keynesian nostrums could point to only twenty-four years of experience with their application; now they can examine more than forty. As a result they have discovered a formidable statistical case against the central Keynesian contention that deficit spending or monetary inflation eliminates or even substantially reduces unemployment. But owing to the multitude of conflicting factors at work in any economy, statistics by themselves can seldom prove any conclusion incontestably; they can at best raise a strong presumption. Our final reliance must be on analysis and deductive reasoning. And though the literature since 1960 has added admirable examples of these, I can think of no major valid criticism of Keynesian doctrine that had not already been put forward prior to 1960.

On the other hand, it would be a profound mistake to conclude that criticism of Keynesian doctrine has already done its work, and that there is no reason to restate, republish, or add to it. It is true that the prevailing drift of academic opinion has changed, and that Keynesian doctrine no longer goes unchallenged. But there are still plenty of Keynesian and other inflationists in the academic community, and they are among its most articulate, publicized and prolific members.

Most ominous of all, the vast majority of politicians and governments today are persistently applying the Keynesian remedies, even though they do not know that they are Keynesians. It is no mere coincidence that as I write these lines, the official estimate of the federal deficit in the current fiscal year—1977—is by far the highest in our history; yet there is overwhelming agreement in Congress and the Administration that this is not nearly enough to reduce current unemployment, and that the federal government must "stimulate" the economy by piling on still more billions of expenditures and cutting taxes. It is no mere coincidence, either, that for the first time in history practically every nation is on a paper basis and every nation is inflating.

The world is verifying what Keynes himself wrote with uncanny clairvoyance in the last paragraph of his *General Theory*: "Practical men, who believe themselves to be quite exempt from any intellectual influences, are usually the slaves of some defunct economist"—now ironically himself—"and the ideas which civil servants and politicians and even agitators apply to current events are not likely to be the newest."

HENRY HAZLITT

April, 1977

ACKNOWLEDGMENTS

I wish to express thanks to publishers of the following for permission to reprint the essays, articles, or excerpts in the anthology:

Quarterly Journal of Economics, vol. 51, 1936-1937; and May 1947.

The Canadian Journal of Economics and Political Science (Toronto), February, 1937.

Revue d'Économie Politique, November-December, 1937.

The Pure Theory of Capital, by F. A. Hayek, American edition, University of Chicago Press, 1941.

The Constitution of Liberty, by F. A. Hayek, University of Chicago Press, 1960.

Econometrica, January, 1944.

Financing American Prosperity, Twentieth Century Fund, 1945.

Commercial and Financial Chronicle (New York), February 8 and 15, 1945.

Harvard Business Review, Summer Issue, 1945.

American Affairs, July, 1946.

The American Economic Review, May, 1948.

The Economics of Illusion, The Squier Publishing Company, distributed by the New York Institute of Finance.

Plain Talk, March, 1948.

The Freeman, October 30, 1950.

Empire Trust Letter, January 1 and February 1, 1950.

Pamphlet, The American Enterprise Association, January, 1952.

The South African Journal of Economics, March, 1954.

The Frontiers of Economic Knowledge, National Bureau of Economic Research, 1954.

The Dollar Dilemma: Perpetual Aid to Europe, by Melchior Palyi, Henry Regnery Co., 1954.

Science, November 21, 1958.

Part of my introduction appeared as an article in *National Review* of November 7, 1959.

H.H.

TABLE OF CONTENTS

I. Introduction [1]

In the course of writing my book, *The Failure of the "New Economics": An Analysis of the Keynesian Fallacies,* I naturally read a good deal not only of the works of Keynes and the Keynesians but of the writers who had criticized Keynes's major theories, particularly the doctrines found in his *General Theory of Employment, Interest and Money.* In only one or two instances, such as Arthur Marget's two formidable volumes on *The Theory of Prices* (1938 and 1942) and L. Albert Hahn's *The Economics of Illusion* (1949), did I find critiques that attempted any full-length or systematic analysis. It was precisely the lack of any thorough chapter-by-chapter or theorem-by-theorem critique, in fact, to offset the immense laudatory literature, that led me to write my own book in an effort to fill this need.

But I did find a refreshing number of instructive and sometimes brilliant short discussions of the *General Theory* or of some of its leading tenets. These discussions were, however, either widely scattered in learned journals, the back numbers of which are available only with difficulty, or consisted of single chapters or a few pages in sometimes lengthy books. It seemed to me that it would not only be serviceable to make these available in permanent book form, but that if assembled within two covers they would complement and reinforce one another, and would have considerably more impact when collected than they had had or could have when published separately, for different audiences, over a wide range of years. This seems even more

1 Part of this Introduction appeared in *National Review*, November 7, 1959, and is reproduced here with its permission.

1

probable when one considers that the political or academic receptivity to any criticism of Keynes was extremely low in the first decade or more after the appearance of the *General Theory*, and that what then seemed to many readers a mere "lack of hospitality to new ideas" might now be recognized as an independence of mind that refused to be swept along by mere intellectual fashion.

The following selections are arranged chronologically, in the order of their appearance, or approximately so. It has seemed to me that this order not only does most justice to the individual contributions, giving credit to those who may have anticipated a particular observation or criticism later made by others, but is likely to be most helpful to the reader, curious to know which weaknesses in the *General Theory* were obvious to the first reviewers and which, if any, were not apparent until later analysis.

It is for this reason that I have included two selections— those from Jean Baptiste Say and John Stuart Mill—that long antedated the *General Theory* itself. The truth of the basic propositions of the *General Theory* rests (on the contention or admission of most Keynesians) on the truth of Keynes's "refutation" of Say's Law. But when we turn to the original statement of this law in the words of the economist after whom it is named, and to its elaboration by the classical economist who argued it most fully, we find that these statements in themselves, particularly the one by Mill, anticipated the objections of Keynes and constituted a refutation of them in advance. I have also included these two "classical" statements because they are today otherwise accessible only with great difficulty.

Each of the selections in the present volume is preceded by a note identifying the author or calling attention to some special aspect of his contribution.

Not the least important function which the present symposium is designed to serve is to make available to the reader a short summary of the theme of Keynes's *General Theory* as well as a short summary of the chief objections to it. In fact, at least half a dozen of the articles included each do that individually. This of course involves some repetition, although each article or extract selects different doctrines for discussion or emphasis and emphasizes different criticisms. But any reader who has not time to read the whole volume will be able to make his own selection, as will the instructor to make his own recommendations or assignments to students.

Having been led, myself, by a desire for fullness and thoroughness, into writing an analysis that ran to 450 pages, I feel that it would be useful if I also offered here a short restatement of a few of my leading criticisms. The argument for each of them, of course, must either be violently condensed or omitted altogether.

I do not think we can point to any one "central" fallacy in Keynes upon which all the others depend, or of which they are all corollaries. The book is not that logical or consistent. It is a succession, rather, of a whole series of major fallacies that are intended to support each other.

But perhaps it is best to begin with a statement of what can *not* be found in the *General Theory*. In spite of the incredible reputation of the book, I could not find in it a single important doctrine that was both true and original. What is original in the book is not true; and what is true is not original. In fact, even most of the major errors in the book are not original, but can be found in a score of previous writers.

On the negative side, the book seems mainly designed to prove that excessive money wage rates are *not* the major cause (or even *a* cause) of unemployment, and that reductions of such money wage rates to marginal-productivity levels will not restore employment. In denying this proposition, it may be pointed out, Keynes is denying what is perhaps the most solidly established of all economic doctrines—to wit, that if any commodity or service is overpriced, some of that commodity will remain unused or unsold: supply will exceed demand; whereas if it is under-priced, a "shortage" will develop: demand will exceed supply.

Yet it is hard to find any place in the *General Theory* where the argument against this proposition is clearly and directly stated. Keynes seems to admit it freely enough when it is applied to commodities; but he makes "labor" an exception. (He even, on occasion, lefthandedly admits it about labor itself, as on pages 264 and 265.) But Keynes's argument on this point is usually obscure and oblique, and seems constantly to shift.

One form of his argument is that the labor unions just won't accept a cut in money wages, and therefore something else must be done. This something else is monetary inflation, which will raise prices. Keynes contends, in other words, that labor unions will not accept a cut in money wage rates but will accept a cut in "real" wage rates. This factual contention, even if it may once have contained a germ of truth, has long been outdated. The major American labor unions today all have their "economists" and "directors of research" who are keenly aware of index numbers of consumer prices and insist that wage rates must at least keep pace with these. But even if this were not so, Keynes's contention would be irrelevant to the "orthodox" doctrine that wage rates in excess of the "equilibrium" point (i.e., of the marginal productivity of labor) will cause unemployment. In fact, Keynes's argument tacitly admits that at least *real* wage rates must be at equilibrium levels if "full employment" is to be achieved.

It is impossible to make sense of the specific arguments that Keynes puts forward to deny the "classical" doctrine. He contends that, if any adjustment were made of wage rates to prices, it would have to be a uniform, *en bloc* adjustment, "a simultaneous and equal reduction in all industries," such as is possible only in a totalitarian economy, or it could not work; and even if it did it would be terribly "unjust." This assumes, of course, that the *previous* interrelationship of wages and prices must have been precisely what it ought to have been! Keynes even puts forward the hysterical argument that if money wage rates were once lowered to adjust them to lower prices and demand, they might "fall without limit."

One of the sources of Keynes's errors on this subject is his failure to distinguish, most of the time, between (weekly, daily, or hourly) wage *rates* and *total wage payments,* (i.e., total payrolls or total wage income). This is because he habitually uses the ambiguous word "wages" to describe either or both. This in turn leads him tacitly to assume that a reduction in wage rates means a corresponding reduction in wage *income,* and hence "reduces purchasing power" and "effective demand" and leads to a descending spiral without limit. But the "classical" contention is simply that those wage rates that are above the equilibrium level should be reduced to that level in order to restore employment and to *increase* and *maximize* the *aggregate* of wages paid.

Another repeated fallacy of Keynes in his discussion of wages is his constant reference to something he calls "an equilibrium with unemployment." But this is simply a misuse of the term "equilibrium." What Keynes is really discussing is a *frozen* situation, a frozen *dis*equilibrium with unemployment. An "equilibrium with less than full employment" is a contradiction in terms.

Keynes tries to refute Say's Law. All Keynesians think that he did so; and many of them think that this was his "greatest achievement" and his chief "title to fame." Say's Law (originally put forward by Jean Baptiste Say, 1767-1832) may be most briefly described as the doctrine that supply creates its own demand. But as elaborated by the classical economists—Ricardo, James Mill, and John Stuart Mill—this was stated merely as an ultimate truth, true only under what today would be called conditions of equilibrium. It was designed to point out chiefly that a *general* overproduction of *all* commodities is not possible. It was never anything so foolish as a contention that money is never hoarded or that depressions are impossible. Keynes "refuted" Say's Law only in a sense in which no serious economist ever maintained it.

Keynes is hailed by his admirers almost as if he alone had discovered the important role of "expectations" in economics. The truth is that he did not sufficiently recognize that role. He saw that expectations affected current output and employment, but seemed to forget that they are also embodied in every current price, interest rate, and wage rate. It is partly because he underrated the central importance of expectations that he denounced "liquidity preference" and "speculation." He failed to see that speculative anticipations and risks are necessarily involved in all economic activity, and that somebody must bear these risks.

Keynes's discussion of the relation of "savings" and "investment" is too confused to be summarized. He alternated constantly between two mutually contradictory contentions: (1) that saving and investment are "necessarily equal" and "merely different aspects of the same thing," and (2) that saving and investment are "two essentially different activities" without even a "nexus," so that saving not only *can* exceed investment but *chronically* tends to do so, and hence brings on deflation.

What we can accurately say about this relationship depends partly, of course, on the particular definitions we choose to give each of these terms. But, assuming the appropriate definitions, I should contend that, under the assumptions of a constant money supply, saving and investment are necessarily at all times equal. When investment exceeds *prior* genuine saving, it is because new money and bank credit have been created. When ordinary saving exceeds *subsequent* investment, it is because the money supply has meanwhile contracted. In other words, it is not, generally speaking, an excess of saving over subsequent investment that *causes* deflation, but deflation that causes the deficiency in subsequent investment. An excess of saving over (subsequent) investment is but another way of describing deflation, and an excess of investment over (prior) saving is but another way of describing inflation—or of saying that it has meanwhile occurred.

Keynes's disparagement of saving in the *General Theory* was not new with him. He had deplored or ridiculed saving for the whole of his writing life, beginning with *The Economic Consequences of the Peace* in 1920. The disparagement came from his failure to understand the nature and function of saving. "Economic growth," higher real wages and living standards, are possible only through new capital formation. And production and saving are both indispensable to the formation of capital.

This is what Keynes tended constantly to overlook. He persistently regarded saving as something merely negative, a mere non-spending, forgetting that it was the inescapable first half of the completed positive act of investment. He could have learned this if he had ever seriously studied Böhm-Bawerk, who had pointed out a generation earlier that: "To complete the act of forming capital it is of course necessary to complement the negative factor of saving with the positive factor of devoting the thing saved to a productive service. . . . [But] saving is an indispensable condition to the formation of capital." And the rate of true "economic growth" is in effect the rate of capital formation.

What Keynes failed to recognize was that, normally, to save is to spend: but to spend on capital goods rather than on consumer goods. And even if, in abnormal conditions, saving takes merely the form of monetary hoarding, it does not lead to unemployment, as Keynes supposed, *unless wages (or prices) are inflexible in the downward direction.* Otherwise, the result would be merely the continuance of the same volume of output and employment at lower prices and wages.

But Keynes had no adequate theory of either capital or interest. He seemed in this field to get everything upside down. He thought that interest was a purely monetary phenomenon, the "reward" that had to be offered to the holders of money to induce them to "part" with their "liquidity." Years before Keynes announced this doctrine it was already very old, and Ludwig von Mises had rightly dismissed it (as early as 1912) as a view of "insurpassable naïveté."

Keynes's theory of interest was, indeed, what Irving Fisher, and before him Böhm-Bawerk, had labeled the Exploitation Theory—the theory that to take interest is, necessarily and always, to take advantage of the debtor; the theory that there ought not to be any interest at all. One form of this theory was developed by the socialists of the Nineteenth Century, notably Proudhon, Rodbertus, and Marx, but in its most naïve form it goes back to the Middle Ages, and, indeed, to Ancient Rome.

It is hardly necessary to add that, as a result of all these theoretical misconceptions, all Keynes's recommendations for practical policy were unsound. He wanted government control and direction of investment—a proposal which, if taken seriously, would lead to full socialism and a totalitarian state. His ideas of creating employment by budget deficits and continuous cheap money policies—i.e., by continuous inflation—got a thorough tryout in both Great Britain and the United States. In Britain they were dramatically and successfully repudiated in 1957, when the Bank of England discount rate was raised to 7 per cent. In the United States they failed miserably, in the entire period from 1930 to 1940, to achieve the goal of eliminating mass unemployment.

But here the Keynesian philosophy remains dominant. Keynesian policies are still the policies of most of our politicians and bureaucrats. At the first sign of recession, they begin to demand increased "public works," increased government spending—whatever will create deficits that in turn will lead to the creation of more paper money. If there is unemployment in any line, or in many, no politician is ever heard to suggest that it might be because wage rates have been forced up too high in those lines and ought to be reduced to levels that would encourage reemployment. The demand is solely that the government spend still more to create more jobs. This demand is, in effect, a demand for more inflation. At every emergence of unemployment, a functioning relationship is to be restored between wages and prices, not by readjusting downward the wage rates of relatively small groups of workers, but by pushing up still further the prices that must be paid by everybody. As Jacob Viner succinctly predicted in a review in 1936, when 'the *General Theory* appeared, Keynes's prescription would lead to "a constant race between the printing press and the business agents of the trade unions." That race has been going on for two decades. It is still going on. And in the foreseeable future it seems more likely to accelerate than to come to a stop.

Behind the triumph of the Keynesian philosophy and nostrums lies an intellectual mystery. How did it happen that a book so full of obscurities, contradictions, confusions, and misstatements was hailed as one of the great works of the Twentieth Century, and its author as a master economist? Perhaps no complete answer is possible; but it is not difficult to point to some of the elements in such an answer.

The Keynesian philosophy seemed to supply a new and more sophisticated rationale, not only for the traditional contention of labor leaders that money wage rates should constantly be raised and under no circumstances reduced, but for the immemorial political recourse of monetary inflation.

But other factors were no less important. Keynes's reputation as a great economist rested from the beginning on his purely *literary* brilliance. Surely a man who could write (in 1919) that Lloyd George found to his horror that "it was harder to de-bamboozle this old Presbyterian [Wilson] than it had been to bamboozle him" must be a very clever dog. If he ridiculed the stodgy old orthodox economists it must be he who was right. Literary men judge specialists by their literary qualities; and among these grace and wit rank higher than rigorous reasoning or a thorough and accurate knowledge of subject matter.

Yet even this hardly seems to apply to the *General Theory*, which with the exception of a few passages is one of the most obscure, awkward, and circumlocutory economic books ever written. But here another element enters. Just as with some of the works of Hegel and Marx, the very mystification added to the book's prestige. Unintelligibility was assumed to be a mark of profundity. One secret of the success of the *General Theory* was its technique of obscure arguments followed by clear and triumphant conclusions.

But there was probably an even more important factor. Keynes had announced in his preface that the composition of the *General Theory* had been "a long struggle of escape . . . from habitual modes of thought and expression." He tauntingly predicted that "those who are strongly wedded to what I shall call 'the classical theory' will fluctuate . . . between a belief that I am quite wrong and a belief that I am saying nothing new." This undoubtedly intimidated many economists, whose greatest dread was to be regarded as "orthodox" and "wedded" to old ideas. As Frank H. Knight put it: "Our civilization today, being essentially romantic, loves and extols heretics quite as much as its direct antecedent a few centuries back hated and feared them. The demand for heresy is always in excess of the supply and its production is always a prosperous business." And the irony was that this heresy in turn became the intellectual fashion, which academic economists could ignore only at the cost of being themselves ignored, or challenge only at the cost of losing status.

But whatever the full explanation of the Keynesian cult, its existence is one of the great intellectual scandals of our age.

HENRY HAZLITT

II

Jean Baptiste Say, the originator of "Say's Law" that supply creates its own demand, was born at Lyons, France, in 1767. He published his principal work, *Traité d'Économie Politique,* in 1803. The last edition which appeared during his lifetime was the fifth, in 1826. The excerpt which follows, containing the statement of "Say's Law," is the whole of Chapter XV of an English translation made from the fourth French edition. It is taken from the fifth American edition of *A Treatise on Political Economy* published in Philadelphia in 1832, the year of Say's death.

Since Keynes attacks Say's Law, and bases his *General Theory* on the explicit assumption that Say's Law is untrue, it seems only fair to present the law in its original formulation by the author whose name it bears. It is also desirable to do so because that formulation has been accessible only with great difficulty. Few economists who have ventured to refute the law in recent years, in fact, reveal any acquaintance with it in its original form.

It will be observed that Say's Law was itself intended as an answer to pre-existing "Keynesian" fallacies. "The encouragement of mere consumption," Say points out, "is no benefit to commerce." "It is the aim of good government to stimulate production, of bad government to encourage consumption."

Say's statement of his law is, of course, incomplete. Although he does consider the effects of tariffs and monopolies, he does not consider those of a monetary deflation or an anticipated fall of price, or of government price-fixing, or of the inflexibility in a downward direction of prices or wages, as a result of custom or monopoly. But when we add

11

the proper qualifications, especially with the aid of the modern concepts of equilibrium and disequilibrium, Say's Law remains both valid and important.

OF THE DEMAND OR MARKET
FOR PRODUCTS

JEAN BAPTISTE SAY

It is common to hear adventurers in the different channels of industry assert, that their difficulty lies not in the production, but in the disposal of commodities; that products would always be abundant, if there were but a ready demand, or market for them. When the demand for their commodities is slow, difficult, and productive of little advantage, they pronounce money to be scarce; the grand object of their desire is, a consumption brisk enough to quicken sales and keep up prices. But ask them what peculiar causes and circumstances facilitate the demand for their products, and you will soon perceive that most of them have extremely vague notions of these matters; that their observation of facts is imperfect, and their explanation still more so; that they treat doubtful points as matter of certainty, often pray for what is directly opposite to their interests, and importunately solicit from authority a protection of the most mischievous tendency.

To enable us to form clear and correct practical notions in regard to markets for the products of industry, we must carefully analyse the best established and most certain facts, and apply to them the inferences we have already deduced from a similar way of proceeding; and thus perhaps we may arrive at new and important truths, that may serve to enlighten the views of the agents of industry, and to give confidence to the measures of governments anxious to afford them encouragement.

A man who applies his labour to the investing of objects with value by the creation of utility of some sort, can not expect such a value to be appreciated and paid for, unless where other men have the means of purchasing it. Now, of what do these means consist? Of other values of other products, likewise the fruits of industry, capital, and land. Which leads us to a conclusion that may at first sight appear paradoxical, namely, that it is production which opens a demand for products.

Should a tradesman say, "I do not want other products for my woollens, I want money," there could be little difficulty in convincing him that his customers could not pay him in money, without having first procured it by the sale of some other commodities of their own. "Yonder farmer," he may be told, "will buy your woollens, if his crops be good, and will buy more or less according to their abundance or scantiness; he can buy none at all, if his crops fail altogether. Neither can you buy his wool nor his corn yourself, unless you contrive to get woollens or some other article to buy withal. You say, you only want money; I say, you want other commodities, and not money. For what, in point of fact, do you want the money? Is it not for the purchase of raw materials or stock for your trade, or victuals for your support? [1] Wherefore, it is products that you want, and not money. The silver coin you will have received on the sale of your own products, and given in the purchase of those of other people, will the next moment execute the same office between other contracting parties, and so from one to another to infinity; just as a public vehicle successively transports objects one after another. If you can not find a ready sale for your commodity, will you say, it is merely for want of a vehicle to transport it? For, after all, money is but the agent of the transfer of values. Its whole utility has consisted in conveying to your hands the value of the commodities, which your customer has sold, for the purpose of buying again from you; and the very next purchase you make, it will again convey to a third person the value of the products you may have sold to others. So that you will have bought, and every body must buy, the objects of want or desire, each with the value of his respective products transformed into money for the moment only. Otherwise, how could it be possible that there should now be bought and sold in France five or six times as many commodities, as in the miser-

---

[1] Even when money is obtained with a view to hoard or bury it, the ultimate object is always to employ it in a purchase of some kind. The heir of the lucky finder uses it in that way, if the miser do not; for money, as money, has no other use than to buy with.

able reign of Charles VI.? Is it not obvious, that five or six times as many commodities must have been produced, and that they must have served to purchase one or the other?"

Thus, to say that sales are dull, owing to the scarcity of money, is to mistake the means for the cause; an error that proceeds from the circumstance, that almost all produce is in the first instance exchanged for money, before it is ultimately converted into other produce: and the commodity, which recurs so repeatedly in use, appears to vulgar apprehensions the most important of commodities, and the end and object of all transactions, whereas it is only the medium. Sales cannot be said to be dull because money is scarce, but because other products are so. There is always money enough to conduct the circulation and mutual interchange of other values, when those values really exist. Should the increase of traffic require more money to facilitate it, the want is easily supplied, and is a strong indication of prosperity—a proof that a great abundance of values has been created, which it is wished to exchange for other values. In such cases, merchants know well enough how to find substitutes for the product serving as the medium of exchange or money: [2] and money itself soon pours in, for this reason, that all produce naturally gravitates to that place where it is most in demand. It is a good sign when the business is too great for the money; just in the same way as it is a good sign when the goods are too plentiful for the warehouses.

When a superabundant article can find no vent, the scarcity of money has so little to do with the obstruction of its sale, that the sellers would gladly receive its value in goods for their own consumption at the current price of the day: they would not ask for money, or have any occasion for that product, since the only use they could make of it would be to convert it forthwith into articles of their own consumption.[3]

[2] By bills at sight, or after date, bank-notes, running-credits, write-offs, &c. as at London and Amsterdam.

[3] I speak here of their aggregate consumption, whether unproductive and designed to satisfy the personal wants of themselves and their families, or expended in the sustenance of reproductive industry. The woollen or cotton manufacturer operates a two-fold consumption of wool and cotton: 1. For his personal wear. 2. For the supply of his manufacture; but, be the purpose of his consumption what it may, whether personal gratification or reproduction, he must needs buy what he consumes with what he produces.

This observation is applicable to all cases, where there is a supply of commodities or of services in the market. They will universally find the most extensive demand in those places, where the most of values are produced; because in no other places are the sole means of purchase created, that is, values. Money performs but a momentary function in this double exchange; and when the transaction is finally closed, it will always be found, that one kind of commodity has been exchanged for another.

It is worth while to remark, that a product is no sooner created, than it, from that instant, affords a market for other products to the full extent of its own value. When the producer has put the finishing hand to his product, he is most anxious to sell it immediately, lest its value should diminish in his hands. Nor is he less anxious to dispose of the money he may get for it; for the value of money is also perishable. But the only way of getting rid of money is in the purchase of some product or other. Thus, the mere circumstance of the creation of one product immediately opens a vent for other products.

For this reason, a good harvest is favourable, not only to the agriculturist, but likewise to the dealers in all commodities generally. The greater the crop, the larger are the purchases of the growers. A bad harvest, on the contrary, hurts the sale of commodities at large. And so it is also with the products of manufacture and commerce. The success of one branch of commerce supplies more ample means of purchase, and consequently opens a market for the products of all the other branches; on the other hand, the stagnation of one channel of manufacture, or of commerce, is felt in all the rest.

But it may be asked, if this be so, how does it happen, that there is at times so great a glut of commodities in the market, and so much difficulty in finding a vent for them? Why cannot one of these superabundant commodities be exchanged for another? I answer that the glut of a particular commodity arises from its having outrun the total demand for it in one or two ways; either because it has been produced in excessive abundance, or because the production of other commodities has fallen short.

It is because the production of some commodities has declined, that other commodities are superabundant. To use a more hackneyed phrase, people have bought less, because they have made less profit; [4] and they have made less profit for one or two causes; either they have found difficulties in the employment of their productive means, or these means have themselves been deficient.

It is observable, moreover, that precisely at the same time that one commodity makes a loss, another commodity is making excessive profit.[5] And, since such profits must operate as a powerful stimulus to the cultivation of that particular kind of products, there must needs be some violent means, or some extraordinary cause, a political or natural convulsion, or the avarice or ignorance of authority, to perpetuate this scarcity on the one hand, and consequent glut on the other. No sooner is the cause of this political disease removed, than the means of production feel a natural impulse towards the vacant channels, the replenishment of which restores activity to all the others. One kind of production would seldom outstrip every other, and its products be disproportionately cheapened, were production left entirely free.[6]

---

[4] Individual profits must, in every description of production, from the general merchant to the common artisan, be derived from the participation in the values produced. The ratio of that participation will form the subject of Book II., *infrà*.

[5] The reader may easily apply these maxims to any time or country he is acquainted with. We have had a striking instance in France during the years 1811, 1812, and 1813; when the high prices of colonial produce of wheat, and other articles, went hand-in-hand with the low price of many others that could find no advantageous market.

[6] These considerations have hitherto been almost wholly overlooked, though forming the basis of correct conclusions in matters of commerce, and of its regulation by the national authority. The right course where it has, by good luck, been pursued, appears to have been selected by accident, or, at most, by a confused idea of its propriety, without either self-conviction, or the ability to convince other people.

Sismondi, who seems not to have very well understood the principles laid down in this and the three first chapters of Book II. of this work, instances the immense quantity of manufactured products with which England has of late inundated the markets of other nations, as a proof, that it is possible for industry to be too productive. (*Nouv. Prin.* liv. iv. c. 4.) But the glut thus occasioned proves nothing more than the feebleness of production in those countries that have been thus glutted with English manufactures. Did Brazil produce wherewithal to purchase the English goods exported thither, those goods would not glut her market. Were England to admit the import of the products of the United States, she would find a better market for her own in those States. The English government, by the exorbitance of its taxation upon import and consumption, virtually interdicts to its subjects many kinds of importation, thus

Should a producer imagine, that many other classes, yielding no material products, are his customers and consumers equally with the classes that raise themselves a product of their own; as, for example, public functionaries, physicians, lawyers, churchmen, &c., and thence infer, that there is a class of demand other than that of the actual producers, he would but expose the shallowness and superficiality of his ideas. A priest goes to a shop to buy a gown or a surplice; he takes the value, that is to make the purchase, in the form of money. Whence had he that money? From some tax-gatherer who has taken it from a tax-payer. But whence did this latter derive it? From the value he has himself produced. This value, first produced by the tax-payer, and afterwards turned into money, and given to the priest for his salary, has enabled him to make the purchase. The priest stands in the place of the producer, who might himself have laid the value of his product on his own account, in the purchase, perhaps, not of a gown or surplice, but of some other more serviceable product. The consumption of the particular product, the gown or surplice, has but supplanted that of some other product. It is quite impossible that the purchase of one

---

obliging the merchant to offer to foreign countries a higher price for those articles, whose import is practicable, as sugar, coffee, gold, silver, &c. for the price of the precious metals to them is enchanced by the low price of their commodities, which accounts for the ruinous returns of their commerce.

I would not be understood to maintain in this chapter, that one product can not be raised in too great abundance, in relation to all others; but merely that nothing is more favourable to the demand of one product, than the supply of another; that the import of English manufactures into Brazil would cease to be excessive and be rapidly absorbed, did Brazil produce on her side returns sufficiently ample; to which end it would be necessary that the legislative bodies of either country should consent, the one to free production, the other to free importation. In Brazil every thing is grasped by monopoly, and property is not exempt from the invasion of the government. In England, the heavy duties are a serious obstruction to the foreign commerce of the nation, inasmuch as they circumscribe the choice of returns. I happen myself to know of a most valuable and scientific collection of natural history, which could not be imported from Brazil into England by reason of the exorbitant duties. (a)

(a) The views of Sismondi, in this particular, have been since adopted by our own Malthus, and those of our author by Ricardo. This difference of opinion has given rise to an interesting discussion between our author and Malthus, to whom he has recently addressed a correspondence on this and other parts of the science. Were any thing wanting to confirm the arguments of this chapter, it would be supplied by a reference to his Lettre 1, à M. Malthus. Sismondi has vainly attempted to answer Ricardo, but has made no mention of his original antagonist. Vide Annales de Legislation, No. 1. art. 3. Geneve, 1820. T.

product can be affected, otherwise than by the value of another.[7]

From this important truth may be deduced the following important conclusions:—

1. That, in every community the more numerous are the producers, and the more various their productions, the more prompt, numerous, and extensive are the markets for those productions; and by a natural consequence, the more profitable are they to the producers; for price rises with the demand. But this advantage is to be derived from real production alone, and not from a forced circulation of products; for a value once created is not agumented in its passage from one hand to another, nor by being seized and expended by the government, instead of by an individual. The man, that lives upon the productions of other people, originates no demand for those productions; he merely puts himself in the place of the producer, to the great injury of production, as we shall presently see.

2. That each individual is interested in the general prosperity of all, and that the success of one branch of industry promotes that of all the others. In fact, whatever profession or line of business a man may devote himself to, he is the better paid and the more readily finds employment, in proportion as he sees others thriving equally around him. A man of talent, that scarcely vegetates in a retrograde state of society, would find a thousand ways of turning his faculties to account in a thriving community that could afford to employ and reward his ability. A merchant established in a rich and populous town, sells to a much larger amount than one who sets up in a poor district, with a population sunk in indolence and apathy. What could an active manufacturer, or an intelligent merchant, do in a small deserted and semi-barbarous town in a remote corner of Poland or Westphalia? Though in no fear of a competitor, he could sell but little, because little was produced; whilst at Paris, Amsterdam, or London, in spite of the competition of a hundred dealers in his own line, he might do business on the largest

[7] The capitalist, in spending the interest of his capital, spends his portion of the products raised by the employment of that capital. The general rules that regulate the ratio he receives will be investigated in Book II., *infrà*. Should he ever spend the principal, still he consumes products only; for capital consists of products, devoted indeed to reproductive, but susceptible of unproductive consumption; to which it is in fact consigned whenever it is wasted or dilapidated.

scale. The reason is obvious: he is surrounded with people who produce largely in an infinity of ways, and who make purchases, each with his respective products, that is to say, with the money arising from the sale of what he may have produced.

This is the true source of the gains made by the town's people out of the country people, and again by the latter out of the former; both of them have wherewith to buy more largely, the more amply they themselves produce. A city, standing in the centre of a rich surrounding country, feels no want of rich and numerous customers; and, on the other hand, the vicinity of an opulent city gives additional value to the produce of the country. The division of nations into agricultural, manufacturing, and commercial, is idle enough. For the success of a people in agriculture is a stimulus to its manufacturing and commercial prosperity; and the flourishing condition of its manufacture and commerce reflects a benefit upon its agriculture also.[8]

The position of a nation, in respect of its neighbours, is analogous to the relation of one of its provinces to the others, or of the country to the town; it has an interest in their prosperity, being sure to profit by their opulence. The government of the United States, therefore, acted most wisely, in their attempt, about the year 1802, to civilize their savage neighbours, the Creek Indians. The design was to introduce habits of industry amongst them, and make them producers capable of carrying on a barter trade with the States of the Union; for there is nothing to be got by dealing with a people that have nothing to pay. It is useful and honourable to mankind, that one nation among so many should conduct itself uniformly upon liberal principles. The brilliant results of this enlightened policy will dem-

---

[8] A productive establishment on a large scale is sure to animate the industry of the whole neighborhood. "In Mexico," says Humboldt, "the best cultivated tract, and that which brings to the recollection of the traveller the most beautiful part of French scenery, is the level country extending from Salamanca as far as Silao, Guanaxuato, and Villa de Leon, and encircling the richest mines of the known world. Wherever the veins of precious metal have been discovered and worked, even in the most desert part of the Cordilleras, and in the most barren and insulated spots, the working of the mines, instead of interrupting the business of superficial cultivation, has given it more than usual activity. The opening of a considerable vein is sure to be followed by the immediate erection of a town; farming concerns are established in the vicinity; and the spot so lately insulated in the midst of wild and desert mountains, is soon brought into contact with the tracts before in tillage." *Essai pol. sur. la Nouv. Espagne.*

onstrate, that the systems and theories really destructive and fallacious, are the exclusive and jealous maxims acted upon by the old European governments, and by them most impudently styled *practical truths,* for no other reason, as it would seem, than because they have the misfortune to put them in practice. The United States will have the honour of proving experimentally, that true policy goes hand-in-hand with moderation and humanity.[9]

3. From this fruitful principle, we may draw this further conclusion, that it is no injury to the internal or national industry and production to buy and import commodities from abroad; for nothing can be bought from strangers, except with native products, which find a vent in this external traffic. Should it be objected, that this foreign produce may have been bought with specie, I answer, specie is not always a native product, but must have been bought itself with the products of native industry; so that, whether the foreign articles be paid for in specie or in home products, the vent for national industry is the same in both cases.[10]

4. The same principle leads to the conclusion, that the encouragement of mere consumption is no benefit to commerce; for the difficulty lies in supplying the means, not in stimulating the desire of consumption; and we have seen that production

---

[9] It is only by the recent advances of political economy, that these most important truths have been made manifest, not to vulgar apprehension alone, but even to the most distinguished and enlightened observers. We read in Voltaire that "such is the lot of humanity, that the patriotic desire for one's country's grandeur, is but a wish for the humiliation of one's neighbours;—that it is clearly impossible for one country to gain, except by the loss of another." *(Dict. Phil. Art. Patrie.)* By a continuation of the same false reasoning, he goes on to declare, that a thorough citizen of the world cannot wish his country to be greater or less, richer or poorer. It is true, that he would not desire her to extend the limits of her dominion, because, in so doing, she might endanger her own well-being; but he will desire her to progress in wealth, for her progressive prosperity promotes that of all other nations.

[10] This effect has been sensibly experienced in Brazil of late years. The large imports of European commodities, which the freedom of navigation directed to the markets of Brazil, has been so favourable to its native productions and commerce, that Brazilian products never found so good a sale. So there is an instance of a national benefit arising from importation. By the way, it might have perhaps been better for Brazil if the prices of her products and the profits of her producers had risen more slowly and gradually; for exorbitant prices never lead to the establishment of a permanent commercial intercourse; it is better to gain by the multiplication of one's own products than by their increased price.

alone, furnishes those means. Thus, it is the aim of good government to stimulate production, of bad government to encourage consumption.

For the same reason that the creation of a new product is the opening of a new market for other products, the consumption or destruction of a product is the stoppage of a vent for them. This is no evil where the end of the product has been answered by its destruction, which end is the satisfying of some human want, or the creation of some new product designed for such a satisfaction. Indeed, if the nation be in a thriving condition, the gross national re-production exceeds the gross consumption. The consumed products have fulfilled their office, as it is natural and fitting they should; the consumption, however, has opened no new market, but just the reverse.[11]

Having once arrived at the clear conviction, that the general demand for products is brisk in proportion to the activity of production, we need not trouble ourselves much to inquire towards what channel of industry production may be most advantageously directed. The products created give rise to various degrees of demand, according to the wants, the manners, the comparative capital, industry, and natural resources of each country; the article most in request, owing to the competition of buyers, yields the best interest of money to the capitalist, the largest profits to the adventurer, and the best wages to the labourer; and the agency of their respective services is naturally attracted by these advantages towards those particular channels.

In a community, city, province, or nation, that produces abundantly, and adds every moment to the sum of its products, almost all the branches of commerce, manufacture, and generally of industry, yield handsome profits, because the demand is great, and because there is always a large quantity of products in the market, ready to bid for new productive services. And, *vice versa,* wherever, by reason of the blunders of the nation or its government, production is stationary, or does not keep pace with consumption, the demand gradually declines, the

[11] If the barren consumption of a product be of itself adverse to re-production, and a diminution *pro tanto* of the existing demand or vent for produce, how shall we designate that degree of insanity, which would induce a gvoernment deliberately to burn and destroy the imports of foreign products, and thus to annihilate the sole advantage accruing from unproductive consumption, that is to say, the gratification of the wants of the consumer?

value of the product is less than the charges of its production; no productive exertion is properly rewarded; profits and wages decrease; the employment of capital becomes less advantageous and more hazardous; it is consumed piecemeal, not through extravagance, but through necessity, and because the sources of profit are dried up.[12] The labouring classes experience a want of work; families before in tolerable circumstances, are more cramped and confined; and those before in difficulties are left altogether destitute. Depopulation, misery, and returning barbarism, occupy the place of abundance and happiness.

Such are the concomitants of declining production, which are only to be remedied by frugality, intelligence, activity, and freedom.

[12] Consumption of this kind gives no encouragement to future production, but devours products already in existence. No additional demand can be created, until there be new products raised; there is only an exchange of one product for another. Neither can one branch of industry suffer without affecting the rest.

III

In his effort to discredit Say's Law, Keynes took as his target a passage from JOHN STUART MILL's *Principles of Political Economy* (Book III, Chap. xiv. Sec. 2). This passage was taken out of context and was presented in truncated form. If Keynes had only gone on to quote the three following sentences of the same passage, he would have allowed Mill to give also his qualifications of balance and proportion—today called "equilibrium"—which he considered essential to the correct statement of Say's Law.

Mill's *Principles of Political Economy* was published in 1848. But as early as 1829 and 1830, when Mill was twenty-four, he had written *Essays on Some Unsettled Questions of Political Economy*. These were not published until 1844. The second of them, here reprinted, "Of the Influence of Consumption on Production," is the fullest and best considered statement of Say's Law to be found in the works of the classical economists.

It is hard to account for the strange neglect of this essay. It is not merely that Keynes's *General Theory* does not mention or show any awareness of it; but in the whole of the Keynesian controversy of the last quarter century it has not been quoted (so far as my knowledge goes) by either the pro- or the anti-Keynesians. Yet it reads almost as if it had been specially written as a refutation of the main contentions of the *General Theory*.

It begins by treating as a "pernicious mistake . . . the immense importance attached to consumption." It admits that "a very large proportion" of capital may be "lying idle," or in seeming idleness, and certainly not in "full employment." But then Mill explains why an effort to bring about "full employment" by a continuous inflationary boom must lead to what we would today call malinvestment (or misdirected investment) and distortions in the structure of production. In this essay Mill recognizes the existence of business cycles (although he did not have the phrase); he expounds Say's Law (although he never mentions it by that name); he discusses "liquidity preference" (again without benefit of having the phrase); and he dismisses the Keynes-Hansen bogey of a "mature economy" (once more without the doubtful advantage of knowing the phrase).

I can only account for the surprising neglect of this essay by its lack of availability. In 1948 the London School of Economics included the work in its "series of reprints of scarce works on political economy" by making a photo-lithographic reproduction of the first edition of 1844. It is reprinted here in full.

OF THE INFLUENCE OF CONSUMPTION ON PRODUCTION

JOHN STUART MILL

Before the appearance of those great writers whose discoveries have given to political economy its present comparatively scientific character, the ideas universally entertained both by theorists and by practical men, on the causes of national wealth, were grounded upon certain general views, which almost all who have given any considerable attention to the subject now justly hold to be completely erroneous.

Among the mistakes which were most pernicious in their direct consequences, and tended in the greatest degree to prevent a just conception of the objects of the science, or of the test to be applied to the solution of the questions which it presents, was the immense importance attached to consumption. The great end of legislation in matters of national wealth, according to the prevalent opinion, was to create consumers.

A great and rapid consumption was what the producers, of all classes and denominations, wanted, to enrich themselves and the country. This object, under the varying names of an extensive demand, a brisk circulation, a great expenditure of money, and sometimes *totidem verbis* a large consumption, was conceived to be the great condition of prosperity.

It is not necessary, in the present state of the science, to contest this doctrine in the most flagrantly absurd of its forms or of its applications. The utility of a large government expenditure, for the purpose of encouraging industry, is no longer maintained. Taxes are not now esteemed to be "like the dews of heaven, which return again in prolific showers." It is no longer supposed that you benefit the producer by taking his money, provided you give it to him again in exchange for his goods. There is nothing which impresses a person of reflection with a stronger sense of the shallowness of the political reasonings of the last two centuries, than the general reception so long given to a doctrine which, if it proves anything, proves that the more you take from the pockets of the people to spend on your own pleasures, the richer they grow; that the man who steals money out of a shop, provided he expends it all again at the same shop, is a benefactor to the tradesman whom he robs, and that the same operation, repeated sufficiently often, would make the tradesman's fortune.

In opposition to these palpable absurdities, it was triumphantly established by political economists, that consumption never needs encouragement. All which is produced is already consumed, either for the purpose of reproduction or of enjoyment. The person who saves his income is no less a consumer than he who spends it: he consumes it in a different way; it supplies food and clothing to be consumed, tools and materials to be used, by productive labourers. Consumption, therefore, already takes place to the greatest extent which the amount of production admits of; but, of the two kinds of consumption, reproductive and unproductive, the former alone adds to the national wealth, the latter impairs it. What is consumed for mere enjoyment, is gone; what is consumed for reproduction, leaves commodities of equal value, commonly with the addition of a profit. The usual effect of the attempts of government to encourage consumption, is merely to prevent saving; that is, to promote unproductive consumption at the expense of reproductive, and diminish the national wealth by the very means which were intended to increase it.

What a country wants to make it richer, is never consumption, but production. Where there is the latter, we may be sure that there is no want of the former. To produce, implies that the producer desires to consume; why else should he give himself useless labour? He may not wish to consume what he himself produces, but his motive for producing and selling is the desire to buy. Therefore, if the producers generally produce and sell more and more, they certainly also buy more and more. Each may not want more of what he himself produces, but each wants more of what some other produces; and, by producing what the other wants, hopes to obtain what the other produces. There will never, therefore, be a greater quantity produced, of commodities in general, than there are consumers for. But there may be, and always are, abundance of persons who have the inclination to become consumers of some commodity, but are unable to satisfy their wish, because they have not the means of producing either that, or anything to give in exchange for it. The legislator, therefore, needs not give himself any concern about consumption. There will always be consumption for everything which can be produced, until the wants of all who possess the means of producing are completely satisfied, and then production will not increase any farther. The legislator has to look solely to two points: that no obstacle shall exist to prevent those who have the means of producing, from employing those means as they find most for their interest; and that those who have not at present the means of producing, to the extent of their desire to consume, shall have every facility afforded to their acquiring the means, that, becoming producers, they may be enabled to consume.

These general principles are now well understood by almost all who profess to have studied the subject, and are disputed by few except those who ostentatiously proclaim their contempt for such studies. We touch upon the question, not in the hope of rendering these fundamental truths clearer than they already are, but to perform a task, so useful and needful, that it is to be wished it were oftener deemed part of the business of those who direct their assaults against ancient prejudices,—that of seeing that no scattered particles of important truth are buried and lost in the ruins of exploded error. Every prejudice, which has long and extensively prevailed among the educated and intelligent, must certainly be borne out by some strong appearance of evidence; and when it is found that the evidence does not prove the received conclusion, it is of the highest importance to see what it does prove. If this be thought not worth inquiring into, an error conformable to appearances is often merely exchanged for an error contrary to appearances; while, even if the result be truth, it is paradoxical truth, and will have difficulty in obtaining credence while the false appearances remain.

Let us therefore inquire into the nature of the appearances, which gave rise to the belief that a great demand, a brisk circulation, a rapid consumption (three equivalent expressions), are a cause of national prosperity.

If every man produced for himself, or with his capital employed others to produce, everything which he required, customers and their wants would be a matter of profound indifference to him. He would be rich, if he had produced and stored up a large supply of the articles which he was likely to require; and poor, if he had stored up none at all, or not enough to last until he could produce more.

The case, however, is different after the separation of employments. In civilized society, a single producer confines himself to the production of one commodity, or a small number of commodities; and his affluence depends, not solely upon the quantity of his commodity which he has produced and laid in store, but upon his success in finding purchasers for that commodity.

It is true, therefore, of every particular producer or dealer, that a great demand, a brisk circulation, a rapid consumption, of the commodities which he sells at his shop or produces in his manufactory, is important to him. The dealer whose shop is crowded with customers, who can dispose of a product almost the very moment it is completed, makes large profits, while his next neighbour, with an equal capital but fewer customers, gains comparatively little.

It was natural that, in this case, as in a hundred others, the analogy of an individual should be unduly applied to a nation: as it has been concluded that a nation generally gains in wealth by the conquest of a province, because an individual frequently does so by the acquisition of an estate; and as, because an individual estimates his riches by the quantity of money which he can command, it was long deemed an excellent contrivance for enriching a country, to heap up artificially the greatest possible quantity of the precious metals within it.

Let us examine, then, more closely than has usually been done, the case from which the misleading analogy is drawn. Let us ascertain to what extent the two cases actually resemble; what is the explanation of the false appearance, and the real nature of the phenomenon which, being seen indistinctly, has led to a false conclusion.

We shall propose for examination a very simple case, but the explanation of which will suffice to clear up all other cases which fall within the same principle. Suppose that a number of foreigners with large incomes arrive in a country, and there expend those incomes: will this operation be beneficial, as respects the national wealth, to the country which receives these immigrants? Yes, say many political economists, if they save any part of their incomes, and employ them reproductively; because then an addition is made to the national capital, and the produce is a clear increase of the national wealth. But if the foreigner expends all his income unproductively, it is no benefit to the country, say they, and for the following reason.

If the foreigner had his income remitted to him in bread and beef, coats and shoes, and all the other articles which he was desirous to consume, it would not be pretended that his eating, drinking, and wearing them, on our shores rather than on his own, could be of any advantage to us in point of wealth. Now, the case is not different if his income is remitted to him in some one commodity, as, for instance, in money. For whatever takes place afterwards, with a view to the supply of his wants, is a mere exchange of equivalents; and it is impossible that a person should ever be enriched by merely receiving an equal value in exchange for an equal value.

When it is said that the purchases of the foreign consumer give employment to capital which would otherwise yield no profit to its owner, the same political economists reject this proposition as involving the fallacy of what has been called a "general glut." They say, that the capital, which any person has chosen to produce and to accumulate, can always find employment, since the fact that he has accumulated it proves that he had an unsatisfied desire; and if he cannot find anything to produce for the wants of other consumers, he can for his own.

It is impossible to contest these propositions as thus stated. But there is one consideration which clearly shews, that there is something more in the matter than is here taken into the account; and this is, that the above reasoning tends distinctly to prove, that it does a tradesman no good to go into his shop and buy his goods. How can he be enriched? it might be asked. He merely receives a certain value in money, for an equivalent value in goods. Neither does this give employment to his capital; for there never exists more capital than can find employment, and if one person does not buy his goods another will; or if nobody does, there is over-production in that business, he can remove his capital, and find employment for it in another trade.

Every one sees the fallacy of this reasoning as applied to individual producers. Every one knows that as applied to them it has not even the semblance of plausibility; that the wealth of a producer does in a great measure depend upon the number of his customers, and that in general every additional purchaser does really add to his profits. If the reasoning, which would be so absurd if applied to individuals, be applicable to nations, the principle on which it rests must require much explanation and elucidation.

Let us endeavour to analyse with precision the real nature of the advantage which a producer derives from an addition to the number of his customers.

For this purpose, it is necessary that we should premise a single observation on the meaning of the word capital. It is usually defined, the food, clothing, and other articles set aside for the consumption of the labourer, together with the materials and instruments of production. This definition appears to us peculiarly liable to misapprehension; and much vagueness and some narrow views have, we conceive, occasionally resulted from its being interpreted with too mechanical an adherence to the literal meaning of the words.

The capital, whether of an individual or of a nation, consists, we apprehend, of all matters possessing exchangeable value, which the individual or the nation has in his or in its possession for the purpose of reproduction, and not for the purpose of the owner's unproductive enjoyment. All unsold goods, therefore, constitute a part of the national capital, and of the capital of the producer or dealer to whom they belong. It is true that tools, materials, and the articles on which the labourer is supported, are the only articles which are directly subservient to production: and if I have a capital consisting of money, or of goods in a warehouse, I can only employ them as means of production in so far as they are capable of being exchanged for the articles which conduce directly to that end. But the food, machinery, &c., which will ultimately be purchased with the goods in my warehouse, may at this moment not be in the country, may not be even in existence. If, after having sold the goods, I hire labourers with the money, and set them to work, I am surely employing capital, though the corn, which in the form of bread those labourers may buy with the money, may be now in warehouse at Dantzic, or perhaps not yet above ground.

Whatever, therefore, is destined to be employed reproductively, either in its existing shape, or indirectly by a previous (or even subsequent) exchange, is capital. Suppose that I have laid out all the money I possess in wages and tools, and that the article I produce is just completed: in the interval which elapses before I can sell the article, realize the proceeds, and lay them out again in wages and tools, will it be said that I have no capital? Certainly not: I have the same capital as before, perhaps a greater, but it is locked up, as the expression is, and not disposable.

When we have thus seen accurately what really constitutes capital, it becomes obvious, that of the capital of a country, there is at all times a very large proportion lying idle. The annual produce of a country is never any thing approaching in magnitude to what it might be if all the resources devoted to reproduction, if all the capital, in short, of the country, were in full employment.

If every commodity on an average remained unsold for a length of time equal to that required for its production, it is obvious that, at any one time, no more than half the productive capital of the country would be really performing the functions of capital. The two halves would relieve one another, like the semichori in a Greek tragedy; or rather the half which was in employment would be a fluctuating portion, composed of varying parts; but the result would be, that each producer would be able to produce every year only half as large a supply of commodities, as he could produce if he were sure of selling them the moment the production was completed.

This, or something like it, is however the habitual state, at every instant, of a very large proportion of all the capitalists in the world.

The number of producers, or dealers, who turn over their capital, as the expression is, in the shortest possible time, is very small. There are few who have so rapid a sale for their wares, that all the goods which their own capital, or the capital which they can borrow, enables them to supply, are carried off as fast as they can be supplied. The majority have not an *extent of business,* at all adequate to the amount of the capital they dispose of. It is true that, in the communities in which industry and commerce are practised with greatest success, the contrivances of banking enable the possessor of a larger capital than he can employ in his own business, to employ it productively and derive a revenue from it notwithstanding. Yet even then, there is, of necessity, a great quantity of capital which remains fixed in the shape of implements, machinery, buildings, &c., whether it is only half employed, or in complete employment: and every dealer keeps a stock in trade, to be ready for a possible sudden demand, though he probably may not be able to dispose of it for an indefinite period.

This perpetual non-employment of a large proportion of capital, is the price we pay for the division of labour. The purchase is worth what it costs; but the price is considerable.

Of the importance of the fact which has just been noticed there are three signal proofs. One is, the large sum often given for the goodwill of a particular business. Another is, the large rent which is paid for shops in certain situations, near a great thoroughfare for example, which have no advantage except that the occupier may expect a larger body of customers, and be enabled to turn over his capital more quickly. Another is, that in many trades, there are some dealers who sell articles of an equal quality at a lower price than other dealers. Of course, this is not a voluntary sacrifice of profits: they expect by the consequent overflow of customers to turn over their capital more quickly, and to be gainers by keeping the whole of their capital in more constant employment, though on any given operation their gains are less.

The reasoning cited in the earlier part of this paper, to show the uselessness of a mere purchaser or customer, for enriching a nation or an individual, applies only to the case of dealers who have already as much business as their capital admits of, and as rapid a sale for their commodities as is possible. To such dealers an additional purchaser is really of no use; for, if they are sure of selling all their commodities the moment those commodities are on sale, it is of no consequence whether they sell them to one person or to another. But it is questionable whether there be any dealers in whose case this hypothesis is exactly verified; and to the great majority it is not applicable at all. An additional customer, to most dealers, is equivalent to an increase of their productive capital. He enables them to convert a portion of their capital which was lying idle (and which could never have become productive in their hands until a customer was found) into wages and instruments of production; and if we suppose that the commodity, unless bought by him, would not have found a purchaser for a year after, then all which a capital of that value can enable men to produce during a year, is clear gain—gain to the dealer, or producer, and to the labourers whom he will employ, and thus (if no one sustains any corresponding loss) gain to the nation. The aggregate produce of the country for the succeeding year is, therefore, increased; not by the mere exchange, but by calling into activity a portion of the national capital, which, had it not been for the exchange, would have remained for some time longer unemployed.

Thus there are actually at all times producers and dealers, of all, or nearly all classes, whose capital is lying partially idle, because they have not found the means of fulfilling the condition which the division of labour renders indispensable to the full employment of capital,—viz., that of exchanging their products with each other. If these persons could find one another out, they could mutually relieve each other from this disadvantage. Any two shopkeepers, in insufficient employment, who agreed to deal at each other's shops so long as they could there purchase articles of as good a quality as elsewhere, and at as low a price, would render the nation a service. It may be said that they must previously have dealt, to the same amount, with some other dealers; but this is erroneous, since they could only have obtained the means of purchasing by being previously enabled to sell. By their compact, each would gain a customer, who would call his capital into fuller employment; each therefore would obtain an increased produce; and they would thus be enabled to become better customers to each other than they could be to third parties.

It is obvious that every dealer who has not business sufficient fully to employ his capital (which is the case with all dealers when they commence business, and with many to the end of their lives), is in this predicament simply for want of some one with whom to exchange his commodities; and as there are such persons to about the same degree probably in all trades, it is evident that if these persons sought one another out, they have their remedy in their own hands, and by each other's assistance might bring their capital into more full employment.

We are now qualified to define the exact nature of the benefit which a producer or dealer derives from the acquisition of a new customer. It is as follows:—

1. If any part of his own capital was locked up in the form of unsold goods, producing (for a longer period or a shorter) nothing at all; a portion of this is called into greater activity, and becomes more constantly productive. But to this we must add some further advantages.

2. If the additional demand exceeds what can be supplied by setting at liberty the capital which exists in the state of unsold goods; and if the dealer has additional resources, which were productively invested (in the public funds, for instance), but not in his own trade; he is enabled to obtain, on a portion of these, not mere interest, but profit, and so to gain that difference between the rate of profit and the rate of interest, which may be considered as "wages of superintendance."

3. If all the dealer's capital is employed in his own trade, and no part of it locked up as unsold goods, the new demand affords him additional encouragement to save, by enabling his savings to yield him not merely interest, but profit; and if he does not choose to save (or until he shall have saved), it enables him to carry on an additional business with borrowed capital, and so gain the difference between interest and profit, or, in other words, to receive wages of superintendance on a larger amount of capital.

This, it will be found, is a complete account of all the gains which a dealer in any commodity can derive from an accession to the number of those who deal with him: and it is evident to every one, that these advantages are real and important, and that they are the cause which induces a dealer of any kind to desire an increase of his business.

It follows from these premises, that the arrival of a new unproductive consumer (living on his own means) in any place, be that place a village, a town, or an entire country, is beneficial to that place, if it causes to any of the dealers of the place any of the advantages above enumerated, without withdrawing an equal advantage of the same kind from any other dealer of the same place.

This accordingly is the test by which we must try all such questions, and by which the propriety of the analogical argument, from dealing with a tradesman to dealing with a nation, must be decided.

Let us take, for instance, as our example, Paris, which is much frequented by strangers from various parts of the world, who, as sojourners there, live unproductively upon their means. Let us consider whether the presence of these persons is beneficial, in an *industrial* point of view, to Paris.

We exclude from the consideration that portion of the strangers' incomes which they pay to natives as direct remuneration for service, or labour of any description. This is obviously beneficial to the country. An increase in the funds expended in employing labour, whether that labour be productive or unproductive, tends equally to raise wages. The condition of the whole labouring class is, so far, benefited. It is true that the labourers thus employed by sojourners are probably, in part or altogether, withdrawn from productive employment. But this is far from being an evil; for either the situation of the labouring classes is improved, which is far more than an equivalent for a diminution in mere production, or the rise of wages acts as a stimulus to population, and then the number of productive labourers becomes as great as before.

To this we may add, that what the sojourners pay as wages of labour or service (whether constant or casual), though expended unproductively by the first possessor, may, when it passes into the hands of the receivers, be by them saved, and invested in a productive employment. If so, a direct addition is made to the national capital.

All this is obvious, and is sufficiently allowed by political economists; who have invariably set apart the gains of all persons coming under the class of domestic servants, as real advantages arising to a place from the residence there of an increased number of unproductive consumers.

We have only to examine whether the purchases of commodities by these unproductive consumers, confer the same kind of benefit upon the village, town, or nation, which is bestowed upon a particular tradesman by dealing at his shop.

Now it is obvious that the sojourners, on their arrival, confer the benefit in question upon some dealers, who did not enjoy it before. They purchase their food, and many other articles, from the dealers in the place. They, therefore, call the capital of some dealers, which was locked up in unsold goods, into more active employment. They encourage them to save, and enable them to receive wages of superintendance upon a larger amount of capital. These effects being undeniable, the question is, whether the presence of the sojourners deprives any others of the Paris dealers of a similar advantage.

It will be seen that it does; and nothing will then remain but a comparison of the amounts.

It is obvious to all who reflect (and was shown in the paper which precedes this) that the remittances to persons who expend their incomes in foreign countries are, after a slight passage of the precious metals, defrayed in commodities: and that the result commonly is, an increase of exports and a diminution of imports, until the latter fall short of the former by the amount of the remittances.

The arrival, therefore, of the strangers (say from England), while it creates at Paris a market for commodities equivalent in value to their funds, displaces in the market other commodities to an equal value. To the extent of the increase of exports from England into France in the way of remittance, it introduces additional commodities which, by their cheapness, displace others formerly produced in that country. To the extent of the diminution of imports into England from France, commodities which existed or which were habitually produced in that country are deprived of a market, or can only find one at a price not sufficient to defray the cost.

It must, therefore, be a matter of mere accident, if by arriving in a place, the new unproductive consumer causes any net advantage to its industry, of the kind which we are now examining. Not to mention that this, like any other change in the channels of trade, may render useless a portion of fixed capital, and so far injure the national wealth.

A distinction, however, must here be made.

The place to which the new unproductive consumers have come, may be a town or village, as well as a country. If a town or village, it may either be or not be a place having an export trade.

If the place had no previous trade except with the immediate neighbourhood, there are no exports and imports, by the new arrangement of which, the remittance can be made. There is no capital, formerly employed in manufacturing for the foreign market, which is now brought into less full employment.

Yet the remittance evidently is still made in commodities, but in this case without displacing any which were produced before. To shew this, it is necessary to make the following remarks.

The reason why towns exist, is that *ceteris paribus* it is convenient, in order to save cost of carriage, that the production of commodities should take place as far as practicable in the immediate vicinity of the consumer. Capital finds its way so easily from town to country and from country to town, that the amount of capital in the town will be regulated wholly by the amount which can be employed there more conveniently than elsewhere. Consequently the capital of a place will be such as is sufficient

1st. To produce all commodities which from local circumstances can be produced there at less cost than elsewhere: and if this be the case to any great extent, it will be an exporting town. When we say *produced,* we may add, or *stored.*

2nd. To produce and retail the commodities which are consumed by the inhabitants of the town, and the place of whose production is in other respects a matter of indifference. To the inhabitants of the town must be added such dwellers in the adjoining country, as are nearer to that place than to any other equally well furnished market.

Now, if new unproductive consumers resort to the place, it is clear that for the latter of these two purposes, more capital will be required than before. Consequently, if less is not required for the former purpose, more capital will establish itself at the place.

Until this additional capital has arrived, the producers and dealers already on the spot will enjoy great advantages. Every particle of their own capital will be called into the most active employment. What their capital does not enable them to supply, will be got from others at a distance, who cannot supply it on such favourable terms; consequently they will be in the predicament of possessing a partial monopoly—receiving for every thing a price regulated by a higher cost of production than they are compelled to pay. They also, being in possession of the market, will be enabled to make a large portion of the new capital pass through their hands, and thus to earn wages of superintendance upon it.

If, indeed, the place from whence the strangers came, previously traded with that where they have taken up their abode, the effect of their arrival is, that the exports of the town will diminish, and that it will be supplied from abroad with something which it previously produced at home. In this way an amount of capital will be set free equal to that required, and there will be no increase on the whole. The removal of the court from London to Birmingham would not necessarily, though it would probably,[1] increase the amount of capital in

[1] Probably; because most articles of an ornamental description being still required from the same makers, these makers, with their capital, would probably follow their customers. Besides, from place to place within the same country, most persons will rather change their habitation than their employment. But the moving on this score would be reciprocal.

the latter place. The afflux of money to Birmingham, and its efflux from London, would render it cheaper to make some articles in London for Birmingham consumption; and to make others in London for home consumption, which were formerly brought from Birmingham.

But instead of Birmingham, an exporting town, suppose a village, or a town which only produced and retailed for itself and its immediate vicinity. The remittances must come thither in the shape of money; and though the money would not remain, but would be sent away in exchange for commodities, it would, however, first pass through the hands of the producers and dealers in the place, and would by them be exported in exchange for the articles which they require—viz. the materials, tools, and subsistence necessary for the increased production now required of them, and articles of foreign luxury for their own increased unproductive consumption. These articles would not displace any formerly made in the place, but on the contrary, would forward the production of more.

Hence we may consider the following propositions as established:

1. The expenditure of absentees (the case of domestic servants excepted,) is not necessarily any loss to the *country* which they leave, or gain to the *country* which they resort to (save in the manner shown in Essay I.): for almost every *country* habitually exports and imports to a much greater value than the incomes of its absentees, or of the foreign sojourners within it.

2. But sojourners often do much good to the *town* or village which they resort to, and absentees harm to that which they leave. The capital of the petty tradesman in a small town near an absentee's estate, is deprived of the market for which it is conveniently situated, and must resort to another to which other capitals lie nearer, and where it is consequently outbid, and gains less; obtaining only the same price, with greater expenses. But this evil would be equally occasioned, if, instead of going abroad, the absentee had removed to his own capital city.

If the tradesman could, in the latter case, remove to the metropolis, or in the former, employ himself in producing increased exports, or in producing for home consumption articles now no longer imported, each in the place most convenient for that operation; he would not be a loser, though the place which he was obliged to leave might be said to lose.

Paris undoubtedly gains much by the sojourn of foreigners, while the counteracting loss by diminution of exports from France is suffered by the great trading and manufacturing towns, Rouen, Bordeaux, Lyons, &c., which also suffer the principal part of the loss by importation of articles previously produced at home. The capital thus set free, finds its most convenient seat to be Paris, since the business to which it must turn is the production of articles to be unproductively consumed by the sojourners.

The great trading towns of France would undoubtedly be more flourishing, if France were not frequented by foreigners.

Rome and Naples are perhaps purely benefited by the foreigners sojourning there: for they have so little external trade, that their case may resemble that of the village in our hypothesis.

Absenteeism, therefore, (except as shown in the first Essay,) is a local, not a national evil; and the resort of foreigners, in so far as they purchase for unproductive consumption, is not, in any commercial country, a national, though it may be a local good.

From the considerations which we have now adduced, it is obvious what is meant by such phrases as a *brisk demand,* and a rapid circulation. There is a brisk demand and a rapid circulation, when goods, generally speaking, are sold as fast as they can be produced. There is slackness, on the contrary, and stagnation, when goods, which have been produced, remain for a long time unsold. In the former case, the capital which has been locked up in production is disengaged as soon as the production is completed; and can be immediately employed in further production. In the latter case, a large portion of the productive capital of the country is lying in temporary inactivity.

From what has been already said, it is obvious that periods of "brisk demand" are also the periods of greatest production: the national capital is never called into full employment but at those periods. This, however, is no reason for desiring such times; it is not desirable that the whole capital of the country should be in full employment. For, the calculations of producers and traders being of necessity imperfect, there are always some commodities which are more or less in excess, as there are always some which are in deficiency. If, therefore, the whole truth were known, there would always be some classes of producers contracting, not extending, their operations. If *all* are endeavouring to extend them, it is a certain proof that some general delusion is afloat. The commonest cause of such delusion is some general, or very extensive, rise of prices (whether caused by speculation or by the currency) which persuades all dealers that they are growing rich. And hence, an increase of production really takes place during the progress of depreciation, as long as the existence of depreciation is not suspected; and it is this which gives to the fallacies of the currency school, principally represented by Mr. Attwood, all the little plausibility they possess. But when the delusion vanishes and the truth is disclosed, those whose commodities are relatively in excess must diminish their production or be ruined: and if during the high prices they have built mills and erected machinery, they will be likely to repent at leisure.

In the present state of the commercial world, mercantile transactions being carried on upon an immense scale, but the remote causes of fluctuations in prices being very little understood, so that unreasonable hopes and unreasonable fears alternately rule with tyrannical sway over the minds of a majority of the mercantile public; general eagerness to buy and general reluctance to buy, succeed one another in a manner more or less marked, at brief intervals. Except during short periods of transition, there is almost always either great briskness of business or great stagnation; either the principal producers of almost all the leading articles of industry have as many orders as they can possibly execute, or the dealers in almost all commodities have their warehouses full of unsold goods.

In this last case, it is commonly said that there is a general superabundance; and as those economists who have contested the possibility of general superabundance, would none of them deny the possibility or even the frequent occurrence of the phenomenon which we have just noticed, it would seem incumbent on them to show, that the expression to which they object is not applicable to a state of things in which all or most commodities remain unsold, in the same sense in which there is said to be a superabundance of any one commodity when it remains in the warehouses of dealers for want of a market.

This is merely a question of naming, but an important one, as it seems to us that much apparent difference of opinion has been produced by a mere difference in the mode of describing the same facts, and that persons who at bottom were perfectly agreed, have considered each other as guilty of gross error, and sometimes even misrepresentation, on this subject.

In order to afford the explanations, with which it is necessary to take the doctrine of the impossibility of an excess of all commodities, we must advert for a moment to the argument by which this impossibility is commonly maintained.

There can never, it is said, be a want of buyers for all commodities; because whoever offers a commodity for sale, desires to obtain a commodity in exchange for it, and is therefore a buyer by the mere fact of his being a seller. The sellers and the buyers, for all commodities taken together, must, by the metaphysical necessity of the case, be an exact equipoise to each other; and if there be more sellers than buyers of one thing, there must be more buyers than sellers for another.

This argument is evidently founded on the supposition of a state of barter; and, on that supposition, it is perfectly incontestable. When two persons perform an act of barter, each of them is at once a seller and a buyer. He cannot sell without buying. Unless he chooses to buy some other person's commodity, he does not sell his own.

If, however, we suppose that money is used, these propositions cease to be exactly true. It must be admitted that no person desires money for its own sake, (unless some very rare cases of misers be an exception,) and that he who sells his commodity, receiving money in exchange, does so with the intention of buying with that same money some other commodity. Interchange by means of money is therefore, as has been often observed, ultimately nothing but barter. But there is this difference—that in the case of barter, the selling and the buying are simultaneously confounded in one operation; you sell what you have, and buy what you want, by one indivisible act, and you cannot do the one without doing the other. Now the effect of the employment of money, and even the utility of it, is, that it enables this one act of interchange to be divided into two separate acts or operations; one of which may be performed now, and the other a year hence, or whenever it shall be most convenient. Although he who sells, really sells only to buy, he needs not buy at the same moment when he sells; and he does not therefore necessarily add to the *immediate* demand for one commodity when he adds to the supply of another. The buying and selling being now separated, it may very well occur, that there may be, at some given time, a very general inclination to sell with as little delay as possible, accompanied with an equally general inclination to defer all purchases as long as possible. This is always actually the case, in those periods which are described as periods of general excess. And no one, after sufficient explanation, will contest the possibility of general excess, in this sense of the word. The state of things which we have just described, and which is of no uncommon occurrence, amounts to it.

For when there is a general anxiety to sell, and a general disinclination to buy, commodities of all kinds remain for a long time unsold, and those which find an immediate market, do so at a very low price. If it be said that when all commodities fall in price, the fall is of no consequence, since mere money price is not material while the relative value of all commodities remains the same, we answer that this would be true if the low prices were to last for ever. But as it is certain that prices will rise again sooner or later, the person who is obliged by necessity to sell his commodity at a low money price is really a sufferer, the money he receives sinking shortly to its ordinary value. Every person, therefore, delays selling if he can, keeping his capital unproductive in the mean time, and sustaining the consequent loss of interest. There is stagnation to those who are not obliged to sell, and distress to those who are.

It is true that this state can be only temporary, and must even be succeeded by a reaction of corresponding violence, since those who have sold without buying will certainly buy at last, and there will then be more buyers than sellers. But although the general over-supply is of necessity only temporary, this is no more than may be said of every partial over-supply. An overstocked state of the market is always temporary, and is generally followed by a more than common briskness of demand.

In order to render the argument for the impossibility of an excess of all commodities applicable to the case in which a circulating medium is employed, money must itself be considered as a commodity. It must, undoubtedly, be admitted that there cannot be an excess of all other commodities, and an excess of money at the same time.

But those who have, at periods such as we have described, affirmed that there was an excess of all commodities, never pretended that money was one of these commodities; they held that there was not an excess, but a deficiency of the circulating medium. What they called a general superabundance, was not a superabundance of commodities relatively to commodities, but a superabundance of all commodities relatively to money. What it amounted to was, that persons in general, at that particular time, from a general expectation of being called upon to meet sudden demands, liked better to possess money than any other commodity. Money, consequently, was in request, and all other commodities were in comparative disrepute. In extreme cases, money is collected in masses, and hoarded; in the milder cases, people merely defer parting with their money, or coming under any new engagements to part with it. But the result is, that all commodities fall in price, or become unsaleable. When this happens to one single commodity, there is said to be a superabundance of that commodity; and if that be a proper expression, there would seem to be in the nature of the case no particular impropriety in saying that there is a superabundance of all or most commodities, when all or most of them are in this same predicament.

It is, however, of the utmost importance to observe that excess of all commodities, in the only sense in which it is possible, means only a temporary fall in their value relatively to money. To suppose that the markets for all commodities could, in any other sense than this, be overstocked, involves the absurdity that commodities may fall in value relatively to themselves; or that, of two commodities, each can fall relatively to the other, A becoming equivalent to B$-x$, and B to A$-x$, at the same time. And it is, perhaps, a sufficient reason for not using phrases of this description, that they suggest the idea of excessive production. A want of market for one article may arise from excessive production of that article; but when commodities in general become unsaleable, it is from a very different cause; there cannot be excessive production of commodities in general.

The argument against the possibility of general over-production is quite conclusive, so far as it applies to the doctrine that a country may accumulate capital too fast; that produce in general may, by increasing faster than the demand for it, reduce all producers to distress. This proposition, strange to say, was almost a received doctrine as lately as thirty years ago; and the merit of those who have exploded it is much greater than might be inferred from the extreme obviousness of its absurdity when it is stated in its native simplicity. It is true that if all the wants of all the inhabitants of a country were fully satisfied, no further capital could find useful employment; but, in that case, none would be accumulated. So long as there remain any persons not possessed, we do not say of subsistence, but of the most refined luxuries, and who would work to possess them, there is employment for capital; and if the commodities which these persons want are not produced and placed at their disposal, it can only be because capital does not exist, disposable for the purpose of employing, if not any other labourers, those very labourers themselves, in producing the articles for their own consumption. Nothing can be more chimerical than the fear that the accumulation of capital should produce poverty and not wealth, or that it will ever take place too fast for its own end. Nothing is more true than that it is produce which constitutes the market for produce, and that every increase of production, if distributed without miscalculation among all kinds of produce in the proportion which private interest would dictate, creates, or rather constitutes, its own demand.

This is the truth which the deniers of general over-production have seized and enforced; nor is it pretended that anything has been added to it, or subtracted from it, in the present disquisition. But it is thought that those who receive the doctrine accompanied with the explanations which we have given, will understand, more clearly than before, what is, and what is not, implied in it; and will see that, when properly understood, it in no way contradicts those obvious facts which are universally known and admitted to be not only of possible, but of actual and even frequent occurrence. The doctrine in question only appears a paradox, because it has usually been so expressed as

apparently to contradict these well-known facts; which, however, were equally well known to the authors of the doctrine,
who, therefore, can only have adopted from inadvertence any
form of expression which could to a candid person appear inconsistent with it. The essentials of the doctrine are preserved
when it is allowed that there cannot be permanent excess of
production, or of accumulation; though it be at the same time
admitted, that as there may be a temporary excess of any one
article considered separately, so may there of commodities generally, not in consequence of over-production, but of a want of
commercial confidence.

IV

Jacob Viner was born in Montreal, Canada, in 1892. He studied at McGill University, and took his master's and doctor's degrees in economics at Harvard University. He has been professor of economics at Princeton University since 1946, as well as visiting professor at various universities here and abroad. He has served as a consulting expert to the U.S. Treasury and State Departments. In 1939 he was president of the American Economic Association. He is author of *Studies in the Theory of International Trade* (1937) and of numerous other works. The following review of Keynes's *General Theory* appeared in the *Quarterly Journal of Economics,* vol. 51, 1936-1937, pages 147-167, published by the Harvard University Press. It was notable, especially, for pointing out so early and succinctly that: "In a world organized in accordance with Keynes's specifications there would be a constant race between the printing press and the business agents of the trade unions."

MR. KEYNES ON THE CAUSES OF UNEMPLOYMENT[1]

JACOB VINER

The indebtedness of economists to Mr. Keynes has been greatly increased by this latest addition to his series of brilliant, original, and provocative books, whose contribution to our en-

---

[1] John Maynard Keynes, The General Theory of Employment Interest and Money, Macmillan and Co., London, 1936.

lightenment will prove, I am sure, to have been even greater in the long than in the short run. This book deals with almost everything, but the causes of and the future prospects of unemployment, cyclical and secular, are its central theme. It brings much new light, but its display of dialectical skill is so overwhelming that it will have probably more persuasive power than it deserves, and a concentration on the points where I think I can detect defects in the argument, tho it would be unfair if presented as an appraisal of the merits of the book as a whole, may be more useful than would a catalogue—which would have to be long to be complete—of its points of outstanding intellectual achievement.

Written tho it is by a stylist of the first order, the book is not easy to read, to master, or to appraise. An extremely wide range of problems, none of them simple ones, are dealt with in an unnecessarily small number of pages. Had the book been made longer, the time required for reading it with a fair degree of understanding would have been shorter, for the argument often proceeds at breakneck speed and repeated rereadings are necessary before it can be grasped. The book, moreover, breaks with traditional modes of approach to its problems at a number of points—at the greatest possible number of points, one suspects—and no old term for an old concept is used when a new one can be coined, and if old terms are used new meanings are generally assigned to them. The definitions provided, moreover, are sometimes of unbelievable complexity. The oldfashioned economist must, therefore, struggle not only with new ideas and new methods of manipulating them, but also with a new language. There is ample reward, however, for the expenditure of time and attention necessary for even partial mastery of the argument.

1. "Involuntary" Unemployment

Mr. Keynes claims that the "classical" [2] economists recognized the possibility only of "frictional" and of "voluntary" unemployment, and that a vitally important chapter of economic theory remains to be written about a third class of unemploy-

[2] Used by him to mean the later economists, such as J. S. Mill, Marshall, Edgeworth, Pigou, who in the main were adherents of the Ricardian tradition; a usage which I shall follow here.

ment, for which there was no place in the "classical" scheme of things, namely, "involuntary" unemployment. The concept of "frictional" unemployment relates to the inevitable loss of time between jobs, and presents no difficulties. "Voluntary" unemployment is defined as the unemployment "due to the refusal or inability of a unit of labor . . . to accept a reward corresponding to the value of the product attributable to its marginal productivity," but is used in such manner as to require the addition to this definition of the proviso that the money wage offered must not be below what the laborer regards as a proper minimum rate of *money* wages. If laborers refuse available employment at a money rate below this minimum, or if employed laborers refuse to permit a prevailing money rate to be lowered and unemployment results for themselves or for others from this refusal, Keynes would apparently regard it as "involuntary" unemployment, but deny its possibility or probability. He defines "involuntary" unemployment as follows: "Men are involuntarily unemployed if, in the event of a small rise in the price of wage-goods relatively to the money wage, both the aggregate supply of labor willing to work for the current money-wage and the aggregate demand for it at that wage would be greater than existing volume of employment," (p. 15). What he seems to mean by this is that any unemployment which would disappear if real wages were to be reduced by a rise in the prices of wage-goods, money wages remaining the same or rising in less proportion, *but not falling,* would be involuntary. It is with "involuntary" unemployment so understood, its causes and its remedies, that Keynes' analysis of unemployment is primarily—and almost solely—concerned.

In Keynes' classification of unemployment by its causes, unemployment due to downward-rigidity of money-wages, which for the "classical" economists was the chief type of cyclical unemployment and the only important type of secular or persistent unemployment, therefore finds no place. As will be seen later, it is excluded on the ground that resistance to reductions in money wage-rates generally does not involve a reduction in the volume of employment and is, if anything, favorable to employment rather than the reverse. The omission charged against the "classical" economists is their failure to note the lesser resistance of labor to reductions in real wages if unassociated with reductions in money wages *per se,* and their failure to recognize the existence of a large volume of unemployment for which the former is an available and practicable remedy, but not the latter. Keynes' reasoning points obviously to the superiority of inflationary remedies for unemployment over money-wage reductions. In a world organized in accordance with Keynes' specifications there would be a constant race between the printing press and the business agents of the trade unions, with the problem of unemployment largely solved if the printing press could maintain a constant lead and if only volume of employment, irrespective of quality, is considered important.

The only clash here between Keynes' position and the orthodox one is in his denial that reduction of money wage rates is a remedy for unemployment. Keynes even follows the classical doctrine too closely when he concedes that "with a given organization, equipment and technique, real wages and the volume of output (and hence of employment) are uniquely correlated, so that, in general, an increase in employment can only occur to the accompaniment of a decline in the rate of real wages" (p. 17). This conclusion results from too unqualified an application of law-of-diminishing-returns analysis, and needs to be modified for cyclical unemployment, as well as for the possibility that the prices of wage-goods and of other goods may have divergent movements. If a plant geared to work at say 80 per cent of rated capacity is being operated at say only 30 per cent, both the per capita and the marginal output of labor may well be lower at the low rate of operations than at the higher rate, the law of diminishing returns notwithstanding. There is the further empirical consideration that if employers operate in their wage policy in accordance with marginal costs analysis, it is done only imperfectly and unconsciously, and the level of wages they can be persuaded to establish is strongly influenced by the profitability of their operations as a whole, and not solely —if at all—by calculations of the marginal contributions of labor to output.

Keynes uses the term "full employment" to signify the absence of any involuntary unemployment (p. 16). He describes it also as the condition which would prevail "when output has risen to a level at which the marginal return from a representative unit of the factors of production has fallen to the minimum figure at which a quantity of the factors sufficient to produce this output is available" (p. 303). There are implied here several questionable propositions. The concept of diminishing marginal productivity is generally used in economics in a partial differential sense to indicate the diminishing increments of output which would result when some particular factor or group of factors was being increased, the remainder of the working combination being held constant. If all the factors are being increased simultaneously and in uniform proportions, it requires some such assumption as that of the general prevalence of external technical diseconomies from increased production if it is to be accepted that output and return per compound unit of the factors must be negatively correlated. There is also implied here the assumption that any increase in real wages (money wages remaining constant, or rising) will result in an increase in the amount of labor available. If, as widely-held opinion since the seventeenth century has maintained, and as Professor Paul Douglas's recent investigations for urban labor in the United States appear to confirm, the supply schedule of labor with respect to real wages is, for part of its range at least, negatively inclined, the volume of employment could conceivably be much greater when there was "involuntary" unemployment than when there was "full" employment, and Keynes' conditions of "full" employment might be met at an indefinite number of levels of employment.

"Full" employment rarely occurs, according to Keynes, and the main immediate responsibility for the persistence of "involuntary" unemployment lies with the persistence of interest rates at levels too high to induce employers to bid for all the labor available at the prevailing money rates of wages. An elaborate and strikingly novel analysis of the causes determining the level of interest rates leads to the conclusion that high "liquidity-preferences" of savers, an excessive disposition to save and a low marginal productivity of investment are responsible for the absence of such a relation between the rates at which savers are willing to lend and the rates at which entrepreneurs are willing to borrow for investment as would result in an approximation to "full" employment.

Mr. Keynes claims further: (1) that there can be "full" employment only when entrepreneurs make investments sufficient to absorb any excess of income paid-out by entrepreneurs over expenditures on consumption by income-recipients; (2) that the amount of investment entrepreneurs are prepared to make, or their "investment demand for capital," is governed by the relation of their anticipations as to the yield of additional investment, or what Keynes calls the "marginal efficiency of capital" [3] to the interest rates at which funds can be borrowed; (3) that the amount which income-recipients are willing to spend of their current income, or their "propensity to consume," a function primarily of the amount of their incomes,[4] determines the quantity of saving; and (4) the rate of interest is determined by (a) "liquidity preferences" and (b) the quantity of cash available to satisfy such preferences. The quantity of cash is generally assumed to be a constant. I accept most of this as valid in its general outlines, but I am unable to accept some of Keynes' account of how these "propensities" operate in practice or his appraisal of their relative strength.

2. THE PROPENSITY TO HOARD

Keynes maintains that for centuries back the propensity to save has been so much stronger than the inducement to invest as to create a substantial barrier to "full" investment. He finds fault with the "classical" economists for their alleged neglect of the gulf between the desire to save and the desire to invest, i.e., for their neglect of "liquidity preferences." It was a shortcoming of the Ricardian wing of the classical school that in the face of strong criticism they steadfastly adhered to their position that hoarding was so abnormal a phenomenon as not to constitute a significant contributing factor to unemployment even during a period of severe deflation. In static equilibrium analysis, in which perfect price flexibility is assumed and monetary changes are abstracted from, there is no occasion for consideration of hoarding. In modern monetary theory it is generally dealt with, with results which in kind are substantially identical

[3] "*Anticipated* marginal efficiency of capital" would seem to me a more accurately descriptive label for the concept.

[4] It is, in my opinion, probably dependent appreciably also on anticipations as to the prospective trend of income, and is surely affected significantly by amount of accumulated wealth at current valuations as well as by current income. See *infra*, §4, for further comments on this point.

with Keynes', as a factor operating to reduce the "velocity" of money. There has been, I believe, common agreement among economists that when price-rigidities are important hoarding could present a serious and continuing problem, and that it is always a significant factor in the downward phase of a short business cycle. Keynes, however, attaches great importance to it as a barrier to "full" employment at almost all times, and apparently irrespective of the degree of flexibility of prices.

There are several reasons why "liquidity preferences" loom so large to Keynes as a source of trouble in the economic process. He takes it for granted that they are ordinarily so strong for the average person in control of liquid resources that a substantial interest rate is required to overcome them; and apparently that they cannot be overcome by *any* rate of interest if a still higher rate of interest is anticipated in the near future. He assigns to them the rôle of sole determinant (given the amount of cash available, which he treats ordinarily as a constant) of the rate of interest. He believes that the marginal productivity function of capital and therefore the investment demand for capital have little elasticity. Finally he assumes in general that nothing can satisfy liquidity preferences except that "cash" whose quantity is one of the determinants of the interest rate.

We have almost no reliable information about the strength of liquidity preferences under varying circumstances, and in the absence of statistical information of a genuinely relevant character discussion must be based largely on conjecture. Nevertheless I venture to present a series of considerations which, in the aggregate, seem to warrant the conclusion that Keynes has grossly exaggerated the extent to which liquidity preferences have operated in the past and are likely to operate in the future as a barrier to "full" employment.

(a) Keynes stresses the pressure which is exercised by the expectation of a rise in the interest rate on potential purchasers of securities, leading them to postpone their purchases in order to escape a capital loss. There are, however, in every country large numbers of investors who have been taught to buy gilt-edge securities on the basis of their yield to maturity and to disregard the fluctuations in their day-to-day market values. Even investors of a speculative type are ordinarily as anxious not to miss a "low" as not to buy too high. There are many opportunities for investment which are—or seem at the time to be—of the "now-or-never" type. There is a widely-prevalent aversion to the waste of "dead" cash.

(b) Keynes seems to exaggerate the actuarial valuation of postponement of investment during a period of anticipated rise in interest rates. Rising interest rates are frequently associated with periods of greater confidence in the security of the investment, as far as payment of principal and interest according to schedule are concerned; or in the case of equity securities, with periods of more favorable anticipations of long-run yields. Hence periods of rising interest rates are often associated with periods of rising rather than falling prices of securities, especially for equity securities. Keynes seems to be in error also when he asserts that, abstracting from the risk of default on principal or interest, it will be equally profitable to hoard as to invest at par in a long-term security paying 4 per cent if the market interest rate is rising by 0.16 per cent per annum. In the first place, hoarding and investment in a long-term security are not the only alternatives. Let it be provisionally granted that hoarding and the purchase at par of a 4 per cent long-term bond would prove equally profitable at the end of the first year if the interest rate during that year had risen by 0.16 per cent. The purchase at the beginning of the year of a one-year maturity security paying anything over 0.16 per cent would then have been more profitable even if it had to be exchanged for cash within six months, and even if the short-term interest rate were also gradually rising by as much as 0.16 per cent per annum. Secondly, even a purchaser of the long-term 4 per cent security would have been richer at the end of the first year than if he had hoarded his cash, unless the security were a *perpetual* bond.

(c) Even if it be granted that liquidity-preferences are as strong ordinarily as Keynes indicates, their operation as a barrier to investment would necessarily be important only if it be assumed (1) that liquidity-preferences can be satisfied solely by the holding of non-investment assets, and (2) that the quantity of such assets does not automatically respond to the demand for them. Keynes takes care of this second qualification by his assumption that the quantity of money—in the assumed absence of a positive central monetary control—is constant. Here, indeed, he concedes more than is necessary, for if liquidity preferences are assumed to be stronger during depressions than during periods of business expansion, then the quantity of money, under such monetary systems as have existed in the past, varies inversely with the strength of liquidity preferences. But he does not give adequate consideration to the first qualification.

The satisfaction of liquidity preference on the one hand and of investment on the other, are opposite phenomena only if the range of assets which can satisfy investment demand corresponds with the range of assets which can satisfy liquidity-preferences, so that it shall be impossible to satisfy both by the same transaction. If liquidity-preferences can be satisfied by the holding of resources which are not identical with the "money" whose surrender satisfies investment demand, the satisfaction of the former does not necessarily entail failure to satisfy the latter. Keynes explains liquidity-preference as a wish to retain one's resources in the form of money. There is no systematic examination of what is to be included as "money" for this purpose, but incidentally to his analysis of one particular form of surrender of liquidity, namely, exchange of money for a debt, he states:

. . . we can draw the line between "money" and "debts" at whatever point is most convenient for handling a particular problem. For example, we can treat as *money* any command over general purchasing power which the owner has not parted with for a period in excess of three months, and as *debt* what cannot be recovered for a longer period than this; or we can substitute for "three months" one month or three days or three hours or any other period; or we can exclude from *money* whatever is not legal tender on the spot. It is often convenient in practice to include in *money* time-deposits with banks and, occasionally, even such instruments as (e.g.) treasury bills. As a rule, I shall . . . assume that money is co-extensive with bank deposits (p. 167, note).

If everything which satisfies liquidity-preference is to be included as money, then money must be broadly defined so as to include not only demand deposits and time deposits, but also short-term securities, any other assets which are readily marketable without serious risk of loss through depreciation of value, and even the command over credit from banks or others. But the conversion of newly-acquired cash into any other form of asset either involves investment directly or transfers the decision as between hoarding and investment to a banker or other intermediary between the original saver and the ultimate borrower for investment. If the banker permits his investments to remain constant while his cash reserves are increasing, or if he maintains the same cash reserves for idle as for active demand deposits, or for time deposits as for demand deposits, or for deposits as for bank-notes in circulation, then the propensity to hoard which manifests itself in the maintenance of idle bank deposits does operate to check investment, but only with the connivance and support of the banking mechanism.

It may be objected that even if liquidity-preferences operate only, or in the main, to check purchases of long-term securities, they still operate as a check to investment; because the latter is and must be largely in durable goods, or in assets far removed from the stage of the consumers' goods. But the relation between the period of investment intended by the saver and that intended, or in fact resulting, by the borrowing entrepreneur is not a simple one of necessary equality. It is highly flexible and approaches to free variability at the discretion of the borrower. Every money market has an elaborate machinery for transmuting short-term loans into long-term investments and long-term loans into short-term investments, to suit the convenience of original lenders and ultimate borrowers. The typical entrepreneur will shift from long-term to short-term borrowing, or vice versa, even tho the time period involved in the particular operation is unchanged, or (as often) unknowable in advance. He may also be able to shift from long-term to short-term investment if the interest rate at which the latter can be financed is much lower than that at which he can conduct admittedly long-term borrowing. If savers have a 5 per cent per annum preference for cash over investment in 10-year bonds but only a $\frac{1}{4}$ per cent preference for cash over time-deposits or short-term securities, and if entrepreneurs want funds for 10 years and are unwilling to incur the sacrifice of their own liquidity which would be involved in the attempt to finance 10-year operations with say 3-month borrowings, middlemen will step in who are prepared to lend on long-term funds which they have borrowed on short-term. The modern money market is fortunately equipped to some extent with procedures for satisfying liquidity-preferences without providing genuine liquidity.

(d) The propensity to hoard exercises its influence as a restraint on investment through its tendency to raise interest rates. But in what seems to me the most vulnerable part of his analysis, his explanation of the determination of the rate of interest, Keynes assigns to the desire for cash for hoarding purposes a grossly exaggerated importance.

Keynes denies the validity of the "classical" doctrine that interest is the reward for saving and is directly determined by the supply schedule of savings with respect to the interest rate and the investment demand schedule for capital, and his exposition leaves the impression that the interest rate is not dependent to any important extent on these two factors. He denies that interest is the "reward" for saving on the ground that, if a man hoards his savings in cash, he earns no interest, tho he saves just as much as before (p. 167), and claims that, on the contrary, it is the reward for surrender of liquidity. By analogous reasoning he could deny that wages are the reward for labor, or that profit is the reward for risk-taking, because labor is sometimes done without anticipation or realization of a return, and men who assume financial risks have been known to incur losses as a result instead of profits. Without saving there can be no liquidity to surrender. The saver who has no concern about liquidity gets the same reward as the person who saved with liquidity as his initial objective but is persuaded by the interest rate to lend; and the return is granted for loans irrespective whether it is reluctance to postpone consumption or reluctance to surrender liquidity which keeps the supply of funds for investment down to the level at which borrowers are willing to pay the prevailing rate of interest for it. The rate of interest is the return for saving without liquidity.

Keynes explains the rate of interest as determined by the schedule of liquidity-preferences and the available quantity of money, the prevailing rate of interest being simply that price for the sacrifice of liquidity at which the desire to hold cash is equated with the quantity of available cash (p. 167). The rate of interest determines the amount of investment, given the investment demand for capital; but a change in the investment demand for capital will not affect the interest rate "if nothing has happened to the state of liquidity-preference and the quantity of money." (See especially the figure on p. 180, and the text on p. 181.)

There have been previous attempts to discover a basis on which the interest rate could be held to be determined independently of the demand for capital, the level of wages, and other important elements in the economy, but the growing recognition of the basic interdependence of all the important economic variables has led to widespread scepticism that any such attempt could succeed. In Keynes' present attempt the fatal flaw is, to repeat, the exaggerated importance attributed to hoarding. In his discussion of liquidity-preferences Keynes distinguishes between the desire for cash for use in the current transaction of personal and business exchanges, and the desire for cash as a security against loss from unsuccessful investment. As I have already argued, the latter consideration should not operate as a barrier to short-term investment, and while it may induce a high long-term interest rate, it will be compensated for in part by a shift of borrowing to the short-term market. The pattern of behavior of the desire for transaction-liquidity is probably very largely the inverse of that of security-liquidity, or hoarding proper. As D. H. Robertson points out in his contribution to this symposium, the transactions-desire for cash is for cash to be used and not for cash to be held unused. It must therefore vary positively with the volume of investment, of income, and of expenditures for consumption. In so far as it consists of demand for cash from entrepreneurs for business uses, it is but a reflection of their investment demand for capital. In so far as it is a demand for cash from consumers who are living beyond their current income, it is the demand for consumption loans of older theory. Whatever its origin, demand for cash for transaction purposes is, dollar for dollar, of equal influence on the rate of interest as demand for cash for hoarding purposes. The demand for capital and the propensity to save (which is the reciprocal of the propensity to consume) are thus restored—tho, I admit, in somewhat modified and improved fashion—to their traditional rôles as determinants of the rate of interest.

While (to repeat again) relevant statistical information is scarce, what we do know about the holders of cash balances in the United States points strongly to the importance of the trans-actions-motive for liquidity and to the relative insignificance in ordinary times of hoarding. It is the corporations, institutions, and governments that hold at all times the bulk of the cash balances, especially if savings deposits are excluded as constituting investments rather than cash. Moreover I suspect (I know of no data on the question) that at least in prosperous times the savers—those who add each year to their estates—who are supposed by Keynes to be a source of so much trouble because of their hoarding propensities, typically hold in cash a smaller percentage of their incomes, let alone of their total resources, than do the spenders. The former have investment habits, and abhor idle cash as nature abhors a vacuum. The latter hold cash until the bills come in for settlement. It would at least be interesting to know whether these are facts or fancies.

The importance of the transactions-demand for cash makes it easy to explain a whole series of historical phenomena which do not fit into Keynes' theory. Because the demand for cash for business use varies positively with the investment demand for capital, and the demand for cash for personal use varies positively with the level of income and of expenditures for consumption, there is no need for treating as a perplexing puzzle the facts, that business is active when interest rates are high and slack when interest rates are low, and that the quantity of money and the interest rate are historically correlated positively rather than negatively. There is an important stabilizing influence, moreover, in these circumstances. During a depression entrepreneurs and spenders release some of the cash to supply the demand of hoarders for security, and during an expansion of business the absorption of cash by business and by spenders, serving as it does to raise the interest rate, keeps the expansion from going beyond bounds; or, Keynes would say, from even approaching reasonable bounds.

3. MONEY-WAGE FLEXIBILITY AND VOLUME OF EMPLOYMENT

Keynes expresses sweeping dissent with the "classical" doctrine that money-wage rigidity is a major cause both of cyclical and of secular unemployment, altho he freely grants that in general increased employment must mean lower real wages. He maintains that labor strongly resists money wage reductions but takes reductions in real wages much more calmly, and therefore that even if money wage-reductions were logically a remedy for unemployment they would not be a practicable one. His view is that a lowering of money wage-rates, unless it proceeded simultaneously and uniformly all along the line, would chiefly alter the relative rates of wages of different labor groups. It would not be likely to increase the aggregate volume of employment of labor, and on the balance of probabilities would be more likely to reduce it. He does not discuss the effects on employment which would result from pressure from labor for *increases* in money-wages, or from increases of money-wages made voluntarily on the part of employers, whether for humanitarian reasons or because of belief that high wages mean prosperity or in response to public opinion.

Keynes presents his own position mainly in terms of a criticism of a theory which he imputes to the "classical" economists, according to which a reduction of money wages and a *simultaneous corresponding reduction in prices* would increase employment because the same volume of monetary expenditures would purchase a greater physical output of commodities. He easily demolishes this by pointing out that, if money wages paid out were to fall in amount and investment by entrepeneurs (measured in wage-units) did not increase, the amount of money income available for expenditures would fall to an equivalent extent. His discussion of the effects of the wage-reduction on the volume of investment is mainly in terms of its influence on the expectations of entrepreneurs as to the future trend of wages, and he concedes that if entrepreneurs are led to expect further changes to be in an upward direction its effect will be favorable. He urges, however, that "it would be much better that wages should be rigidly fixed and deemed incapable of material changes than that depressions should be accompanied by a gradual downward tendency of money-wages" (p. 265).

This does not meet the argument for wage-reduction—or rather money-cost reduction [5]—during a depression which I had

[5] From the point of view of effect on *output*, the reduction of any part of variable costs is dollar for dollar of the same importance as the reduction of any other part of such costs, and it is only as against reduction of outstanding fixed costs, to the extent that they also do not consist of labor costs, that there

understood to be the prevalent one in recent years. In this other doctrine, factor-prices are to be reduced, but not, or not in the same degree, the prices of consumers' goods. In Keynes' analysis perfect and active competition is assumed, and prices are supposed to fall immediately and in full proportion to the fall in marginal variable [6] costs. If this occurred, and output remained the same, prices per unit would fall in greater absolute amount than would average variable costs,[7] and even more, if current labor cost were a negligible element in the fixed costs, than would average aggregate costs. The profit status of entrepreneurs would then be less favorable than before. What I understand to be the current doctrine is different. It looks to wage-reductions during a depression to restore profit-margins, thus to restore the investment-morale of entrepreneurs and to give them again a credit status which will enable them to finance any investment they may wish to make. It relies upon the occurrence of a lag between the reduction in wage-rates and a response in reduced volume of sales at the previous prices, during which interval entrepreneurs find prices to be higher than marginal costs and extensions of output therefore profitable, provided buyers can be found for the increased output. Increase in expenditures to restore depleted

---

is anything to be said for reducion of labor costs in preference to other costs. But from the point of view of the effect on the employment of *labor,* the reduction of labor cost is more favorable than the reduction to an equivalent amount of any other cost, because it will tend to lead to a substitution of labor for other factors, tho it will not be as favorable as the reduction of both or *a fortiori* of all costs simultaneously and in the same proportions.

[6] Keynes distinguishes between "factor costs" and "user costs," the two combined comprising "prime" costs. By user costs he means the amounts paid out to other entrepreneurs for purchases from them and sacrifices incurred (extra wear and tear presumably) in employing equipment instead of leaving it idle. He claims that economists have generally equated supply price with marginal factor cost, ignoring user cost, whereas it should be equated with prime cost. I see no point in the distinction between purchases from entrepreneurs and direct purchases of the services of the factors. What is the point in distinguishing between the cost of coal to a steel mill according as it is bought from an outside mine or produced in its own collieries? Where is the line to be drawn between entrepreneurs and "factors"? I am sceptical as to whether any economists have, explicitly or by implication, excluded cost of purchased materials or depreciation of equipment through use from the costs supposed to determine supply price.

[7] Because marginal costs would fall in the same proportion as average variable costs but would be greater in amount per unit than average variable costs.

inventories and to replace inefficient equipment is relied upon
to increase pay rolls sufficiently to provide the incomes with
which the increased output can be bought, and the gain in
employment—and in security of employment for those previously employed—is expected to release for expenditure the
emergency reserves of the wage-earning class. On the assumption that a large part of an entrepreneur's expenditures are
ordinarily of the postponable class in the sense that they can
be deferred without forcing a reduction of the scheduled rate
of current output, even tho not without increasing the current
cost of production; and on the further assumption that operations at a loss are conducive to the postponement of every expenditure not essential for current operation, the supporters
of this doctrine maintain that recovery of a profit margin can
lead for a time to an increase in entrepreneurs' expenditures
many times the increase in their net income, or, alternatively,
the reduction in their net loss. They do not contend that this
is certain to occur, but on the ground that the chief factor in
governing the action of entrepreneurs with respect to postponable expenditures is the current profit status of their operations as compared to their immediately preceding experience,
they say that it is a reasonable probability. Where external
pressure on prices in the face of rigid costs has been an important factor in the depression, they also expect a favorable
influence on the volume of employment from the effect of a
wage-reduction on profits and therefore on the volume of postponable expenditures, rather than from its effect on prices.
While Keynes' analysis provides materials for strengthening
this doctrine at a number of points, I cannot find in it any
refutation of its general validity.

4. Propensity to Consume

Mr. Keynes himself tells us that the functional relationships
of the various economic variables are more complex in fact
than is formally recognized in his analysis. Simplification of
this sort is inevitable, if analysis is to proceed at all. In the
case, however, of Keynes' "propensity to consume" function,
it seems to me that the simplification has been carried further
than is necessary to prevent the analysis from becoming en-
tangled in its own complexities, and further than is permissible

if the concept is to be used fruitfully in the analysis of the short cycle.

Keynes explains the propensity to consume as a functional relationship between the amount of consumption measured in money-wage units and the amount of income similarly measured. On the assumption that income in terms of money wage-units corresponds substantially in its variations with the variations in level of employment, it is concluded that income, consumption, and level of employment are related to each other in a simple pattern. Writing C_w for amount of consumption in wage-units and Y_w for income in wage-units, and accepting as a close approximation that Y_w is a unique function of the level of employment, he states the propensity to consume function as: $C_w = \chi (Y_w)$ (p. 90).

Keynes lists a number of factors, (p. 96) "subjective" and "objective," which might affect the value of χ, Y_w remaining constant, but he assumes in general that the "subjective" factors remain constant, at least over short periods, and that, given Y_w, χ depends only on changes in the "objective" factors, which in the aggregate he takes to be of minor importance as compared to changes in Y_w. Several "objective" factors which he does not appear to have taken into account seem important enough in the short cycle to be deserving at least of mention.

Keynes believes that, apart from the effect of a change in the wage-unit on the distribution of income between entrepreneurs and rentiers, who might have different propensities to consume, he has made adequate allowance in his formula for changes in expenditure resulting from changes in the wage-unit by measuring both consumption and income in wage-units. This disregards the possibility that, for short periods at least, the distinction which Keynes' makes in his supply function of labor between the response of labor (1) to changes in real wages accompanied by corresponding changes in money wages, and (2) to changes in real wages resulting from the changes in the prices of wage-goods, money wages remaining the same, may have a parallel in the propensity to consume function. The response of consumption to a reduction in real income may be, for a time, substantially different if the reduction takes the form of a decrease in money-income, prices remaining the same, from what it would be if money-income remained the same but prices increased.

Mr. Keynes claims that in general rich countries are worse off than poor countries with respect to avoidance of "involuntary" employment because of the lesser propensities to consume in the former than in the latter, and thus the greater potential importance of hoarding. Since I would contend that over long periods, given a flexible price system, the propensity to consume will affect the rate of capital accumulation rather than the volume of employment, I will confine myself to a consideration of the comparative situation of the rich and poor countries with respect to the short cycle. The possession of large accumulated resources should operate to level out the rate of consumption in the face of fluctuations in income, and therefore to check both the downward and the upward phases of the cycle. Corresponding to the charges against the entrepreneur's budget which are fixed in aggregate monetary amount regardless of current output, there are in the ordinary consumer's budget items of monetary expenditure which are fixed for a time, very much regardless of changes in his money income as far as reductions therein are concerned, and which tend to be increased only as the result of careful deliberation in response to anticipation of a change of some duration in the individual's economic status. Aside from the probability that such fixed charges are ordinarily a greater proportion of the expenditures of the rich than of the poor, the poor in times of severe depression have a partial means of escape from them, in the form of defaults, to which those with resources subject to levy cannot resort. What this amounts to is that C_w should be treated as a function not only of Y_w, but also of the amount of accumulated resources measured in wage units held by the individual. In so far as the possession of resources operates in the manner suggested here, wealth becomes a stabilizing rather than a disturbing factor. The explanation of the apparently indisputable fact that the cyclical disturbances are more severe in rich than in poor countries would then have to be sought elsewhere than in the differences between rich and poor in propensities to consume. My own guess is that it is to be sought largely in the differences between the cyclical behavior of rich and poor with respect to the disposition of the income which they do not spend. The rich hoard only during depressions and dishoard for investment during prosperity, whereas the poor hoard some of their emergency reserves during prosperity and dishoard during depression.

Mr. Keynes says that a fundamental psychological law, upon which we have a right to depend both on *a priori* grounds and on the basis of experience is that $\frac{dC_w}{dY_w}$ is positive and less than unity; i.e., that in terms of wage-units consumption varies in the same direction as income, but in smaller absolute amount than income (p. 96). This seems altogether reasonable. It leaves unanswered, however, a question of some interest: does C_w ever, except perhaps under war conditions, exceed Y_w? Since the community excess of Y_w over C_w constitutes new investment, if C_w never exceeded Y_w there would be continuous, tho fluctuating, accumulation of capital resources, even through the depths of depression. Mr. Keynes apparently must believe that for the world as a whole the C_w's must often and substantially exceed the Y_w's, for he holds that in spite of "several millennia of steady individual saving" the world is poor in accumulated capital assets.[8] But what evidence there is seems to indicate that, if any acceptable mode of measuring physical amount of capital could be found and applied, it would show that the western world has been getting wealthier fairly steadily during say the past century and a half, not only in terms of aggregate resources but per capita, in spite of a three-or four-fold increase of population.

In connection with the propensity to consume concept, as with most of Keynes' concepts, the question arises in my mind how these concepts would have to be restated in order to provide specifications for the construction of statistical series by which his conclusions as to the nature and mode of behavior through time of the various functions could be inductively tested, and I regret that no suggestions of this sort are provided in this book. I am disposed to support Mr. Robertson in his

---

[8] "That the world after several millennia of steady individual saving, is so poor as it is in accumulated capital-assets, is to be explained, in my opinion, neither by the improvident propensities of mankind, nor even by the destruction of war, but by the high liquidity-premiums formerly attaching to the ownershp of land and now attaching to money" (p. 242).

claim that concepts expressed in more "monetary" terms, and expressions for the relationships between variables which make specific allowance for time-lags instead of assigning uniform time-units to all the variables, have for purposes of *a priori* analysis some points of superiority over Keynes' "propensity" concepts expressed in terms of a single time-unit. For purposes of inductive verification, assuming that the statistical data available will ever be in a form relevant to the answer of important questions, it seems obvious to me that the analysis would have to be extensively restated in terms of directions and degrees of time-lags.

V

FRANK H. KNIGHT was born in Illinois in 1885. He has been professor of economics at the University of Chicago since 1928, and was president of the American Economic Association in 1950. His best known work is *Risk, Uncertainty and Profit,* 1921 (reprinted London, 1933). He is also the author of numerous other works, including *The Ethics of Competition, and Other Essays,* 1935, 1951; *Freedom and Reform,* 1947; *The Economic Organization,* 1951; *On the History and Method of Economics,* 1956. The review that follows appeared in *The Canadian Journal of Economics and Political Science* (Toronto) of February, 1937, pages 100-123.

[*Note added by Professor* Knight *in December, 1959—* On the occasion of republication of this review article, the writer would like to remind readers that after all that has happened in this field of discussion in the past twenty-odd years, such a composition would run in somewhat different terms if written now. Of course it was then viewed as timely, with no thought of permanence. The main theme would still be disagreement with the position of the book. But this is not the place to give details, and doubtless this note is superfluous, but the absence of any word of apology or disclaimer might be misinterpreted.]

[*Note added by the editor—*It was my own misfortune that I did not encounter Professor Knight's article until the manuscript of my own book on Keynes, *The Failure of the "New Economics,"* was in the hands of the printers. References to his article, therefore, had to be confined to footnotes added on the galley proofs.]

UNEMPLOYMENT:
AND MR. KEYNES'S REVOLUTION
IN ECONOMIC THEORY[1]

FRANK H. KNIGHT

1. The Revolutionary Approach to the Problem

What Mr. Keynes ostensibly does in his already widely discussed volume published over a year ago is to effect a revolution
in general economic theory. His work does not purport to be
an extension of theory in the way of removing abstract generalizations and bringing it into closer touch with reality under
particular conditions; rather its fundamental assumptions are
rejected outright and others are substituted. These are still
more general, and the accepted notions are treated as "special
case" propositions not justified by the facts. The general character of the argument is indicated by the title, which is not
"The Theory of Unemployment," but in contrast, "The
Theory of Employment." In particular, the book is not ostensibly or directly a treatise on the business or trade cycle, to
be incorporated into, and by qualifying to supplement, a general theory of stable equilibrium. It claims to be itself a theory
of stable equilibrium, like the conventional systems in being
free from cycles, but different in that instead of full employment a large amount of unemployment, involuntary and not
due to friction, is characteristic of the equilibrium position.

I may as well state at the outset that the direct contention
of the work seems to me quite unsubstantiated. Its value is,
I think, to be sought in the opposite direction from that of its
pretensions, as just indicated; *i.e.,* the treatment suggests modi-

[1] *The General Theory of Employment, Interest, and Money.* By JOHN
MAYNARD KEYNES. London: Macmillan and Co. [Toronto: The Macmillan
Company of Canada.] 1936. Pp. xii, 403. ($1.50) In view of the late date of this
review, and particularly of the number of extensive reviews already published,
some familiarity with the content of the book may be assumed, and this
article will be made primarily critical in character.

fications of conventional equilibrium analysis to account for temporary, possibly more or less chronic, disequilibrium conditions or, in other words, makes indirect contributions to the theory of business fluctuations. The argument, therefore, requires extensive re-interpretation and integration with a general theory running in terms of equilibrium with full employment, before it can be accepted as sound or useful.

Mr. Keynes himself sets his position in contrast with that of "the classical economics" at every opportunity. He begins with an introductory chapter of a single short paragraph which, repeating statements in his Preface, condemns the classical economics for dealing with a "special case," the characteristics of which "happen not to be those of the economic society in which we actually live," and follows with a full-length chapter entitled "The Postulates of the Classical Economics." In this chapter and throughout the book, his references under this phrase are, in general, the sort of caricatures which are typically set up as straw men for purposes of attack in controversial writing. I mean, of course, that that is the way in which they impress me. In the great majority of cases the doctrines so labelled seem to be quite at variance with, and often contradictory to, anything I was ever taught as classical doctrine in any modern sense—and I went through the academic "mill"; and they are certainly alien to anything I have ever taught as such, and I have been rated, and have supposed myself, an adherent of the general type of position referred to by the term. On the other hand, many of Mr. Keynes's own doctrines are, as he would proudly admit, among the notorious fallacies to combat which has been considered a main function of the teaching of economics. The general issue—in so far as there is an issue, and not merely the sort of amiable misrepresentation customarily assumed to be necessary to make an interesting fight—has to do with procedure in analysis. The accepted view among theorists has been that theory must begin with drastically simplified situations, described in abstract and over-general terms, and must proceed by stages toward the complexity of real life. In particular, it has been assumed that the theorist must consider a society free from the complications of speculation and of monetary changes, and hence from cyclical unemployment, before taking up these phenomena.[2] In the interest of clarity as to the underlying meaning, the reader of Mr. Keynes's book would do well to keep in mind that references to "the classical economics" are to be interpreted as relating to economic analysis *at the stage* at which uncertainty and monetary disturbances are assumed absent. It may also be helpful to suggest that Mr. Keynes's own procedure is typically that of replacing conventional assumptions which do not tell the whole story, and were never represented as doing so, with some antithetical proposition, or familiar qualification, which is then treated as quite general, though the context of the book itself makes it clear enough that the argument cannot be taken as meaning what it says.

In chapter 2, Mr. Keynes states two "postulates," both having to do with labour and wages. The first is that "the wage is equal to the marginal product of labour"; the second, that "the utility of the wage when a given volume of labour is employed is equal to the marginal disutility of that amount of employment." The first is accepted, "subject only to the same qualifications as in the classical theory" (p. 17), the second rejected. The argument on this point need not be considered in detail; the main conclusion is that money wages are not revised downward in case of involuntary unemployment, because "fortunately," the workers are "instinctively more reasonable economists than the classical school" (p. 14).[3] In more general terms, the contention is that in the labour market the prevalence of a price which leaves a large quantity of the commodity in question unsalable but with the owners willing and anxious to sell, produces no effective tendency to reduce the price to a level which will "clear the market." It is almost, if not quite expressly, stated that workers bargain through an organization as a unit, *i.e.,* a monopoly, yet the situation conspicuously is not brought under the principles of monopoly price, and, of course, nothing is said of any arrangement for distributing the burden of loss of sale (*i.e.,* of unemployment). Mr. Keynes

[2] On page 292 the author finally mentions satirically the fact that traditional economics may get around to monetary phenomena, "in Vol. II, or more often in a separate treatise."

[3] Chapter 19, entitled "Changes in Money-Wages," deals with the *effects* of wage *increases*.

states repeatedly that the normal presence of a large amount of involuntary and non-frictional unemployment is a fact of common observation (pp. 7, 10, 16, 32, *etc.*). There is no reference to depression conditions. As neither the relation to friction nor even the involuntariness of unemployment is open to direct observation, the conclusion must be that his belief is based on deduction from the principles of his "system,"—just the crime of which he accuses the classical writers (p. 16) in connection with the contrary conviction.

2. THE GENERAL STATEMENT OF THE THEORY

It is imperative to keep the fundamental position above stated clearly in mind in interpreting the book as a whole, for little more is said about it, yet it is assumed throughout. It represents the first main step in the author's argument. Viewed as a theory of unemployment, the drift of this argument may be sketched as follows (as far as I am able to figure it out). To explain unemployment, Mr. Keynes first *assumes* (*a*) unemployment, and (*b*) such a price situation, and (*c*) such a mode of operation of the price mechanism, that growth in employment is blocked. This blocking is the fundamental mystery. It does not seem to be a matter primarily of wages being too high in relation to product prices, plus wage and price "stickiness," but rather a matter of rigidity in the total monetary circulation, plus rigidity as regards decline in both prices and wages. The first step in the argument is intended to dispose of the popular heresy (derived from "classical" reasoning) that employment might be increased through a downward adjustment of wages. It has been argued (in chapter 2) (*a*) that the pressure of unemployment does not tend effectively to lower wages, and (*b*) that if it did, or if effective pressure in this sense were somehow brought to bear, wage reduction would not tend to increase employment, and hence "ought" not to happen. The bulk of the book, then, assuming initially more or less "correct" relative levels of wages and product prices, attempts to explain the failure of employment to increase spontaneously, and to suggest the type of social policy to be pursued in connection with the problem. The explanation runs in terms of the workings of the monetary system, especially in relation to the investment market.

In chapter 3, "The Principle of Effective Demand," the main argument of the book is sketched out in the form of a relation between aggregate demand and supply functions, *i.e.*, functions expressing supply-price and demand-price of amounts of employment (labour) as functions of the amount. The demand-price for labour (D in Mr. Keynes's notation) is the "proceeds" to be expected by entrepreneurs from employing a given amount. The supply-price is represented by Z and the quantity of employment by N. We read (p. 25):

Now if for a given value of N the expected proceeds are greater than the aggregate supply price, *i.e.*, if D is greater than Z, there will be an incentive to entrepreneurs to increase employment beyond N and, if necessary, to raise costs by competing with one another for the factors of production, up to the value of N for which Z has become equal to D. Thus the volume of employment is given by the point of intersection between the aggregate demand function and the aggregate supply function; for it is at this point that the entrepreneurs' expectation of profits will be maximized. The value of D at the point of the aggregate demand function, where it is intersected by the aggregate supply function, will be called *the effective demand.* . . . This is the substance of the General Theory of Employment, . . .

For "factors of production," we clearly should read "labour," and for "costs," "wages." In view of the fixity (against downward change) of the wage-level, this ought to say that there is a tendency to increase N until D is lowered, in consequence of diminishing returns, to equality with Z. What is meant by maximizing profits, I cannot see (the same statement is repeated on page 89), as the author surely does not assume that all entrepreneurs are organized as a monopoly, and if they were, the marginal productivity of labour would not be made equal to wages—the first "assumption of the classical economics," which he has said he accepts.

The page following the paragraph quoted again emphasizes the contrast with "the classical doctrine." The contrast is exceedingly strained and almost seems designed to distract attention from the essential assumption of the (downwardly) fixed supply-price for labour. The "special assumption as to the relation between these two functions" which classical economists are accused of making (p. 24 at bottom), which Mr.

Keynes forcibly identifies with "Say's Law," actually means precisely the assumption that there is no such fixity of price preventing an adjustment which will clear the market.[4]

In the following section (of the same chapter, ch. 3) is given a "brief summary of the theory of unemployment to be worked out in the course of the following chapters." We read (pp. 27-8):

The outline of our theory can be expressed as follows. When employment increases, aggregate real income is increased. The psychology of the community is such that when aggregate real income is increased aggregate consumption is increased, but not by so much as income. Hence employers would make a loss if the whole of the increased employment were to be devoted to satisfying the increased demand for immediate consumption. Thus, to justify any given amount of employment there must be an amount of current investment sufficient to absorb the excess of total output over what the community chooses to consume when employment is at the given level. For unless there is this amount of investment, the receipts of the entrepreneurs will be less than is required to induce them to offer the given amount of employment. It follows, therefore, that, given what we shall call the community's propensity to consume, the equilibrium level of employment, . . . will depend on the amount of current investment. The amount of current investment will depend, in turn, on what we shall call the inducement to invest; and [this] will . . . depend on the relation between the schedule of the marginal efficiency of capital and the complex of rates of interest. . . .[5]

---

[4] Mr. Keynes quotes Mill on Say's Law, but does not mention either Mill's explicit exception for crisis conditions which occurs a few pages previously in his *Principles,* or, of course, Mill's doctrine that the demand for products is not a demand for labour, which (however absurd) was one of his chief bids for fame.

[5] The first difficulty in following up and interpreting this statement is the confusion between what is dependent upon the actual magnitude of a variable and what is dependent on changes in that variable. It is no exaggeration to say that the book is "packed" with examples of this confusion. If we interpret the statement in accord with what it actually says, the questions raised have to do with speed of change and differences in speed of change between independent and dependent variables, *i.e.*, with "lags" in response, and the length of time required to establish a new equilibrium of the same sort which must be assumed as the starting point of the initial change, to make sense of the statement. But this view is contradictory to the conception of equilibrium in terms of which the theory as a whole is couched. The main assumption as to the psychology is repeatedly referred to in the book as a "law." The statements alternate more or less at random between the form of a relation between changes (almost

3. The Monetary Demand for Labour

So far we have been dealing with what is essentially introductory material; the title above (of this present section of our study) is practically the subject of Mr. Keynes's book. (On page 89, he remarks that the aggregate supply function involves few considerations which are not already familiar, that it is the part played by the aggregate demand function which has been overlooked.) The thesis of the work is, first, that unemployment is due to the failure of effective demand, that neither actually nor properly, naturally nor artificially, is unemployment to be remedied otherwise than by an increase in the effective (monetary) demand for labour.[6] The reader's task could have been made indefinitely lighter if key sentences in the early part of the book had been so worded as to make it clear that, theoretically in the course of nature, and practically as a matter of policy, supply-price is fixed and the adjustment is all on the demand side, instead of being worded so as to give the impression that the supply-price function is a real function in the sense ordinarily understood.[7]

always increases) in income and changes (increases) in "non-consumption" (as to saving, see below) and the form of a relation between income itself and non-consumption. For the latter, see page following quotation (p. 28 at bottom) and the apparently crucial definition on page 90, which calls the propensity to consume the functional relation between income and expenditure on consumption out of that income. But on page 96 "the fundamental psychological law" is again a relation between increases, and on page 97 the two formulations are apparently identified. (Cf. also pp. 115, 121, 251, 247.)

It is to be noted as a separate source of confusion that a relation between changes in one direction does not necessarily hold for changes in the other. A sufficiently industrious and painstaking reader will finally discover that in this case the reverse change, decrease in monetary flow, is supposed not to occur. (Cf. p. 307, at middle, and discussion below in this review.)

[6] Secondly, as we shall presently see, the thesis is specifically that the failure occurs in the demand for labour for use in connection with investment, not in connection with consumption.

[7] Immediately following the last long quotation above (General Theory, p. 28), the author reiterates his special-case accusation (without using the words "classical economics"), asserting that the equilibrium level of employment cannot correspond to more than full employment, since wages cannot exceed marginal productivity, but that there is no reason for expecting employment to be as much as full, that this will be the case only "when the propensity to consume and the inducement to invest stand in a particular relationship to one another." He means when they stand in a particular relationship to wages, the interest-rate, and general prices, which is obvious. What is mysterious and difficult to state clearly is the manner in which Mr. Keynes sets up an economic

After dividing the monetary demand for labour into the two parts, demand for consumption purposes and demand for investment, the logical order of procedure might seem to be that of examining the forces which control the division of money income between the two fields and then following through the course taken by the "money" in the two channels until it either results in a demand for employment or for some explained reason fails to do so. But before taking the suggested next step, Mr. Keynes finds it necessary to insert a group of four general chapters under the caption, "Definitions and Ideas" (book II, chs. 4-7). These are chiefly devoted to explaining the meaning of investment.

The main task of chapter 4, on "The Choice of Units," is to assume out of existence the complicating circumstance that the demand for labour is a two-stage affair of prices, a price offered by entrepreneurs to secure the labour for use in making products which either are to be sold at prices or have an estimated money value to the entrepreneurs themselves. It might well have been made clear that the discussion of the chapter deals only with the demand for consumers' goods, since in Mr. Keynes's set-up only these are assumed to be sold by entrepreneurs in the market. Capital goods are held by them for use. The nominal capitalized value of such goods is, however, the crucial factor in the workings of the author's theoretical system. The argument advanced for treating the demand-function for labour as a single function is that the notion of a general price level is unnecessary and lacks "perfect precision—such as our analysis requires." The subject of prices is henceforth almost entirely avoided, sometimes apparently with effort, until the last chapter in the body of the work. The assumption is that prices, like wages, are fixed in one direction; they may go up, but never go down. This is virtually stated in so many words in chapter 21 (p. 307). And again, the sellers who according to the theory never cut prices, are, like the workers who refuse to accept lower wages, held to be pursuing

---

system on the basis of assumptions which imply that these variables or variable-complexes are either fixed or are determined by other forces than the mutual adjustment of supply and demand, i.e., by "bargains" or public authority, or "psychology," or some other *deus ex machina*.

the right policy (though in this case their superiority in wisdom to classical economists is not explicitly asserted).[8]

The consumption demand for employment (for labour) need not detain us much longer, as it is the failure of demand in the investment field which is the crux of the theory. It may be observed that labour applied to given equipment is assumed to be subject to diminishing returns (pp. 17, 40, *etc.*) and that this fact is made to imply rising prices with increasing employment (p. 249, *etc.*). The reasoning is doubtfully sound under the actual conditions in which serious unemployment occurs, *i.e.*, when the equipment has been built for use with a much larger complement of labour; but it would hold under ideal and instantly effective competition, and in any case the point plays no important role in the general argument. We pass for the present over chapter 5, on "Expectations," which contains important matter but it is properly relative to the theory of investment, and is badly stated, out of order, and not effectively integrated with the main argument. Chapter 6, on "The Definition of Income, Saving and Investment," begins with a discussion of production in terms of revenue and cost. This seems intended to illuminate the relation of costs, especially capital depreciation (a special formulation of which is here called user cost), to the producer's decisions affecting volume of produc-

[8] As already remarked, the question of the reversibility of functional relations predicated for change in one direction is a confusing feature of Mr. Keynes's argument as a whole. The most general and pervasive example is the fact that the whole work explains unemployment by showing why increase in employment is brought to a stop, or blocked before it can get started. Except in chapter 22, "Notes on the Trade Cycle," which is really an appendix with a different point of view, little or no intimation is ever given that unemployment might result from a decrease in employment. In historical fact, as far as I know, unemployment on the scale of a serious social problem is not a typical state of affairs, and in every known case such a situation has followed at no long remove a period of relatively full employment—and has followed upon a sequence of change fairly uniform and familiar in its more general features and, similarly, periods of serious unemployment have in due course come to an end. But the question of how unemployment comes to pass is excluded from this work by the predetermination to make it a "normal" phenomenon, characteristic of an enterprise economy in stable equilibrium. It always follows upon equal or greater unemployment, never upon more employment. In this connection the interpretation of Mr. Keynes by Professor Alvin H. Hansen (*Journal of Political Economy*, Oct. 1936) is interesting in that the position of equilibrium is established on the way down and not on the way up, as in the book itself.

tion. But the argument is confused and unrealistic, and is hardly used in the later discussion, where marginal wage cost seems to be treated as controlling.[9]

The outstanding point made in book II is that saving and investment are so defined as to be necessarily and continuously equal. What this amounts to in the first place is simply that saving money is treated as "investing" in money, which is logically correct from the point of view of the saver. But in Mr. Keynes's first definition of investment, "current" investment is defined as "the current addition to the value of the capital equipment which has resulted from the productive activity of the period" (p. 62). This is correct only if the "productive activity" is interpreted to include everything that has happened during the period in question which affects values in any way, especially any shrinkage in general values due to money saving *not* resulting in investment as ordinarily understood and as implied in the phrase "productive activity"; and it must include any change in values in either direction consequent upon any monetary changes. Mr. Keynes's exposition seems calculated to conceal these facts, though in them lies the core of the explanation of depression and unemployment in accord with his own theory, if the latter is interpreted so as to make it defensible or intelligible. In this connection we may quote what seem to be the two most important sentences in the book (pp. 83-4): "The error [in the "old-fashioned view that saving always involves investment"] lies in proceeding to the plausible inference that, when an individual saves, he will increase aggregate investment by an equal amount. [This] conclusion . . . fails to allow for the possibility that an act of individual saving may react on someone else's savings and hence on someone

9 It is difficult to tell what is Mr. Keynes's conception of the relation between short-run and long-run conceptions and of their role in managers' decisions. The weakness of chapter 5 is again in point. It should be recognized that in the shortest short-run all, or virtually all, production of goods is for stock (in possession of some one) and all sales are sales from stock, hence that both are a matter either of speculative conversion of investment between goods and money, or of choice between consumption and investment. On the other hand, in the ultimate long-run there are no fixed costs, and for a system in equilibrium, stationary, or with growth (*i.e.,* unless the system as a whole is decadent), there is no capital charge except interest. In the "theoretical" long-run, moreover, there is no speculative factor; but in reality the farther ahead plans must look the greater this factor becomes.

else's wealth." In familiar language this, of course, means simply that the saving may be hoarded and by reducing monetary circulation lead to sales reductions or price declines with all the consequences of these in train; but familiar terms and modes of expression seem to be shunned on principle in this book.

In book III ("The Propensity to Consume," chs. 8-10), we finally arrive at the author's development of his view as to the forces determining the division of individual money income between consumption and saving. In substance, little is added to the "psychological law" first stated in the summary of the theory in chapter 3 (already cited) and several times repeated in the meantime. Objecting (characteristically) to any designation already in use, the author has in the meantime regularly referred to the determining psychological principle or attitude by the name which is used as a title to book III. (See especially, at end of chapter 6, p. 65.) As already indicated above, the point emphasized is that the amount saved out of income increases when the income increases, *i.e.,* a part of the increase will be saved. The amount saved is supposed to be dependent only on the size of the income (or change in its size), or at least substantially independent of other influences, notably the interest rate. There is nothing novel in this last view; it is familiar in "classical" writings, where it is commonly emphasized that saving is an "institutional" matter, dependent upon social psychology rather than economic comparisons in terms of price. More interesting is the fact that in an elaborate analysis filling three chapters, the prices of consumption goods (or their price changes) are not mentioned. Perhaps they are assumed to be tied to the wage level, for it is specified that income is measured in wage units.[10]

It would have helped the reader to avoid confusion if the author had stated explicitly that by "amount" saved he meant the absolute amount, and not the proportional amount or fraction of the income. (At least this reader puzzled some time over the question as to just why the author so emphasized the in-

---

[10] As already noted, it is expressly stated (p. 249) that prices rise, in terms of wage-units, with increasing employment—which seems to be the same as increasing income—in consequence of increasing cost (diminishing returns) in the short period.

crease of saving with increased income, making the natural assumption that an increase meant an increased proportion.) The importance of the "psychological law" is, in fact, that while money spent on consumption may supposedly be counted upon to result in demand for employment, that which is "saved" may fail to do so.[11] What is essential is that social money income shall increase with increased employment. This presumably must happen if wages are fixed as to decline, as the entire increase in total wages would hardly come out of profit or other outlay cost. Again, it would have been an aid in following the argument if Mr. Keynes had been clearer as to the nature of his organization set-up, particularly as to what decisions are made by whom. It seems to be assumed for the most part that wages represent the only outlay cost, or certainly the only variable outlay cost (apart, in chapter 6, from differential depreciation), and the express statement that interest paid is considered a part of profit (p. 290) indicates that wages and profit are the only forms of income. It would be particularly interesting to know whether anyone except the labourer is supposed to save (money).

As Mr. Keynes states the theory, the fact that some fraction of an increment of income "would be" saved "if" it were disbursed prevents its being disbursed in the first place, unless some "special conditions" insure that investment will keep pace with monetary saving. (The unconscious assumption that such conditions always obtain is the most important flaw found in classical theory.) In this form the theory seems to depend on the assumption that all entrepreneurs are organized and act as a unit, or at least that the consumption-goods and investment-goods industries are carried on in combination by the same firms. Under competition, the fact that employing an additional labourer in one enterprise would cause disemployment in another would not prevent the first increase in employment,

[11] On page 83 (quoted above) it "may" fail. When we come to Mr. Keynes's theory of interest, we shall see that there is no indication of any way in which monetary saving, though it "is" an equal investment, can lead to any investment in the sense of technical production. The questions whether money savings are made by entrepreneurs as well as "owners of productive factors" (and *rentiers?*) and whether "owners of factors" means simply labourers, become important in connection with the effort to form any inclusive picture of the motives of saving and the way in which they operate; but I have not been able to find answers to them.

and to establish equilibrium this process would have to be followed through to a defensible general adjustment, in which no single employer and unemployed worker would find it advantageous to make an employment agreement.[12]

This brings us to the theory of the "Multiplier," to which chapter 10 is largely devoted. It represents a drastic simplification of an argument developed by Mr. R. F. Kahn [13] to afford some basis for estimating the additional employment consequent upon "repercussions," beyond what would be directly provided by an expenditure on public works or the like. Mr. Keynes assumes (as he has done throughout the argument just summarized) that an increment of investment is made and paid for with new money from "somewhere," that the expenditure is divided by its recipients (owners of unemployed productive factors, *i.e.*, labourers) between consumption and "savings" (meaning hoarding) in the proportions corresponding to the prevalent "propensity to consume," and that the fraction devoted to consumption is divided in the same way by its recipients, and so on *ad infinitum.* The result, easily calculated, is that if the propensity to consume is represented by $\dfrac{r-1}{r}$, the total employment due to repercussions will be r times the direct expenditure (if the public spends three-fourths of its income and hoards one-fourth, the multiplier is 4). As usual, Mr. Keynes's arithmetic is correct, but the result is somewhat strange. It is undoubtedly true that "the logical theory of the multiplier . . . holds good continuously, without time lag, at all moments of time . . ." (p. 122). This is rigorously correct because all money which exists at all must exist in some "hoard" at any moment of time. But it would surely be more realistic to assume that an addition to the monetary circulation simply continues to circulate at the prevalent velocity (or some other, to be explained), which would yield entirely different results.

Leaving the underlying usable meaning of the entire scheme

[12] As already suggested, Mr. Keynes's whole argument in connection with labour apparently assumes that it bargains as a unit, and that the complete unemployment of particular individuals (leaving them with no income? or none except "relief"?), will affect the supply price of labour in the same way as a fractional reduction in the employment and wages of a given group of employed men.

[13] *Economic Journal,* June, 1931.

for later consideration, we turn now to the theory of the investment demand for employment. This is necessarily the crux of any theory of unemployment and cycles, since it is a well-known empirical fact that it is in the capital-goods industries that boom and depression—and unemployment as a phase of the latter—are largely concentrated.

4.   THE INVESTMENT DEMAND FOR LABOUR

This topic is the pivotal one for Mr. Keynes's new theoretical system as well as for any realistic treatment of the problem of unemployment. It is discussed especially in book IV, "The Inducement to Invest," which occupies eight chapters (11-18) and well over a third of the volume, apart from two chapters which are really appendices. It is certainly in connection with this subject that we meet the most important ideas in the work, and also the most confused thinking and exposition. To begin with, the title of book IV is hardly in strict accord with the author's new-fangled definitions of investment and saving, as the intention clearly is not that of discussing the inducement to invest in the sense in which the latter is automatically and identically equal to saving. The reference is to investment in the ordinary acceptation, the use of money to hire productive services to create capital goods, which is done by entrepreneurs. In chapters 11 and 12 is discussed a "reformulation" of the doctrine of the marginal productivity of capital, renamed "marginal efficiency" for the purpose of emphasizing appreciation as an element in yield. (It is said to have been left out of account in "classical" theory.) The next two chapters (13, 14) deal with the rate of interest, contrasting Mr. Keynes's own theory with classical theory (Mr. Keynes's version). The significance of the rate of interest, for Mr. Keynes as in part for "classical" economists, is that it is the negative inducement, the impediment, to investment in the real sense. Chapter 15 ("The Psychological and Business Incentives to Liquidity") discusses the grounds of choice between holding money and holding wealth, apparently from the standpoint of entrepreneurs considering (real) investment. This argument must then be seen in relation to that of book III, where grounds of choice between "saving" (hoarding) and spending for consumption are treated from the standpoint of the income-receiver (in this system, the labourer, and possibly also the *rentier*). The next two chapters (16, 17) contain various observations on capital, money, and interest, and chapter 18 is a general restatement of the theory as a whole.

The crucial assumptions in this crucial part of Mr. Keynes's system, viewed as a theory of unemployment, relate to the decision to save money and the decision to invest money in the creation of real capital. The two decisions are absolutely separated, as suggested above; they are made by two different sets of persons, with apparently no possibility of contact between their spheres of action in this connection. The rate of interest, it is to be observed, has nothing to do with the first decision, but is decisive in connection with the second; men do not save to get interest and never invest (in real production) except at the cost of interest. Saving, which appears to be done exclusively by owners of factors (labourers), neither influences the rate of interest nor is affected by it. (The novelty is in the first of these two positions.) Mr. Keynes's theory of interest is even more original than his theory of wages, but runs along somewhat the same lines. It is curious that no mention was made of it in his opening chapter dealing with the postulates of the classical economics, for it is much more important in the system and more of a departure from orthodox doctrine. In the capital market, saving has no influence on the interest rate, while on the other side demand is similarly without effect on price, even, apparently, in an upward direction. Men get control of capital through borrowing money, but there is never any connection between saving money and the offer of funds in the loan market. It almost seems as if the money which is saved is completely distinct from the money which is lent and borrowed, and that the former, if it ever reaches a bank, or any lending agency, is still kept entirely separate. The theory of interest is the most difficult part of the whole construction to take seriously.[14]

According to Mr. Keynes, interest is a purely monetary phenomenon. He is repeatedly explicit and emphatic that "the

[14] In the first of the chapters on "The Propensity to Consume" (ch. 8, p. 93), the rate of interest is referred to as being nearly the same thing as the ratio of exchange between present and future goods. But in the text no move is made to integrate this notion with the theory of interest. There is no indication of any causal relation either way between the interest rate and the exchange ratio or between either and the general price level. (*Cf. General Theory*, 140-1, reference to Fisher.)

rate of interest at any time, being the reward for parting with liquidity, is a measure of the unwillingness of those who possess money to part with their liquid control over it. The rate of interest is *not* the 'price' which brings into equilibrium the demand for resources to invest with the readiness to abstain from present consumption. It *is the 'price' which equilibrates the desire to hold wealth in the form of cash with the available quantity of cash . . .*" (my italics; *cf.* also pp. 174, 236, 246, ch. 14 *passim, etc.*). The positive part of the statement, asserting that the rate of interest does, at any time, equilibrate the desirability of holding cash with the quantity of cash, is not only badly worded (a desirability is not comparable with a quantity of cash), but is definitely beside the point. The things equilibrated are the desirability of holding cash and the desirability of holding wealth in any other form, the relation between the two being dependent upon the relative quantities of cash and of other forms of wealth—and upon other factors, among which the money prices of other wealth items can hardly be ignored!

The negative part of the statement is entirely indefensible; it is self-evident that at any time (and at the margin) the rate of interest equates *both* the desirability of holding cash with the desirability of holding non-monetary wealth *and* the desirability of consuming with that of lending and so with both the other two desirabilities. For, to any person who has either money or wealth in any form, or to anyone who holds salable service-capacity, all three of these alternatives are continuously open. He can consume or hold wealth, and if he holds wealth he can hold it in the form of money or real things—and the latter, of course, in innumerable forms, and with various sorts of claims to money as intermediaries, other wealth being always the security back of such claims. The statement also involves all the abstractions which are involved in assuming that the rate of interest is merely a price ratio between present and future income, *i.e.,* that there always is a single known interest rate in terms of which either capital value or yield is known when the other is known.[15]

15 It will be noticed that Mr. Keynes's discussion of the interest rate (the terms of investment) comes in between the treatments respectively of the two alternatives compared by the entrepreneur who makes a real investment, namely, the incentive to invest and the incentive to hold cash, the latter called

In the first two chapters of book IV, which bear directly on the incentive to invest, the main point emphasized is the speculative element involved in any decision to produce durable wealth. It is, I think, a point which has needed more emphasis than it has received and a matter on which the book should render service. (But as to its novelty, *cf.* again Mr. Keynes's reference to Fisher, p. 140.) My criticism of Mr. Keynes's treatment of anticipation, apart from the exasperating difficulty of following his exposition, would be that he does not follow through in accord with the importance and universality of the speculative aspect of capital production (and, in a lesser degree, capital-maintenance) in real life. In a pecuniary enterprise economy, production only very exceptionally takes place on direct order for the final consumer; consequently, as already noted, every act of production is a speculation in the relative value of money and the good produced. (This, of course, applies only to the production of goods, not of services from given agencies; *i.e.,* it applies to capital production.) The speculative element varies directly with the length of time the good may be expected to remain in the possession of the producer, and affects every purchaser of anything for resale, as well as technical producers; it varies inversely with the development of a market for the article in question. Above all, in practical import, such speculation affects producers or purchasers of durable goods for actual use, whether in consumption or in production. It does not seem to me an improvement in terminology to insist on lumping value changes into the concept of the productivity of capital, without discrimination. This is particularly dubious because, in the cases which are crucial for the problem of the cycle and of unemployment, the value change is due to something that has happened outside the field of real supply and demand for the particular good, namely in the field of money. It seems to me imperative rather to keep the different factors entering into demand and supply sharply separate, but, of course, that does not excuse neglecting any of them, as has perhaps happened until recently with respect to speculative anticipation.

"the incentive to liquidity." But in fact neither of these alternatives has any reality apart from the other, or from the necessity of comparing them and making a choice.

The point which I think Mr. Keynes is really trying to get at is that the decision to produce is a speculation on the general price level, thought of as controllable from the money side. Again, his use of the term "liquidity" to designate everything that makes it desirable to hold money, apart from its purely relative character, already noted, does not seem to be an advance or justifiable. Of the four specified and numbered motives for holding money, the first two, income motive and business motive, might be lumped together as the convenience motive. The real issue for cycle and unemployment theory arises in connection with the third and fourth—the precautionary motive and the speculative motive—which are different cases of the speculative motive. Convenience and speculation or provision against contingencies are factors in any decision and are only conceptually separable, but it is the second of these which is suggested by the word liquidity, the general "feeling" that money is for the time being the safest form of property to hold. The feeling may, of course, be present when in fact the value of money is an especially dubious risk. The convenience motive is the familiar non-coincidence of barter of "classical' phraseology. There is finally no distinction between the two functions. For, as we approach the ideal of the perfectly stationary state with all economic activity reduced to an unvarying routine, uncertainty, and with it the need for money, tends to disappear. The essential function of money is that of meeting contingencies, and in the ultimate limit velocity becomes infinity, cash holdings, or "M," zero; physical money is replaced by some conventional unit of account or *numéraire*. In any case, why not call the general psychological attitude simply the "relative money preference," and keep the elements in, or grounds for, it a matter for separate discussion?

And in any case, it is the speculative motive for holding money which varies widely in connection with the cycle and immediately causes the trouble. (What causes this variation is the central problem of cycle theory.) Of course this is not necessarily true of the individual "holder." A man with an obligation to meet in a specified number of money units on a specified day will try harder to accumulate cash, apart from his own speculative feelings, when loans are costly and especially when they are precarious; for at such times it is quite erroneous to assume a perfect market for the use of cash.[16] This applies to anyone in business when there comes to be a general demand for, and premium on, cash. Practically speaking—apart from the short period of crisis when there is danger of actual inability to secure cash for contractual or otherwise fixed needs—the speculative consideration which causes the trouble is opinion or fear as to prospective unfavourable change in the price-level or such a change in the relation between product prices and cost prices as results directly from changes in the general level. In the ordinary course of events, changes in relative prices are a risk of the individual business and are related only as effect, not as cause, to cycles, depression, or general unemployment.

Conversely,—as Mr. Keynes, like most writers on capital, fails to see or to make clear—in every case where either risk or futurity in any form is in question, the activity is necessarily one of investment, or disinvestment. Any act or outlay by way of production which does not yield its fruit instantly and finally in the form of a service enjoyed, yields it in the form of an addition to the value of some specifiable thing, hence a quantity of capital. If it does not instantly yield either service or capital value, it is not productive, and if intended to be, represents failure and waste. The opening sentences of chapter 5, for example, are ambiguous and will undoubtedly be generally read in a sense which commits the author to the widely accepted but fallacious doctrine that present production typically results in a future value. The discussion in chapter 16 (pp. 213 ff.) endorsing the old classical (as well as pre-classical) view that everything is produced by labour, still further commits him to this untenable position. (What *can* anyone think he means by a physical unit of labour? Yet from beginning to end Mr. Keynes treats labour as a homogeneous fluid with a uniform price per unit.) Moreover, in a world in which capital goods were actually produced by labour, or any "primary factors," and worn out in use in a fairly short period, the Austrian view

[16] It would surely have been in accord with Mr. Keynes's line of attack to emphasize the fact that at a time of deep depression there is little relation between the prices of capital goods or even securities (relative to yield) and any market rate of interest. Interest rates and capital values are both abnormally low. See above, p. 82, and below, p. 87.

that "capital formation occurs when there is a lengthening of the period of production" would be sound, and Mr. Keynes has expressly repudiated it (p. 76). In contrast with his general position in this connection, which is muddy if not unequivocally wrong, we find on page 105 the correct statement that wants are satisfied by objects produced previously only in connection with disinvestment. However, we still lack anything definitive, since real disinvestment means disinvestment at one point in a capital system without reinvestment somewhere else in the system, and everything depends on what are considered to be the boundaries of the "system."

What this all finally amounts to for a theory of employment or unemployment, we have another chance to attempt to find out in the last three chapters of book IV, especially the last (18), which is a formal restatement. I cannot see that we are really carried beyond the argument developed in the earlier summary chapters already summarized, including especially the statement quoted from *General Theory*, pp. 83-4 (see above, p. 76), but with the predicate regarding possible effects of monetary saving changed from a contingency to a positive assertion. We must take as the starting point, as given and unexplained, an economic system in which there is (*a*) extensive unemployment, (*b*) such an adjustment and pegging of prices and of quantity and distribution of exchange medium, and (*c*) such attitudes, especially such a relative desire to own "money" in comparison with other forms of wealth (at existing prices?) that the only possibility for absorbing unemployment is an interference by some "god" outside the economic system leading to increased real investment. Any new light on the question why this is so must be obtained from such statements as the following, which surely deserves quotation as a sample of lucid exposition (p. 236).

Our conclusion can be stated in the most general form (taking the propensity to consume as given) as follows. No further increase in the rate of investment is possible when the greatest amongst the own-rates of own-interest of all available assets is equal to the greatest amongst the marginal efficiencies of all assets, measured in terms of the asset whose own-rate of own-interest is greatest.

In a position of full employment this condition is necessarily satisfied. But it may also be satisfied before full employment is reached, if there exists some asset, having zero (or relatively small) elasticities of production and substitution, whose rate of interest declines more slowly, as output increases, than the marginal efficiencies of capital-assets measured in terms of it.

This, if I understand it at all, is, taken with the context, Mr. Keynes's way of saying that if new capital wealth is to be produced, its anticipated yield, including appreciation, must exceed interest on the money expended in its production. Possibly this is a revelation in economic insight. There is no reference to any possible difference between interest actually paid and interest which might have been received, and apparently the author assumes a perfect market, in which there would be no difference; there is also no reference to any speculative element in either the holding or the lending of money.[17] In reality, of course, every choice between forms in which wealth is to be held, including money, reflects a speculative comparison, a comparison between speculative prospects.

Discussion of this section may be brought to a conclusion by noticing one or two statements of the implications of the system as regards policy, which serve as a basis for the positions taken in the final chapter of the book, to which we must now turn. In the final section of chapter 16, we read (p. 220) of "steps to be taken" to "ensure that the rate of interest is consistent with the rate of investment which corresponds to full employment." This means, of course, that the rate is to be artificially kept down to such a point. Immediately following we are asked to assume that "state action enters in" to regulate "the growth of capital equipment." This is followed with a statement of conviction that it would be "comparatively easy to make capital-goods so abundant that the marginal efficiency of capital is

[17] This is probably more or less in accord with the general thinking of the business community, which fact, and its relation to the realities of the situation, might have been worth noting. Mr. Keynes makes no reference to the patent fact of the business cycle that men rarely borrow money to hold money, but do so to hold other forms of wealth (or to pay off some other debt) and that the rate of interest is highest when exchange medium is most abundant and its velocity of circulation most rapid (with the exception of the brief period of acute crisis, when the demand for cash rests primarily on actual, prospective, or feared needs to meet contractual or other obligations fixed in monetary terms).

zero" (p. 221).[18] The rest of the section briefly argues for the desirability of this result.

5. SOCIAL-PHILOSOPHICAL IMPLICATIONS OF THE NEW THEORETICAL SYSTEM

In his final chapter (24, following two chapters which are really digressions), Mr. Keynes sets down a number of "inferences" from his general theory which have to do with the problem of social-economic reform, reconstruction, or revolution, as the case may be. This section is of especial interest to the present writer—as one inclined to take economics as a "serious subject" rather than an intellectual puzzle for the diversion or even the improvement of the mind.

The first inference drawn is that the new economic theory removes "one of the chief social justifications of great inequality of wealth." For "in contemporary conditions the growth of wealth, so far from being dependent on the abstinence of the rich, as is commonly supposed, is more likely to be impeded by it" (p. 373).[19] This inference is held to affect particularly our attitude toward death duties; but even within any given generation, "much lower stakes will serve the purpose equally well, as soon as the players are accustomed to them," in stimulating those "valuable human activities which require the motive of money-making and the environment of private wealth-ownership for their full fruition" (p. 374). From the standpoint of moral idealism, this is an agreeable conclusion to draw, and is not implausible, with sufficient emphasis on the qualification, "as soon as they are used to it," with what it may be taken to imply regarding caution and gradualness in taking measures.

It is not so clear what the conclusion has to do with Mr. Keynes's particular theories, or, still less, what "measures" would be implied. The indirect and subtle social-psychological accompaniments of wealth ownership are (in my opinion) far more important than its direct consequences, and the same applies even more to any political substitute for the economic machin-

[18] I think this idea fantastic, but the issue cannot be argued here.

[19] This indeed is qualified to apply "up to the point where full employment prevails" (p. 372), but the text of this chapter, as well as the book as a whole, makes it clear that the qualification is essentially "theoretical."

ery of private property; and some political substitute is the only conceivable possibility, unless one plans for such a moral-religious conversion of human nature as would make a completely anarchistic utopia feasible. Such facts make the issues much less simple to me than they evidently seem to Mr. Keynes. When he goes on, for example, to say that institutional saving is now "more than adequate" (p. 373), very large questions regarding ideals of policy, as well as regarding facts, are raised in my mind. The difficulties, and dangers, in any ambitious programme of deliberate social reorganization make too large a topic to go into here.[20] In my own opinion, the distribution of actual consumption not only is rather a side issue in importance (the statistical facts set narrow limits to the possible gains from mere redistribution), but in addition, the distribution could not be much less unequal under any conceivable system of socialism, and the concentration of power, which is a more important issue, would certainly be much greater.

In any event, the mere mechanical problem of securing a supply of capital presents no serious difficulty, if productive efficiency is maintained. Any government in effective control of the economic life of a nation can certainly set aside any fraction of the social product it may decide upon, and can also invest it in any way it pleases. It is pertinent to note that Mr. Keynes has explicitly provided for all that, in advocating "a somewhat comprehensive socialization of investment" in addition to "the influence of banking policy on the rate of interest" as "the only means of securing an approximation to full employment" (p. 378). I can only comment that phrases like socialization of investment, with no indication of what procedure is in mind, sound (to me) more like the language of the soap-box reformer than that of an economist writing a theo-

[20] One difficulty which may be mentioned is that if modern technology, with specialization and large scale organization of production, is not to be simply scrapped, great concentration of authority in the hands of individual human beings, or committees or "boards," is unavoidable, and the issue is one of methods of selecting, motivating, and remunerating such functionaries, and of maintaining "responsibility" in the face of social objectives which must also be formulated through the workings of the social system itself. Reformers seem characteristically to pass somewhat lightly over the fact that these are human problems, essentially political problems, that there is no way which men will generally agree upon as valid to call in God and the angels to make the decisions and carry out the policies.

retical tome for economists. Even the "influence of banking policy" cannot, in fact, be carried far without the banking authority passing upon the soundness of, and taking responsibility for, real investment for long periods, which would necessitate a large measure of actual management. That is, this in itself involves socialization of investment, which again certainly cannot be carried far without largely "socializing" economic life in general, and this means taking it out of business and putting it into politics. More specifically, it is hard for me to believe that Mr. Keynes has tried very hard to picture in his mind the effects on the competitive economy of having a political banking authority dedicated to the permanent policy of maintaining an artificially low rate of interest. He calls such suggestions "moderately conservative" (p. 377)! (I wish to state explicitly that—as I think Mr. Keynes might also have recognized—any statement as to what would, or would probably, happen in consequence of any considerable politico-legal-administrative measure is a political rather than an economic prediction.)

The second inference drawn by Mr. Keynes, and labelled "much more fundamental," repeats a statement already quoted, along the same general line. It is that since "the extent of effective saving is necessarily determined by the scale of investment and [since] the scale of investment is promoted by a *low* rate of interest" (up to full employment), "it is to our best advantage to reduce the rate of interest to that point relatively to the schedule of the marginal efficiency of capital at which there is full employment" (pp. 374-5). Passing over the fact that there is no way of knowing at all accurately when there is full employment, meaning no "involuntary" or "frictional" unemployment, there are two notable omissions. Again, nothing is said either as to the consequences, monetary and other, of having a central bank unremittingly pumping money into the system by an arbitrarily low interest rate, or as to the political status of the official or board by whom it would be done. It surely requires an optimist to believe that it would or could be done without resulting in an unbalanced capital structure in industry, and more of an optimist to believe that the resulting situation could be cured—as Mr. Keynes must imply—

by a further overdose of the same medicine which would have brought it about.

Mr. Keynes ends his chapter and volume with a short and very optimistic section on the favourable effects for world peace which would result from abandoning the international gold standard, and a final short section on the great power and influence of economists' ideas. Whether this faith is also optimistic or not depends on one's opinion of the quality of economists' ideas, and whether the faith itself is justifiable is another question.

6. CONCLUDING SUMMARY AND COMMENT

From the standpoint of economic theory, the important fact is that all these conclusions are supposed to depend on the principles of Mr. Keynes's system. These are formally summarized at the beginning of chapter 18 (pp. 245 ff.): "We take as given the existing skill and quantity of available labour, the existing quality and quantity of available equipment, the existing technique, the degree of competition, the tastes and habits of the consumer, the disutility of different intensities of labour . . . the social structure." "Our independent variables are, in the first instance, the propensity to consume, the schedule of the marginal efficiency of capital and the rate of interest."

The schedule of the marginal efficiency of capital depends, however, partly on the given factors and partly on the prospective yield of capital-assets of different kinds; whilst the rate of interest depends partly on the state of liquidity-preference (*i.e.*, on the liquidity function) and partly on the quantity of money measured in terms of wage-units. Thus we can sometimes regard our ultimate independent variables as consisting of (1) the three fundamental psychological factors, namely, the psychological propensity to consume, the psychological attitude to liquidity and the psychological expectation of future yield from capital-assets, (2) the wage-unit as determined by the bargains reached between employers and employed, and (3) the quantity of money as determined by the action of the central bank.

"Our dependent variables are the volume of employment and the national income . . . measured in wage units.[21] It would

[21] As to the import of the "sometimes" I have no inkling. Why the national income is measured in wage units is also obscure to me; presumably there is

surely appear that if one is willing to make assumptions of this sort—along with those already pointed out, namely, that there *is* unemployment, that wages and prices cannot fall (but are free to rise), that wages are uninfluenced by the supply-offering of labour, that the price of capital-service is dependent only on the speculative attitude of the public toward money (*i.e.*, toward general prices) and the quantity of money fixed by the arbitrary fiat of a central banking authority entirely uninfluenced either by saving or by the demand for capital—one should indeed find little difficulty in revolutionizing economic theory in any manner or degree or in rationalizing any policy which one might find appealing.

The next general comment which must be made on Mr. Keynes's book as a whole is that it is inordinately difficult to tell what the author means. This is true in particular because on general issues it appears certain that he does not mean what he says. The theory is ostensibly one of equilibrium with extensive involuntary unemployment, and with the things taken as given, or independently variable, which have been set out in our preceding paragraph. Moreover, as already emphasized, it is an equilibrium reached "on the way up," and in the bulk of the exposition there is no explicit reference to cycles or oscillations and little hint that such phenomena exist. Now I for one simply cannot take this new and revolutionary equilibrium theory seriously, and doubt whether Mr. Keynes himself really does so. Scattered through the work are innumerable references to the short period, several which indicate that reactions are more or less reversible (*e.g.*, pp. 248, 251), and a few which run frankly in terms of comparative stability or stickiness rather than fixity (pp. 236, 237); in particular, there

---

some connection with the dictum in the next section of the chapter, where it is explained that an increase in employment will increase the demand for money because of increased quantity and value of output, the latter in turn being due to rising wages and diminishing returns from labour "in the short period." Why either money or real wage rates should rise before unemployment is absorbed is not explained and the increase in labour cost under conditions of unemployment is dubious; and granting both, the rise in prices rests on the dogma that they "must" equal or correspond to wage cost, which is the kind of reasoning we have been told earlier (p. 12) would have been expected of the classical school. More interesting is the fact that in the formal classification itself, prices were not mentioned, either as given, as independent variable, or as dependent variable.

is a reference (p. 249) to the capacity of the economic system for remaining in a "chronic" condition of sub-normal activity for a "considerable period." This is a far cry from the "stable equilibrium" of page 30 and the tone of most of the book. Then, of course, there is chapter 22, "Notes on the Trade Cycle," which hardly seems to be a part of the book, but, along with a few other allusions to cycles, cannot be left entirely out of the picture.

As suggested at the beginning of this article, it is my own conviction that we must simply "forget" the revolution in economic theory and read the book as a contribution to the theory of business oscillations. This, of course, involves laborious interpretation, amounting to rewriting the book as one reads—or re-reads for the rth time. Even from this point of view, I cannot see that it gets very far or says anything very original, but perhaps its wild overstatement may serve to emphasize some factors which have been relatively neglected. In my own case, which is that of one who has happened to work primarily in economic theory at the more general levels, and who pretends to no expert knowledge of monetary and cycle theory, the book has been useful in emphasizing the need of more effective integration of monetary theory and general equilibrium economics.[22] Perhaps I may also be allowed to add

[22] This, of course, is a line on which a number of thinkers have been working and writing in recent years. I am thinking especially of the work of Mr. Hawtrey, the Swedish school, and Mr. Robertson; but only an authority on subject-matter can be an authority on the literature.

In the very first paragraph of his Preface, Mr. Keynes says: "Those, who are strongly wedded to what I shall call 'the classical theory,' will fluctuate, I expect, between a belief that I am quite wrong and a belief that I am saying nothing new. It is for others to determine if either of these or the third alternative is right." The prediction has been largely correct in my own case, though I should say that my difficulty (and no little annoyance) has been that of choosing between interpretations, one apparently nonsensical and the other more or less commonplace. "It is for others to determine" whether such a result proves that the one who arrives at it is "wedded" to some antique mode of thought. This, of course, is one of two "arguments" regularly hurled by revolutionary thinkers at those who do not immediately join up, the other being that the refusal is based on a vested interest. This the revolutionary is sometimes "polite" enough to imply is done unconsciously (i.e., blindly instead of intelligently); Mr. Keynes may be thanked for omitting the second. Since it has become quite the fashion to account for differences in intellectual position by psycho-analysing, or somehow "explaining," one's opponent (and the example of following the fashion having in this case been set by Mr. Keynes), it may be permissible to note that our civilization of to-day, being essentially romantic,

that as a theorist, I have always made a special point of emphasizing (along with rigour in theorizing) not only the dangers of drawing conclusions from the propositions of a theoretical construction without carefully making allowance for all the factors ignored in building it, but also the dangers of taking any step in the theoretical construction itself without full awareness of all the abstractions involved. Among these abstractions (or "disturbing factors"—speaking from the standpoint of practical implications), "monetary repercussions" constitute an item or a group of items the importance of which can hardly be overestimated.

Whether this point has been neglected, or especially needed urging against the "classical" economics is a matter of opinion. Personally I had not been aware of any striking dearth of publication in the field indicated, in the period in which I have been a student and teacher of economics, and am inclined to guess that the issue is one of kind and quality rather than quantity; but that may be a prejudice. Speaking from the same point of view, I am disposed to echo and to underline the doubt expressed by Mr. Robertson whether the "multiplier"—and I should add the other novel conceptions of Mr. Keynes, in so far as they are novel—constitute much advance over more crudely "monetary" weapons of thought; [23] and I would also insert the adjective "classical" before the word "monetary." It seems to me that the value of the book is in emphasizing the need of a sound monetary theory, rather than in contributing to the construction of such a theory. At least, after much labour spent in trying, I have extremely little conception of Mr. Keynes's monetary theory, if he has one. It seems to me reasonable to interpret the entire work as a new system of political economy, built around, and built to support, Mr. Keynes's conception of inflation as the cure for depression and unemployment—with especial reference to a situation in which this condition has

---

loves and extols heretics quite as much as its direct antecedent a few centuries back hated and feared them. The demand for heresy is always in excess of the supply and its production always a prosperous business. Where once it was necessary in writing to pose as merely restating and interpreting doctrine handed down from the Fathers, the surest way to public interest and acclaim now lies through pulling down and overturning everything established or accepted.

[23] See *Quarterly Journal of Economics*, Nov., 1936, p. 175.

become more or less "stabilized," such as Mr. Keynes's own country in and since the later 1920's. With this general position, I happen to be in sympathy—for whatever that statement may be worth. But I had hopes of learning more about the problems involved, especially whether society should wait until such a situation is existent before taking action or should rather take steps to prevent its arising; and also what concrete measures are likely to be effective without aggravating the situation, or preparing for a recurrence, possibly worse, or introducing other evils more than offsetting the gain. In this regard, I must confess that the labour I have spent on *The General Theory of Employment, Interest, and Money* leaves me with a feeling of keen disappointment. The chief value of the book has seemed to lie in the hard labour involved in reading it, which enforces intensive grappling with the problems.[24]

[24] Perhaps a constructive suggestion from a "mere theorist" may not be entirely out of order. It has long been in my mind that in the welter of cycle theories (most of which have merit in pointing to real factors in the problem) one point is still neglected which must be of some importance. It has been recognized for at least a century that within some limits speculative psychology tends to give rise to a kind of momentum or cumulative tendency in price changes. The equilibrium point being uncertain, the tendency of speculation for a rise to create a rise in the price of any commodity within limits outweighs the "force" tending toward equilibrium—and conversely. Reasoning which cannot be developed here would show that this tendency should be especially strong in the case of money, the essential function of which is to be held speculatively. I should not be surprised if this is the most important factor in the general tendency to oscillation in an economic system—in contrast with specific "cycles" affecting particular commodities, which according to the laws of chance should be distributed in periodicity and phase and so cancel out for the system as a whole.

VI

Étienne Mantoux, son of the distinguished French Historian, Paul Mantoux, was born in Paris in 1913. After graduating from the University of Paris and the École des Science Politiques, he was attracted to economic studies and went to the London School of Economics (1935-36) on a research scholarship. His only book was *The Carthaginian Peace—or The Economic Consequences of Mr. Keynes* (1946), by far the fullest and ablest attack on the contentions of Keynes's *The Economic Consequences of the Peace*. But Étienne Mantoux did not live to see its publication. As his father wrote in a touching foreword: "The author of the following pages was killed on active service near a Bavarian village in the Danube Valley, on 29 April, 1945—hardly more than a week before the bells rang for victory and peace. What was meant to be his first message to the public, opening discussions he was eagerly expecting, now comes to us from beyond the grave." Yet Étienne Mantoux's first message (though a brief one) had, fortunately, come years earlier, in the following essay from the *Revue d'Économie Politique* of November-December, 1937, published by Editions Sirey, 22, rue Soufflot, Paris 5e, France. Written when its author was only twenty-four, it reveals, no less than *The Carthaginian Peace,* what a brilliant mind was lost to economics by his premature death.

This is the essay's first publication in English. The translation is by Philip Cortney and Henry Hazlitt.

MR. KEYNES' "GENERAL THEORY" [1]

ÉTIENNE MANTOUX

When he published *The General Theory of Employment, Interest and Money* [2] last year at the sensational price of 5 shillings, J. M. Keynes perhaps meant to express a wish for the broadest and earliest possible dissemination of his new ideas. At all events, the book reads more like an invitation to open discussion, an encouragement to debate, than like a definitive affirmation. And yet, as Keynes himself tells us in the Preface, the book is addressed to his fellow economists, rather than to the general public. The most arduous problems are examined there, and the most exacting specialists will find matter to exercise their powers of abstraction—often, perhaps, of divination—more even than in the *Treatise*. Where is the lucid style, the vigorous clarity, of Keynes of *The Economic Consequences of the Peace* and *Monetary Reform?* The problems he then so powerfully helped to illuminate seem quite transcended in his present preoccupations. The result is a degree of obscurity without precedent in his past work—though not, to be sure, in the annals of economic thought; the complaints one might make upon this head were to be heard long ago, when the same problems were already being argued, and when the very authors now attacked by Keynes were already under fire. *"Omne ignotum pro magnifico,"* cried Samuel Bailey, in 1825, "is not without example among us, and an author's reputation for the profundity of his ideas often gains by a small admixture of the unintelligible!" [3] And yet I should not be surprised to learn that this latest book, so great is its author's reputation, so engrossing the issues of which it treats,

[1] This article is a sequel to that of Mr. J.-M. Jeanneney, "L'oeuvre scientifique de quelques économistes étrangers, VIII: John Maynard Keynes," *Revue d'Économie Politique*, March-April 1936, pp. 532ff.

[2] *The General Theory of Employment, Interest and Money*, New York: Harcourt, Brace and Co., 1936, 403 p.

[3] *A Critical Dissertation on the Nature, Measures, and Causes of Value; chiefly in reference to the writings of Mr. Ricardo and his followers;* p. xvii.

did bring him a return he had not hoped for. However that may be, the *General Theory*, once published, has been the staple diet of discussion—frequently animated—in the economics seminars of the English universities. Several books have already been more or less directly inspired by it.[4] Few men, indeed, enjoy comparable intellectual prestige in their generation. In 1919, he appeared to an exhausted Europe, still blinded by violent passions, as the clear-eyed and courageous champion of fair play and common sense. But it is not by the play of cold reason that Keynes has gained renown; the warlike humor of the polemicist, the powerful gift of imagery in analysis or repartee, and the literary charm about everything he writes, though they may have troubled the needful serenity of the scientist, have nonetheless contributed to the fascination felt by most young British economists and students, which has made him the leader of a School—albeit as yet undefined.

For with his fascination Keynes combines another of the serpent's attributes—his disconcerting ability to molt at more or less frequent intervals, leaving his former conceptions behind him like so many old integuments from which the reader, somewhat disconcerted, must proceed to extricate his own thinking, having previously been at no little trouble to get it in.[5] In fact, one of Keynes' rarer virtues is to be often right in difficult situations, and another, rarer still, is never to hesitate in public retraction when convinced or persuaded of error. Thus when Alvin Hansen, for example, made an important correction in the first of his fundamental equations, Keynes assented freely.[6] On the other hand, his dispute with F. A. von Hayek did not so quickly reach an agreeable con-

---

[4] See particularly R. F. Harrod, *The Trade Cycle,* Oxford, 1936; J. E. Meade, *An Introduction to Economic Analysis and Policy,* Oxford, 1936; A. L. Rowse, *Mr. Keynes and the Labour Movement,* Macmillan, 1936; R. G. Hawtrey, *Capital and Employment,* Longmans Green, 1937; Joan Robinson, *Essays in the Theory of Employment,* Macmillan, 1937.

[5] Keynes was already quite solicitous of the readers of his *Treatise:* "Those still greatly attached to the old point of view cannot see that they are being asked to put on a new pair of trousers, and insist that it is only an alteration of the one they have been wearing for years." (*Economica,* November, 1931, p. 390.)

[6] A. H. Hansen, "A Fundamental Error in Keynes' *Treatise on Money,*" *American Economic Review,* September 1932.

clusion.[7] It is even to be regretted that in this new work, the difficulties raised by the clash between Keynes' views and those of the "Austrian," or "neo-Austrian," school, are not dealt with except by occasionally devious allusions.[8]

Still, the *Treatise* itself was a way station, and quite plainly a transitional work. The *General Theory* is now offered to us as the outcome of "a long struggle of escape . . . from habitual modes of thought and expression" (Preface, p. viii). Why "general" theory? Because, in Keynes' opinion, the conclusions of the classical school apply only to a special case, and depend on an implicit hypothesis that is seldom satisfied. "General," then, is here opposed to "classical"; we are to witness a revolution. At least so one would gather from some of the more enthusiastic reviews, which go so far as to make Keynes (much to his disgust, no doubt) the direct successor of Karl Marx.[9] "My undertaking is one that has had no equal, that none will ever equal. I would change the basis of society, shift the axis of civilization. . . ." [10] Is it facetious to place Proudhon's ironic boast beside Keynes' ambitious sureness? Yet their two proposals are not so very unlike; for it is by decline of the rate of interest to zero that the latter would see our economic ills remedied. Curious that the most sharp-tongued economist of our time should come back, by this unexpected route, to the thought of the famous inventor of "crédit gratuit."

What is the idea? In the *Treatise*, as Keynes tells us, his

[7] F. A. Hayek, "Reflections on the Pure Theory of Money of Mr. Keynes," *Economica*, August 1931 and February 1932; and Keynes' reply, *Economica*, November 1931.

[8] One can hardly interpret otherwise, for example, the passages devoted to excess of depreciation allowances and the financial prudence of enterprises in periods of rising prices. These excesses may have been sufficient to start the 1929 crisis (p. 100)! It would be interesting to know what Keynes thinks of the phenomenon of "Kapitalaufzehrung."—On this point, (see recent report of economic section of the League of Nations, *Prospérité et Dépression*, by G. v. Haberler, p. 53), Keynes himself was recently alarmed by the danger of mistaken employment of the profits from the present boom; *Times*, January 12, 1937.—See also *General Theory*, pp. 76 and 329.

[9] See particularly account by G. D. H. Cole, *New Statesman*, February 15, 1936: "The most important theoretical economic writing since Marx's *Capital*, or, if only classical economics is to be considered as comparable, since Ricardo's *Principles*." Sir Josiah Stamp in 1930 greeted the *Treatise* as "the most penetrating and significant work since Ricardo."

[10] *Le Peuple*, February 19, 1849, "Démonstration du socialisme théorique et pratique, ou Révolution par le crédit."

monetary theory attempted to deal with output in general; but his fundamental equations reflected only a momentary situation, for a given total output. It remained to determine the effects of changes in the total volume of output. Here attention shifts, and takes a step backward, as it were; for Keynes' analysis is addressed to variations in employment. The classical writers had not only taken the quantity of products to be distributed as given; they had based their perfectly logical and consistent theory of prices and distribution on the tacit hypothesis of a state of equilibrium in which all the factors of production were being employed. The expression "full employment" lends itself unreadily to translation, and its use in the contemporary English literature of economics is universal. Through the persistence of worklessness—a sore subject with British economists, and an outrage to their theoretical position—the happy state of affairs implied by this term "full employment" has become the aim and the ideal of all political economy:

What is the criterion of improvement of the economic situation? [asks *The Economist;* [11]] the classical economists would have replied unhesitatingly, "Increase of the average real income!" . . . It was not until the first decade of this century that a full volume of employment gained equal status with the rise of real income as a criterion of economic efficacy. Since the war, we may have gone too far in this direction. There is today among statesmen and economists a tendency to concentrate attention on reducing the ranks of the unemployed at the expense not only of the real income of the employed, but also of the average income of the population as a whole.

Now that is just the point. It is true that the classical economists paid too little attention to the forces determining the level of employment; but today the pendulum seems to have swung in the opposite direction. If increase of real income and consumption of that income are the ends of all economic activity, then control of employment (of capital as well as of men) is of course only a means. Yet one would have to conclude, with Keynes, that economic theory has got ahead of itself, and that before we can say how much consumable wealth will be produced and distributed, we must try to learn why workers cannot

[11] June 13, 1936.

all find steady occupation in a growing society. So we must turn back. How humiliating! How gratifying to those who ridicule the inability of economic science to solve pressing problems and the continual lack of agreement among its foremost exponents! The issue raised was, from the beginnings of the science, a subject of embittered dispute. It was this that embroiled Ricardo and Say with Malthus, Sismondi and many others:

This theorem, that to purchase produce is not to employ labor; that the demand for labor is constituted by the wages which precede the production, and not by the demand which may exist for the commodities resulting from the production . . . is, to common apprehension, a paradox; and even among political economists of reputation, I can hardly point to any, except Mr. Ricardo, and M. Say, who have kept it constantly and steadily in view. Almost all others occasionally express themselves as if a person who buys commodities, the produce of labor . . . created a demand for [labor] as really . . . as if he had bought the labor itself directly, by the payment of wages. It is no wonder [Mill adds ruefully] that political economy advances slowly, when such a question as this still remains open at its very threshold.[12]

Has the science made any progress since? Keynes's book, which reopens the whole subject, might lead us to doubt it. And in what degree can we now speak of science?

When after all sorts of arrangements and preparations, new difficulties are encountered just as one believes himself in sight of the goal—when, to reach it, one is often obliged to retrace one's steps and take a different road—or when agreement cannot be had among those working in the field concerning the manner in which the common end should be pursued—then one may be sure that inquiry has yet to enter upon the path of science, and is merely groping.[13]

If economic thought is indeed still at such a point as to require remolding from the bottom up in order to arrive at a judgment of phenomena in the world of today that will give us a basis for positive action, Keynes will have done us a real service. But if his new theory is after all not so revolutionary as he claims— more, if it is only an analytical rationalization of a policy dear

[12] *Principles of Political Economy*, book I, chapter V, section 9.
[13] Kant, *Critique of Pure Reason*, preface to 2nd edition.

to him, and one we have long known to be so—was it necessary not only to sow discord among economists, but to cast ridicule upon that portion of our hard-gained and laboriously disseminated knowledge, which the public so willingly blames for mistakes whose consequences it suffers? Keynes is here without indulgence for his predecessors, in particular for his teacher, Marshall, to whom, as he himself acknowledges in a masterly biography, he owes the best of his theoretical training. And he admits that his own book is utterly at variance with what he had once learned and then taught for years afterwards.

What, then, is the essential novelty of the General Theory?

What might catch public attention first of all is of course the new identity between investment and saving. The *Treatise* rested wholly on a distinction between the two, through a very special definition of income that excluded profit, or at least "abnormal" profit (*General Theory*, p. 61). But Keynes has by no means given up explaining economic fluctuations by anomalies of the mechanism of saving.[14] This particular phenomenon has always intrigued him. It will be recalled how he placed it in his striking portrait, drawn in 1919, of nineteenth century Europe:

The capitalist classes were allowed to call the best part of the cake theirs and were theoretically free to consume it, on the tacit underlying condition that they consumed very little of it in practice. . . . There grew round the non-consumption of the cake all those instincts of puritanism which in other ages has withdrawn itself from the world and has neglected the arts of production as well as those of enjoyment. And so the cake increased; but to what end was not clearly contemplated.[15]

14 Mr. Rist wrote on this subject: "J. M. Keynes, having sought diligently in a theory of investments and savings for an adequate explanation of the price level, has just affirmed, in a ringing article, the importance he assigns to the recent increase in the output of gold." (*Revue d' Économie Politique*, September-October 1936, p. 1521.) Keynes has never denied the part played by gold in price movements, and the article to which Mr. Rist refers ("The supply of gold," *Economic Journal*, September 1936, p. 412) does not appear to me, in this respect, so much of an innovation. Keynes merely discusses some probable effects of the present gold inflation. Monetary abundance due to accelerated production of gold, for the Keynes of the *Treatise*, would be only a special case of excess of investment over saving. According to the new terminology of the *General Theory*, it would have the same effects on the capital market, but by strengthening the liquidity of the banking system.

15 *The Economic Consequences of the Peace*, p. 20.

The tone became more ironical in *Monetary Reform* (1923):

To save and to invest became at once the duty and the delight of a large class. . . . The morals, the politics, the literature, and the religion of the age joined in a grand conspiracy for the promotion of saving. God and Mammon were reconciled. Peace on earth to men of good means. A rich man could, after all, enter into the Kingdom of Heaven—if only he saved. . . .[16]

But this playfulness conceals an imperfectly satisfied curiosity. "Were the Seven Wonders of the World built by Thrift?" he asked in the *Treatise;* "I deem it doubtful."[17] It became apparent that the total capital being accumulated was not equal to the aggregate amount of savings. The celebrated distinction between "saving" and "investment" might help clear up the mystery, provided it were stated in what the difference consisted. Keynes was aware in 1931 that if profit was included in income, the identity of saving and investment became obvious.[18] Such an identity today, then, is only a consequence of a new terminology, and does not imply so great an overturn as might be imagined.

The mystery, however, does not seem to be explained very clearly in the *General Theory;* it appears to reside in the relationship of these concepts to time. At this point Keynes brings in the factor of expectations, and throughout his book it is in terms of forecasts that the new entities are defined. We shall have occasion to return to this major innovation shortly. But where it might have been most felicitously applied, Keynes leaves us still in doubt; savings (p. 63) are equal to the difference between income and consumption; and, by definition, income corresponds to the total value of output, which is to say to the sum of consumption and investment. It follows quite naturally that saving and investment are equal, if not identical. The manifest contradiction between this definition and that of the *Treatise* is explained when it is considered that any saving amounts to the acquisition of an asset, whether in liquid money or in actual goods; [19] conversely, the establishment of an in-

---

16 *Monetary Reform,* (American edition, 1924, pp. 9-10).

17 *Treatise,* vol. II, p. 150.

18 *Economica, op. cit.,* November 1931.

19 Mr. A. P. Lerner (*Revue internationale du travail,* October 1936, p. 477) points out that the appearance of "hoarding" does not interfere with equality

vestment through the banking system is necessarily attended on the other hand by an equivalent diminution of the share of income devoted to consumption.

But Keynes does not clearly tell us that this diminution is not instantaneous and that the mechanism of saving must be understood in terms of two successive "periods," as would appear from D. H. Robertson's terminology, which he nevertheless regards as an alternative to his own. Nor does he approve the use of the term "forced saving" (p. 79); but, as Robertson brought to his attention,[20] he does recognize the fact of an imbalance between the total quantity of capital in existence at a given time and the corresponding quantity of "voluntary" savings; it may be, as he contends, that a standard rate of saving must first be defined in order to specify the quantity of investments deriving from another source. But the fact of the imbalance is not to be doubted, and continues moreover to underlie the General Theory.

If Keynes had resorted more explicitly in this part of his exposition to his original use of "expectations," the difficulty would have been much less. On this particular problem, the suggestion made by Ohlin brings some enlightenment; though Keynes says (p. 77) that his mistake in the *Treatise* had been not to distinguish between anticipated and realized return, he does not yet make use of this distinction in his new terminology of savings. Ohlin, on the other hand, points out [21] that if we consider the plans and forecasts of entrepreneurs, there is not necessarily, beforehand, identity between the sums of money which some decide to save and others to invest. But retrospectively, behindhand, the results realized generally differ from

---

of the two terms according to the new definition. For according to him, though the individual can hoard, and though individual investments and saving can of course be different, there can be no *net* hoarding for society as a whole unless the total stock of money increases; otherwise, all individual hoarding implies de-hoarding elsewhere. This assertion can be understood only insofar as Mr. Lerner allows changes in the velocity of circulation to depend only on those in quantity of money held. It seems to me, however, that any slowing in velocity of circulation, any lengthening of the interval between two consecutive payments, amounts to hoarding, without necessarily bringing in an overall increase of the stock of money.

[20] Some Notes on Mr. Keynes' General Theory of Employment," *Quarterly Journal of Economics*, vol. 51, 1936, p. 178.

[21] "Some Notes on the Stockholm Theory of Savings and Investments," *Economic Journal*, March 1937, pp. 64-65.

expectations because the quantity of capital invested cannot but correspond to the existing volume of savings. Whether the difference between expectation and results is called "forced savings" according to the current terminology, or, according to the quite recent one of R. G. Hawtrey,[22] "passive investment," it is still understood that the causes of general imbalance are to be found in the capital market. The monetary theory of saving remains the pivot of the demonstration, but the new identity hardly helps us to understand the complex phenomena that come in with money. However, Keynes feels that it gets closer to reality, and besides, the use of unaccustomed devices is to give us the answer to the riddle of unemployment.

*   *   *

What, then, is to be proved? Essentially this: That in a society where not all the productive forces are employed, the classical analysis is inapplicable; and since it is necessary precisely to know why unemployment exists—how there can be a state of equilibrium without "full employment"—we should inquire what forces determine this state of equilibrium. Over against the classical theory of balancing of the labor and capital markets by the interplay of supply and demand, Keynes sets the new variables of the general theory: the propensity to consume, the marginal efficiency of capital, and liquidity preference.

THE PROPENSITY TO CONSUME

It is correct to say that most "classical" analyses of the operation of production, and more especially of the capital market, rest on the hypothesis of absence of unemployment. And most of the time this hypothesis does remain implicit. In the course of more recent analysis, however, its necessity to rigorous argument has been so felt that it has often been expressed with all the clarity one could wish: "We shall assume," writes Mr. Rist, "a society in which the forces of production are all employed." [23] In such a case, the classical analysis was correct, upon condition,

---

22 *Capital and Employment*, p. 176.
23 *Essais sur quelques problèmes économiques et monétaires*, p. 205.—See also, for an analytical justification of this hypothesis, F. A. Hayek, "The Paradox of Saving," *Economica*, May 1931, p. 140.

says Keynes, of appealing to two more hypotheses (p. 21): the classical theory of wages, and Say's Law.

The traditional theory of wages required that the utility of the wage be equal to the marginal disutility of the labor performed; otherwise stated, a decline in the demand for labor should normally lead wage earners to accept a reduction in the level of their wages until their value coincides with the marginal productivity of labor. This rule is compatible with the existence of unemployment due to "friction" (seasonal variations, incomplete mobility of workers from job to job or from region to region) and of voluntary unemployment. But the classical theory cannot logically accept the possibility of "involuntary" unemployment, defined by Keynes as follows: "Men are involuntarily unemployed if, in the event of a small rise in the price of wage-goods [consumers goods: products bought with wages] relatively to the money-wage, both the aggregate supply of labour willing to work for the current money-wage and the aggregate demand for it at that wage would be greater than the existing volume of employment" (p. 15).

The distinction between money wage and real wage affords an exploration of the consequences of this definition. By the "classical" theory, a slight decline in real wages sufficed to increase the demand for labor; it assumed that the demand curves shift with all price movements. Now in actuality it is the money wage that the workers look to. French readers of Simiand will perhaps recognize this as a familiar theme. But does the experience of certain recent events encourage us to see the money wage as the only factor determining the movements of supply and demand? Of course, it is often urged, it is well known that in times of prosperity and rising prices, workers are stimulated by the high profits of enterprises to demand wage increases. But for some time now, it has not been only in time of prosperity that such movements occur! "Having regard to human nature and our institutions, it can only be a foolish person who would prefer a flexible wage policy to a flexible money policy . . ." (p. 268). It would seem that Keynes acknowledges the necessity of reducing real wages to diminish unemployment. If so, he is being perfectly classical,[24] or if you will, traditional.

[24] J. Viner, "Mr. Keynes and the Causes of Unemployment," *Quarterly Journal of Economics*, vol. 51, 1936-1937, p. 158.

But it is hard to tell whether he regards this policy as economically necessary, or whether, in order to render it more palatable to the public, he brings in considerations of fairness and practical politics while arriving at it indirectly through monetary manipulations. In any case, he will have to reckon with the practical experience of union negotiators; even if they have not read the *General Theory,* it would seem that the various postwar monetary upheavals, and certain incidents more recent still, have today enabled many a layman to grasp the distinction between money wages and real wages.

Are we moreover to assume that reduction of nominal wages is in no case an effective means of combatting unemployment? This is where those celebrated "expectations" came in. The volume of employment depends, at all events, on the sums that entrepreneurs have decided to invest in production. These in turn depend only indirectly on prices existing at the time; for it is the entrepreneurs' expectations that determine the volume of sums to be invested; a decline in wages, opening up the prospect of a further decline, will not serve to increase the demand for labor (p. 263). It is upon probable consumption expenditures that the expectations are based. These future expenditures, or the "effective demand," correspond to the point of intersection of the entrepreneurs' over-all supply and demand functions (expressed in "anticipated" prices). Keynes gives the name of *"propensity to consume"* to the ratio of consumption expenditures to the total income of the community (the marginal propensity $\frac{dC}{dY}$ being (p. 115) the ratio of infinitesimal increments of the two variables). Now the volume of employment is controlled by that of investments. What part, then, is played by the propensity to consume?

This brings us to the multiplier theory, under which Keynes merely develops some reflections due to R. F. Kahn on the incremental effects of a capital investment.[25] Obviously the movements of capital entailed by investing a certain sum devoted,

[25] "The Relation of Home Investment to Unemployment," *Economic Journal,* June 1931. See also an excellent analysis of this complicated question in J. M. Clark, *The Economics of Planning Public Works,* pp. 80ff., and E. R. Walker, "Public Works as a Recovery Measure," *Economic Record,* vol. 11, December 1935.

say, to the execution of a given public works program, will not be confined to the original sum, and a certain amount of additional investments will result, after a varying interval of time, from that initial outlay. The sums invested will more or less rapidly permeate the structure of production, first leading to expenditures among enterprises, and later, when they reach the consumer through payment of wages or other income, causing a demand for consumption goods, which in turn will step up demand for intermediate goods, and so on.

Most analyses of this highly complex phenomenon assume, as we have seen, that all the factors of production are employed. In that case a new investment can only have the effect, in production as a whole, of transferring factors from one branch to another, most often from the consumption goods to the production goods market. It then becomes difficult to speak of *net* secondary effects of the initial investment, since their addition does not go to augment total output. Kahn's multiplier measured the ratio of the immediate increment of employment, due to a given investment, to the total increment. Keynes here defines his investment multiplier as the ratio of the total increment of income brought about by a given increment of investments, to this original increment (Y income, I investment, multiplier $k = \dfrac{\Delta Y}{\Delta I}$).

One might first point out that it is very hard to tell what moment to choose for evaluating the final result Y. The interval between the initial outlay and the time when the money invested reaches consumers is not only highly variable, but scarcely amenable to averaging without recourse to some concept like the "Austrian" theory's "period of production"— apparently not very congenial to Keynes (p. 76). His "period of production" (p. 287), defined in terms of the time elapsed before increased demand for a given product expresses itself in a diminished elasticity of employment, looks very much like a *petitio principii*. But the effects of the multiplier, approximate as they are, are indubitable. Far more debatable is the function making the multiplier depend on the propensity to consume. The latter is equal, by definition, to $1 - \dfrac{1}{k}$, since income is divided between consumption expenditures and investment expenditures.

Given the definition of the multiplier, the propensity to consume therefore becomes equal to $1 - \frac{1}{k}$, which amounts to saying that as the propensity to consume approaches unity, meaning if the community applies the totality of its income to consumption expenditures, the secondary effects of a primary investment would approach infinity. Remarkable! Back in 1933, Keynes thought the multiplier, in Great Britain, was slightly greater than 2.[26] It is altogether reasonable to use a term such as the "multiplier" to express a fact patent to everyone; one may go on to regard the proportion of income devoted to consumption as an independent function; lastly, it is quite permissible to make a certain function, called the "multiplier," depend *by definition* on a certain variable called the "propensity to consume." It is another matter to turn this formal relationship into a causal relationship.[27]

The entire demonstration, it would seem, nevertheless rests on this function. The volume of employment depends on the over-all demand function, the propensity to consume, and the volume of investments. When the volume of employment increases, income increases also; but, "when aggregate real income is increased, aggregate consumption is increased, but not by so much as income" (p. 27; pp. 96, 116). The propensity to consume is less than unity. Savings accumulate more rapidly, too rapidly to allow entrepreneurs to base their expectations on an increase in effective demand.

So it is not surprising that "Say's Law" should be altogether abandoned by Keynes. In his biographical essay on Malthus,[28] he was apparently already struck by the latter's ideas, expressed in his correspondence with Ricardo, on the respective effects of consumption and accumulation. Ricardo's opinion appears clearly enough in a letter of September 16, 1814:

Effectual demand consists of two elements, the *power* and the *will* to purchase; but I think the will is very seldom wanting where the

[26] *The Means to Prosperity*, p. 11.—See also a recent article in the *Times*, March 11, 1937 ("Is it Inflation?"), where he puts the multiplier close to 3 in present circumstances.

[27] See the penetrating criticism by G. v. Haberler, *Zeitschrift für Nationalökonomie*, vol. VII, no. 3, August 1936.

[28] *Essays in Biography*, 1933, pp. 95ff.

power exists, since desire of accumulation will occasion demand just as effectually as a desire to consume; it will only change the objects on which the demand will exercise itself.[29]

Malthus replied:

I must admit that I see no other cause for the diminution of profits which, you will acknowledge, follows accumulation, than in the fall of prices of the product compared to the costs of production, or in other words in the diminution of effective demand.

In 1821, the discussion was resumed, but Malthus and Ricardo stood upon their respective positions. Malthus wrote on July 16, 1821,

You will yourself agree that a temporary increase in savings at a time when profits are high enough to encourage it, may entail a division of income capable of banishing any motive for increasing production. If such a state of affairs is not to be called stagnation, I know not what to call it. The more so as this stagnation must inevitably leave the new generation without employment. . . .

He wrote again in his treatise,[30]

The opinion of M. Say which states that, *un produit consommé . . . est un débouché fermé,* appears to me to be . . . directly opposed to just theory and . . . uniformly contradicted by experience. . . . What, I would ask, would become of the demand for commodities, if all consumption except bread and water were suspended for the next half-year? What an accumulation of commodities! *Quels débouchés!* What a prodigious market would this event occasion!

What would become of the commodities? Wrote J.-B. Say to Malthus,[31]

Well! Sir, they would sell for every bit as much. After all, what was thereby added to the sum of capital would buy beer, coats, shirts, shoes, furniture from the producer class, which the sums saved would put to work.

Sound reasoning, if we suppose, once more, that all the productive forces are employed; for the mechanism of saving has no other meaning than, in such a case, to allocate consumable

[29] *Letters of Ricardo to Malthus,* Bonar 1887, p. 43.
[30] *Principles of Political Economy,* p. 363, quoted in *General Theory,* p. 362.
[31] Letters to Malthus, *Oeuvres diverses,* Guillaumin, p. 470.

wealth to the making of intermediate goods, to the expansion of capital, to be expressed in an increment of future real incomes, but necessarily at the expense of immediate income. The celebrated theory of the wage fund, which, properly interpreted, contains a basic truth, too often disregarded, says nothing else: the real income commanded by the community, which is to say the aggregate of its consumption goods, is limited by the existing amount of capital, and is capable of increment only within very narrow limits; hence the "real-income fund" can increase only in the long run, through an increase in capital, and consequently requires a prior increment of saving.

Now among the numerous critics of this theory, some appear, with Malthus, to have had an intimation of the ultimate role of demand and of the paradox inherent in the mechanism of the formation of capital—the weak point in Say's reply; for new investments will not develop unless the state of demand for the goods to be produced warrants the expectation of selling them; if demand decreases and prices fall because of saving, the deflation in the consumer-goods industries is apt to be echoed at the higher levels. Ultimately, then, the real-income fund depends on consumer demand. Hermann, who opposed the classical economists by asserting that all demand for commodities is a demand for labor, implied that the elasticity of the fund was limited by that demand only. We find a kindred idea in Keynes, since his entire theory rests on the assumption of very great elasticity in the production of consumption goods.

For the classical analysis applies only to the special situation in which all the productive resources are employed, the case of "full employment," and so long as there exists unused wealth, ready to be allocated to production, it becomes unnecessary to diminish present consumption in order to increase capital, or, if one prefers, to promote investments. It is certainly true that the theory of saving requires revision at this point. But the conception of "full employment" as here presented surely does not suffice to clarify the problem. That state is not achieved, for Keynes, until there is no more involuntary unemployment, defined as we have seen, or again, until aggregate employment ceases to increase despite an increase in the effective demand for its output (p. 26), in other words until aggregate employment becomes inelastic. To this definition is added a new theory of prices, in the form of a statement of the quantity theory of money (p. 304), for so long as aggregate output increases under the impetus of effective demand due to involvement of unused resources, an increase in monetary circulation will not necessarily raise prices.

So long as there is unemployment, *employment* will change in the same proportion as the quantity of money; and when there is full employment, *prices* will change in the same proportion as the quantity of money (p. 296).

But why seize upon the criterion of unemployment alone? If by "full employment" we mean *emploi complet,* the height of activity of all resources, men and capital alike, the definition of the term presents great difficulties. One would suppose that so long as the productive system is not operating at its maximum productivity, so long as all the resources employed are not yielding the technical output of which they are capable, the true state of "full employment" has not been reached. In that case, logic would require that the General Theory apply whenever the point of diminishing returns itself has not been reached. What difference is there, from the point of view of aggregate output, between a man involuntarily unemployed and a skilled worker whose abilities are ill utilized, a poorly maintained machine, a mistaken investment? Are we justified, in any of the latter three cases, in speaking of "full employment," even if, following Keynes' definition, there is no involuntary worklessness?

Now what Keynes has in mind is essentially the elimination of unemployment. As we have seen, this aim has today become the alpha and omega of economics and political economy in Great Britain: "Our present object is to discover what determines at any time the national income of a given economic system and (which is almost the same thing) the amount of its employment" (p. 247). But that is where the difficulty begins: *Is* it almost the same thing? A policy of combatting unemployment can always succeed, at least for a time, if one will *at all costs* put people to work, without regard to the productivity of the works undertaken. Can we flatter ourselves that we have then killed two birds with one stone, reducing unemployment and increasing national income at the same time? Far from being blind to the absurdity of the policy of unproductive public works, Keynes finds in it one more weapon to support his own theory:

If the Treasury were to fill old bottles with banknotes, bury them at suitable depths in disused coal mines which are then filled up to the surface with town rubbish, and leave it to private enterprise on well-tried principles of *laissez-faire* to dig the notes up again (the right to do so being obtained, of course, by tendering for leases of the note-bearing territory), there need be no more unemployment and, with the help of the repercussions, the real income of the community, and its capital wealth also, would probably become a good deal greater than it actually is. It would, indeed, be more sensible to build houses and the like; but if there are political and practical difficulties in the way of this, the above would be better than nothing (p. 129).

Between this *reductio ad absurdum* of the big-projects policy and the gold mining industry, Keynes sees a complete analogy; by virtue of the multiplier, an investment, though unproductive, must at last express itself in an increment of effective demand, hence of employment, hence of national income. So the policy of public works becomes, in the *General Theory*, the practical application of the ideas of Malthus, who in his *Principles* suggested unproductive expenditures to remedy the evils of the 1815-1820 crisis. "If only Malthus, instead of Ricardo, had been the parent stem from which nineteenth century economics proceeded, what a wiser and richer place the world would be today!" [32] But the ascendancy of Ricardo, "that able but mistaken mind," said Jevons, was absolute.[33] Ricardo wrote in a note on Malthus' *Principles:*

[32] *Essays in Biography*, p. 144.

[33] "Ricardo conquered England as completely as the Holy Inquisition conquered Spain" (p. 32). But Keynes is at least inaccurate when he later says that Effective Demand is not mentioned even once in Marshall's works (see *Principles*, 8th ed., pp. 511 and 699). Keynes gives us, moreover, a rather strange picture of what he calls the "classical" school, embracing under this term, apart from Ricardo's forerunners (in Marx's sense), "the *followers* of Ricardo, . . . including (for example) J. S. Mill, Marshall, Edgeworth and Prof. Pigou" (p. 3). He tells us elsewhere that his "classical" critics will be in doubt "whether what I am saying is utterly false, or whether I am saying nothing new." One might well be in doubt, for example, whether the new conception of "user cost" (p. 53 and appendix to chapter VI, p. 65) is much different from Marshall's (*op. cit.*, pp. 360 and 421). Again, it is certainly untrue to say that

If, of the two things necessary to demand, the will and the power
to purchase, the will should prove wanting, and we should consequently suffer a general depression of trade, we could do no better
than follow Mr. Malthus' advice and have the government step in
where the public is holding back. We must then petition the Crown
to dismiss the economic ministers and appoint others able to provide more effectively for the best interests of the country by encouraging luxury and public spending.[34]

Ricardo thought he was being very ironical.

THE RATE OF INTEREST

At one end of the system, then, Keynes finds that inadequacy
of effective demand is at the bottom of the imbalances which
Say's Law failed to explain. But the entrepreneur, in order to
be able to produce, must not only rely on the future proceeds
of his sales; he must also be able to borrow at reasonable rates.
The *General Theory* gives us a new explanation of interest,
and leads us to a policy perhaps less new, for one acquainted
with Keynes, but quite considerably different from that of the
Treatise.

The theory of interest, of all elements of economics, is certainly the one that, since its beginning, has suffered most vicis-
situdes. It is perhaps the best example of the nature of this
science, of its scope, and of the chief difficulties it encounters,
combining nearly all of them: notably those of distinguishing
between lawfulness and necessity, between ethics and expository
theory; that of looking behind monetary phenomena for actual
consequences; those, lastly, associated with the "time factor."
Here again, Keynes would have us replace the "classical"
theory with his "general theory"; but between the two, the
theory of interest has a long history to look back upon. If we
take the classical theory back to Hume, we shall already find
the two main ideas that were to dominate the endeavors of
later authors: first, the influence on the rate of interest of the
quantity of money; and secondly, its relationships to the commercial rate of profit.

---

the idea of a difference between *savings* and *investment* only appeared in some
post-war theories (*Economic Journal*, June 1937, p. 249). The distinction is very
clearly made in Bagehot, *Lombard Street,* chapter VI.

[34] See David Ricardo, *Notes on Malthus*, ed. Hollander and Gregory, 1928,
p. 162. The introduction contains an excellent summary of the argument.

Hume showed clearly that money could accumulate in a country without affecting the rate of interest, and that the latter depended on three circumstances: demand by borrowers, supply of "wealth" by lenders, and the profit drawn from trade. Hume was already distinguishing between interest, the price asked and paid for a loan of money, and the commercial profit which enabled the borrower to pay that price, and he emphasized that the bond between them was a relationship of mutual dependence ("they mutually forward each other").[35] Later, however, the two terms were frequently confused. Still, the classical form of the quantity theory of money rested upon utter elimination of the role of the interest rate from the monetary mechanism of establishment of prices.

It is only with Wicksell[36] that we find the first attempt at unification.[37] Wicksell's contribution, in fact, was twofold. First he separated the monetary rate of interest from the hypothetical "natural" rate that would have resulted from equilibrium of capital supply and demand in a barter economy, and he assumed that as a result of the presence of money alone, the effective market rate could fail to correspond to this ideal rate in actuality. Next he supposed that through the mechanism of credit, the rate of interest had an influence on prices; that a rise of the monetary rate above the "natural" level produced a fall, and a decline below that level a rise, in prices. But Wicksell went on to conclude that if the natural rate coincided with the monetary rate, stability of prices would follow. Davidson then pointed out that in a progressive economy where accumulation of wealth takes place normally, the equilibrium rate between capital supply and demand was necessarily greater than would correspond to a stable price level, in which case such stability could be obtained only by swelling monetary circulation.[38] But Keynes, who acknowledged in the *Treatise* what his ideas owed to Wicksell, adopted the concept of a natural rate, the one placing investments and savings in equilibrium. From this theory he derived a banking policy intended

[35] *Essays*, ed. Routledge, p. 221.

[36] *Geldzins und Gütterpreise*, Jena 1898. Recently translated into English by R. F. Kahn: *Interest and Prices*, Macmillan, 1936.

[37] See Rist, "Théories relatives à l'or, au taux de l'escompte et aux prix," *Revue d'Economie Politique*, September-October 1935.

[38] See Hayek, *Monetary Theory and the Trade Cycle*, pp. 113-114.

to avoid excessively violent price fluctuations by manipulating the rate of discount.

Side-by-side with the "natural rate" theory of Wicksell and the neo-Wicksellians, that of the "real rate" suggested by Marshall and further developed by I. Fisher, served to explain how price movements, or rather anticipation of price movements, reacted upon the rate of interest, and why long-term interest rate rises coincided with periods of rising prices, and vice versa. Between these two theories, there was no room for any contradiction or paradox; but neither of them made interest an exclusively monetary phenomenon. It would seem that Keynes burdens the "general" theory of interest with this exclusiveness; whether in the circumstances determining its establishment or in its effects on the productive system, it is in fact money that now assumes the main role, not real factors.

Keynes distinguishes two rates: First, the marginal efficiency of capital (*efficacité marginale du capital;* in the previously cited article by Lerner, *Revue internationale du travail,* p. 481, the French translator adopts the convenient term *rendement-limite* "limit of yield"), which agrees fairly closely with Fisher's "rate of return over cost" [39] (taux de rendement par rapport au coût), expresses the rate that would equate the present value of the annuities yielded by a given capital to its supply price, or, if one prefers, its replacement cost (p. 135). The rate of yield is consequently the limit of the price that entrepreneurs will pay, on the basis of expectations, to obtain the requisite capital for an undertaking. This is the demand price of capital, the price bid by the borrowers; not to be confused with the rate of interest, which is the price asked by lenders in exchange for a sum of liquid money. The former rate expresses no actual ratio of productivity, but only the effect of expectations, and will decrease when the aggregate volume of capital invested increases, both because the replacement cost in that case itself increases, and because the anticipated yield decreases. The schedule of marginal efficiency of capital thus gives us the demand curve, or demand schedule, of investments (p. 126). Thus the volume of investments will be adjusted to the point where the marginal efficiency of capital exactly corresponds with the level of the current rate of interest.

[39] *Théorie de l'intérêt,* French ed., p. 155; *General Theory,* p. 140.

LIQUIDITY PREFERENCE

But this point of equilibrium tells us nothing, because the rate of interest is itself a datum in the system, not depending, according to the classical formula, on supply of and demand for savings, nor on psychological factors called in turn by the names of "abstinence," "waiting," "time preference," "impatience," but on a new function, *"liquidity preference,"* which serves to explain the role of money in the economic system (p. 168): the basic property of money is to be a means of liquid payment, so to lend one's money involves at once an immediate disadvantage and a risk. It is to offset this loss of liquidity that lenders exact interest, varying with the strength of their preference for liquid effects. The supply curve of capital (which actually has the form of an ordinary demand curve) thus expresses the relation $M = L(r)$, and the rate of interest decreases as the quantity of money increases. The propensity to hoard becomes a sufficient explanation of the rate of interest, which depends on "money supply and demand," or again, serves to equilibrate "supply and demand for hoarding." [40]

The rate of interest thus becomes a purely monetary and at all events a purely conventional phenomenon (p. 203). For the operation of our economic system depends on individual decisions based on expectations, and insurance against the unforeseeable risks of the future, immediate or more remote, finds its simplest expression in the accumulation of a reserve of liquid money. Money acts, so long as its rate of circulation is not infinite, as a means of waiting, as a link between present and future. Knight [41] had pointed out that interest was hardly conceivable except in a society where the future did not admit of firm predictions. Keynes, by introducing into his theory of interest the part played by expectations, quite felicitously connects the "pure," or "real," theory to the money theory: "The classical school have had quite a different theory of the rate of interest in Volume I dealing with the theory of value from what they have had in Volume II dealing with the theory of money" (pp. 182-183). " 'Interest' has really no business to

[40] *Economic Journal,* June 1937, pp. 241 and 250.
[41] *Risk, Uncertainty and Profit,* pp. 168 and 321.

turn up at all in Marshall's *Principles of Economics,*—it belongs to another branch of the subject" (p. 189). In so doing, however, he definitely abandons the neo-Wicksellian line of thought. In the General Theory, there is no place for a natural rate, even though he grants (p. 242) that a "neutral" rate might be defined as that prevailing in a state of "full employment."

Does the liquidity-preference function suffice to explain the phenomenon of interest? Keynes seems to think so. The liquidity-preference schedule shows us the rate of interest decreasing as the quantity of money increases. Here we have indeed come a long way from Hume and the classical theory. But, Keynes adds, "the most stable . . . element in our contemporary economy has been hitherto, and may prove to be in future, the minimum rate of interest acceptable to the generality of wealth-owners" (p. 309). Be that as it may, there have been very considerable fluctuations of the rate of interest since the beginning of the nineteenth century, especially the past forty years. Perhaps Keynes refers only to the lower limit, defined by Cassel in his *Nature and Necessity of Interest,* and still expressed in the celebrated Victorian saying, "John Bull can stand many things, but he cannot stand 2 per cent" (p. 309). However that may be, it is the rate of interest thus determined that sets a limit on the capacity of entrepreneurs to borrow. For the marginal efficiency of capital may be less than the rate of interest: in that case, investments are inadequate, and unemployment appears.

Furthermore, there is no mechanism able to bring about equilibrium, and this is where Keynes finds the classical theory particularly at fault. For there is no rate determined by the supply and demand for savings, or rather, that mechanism does not tell us at what level the rate will be set and in what degree it will diverge from the marginal efficiency of capital; in fact, the amounts offered on the market depend far less on movements of the rate of interest than on those of income. The sums invested, on the other hand (the demand for capital), depend narrowly on the rate of interest; so variations in this rate directly affect investments, hence employment, hence incomes. When the rate of interest rises, the sums invested decrease at once, and so at the same time incomes contract (p. 181). The sums saved out of these incomes decrease, or at least do not necessarily increase in response to a higher rate. We cannot know the new point of equilibrium and the locations of the supply and demand curves unless we know, on the basis of the new income, how liquidity preference and hence the rate of interest have changed. At all events, the latter has to be a datum:

Thus the traditional analysis is faulty because it has failed to isolate correctly the independent variables of the system. Saving and Investment are the determinates of the system, not the determinants. They are the twin results of the system's determinants, namely, the propensity to consume, the schedule of the marginal efficiency of capital and the rate of interest (pp. 183–184).

> "And, sure, a reverent eye must see
> A Purpose in Liquidity,"

sang Rupert Brooke's fishes. The nature of this function is as yet vague. Yet liquidity preference helps us to clarify some of the most complex problems of the monetary mechanism. We know well enough that the entire banking structure rests, in the last analysis, on the need to be "liquid." But since in a society where production takes any appreciable time, there can never be real liquidity, in the sense that liquidation of an asset means final payment, the last step placing it in the hands of the consumer, the full maturity of the real asset, it is obvious that no productive system can ever be wholly and simultaneously liquid. In most cases, however, people call liquidity the possibility of transferring an asset, of exchanging a claim collectible at a given term for another whose date of liquidation is nearer at hand.[42] The existence of such institutions as stock exchanges has no other purpose than to render investments liquid for the individual that cannot be so for the community as a whole. "Of the maxims of orthodox finance none, surely, is more anti-social than the fetish of liquidity, the doctrine that it is a positive virtue on the part of investment institutions to concentrate their resources upon the holding of 'liquid' securities" (p. 155). Liquidity by transfer can have no effect on that of the system as a whole, and by definition, the larger the sums invested, the less liquid the system. When the

[42] H. G. Moulton, *Journal of Political Economy*, vol. XXVI, 1918.

members of the community, under the influence of a panic, try to "become liquid," it soon becomes apparent that they are attempting the impossible. The most sinister aspects of great speculative upheavals are all to be accounted for by this phenomenon.

So the mechanism of economic life, at all events that of investment, is little more than a game, in which the success of each depends on his ability first to guess his neighbor's expectations, and then to unload losses on him at the favorable moment. Thus decisions are taken at the third, fourth or fifth remove, and so on, for when we have managed to guess each other's thoughts, we must turn to guessing "what average opinion expects the average opinion to be" (p. 156). One is reminded of Poe's famous story of the little boy who won marbles by guessing what his opponents thought he was thinking. "When the capital development of a country becomes a by-product of the activities of a casino, the job is likely to be ill-done. The measure of success attained by Wall Street, regarded as an institution of which the proper social purpose is to direct new investment into the most profitable channels in terms of future yield, cannot be claimed as one of the outstanding triumphs of *laissez-faire* capitalism" (p. 159). However, Keynes is not yet ready to eliminate capitalism entirely. Though some English socialists have received this new book with enthusiasm,[43] and are trying to persuade Keynes that there is nothing left for him to do but to join them, the policy he envisages is still, as he himself says, "reasonably conservative." Non-socialist though it may be, however, its consequences would nevertheless modify the existing social order quite profoundly.

*   *   *

In this sense, the general philosophy Keynes presents to us is not very greatly different from what we have long since come to expect from him. The economic difficulties in which the world is floundering irritate him because a little reflection, as it seems to him, should be enough to solve them. After the effort he has had to make, by his own admission, and then demand of his readers, to rediscover the secret of the workings

[43] A. L. Rowse, *op. cit.*

of our economic system, one might think the difficulties were not so trifling. "The economic problem is not so difficult," he wrote one day, remarking upon Wells' interview with Stalin; "leave that to me, I'll take care of it." This sally is not so great an exaggeration of his attitude. An upheaval of our society from top to bottom has always seemed to him quite unnecessary. But today he considers that the extreme inequality of fortunes characteristic of the present capitalist system must be eliminated—an inequality that was justified, in the view of economists of the last century, by the part large incomes played in the accumulation of capital. Above all, we must maintain the propensity to consume. ". . . the growth of wealth, so far from being dependent on the abstinence of the rich, . . . is more likely to be impeded by it" (p. 373). So one of the economic bases of inequality of fortunes, in his view, disappears.

But is this enough to make Keynes a socialist? Appropriation of the means of production by the state seems to him no more necessary than before. It is much more important to centralize the control and direction of investment in its hands. Just recently, Keynes suggested establishment of a Public Office of Investment to draw up programs ready to be put into effect at the first sign of crisis.[44] The boom in England is giving him some cause for concern. But the last thing to do, if one would avoid it, would be to raise the rate of interest.

Interest policy, in fact, remains the heart of the system. Though he says (p. 164) that a purely monetary policy intended to affect the rate of interest seems to him inadequate today, that policy is still the necessary condition for a state of "full employment." One does not quite see how Keynes proposes to diminish liquidity preference, since it is not a matter of "injecting" a little money, in time of crisis, to "prime the pump," according to the familiar formula of reflation, and the General Theory is not basically an explanation of the business cycle. (Chapter 22, "Notes on the Trade Cycle," contains only some passing comments, and attributes the phenomenon to variations in the marginal efficiency of capital, to successive waves of optimism and pessimism.) Keynes nevertheless looks to a future when the State will have pushed capital development to a saturation point such that the marginal efficiency is re-

44 London *Times*, January 14, 1937, "How to Avoid a Slump."

duced to zero. This result might be brought about within a generation (p. 220).

Is it credible that the present wealth of the world warrants such optimism, and that Mill's famous "stationary state," the mere thought of which sent Paul Leroy-Beaulieu into raptures, can be so close? Keynes believes, though, that despite the disappearance—euthanasia—of the rentier (p. 375), the rate of interest will not fall absolutely to zero, and that enterprise may quite well persist, paying no more for the use of capital than its depreciation through wear and obsolescence, plus a margin required to cover risk and the exercise of skill and judgment (p. 221). In other words, profit properly so called would remain, but pure "interest" would be nil. Pending this state of bliss,[45] monetary policy should attempt, by diminishing liquidity preference, to keep the rate of interest below the marginal efficiency of capital.

Is not this policy likely to beget inflation pure and simple, and present us once more with the excesses that have characterized all great crises, and that were indulged in *con molto brio* during the last? For Keynes, apparently, there can be no inflation so long as there is not full employment. "It is when an acceleration of demand cannot significantly increase the volume of employment, and expresses itself merely in rising prices, that we can speak of true inflation."[46] England, with its 1,570,000 unemployed, is therefore approaching this limit today in his opinion, since prices (especially the cost of living) have been accelerating alarmingly for the past year (though much progress is still to be made in the "distressed areas" before true inflation need be feared). In that case one may wonder what is really meant by "full employment"! If Keynes considers that rising prices are a sufficient sign to serve as the criterion, many of the unwillingly unemployed may not agree with him. At any rate, this might put the famous "irreducible minimum" pretty high.

Keynes, then, is not blind to the dangers of a coming crisis.

[45] J. E. Meade (*op. cit.*, p. 277), for convenience of exposition, adopts the term "state of bliss" to designate the time when the stock of capital has reached the point where its marginal return is zero. In that condition the real income of the community is a maximum and the real satisfaction of economic wants as great as possible.
[46] London *Times*, March 11, 1937.

But the General Theory gives us no prescription against acceleration of the speculative boom. The persistence in London of rates never before reached, even at the low points in the latter years of the last century, is certainly an effect of the now inveterate belief in the enduring virtue of cheap money. If you ask a financier in the City today what will happen when the Bank of England rate goes up again, he will tell you without a smile (or nearly) that he sees no reason why it ever should. It will be curious to see what reaction that inevitable rise will produce, in the more or less early future, on the London market.[47] Will it cause more of a shock, the more the public has become convinced that the 2 per cent level must not be abandoned except under very serious circumstances, and especially so if there is a conviction that a rise in the discount rate must precipitate a crisis? Or will British sang-froid, allied with the spirit of the third and fifth removes, serve to avoid a panic rendered more dangerous than ever by the persistence of that ideology?

For this ideology, of course, Keynes is not alone responsible. At all times there have been hymns in praise of lowering the rate of interest. But it has only been for a few years now that British opinion—which has humiliating and anguished memories of the "deflation" following the return to the gold standard in 1925, those grim years when industry stopped, exports languished, and unemployment continued in a time of world prosperity—has seen the gold standard and the so-called orthodox monetary policy as the root of all evil.

Recently, practical bankers in London have learnt much, and one can almost hope that in Great Britain the technique of bank rate will never be used again to protect the foreign balance in conditions in which it is likely to cause unemployment at home (p. 339).

Certainly events count for something in the molding of contemporary ideas, if only of Keynes' own. But cannot Keynes, who has so much interest in the history of ideas, boast today of having failed not only to predict, but even to persuade? On March 7, 1931, an article appeared that ended, for generations perhaps, an era begun by Adam Smith in 1776. Keynes had

[47] Written in 1937. In 1957 the Bank of England discount rate was raised to 7 per cent.—Ed.

always wondered whether he was really a liberal. But the general staff of that army, now without troops, counted him among the strongest adversaries of protectionist remedies. "If there is one thing Protection can *not* do, it is cure Unemployment." [48] In 1931, his prestige turned the balance. And for many liberals, attached to free trade as the last symbol of their convictions, his conversion must have been a real tragedy. But then as always, Keynes acted in the best of faith. Today he has come round to an esoteric justification of the preconceptions of the man in the street, whose intuition, as he likes to say, is sounder than the classical economist's. "Now that Gavroche and Mr. Homais have come straight to the last word in philosophy, and with so little trouble too," wrote Renan, "a man has a hard time thinking."

After all this manifestation of candor, Keynes may be yielding to the temptations of his genius for mystification. When, for example, he rediscovers the neglected merits of the mercantilists, or pays belated homage to Silvio Gesell, the inventor of stamped (shrinking) money, to J. A. Hobson and to Major Douglas, or quotes Mandeville and his *Fable of the Bees* interminably in support of the virtues of prodigality, he certainly hopes to scandalize his more orthodox and less alert colleagues. And in that sense, he still belongs, in the field of economics, to the antipuritan and anti-Victorian tradition so well represented in the field of letters by Wells and Shaw. But behind this foolery, do we not sense some discomfiture, after a long and painful effort of conscience in quest of truth forlorn— *à la recherche de la vérité perdue?*

[48] *Nation and Athenaeum,* November 4, 1923, quoted by Keynes himself, *General Theory,* p. 334.

VII

F. A. HAYEK was born in Vienna in 1899. He acquired doctorates in law and economics at the University of Vienna and later taught economics there. In 1926 he became director of the Austrian Institute of Economic Research. In 1931 he was appointed Tooke professor of economic science and statistics at the University of London, where he remained until 1950, in which year he accepted the invitation to become professor of social and moral science at the University of Chicago—a position he still holds. Professor Hayek is the author of nearly a dozen books. Among the best known are: *Prices and Production,* 1931; *The Pure Theory of Capital,* 1941; *The Road to Serfdom,* 1944; and *The Constitution of Liberty,* 1960.

The following short excerpt is from *The Pure Theory of Capital,* pages 373-376. The American edition of which was published by the University of Chicago Press in 1941.

The paragraph under the heading "What 'Full Employment' Policy Means" is from *The Constitution of Liberty,* page 280, published by the University of Chicago Press in 1960.

The paragraph under the heading "Après Nous le Déluge" is also from *The Pure Theory of Capital,* page 409.

THE ECONOMICS OF ABUNDANCE

F. A. HAYEK

Now such a situation, in which abundant unused reserves of all kinds of resources, including all intermediate products, exist, may occasionally prevail in the depths of a depression. But it is certainly not a normal position on which a theory claiming general applicability could be based. Yet it is some such world as this which is treated in Mr. Keynes' *General Theory of Employment, Interest and Money,* which in recent years has created so much stir and confusion among economists and even the wider public. Although the technocrats, and other believers in the unbounded productive capacity of our economic system, do not yet appear to have realised it, what he has given us is really that economics of abundance for which they have been clamouring so long. Or rather, he has given us a system of economics which is based on the assumption that no real scarcity exists, and that the only scarcity with which we need concern ourselves is the artificial scarcity created by the determination of people not to sell their services and products below certain arbitrarily fixed prices. These prices are in no way explained, but are simply assumed to remain at their historically given level, except at rare intervals when "full employment" is approached and the different goods begin successively to become scarce and to rise in price.

Now if there is a well-established fact which dominates economic life, it is the incessant, even hourly, variation in the prices of most of the important raw materials and of the wholesale prices of nearly all foodstuffs. But the reader of Mr. Keynes' theory is left with the impression that these fluctuations of prices are entirely unmotivated and irrelevant, except towards the end of a boom, when the fact of scarcity is readmitted into the analysis, as an apparent exception, under the designation of "bottlenecks".[1] And not only are the factors which de-

---

[1] I should have thought that the abandonment of the sharp distinction between the "freely reproducible goods" and goods of absolute scarcity and the

termine the relative prices of the various commodities systematically disregarded; [2] it is even explicitly argued that, apart from the purely monetary factors which are supposed to be the sole determinants of the rate of interest, the prices of the majority of goods would be indeterminate. Although this is expressly stated only for capital assets in the special narrow sense in which Mr. Keynes uses this term, that is, for durable goods and securities, the same reasoning would apply to all factors of production. In so far as "assets" in general are concerned the whole argument of the *General Theory* rests on the assumption that their yield only is determined by real factors (*i.e.*, that it is determined by the given prices of their products), and that their price can be determined only by capitalising this yield at a given rate of interest determined solely by monetary factors.[3] This argument, if it were correct, would clearly have to be extended to the prices of all factors of production the price of which is not arbitrarily fixed by monopolists, for their prices would have to be equal to the value of their contribution to the product less interest for the interval for which the factors remained invested.[4] That is, the difference between costs and prices would not be a source of the demand for capital but would be unilaterally determined

---

substitution for this distinction of the concept of varying degrees of scarcity (according to the increasing costs of reproduction) was one of the major advances of modern economics. But Mr. Keynes evidently wishes us to return to the older way of thinking. This at any rate seems to be what his use of the concept of "bottlenecks" means; a concept which seems to me to belong essentially to a naïve early stage of economic thinking and the introduction of which into economic theory can hardly be regarded as an improvement.

[2] It is characteristic that when at last, towards the end of his book, Mr. Keynes comes to discuss prices, the "Theory of Price" is to him merely "the analysis of the relations between changes in the quantity of money and changes in the price level" (*General Theory*, p. 296).

[3] Cf. *General Theory*, p. 137: "We must ascertain the rate of interest from some other source and only then can we value the asset by 'capitalising' its prospective yield."

[4] The reason why Mr. Keynes does not draw this conclusion, and the general explanation of his peculiar attitude towards the problem of the determination of relative prices, is presumably that under the influence of the "real cost" doctrine which to the present day plays such a large rôle in the Cambridge tradition, he assumes that the prices of all goods except the more durable ones are even in the short run determined by costs. But whatever one may think about the usefulness of a cost explanation of relative prices in equilibrium analysis, it should be clear that it is altogether useless in any discussion of problems of the short period.

by a rate of interest which was entirely dependent on monetary influences.

We need not follow this argument much further to see that it leads to contradictory conclusions. Even in the case we have considered before of an increase in the investment demand due to an invention, the mechanism which restores the equality between profits and interest would be inconceivable without an independent determinant of the prices of the factors of production, namely their scarcity. For, if the prices of the factors were directly dependent on the given rate of interest, no increase in profits could appear, and no expansion of investment would take place, since prices would be automatically marked to make the rate of profit equal to the given rate of interest. Or, if the initial prices were regarded as unchangeable and unlimited supplies of factors were assumed to be available at these prices, nothing could reduce the increased rate of profit to the level of the unchanged rate of interest. It is clear that, if we want to understand at all the mechanism which determines the relation between costs and prices, and therefore the rate of profit, it is to the relative scarcity of the various types of capital goods and of the other factors of production that we must direct our attention, for it is this scarcity which determines their prices. And although there may be, at most times, some goods an increase in demand for which may bring forth some increase in supply without an increase of their prices, it will on the whole be more useful and realistic to assume for the purposes of this investigation that most commodities are scarce, in the sense that any rise of demand will, *ceteris paribus,* lead to a rise in their prices. We must leave the consideration of the existence of unemployed resources of certain kinds to more specialised investigations of dynamic problems.

This critical excursion was unfortunately made necessary by the confusion which has reigned on this subject since the appearance of Mr. Keynes' *General Theory.*

WHAT "FULL EMPLOYMENT" POLICY MEANS

In order to understand the situation into which we have been led, it will be necessary to take a brief look at the intellectual sources of the full-employment policy of the "Keynesian" type. The development of Lord Keynes's theories started from the correct insight that the regular cause of extensive unemployment is real wages that are too high. The next step consisted in the proposition that a direct lowering of money wages could be brought about only by a struggle so painful and prolonged that it could not be contemplated. Hence he concluded that real wages must be lowered by the process of lowering the value of money. This is really the reasoning underlying the whole "full-employment" policy, now so widely accepted. If labor insists on a level of money wages too high to allow of full employment, the supply of money must be so increased as to raise prices to a level where the real value of the prevailing money wages is no longer greater than the productivity of the workers seeking employment. In practice, this necessarily means that each separate union, in its attempt to overtake the value of money, will never cease to insist on further increases in money wages and that the aggregate effort of the unions will thus bring about progressive inflation.

"Après Nous le Déluge"

I cannot help regarding the increasing concentration on short-run effects—which in this context amounts to the same thing as concentration on purely monetary factors—not only as a serious and dangerous intellectual error, but as a betrayal of the main duty of the economist and a grave menace to our civilization. To the understanding of the forces which determine the day-to-day changes of business, the economist has probably little to contribute that the man of affairs does not know better. It used, however, to be regarded as the duty and the privilege of the economist to study and to stress the long effects which are apt to be hidden to the untrained eye, and to leave the concern about the more immediate effects to the practical man, who in any event would see only the latter and nothing else. The aim and effect of two hundred years of continuous development of economic thought have essentially been to lead us away from, and "behind," the more superficial monetary mechanism and to bring out the real forces which guide long-run development. I do not wish to deny that the preoccupation with the "real" as distinguished from the monetary aspects of the problems may sometimes have gone too far. But this can be no excuse for the present tendencies which have already gone far towards taking us back to the pre-scientific stage of economics, when the whole working of the price mechanism was not yet understood, and only the problems of the impact of a varying money stream on a supply of goods and services with given prices aroused interest. It is not surprising that Mr. Keynes finds his views anticipated by the mercantilist writers and gifted amateurs: concern with the surface phenomena has always marked the first stage of the scientific approach to our subject. But it is alarming to see that after we have once gone through the process of developing a systematic account of those forces which in the long run determine prices and production, we are now called upon to scrap it, in order to replace it by the short-sighted philosophy of the business man raised to the dignity of a science. Are we not even told that, "since in the long run we are all dead," policy should be guided entirely by short-run considerations? I fear that these believers in the principle of *après nous le déluge* may get what they have bargained for sooner than they wish.

VIII

FRANCO MODIGLIANI was born in Rome, Italy. He became a Doctor in Jurisprudence at the University of Rome in 1939, and a Doctor in Social Science at the Graduate Faculty of Political and Social Science of the New School for Social Research, New York, in 1944. At the time of publication of the following article he was on the faculty of Bard College of Columbia University. He was research associate and chief statistician of the Institute of World Affairs from 1945 to 1948; associate professor and then full professor of economics at the University of Illinois from 1949 to 1952; and since 1952 has been professor of economics and industrial administration at the Carnegie Institute of Technology at Pittsburgh.

W. H. Hutt (see p. 397) has written: "Modigliani (whose 1944 article quietly caused more harm to the Keynesian thesis than any other single contribution) seems, almost unintentionally, to reduce to the absurd the notion of the coexistence of idle resources and price flexibility."

Modigliani's article, which appeared in *Econometrica* of January 1944, pages 45-88, seems to have particularly impressed the Keynesians because, beginning with the Keynesian vocabulary and many of the Keynesian concepts, he made alternative assumptions that led to some quite unKeynesian conclusions.

Modigliani has taken the opportunity offered by this reprinting to add a postscript acknowledging certain errors in section 13, and outlining needed corrections.

131

LIQUIDITY PREFERENCE AND THE THEORY OF INTEREST AND MONEY

FRANCO MODIGLIANI

PART I

1. INTRODUCTION

The aim of this paper is to reconsider critically some of the most important old and recent theories of the rate of interest and money and to formulate, eventually, a more general theory that will take into account the vital contributions of each analysis as well as the part played by different basic hypotheses.

The analysis will proceed according to the following plan:

I. We start out by briefly re-examining the Keynesian theory. In so doing our principal aim is to determine what is the part played in the Keynesian system by the "liquidity preference," on the one hand, and by the very special assumptions about the supply of labor, on the other. This will permit us to distinguish those results that are due to a real improvement of analysis from conclusions that depend on the difference of basic assumptions.

II. We then proceed to consider the properties of systems in which one or both Keynesian hypotheses are abandoned. We thus check our previous results and test the logical consistency of the "classical" theory of money and the dichotomy of real and monetary economics.

III. From this analysis will gradually emerge our general theory of the rate of interest and money; and we can proceed to use this theory to test critically some recent "Keynesian" theories and more especially those formulated by J. R. Hicks in *Value and Capital*[1] and by A. P. Lerner in several articles.

IV. Finally, to make clear the conclusions that follow from our theory, we take issue in the controversial question as to

---

[1] J. R. Hicks, *Value and Capital*, Oxford University Press, 1939, 331 pp.

whether the rate of interest is determined by "real" or by monetary factors.

In order to simplify the task, our analysis proceeds in general, under "static" assumptions; this does not mean that we neglect time but only that we assume the Hicksian (total) "elasticity of expectation" to be always unity. In Hicks's own words this means that "a change in current prices will change expected prices in the same direction and in the same proportion." [2] As shown by Oscar Lange, this implies that we assume the "expectation functions," connecting expected with present prices, to be homogeneous of the first degree.[3]

Since all the theories we examine or formulate in this paper are concerned with the determinants of equilibrium and not with the explanation of business cycles, this simplification, although it is serious in some respects, does not seem unwarranted.

2. Three Alternative Macrostatic Systems

As a first step in the analysis, we must set up a system of equations describing the relation between the variables to be analyzed. In doing this we are at once confronted with a difficult choice between rigor and convenience; the only rigorous procedure is to set up a complete "Walrasian" system and to determine the equilibrium prices and quantities of each good: but this system is cumbersome and not well suited to an essentially literary exposition such as we intend to develop here. The alternative is to work with a reduced system: we must then be satisfied with the rather vague notions of "physical output," "investment," "price level," etc. In what follows we have chosen, in principle, the second alternative, but we shall check our conclusions with a more general system whenever necessary.

The equations of our system are:

(1) $$M = L(r, Y),$$
(2) $$I = I(r, Y),$$
(3) $$S = S(r, Y),$$
(4) $$S = I,$$

[2] *Ibid.*, p. 205.
[3] Cf. O. Lange, "Say's Law: a Restatement and Criticism" in *Studies in Mathematical Economics and Econometrics*, edited by Lange, McIntyre, and Yntema, The University of Chicago Press, 1942, pp. 67-68.

(5) $Y \equiv PX,$
(6) $X = X(N),$
(7) $W = X'(N)P.$

The symbols have the following meaning: Y, money income; M, quantity of money in the system (regarded as given); r, rate of interest; S and I, saving and investment respectively, all measured in money; P, price level; N, aggregate employment; W, money wage rate; X, an index of physical output.[4] We may also define C, consumption measured in money, by the following identity:

(8) $C \equiv Y - I.$

Identity (5) can be regarded as defining money income. There are so far 8 unknowns and only 7 equations; we lack the equation relating the wage rate and the supply of labor. This equation takes a substantially different form in the "Keynesian" system as compared with the "classical" systems.

In the classical systems the suppliers of labor (as well as the suppliers of all other commodities) are supposed to behave "rationally." In the same way as the supply of any commodity depends on the relative price of the commodity so the supply of labor is taken to depend not on the money wage rate, but on the real wage rate. Under the classical hypothesis, therefore, the last equation of the system takes the form:

(9a) $N = F\left(\dfrac{W}{P}\right)$; or, in the inverse form: $W = F^{-1}(N)P.$

The function F is a continuous function, although not necessarily monotonically increasing.

The Keynesian assumptions concerning the supply-of-labor schedule are quite different. In the Keynesian system, within certain limits to be specified presently, the supply of labor is assumed to be perfectly elastic at the historically ruling wage rate, say w_0. The limits mentioned above are given by equation (9a). For every value of W and P the corresponding value of

---

[4] This system is partly taken from earlier writings on the subject. See especially O. Lange, "The Rate of Interest and the Optimum Propensity to Consume," *Economica*, Vol. 5 (N. S.), February, 1938, pp. 12-32, and J. R. Hicks, "Mr. Keynes and the 'Classics'; A Suggested Interpretation," ECONOMETRICA, Vol. 5, April, 1937, pp. 147-159.

N from (9a) gives the maximum amount of labor obtainable in the market. As long as the demand is less than this, the wage rate remains fixed as w_0. But as soon as all those who wanted to be employed at the ruling real wage rate w_0/P have found employment, wages become flexible upward. The supply of labor will not increase unless the money wage rate rises relative to the price level.

In order to write the last equation of the "Keynesian" form of our system, we must express this rather complicated hypothesis in functional form. Taking (9a) as a starting point, we may write:

$$(9) \qquad W = aw_0 + \beta F^{-1}(N)P,$$

where a and β are functions of N, W, P, characterized by the following properties:

$$(10) \qquad \begin{aligned} a &= 1, & \beta &= 0, & \text{for} \quad N &\leqq N_0, \\ a &= 0, & \beta &= 1, & \text{for} \quad N &> N_0, \end{aligned}$$

where N_0 is said to be "full employment." Equations and inequalities (10) thus state that, unless there is "full employment" ($N = N_0$), the wage rate is not really a variable of the system but a datum, a result of "history" or of "economic policy" or of both. Equation (9) then reduces to $W = w_0$. But after "full employment" has been reached at wage rate w_0, the supply of labor ceases to be perfectly elastic: W becomes a variable to be determined by the system and (9) becomes a "genuine" equation. We should add that, even in the "Keynesian" system, it is admitted that the wage rate will begin to be flexible downward before employment has reached the zero level: but in order not to complicate equation (9) still further we can, without serious harm, leave the hypothesis in its most stringent form.

For generality we may also use equation (9) as it now stands, as the "supply of labor" function of the "classical" theory. But instead of conditions (10) we have the identities (for all values of N)

$$(11) \qquad a \equiv 0, \qquad \beta \equiv 1.$$

Some remarks are also necessary concerning the "demand for money" equation. According to the "quantity theory of money," the demand for money does not depend on the rate of interest but varies directly with money income. Under this hypothesis equation (1) reduces to

(1a) $M = kY$.

By properly combining the equations and conditions written above, we obtain three different systems which we will analyze in turn.

I. A "Keynesian" system consisting of equations (1) to (7) and (9) and conditions (10).

II. A "crude classical" system consisting of equations (1a), (2) to (7), and (9), and identities (11).

III. A "generalized classical" system consisting of the equations listed under II but with (1a) replaced by (1).

3. A RECONSIDERATION OF THE KEYNESIAN THEORY

In reconsidering the Keynesian system we shall essentially follow the lines suggested by J. R. Hicks in his fundamental paper, "Mr. Keynes and the 'Classics.' " [5] Our main task will be to clarify and develop his arguments, taking into account later theoretical developments.

Close consideration of the Keynesian system of equations [equations (1) to (7) and (9) to (10)] reveals that the first 4 equations contain only 4 unknowns and form a determinate system: the system of monetary equilibrium. We therefore begin by discussing its equations and its solution.

4. THE TRANSACTION DEMAND FOR MONEY

In a free capitalistic economy, money serves two purposes: (a) it is a medium of exchange, (b) it is a form of holding assets. There are accordingly two sources of demand for money: the transaction demand for money and the demand for money as an asset. This is the fundamental proposition on which the theory of the rate of interest and money rests; it is therefore necessary to analyze closely each source of demand and the factors that determine it.

The transaction demand for money is closely connected with the concept of the income period. We may define the income period as the (typical) time interval elapsing between the dates at which members of the community are paid for services rendered. We shall assume for the moment that this income period is approximately the same for every individual and that it coincides with the expenditure period.[6]

Each individual begins the income period with a certain income arising out of direct services rendered or out of property and with assets (physical and nonphysical) having a certain market value. In his endeavor to reach the highest level of satisfaction he is confronted with two sets of decisions: (a) he must decide what part of his income he will spend on consumption and what part he will save, (b) he must determine how to dispose of his assets.

The first set of decisions presents no special difficulty of analysis. On the basis of his tastes, his income, and market prices he will make a certain plan of expenditure to be carried out in the course of the income period. The amount of money that is necessary for individuals to carry out their expenditure plans is the *transaction demand for money by consumers,* as of the beginning of the period. The average transaction demand, on the other hand, depends on the rate at which expenditure takes place within the period.[7]

The difference between the individual's money income and the amount he decides to spend in the fashion discussed above is the money value of his savings (dissavings) for the income period. It represents the net increment in the value of his assets.

5. THE DEMAND FOR MONEY AS AN ASSET

Having made his consumption-saving plan, the individual has to make decisions concerning the assets he owns. These assets, let us note, consist of property carried over from the preceding income period *plus current savings.*

There are essentially three forms in which people can keep

[6] This means, for instance, that people are required by custom or contract to pay within the income period for what they have consumed in the period (rent, grocery bill, etc.) or else must rely on "consumers' credit."

[7] Thus if expenditure should proceed at an approximately even rate, it would be one-half the initial demand.

their assets: (a) money, (b) securities,[8] and (c) physical assets.

We shall for the moment eliminate the third alternative by distinguishing between entrepreneurial and nonentrepreneurial decisions. We consider as entrepreneurs individuals who hold assets in physical form; decisions concerning the acquisition or disposal of physical assets will accordingly be treated as entrepreneurial decisions and will be analyzed in connection with the schedule of the propensity to invest [equation (3)]. An individual's decision to acquire directly physical assets (say a house) or to reinvest profits in his enterprise can be split into two separate decisions, a decision to lend (to himself) and a decision to increase his entrepreneurial risk by borrowing (from himself).

We are therefore concerned here exclusively with decisions concerning nonphysical assets and with those factors that influence the choice between the first two alternatives. Our problem is to determine whether there is any reason for individuals to wish to hold some or all of their assets in the form of money and thus to demand money over and above the quantity they need for transactions.

In this respect there is little to add to the exhaustive treatment that this subject has received in recent literature.[9]

There are two properties that all assets, whether physical or not, share in different degrees: liquidity and risk. Following a criterion particularly stressed by Jacob Marschak, we shall define liquidity of an asset in terms of the perfection of the market in which it is traded. An asset is liquid if this market is perfect, i.e., an individual's decision to buy or sell does not affect the price finitely; it is illiquid in the opposite case. It is riskless if the price at which it sells is constant or practically so; it is risky if the price fluctuates widely.

8 Under the name of securities we include both fixed-income-bearing certificates and common stocks or equities. From the strictly economic point of view, common stocks should perhaps be considerd as a form of holding physical assets. For institutional reasons, however, equities have very special properties which make them in many respects more similar to bonds than to physical assets.

9 See, for instance, J. R. Hicks, *Value and Capital,* Chapters XIII and XIV and *passim;* J. M. Keynes, *The General Theory of Employment, Interest and Money,* New York, Harcourt, Brace and Company, 1936, 403 pp.; Mabel Timlin, *Keynesian Economics,* University of Toronto Press, 1942, Chapters V and VI; etc.

Securities clearly share with money the property of being highly liquid assets. Where there is an organized market, securities will not be significantly inferior to money in this respect. They have, however, two clear drawbacks in comparison with cash:

(a) They are not a medium of exchange. Assets generally accrue in the form of money through savings, and a separate transaction is necessary to transform them into securities. This transaction involves both subjective and objective costs.

(b) They are more risky than money since their market price is not constant. Even the "safest" type of securities, on which the risk of default can be neglected, fluctuates in price as the rate of interest moves. There are, it is true, some types of loans for which this last risk can be neglected, namely very-short-term loans. Let us assume, for the sake of precision, that the money market is open only on the first day of the income period; then the shortest type of loans will be those that mature at the end of said period. These types of assets will not be subject to the risk mentioned under (b) since, by assumption, the rate of interest cannot change while they are outstanding.[10]

It is just for this type of assets, however, that the disadvantage mentioned under (a), namely the cost of investment, weighs more heavily: for the yield they promise for the very short duration of the loan can only be small, so that even a moderate cost is sufficient to wipe it out. If, as is likely, the cost of investment does not rise in proportion to the amount invested, then short loans may be an interesting investment for large sums, but not so for small investors. Thus, if this were the only possible form of investment, we should expect that any fall in the rate of interest, not accompanied by a corresponding fall in the cost of investing, would induce a growing number of potential investors to keep their assets in the form of money, rather than securities; that is to say, we should expect a fall in the rate of interest to increase the demand for money as an asset.

In this respect, securities of longer maturity would appear to be superior, since the yield to be gathered by holding them

---

10 Even if this assumption were relaxed, the possible fluctuations in the rate of interst would be negligible and the extent to which they would affect the present value of the securities mentioned above could be disregarded.

until maturity is larger, while the cost of acquiring them need not be different. But as the importance of the cost element decreases, the importance of the risk element grows. As is well known, a given change in the rate of interest will affect most the present value of those bonds whose maturity is furthest away. If the only reason for owning assets were to earn the income they produce, these price fluctuations would not be so important. For, as long as the owner is in a position to hold the asset until maturity, there would be only a potential loss, a loss of better opportunities. There can be little doubt, however, that for a large part of the community the main reason for holding assets is as a reserve against contingencies. A form of assets whose value is not certain must be, *ceteris paribus,* inferior to one whose value is certain, namely money.

This very fact, besides, gives an additional reason why bonds of longer maturity should be a less safe form of holding assets. For there is much less certainty about faraway income periods than there is about the near future and the possibility that one will have to realize the assets before their maturity, if any, increases accordingly; while, on the other hand, it becomes increasingly difficult to make reliable forecasts about the level of the rate of interest and the future market value of the assets.

Securities, on the other hand, are clearly superior to money in that they yield an income. The ruling rate of interest measures the remuneration to be obtained by accepting the drawbacks and assuming the risks that are characteristic of securities as compared with money. Or, to look at it from another point of view, it measures the cost of holding money instead of securities in terms of foregone income. Thus a fall in the rate of interest has, in any event, the effect of making cash cheaper and hence more attractive as a form of holding assets.

In addition, several other reasons can be mentioned that cause a low rate of interest to discourage the holding of securities. In the first place, the risk element involved in holding securities becomes more pronounced when the rate of interest is low, for a smaller fall in the capital value of the asset is sufficient to wipe out the income already earned by holding the asset. Thus, for instance, the smaller the rate of interest, the smaller is the *percentage change* in the rate itself necessary to absorb the yield obtained by holding the asset a given length of time. Again, it has been pointed out by some authors that, as the rate of interest becomes lower, there is some ground to expect that possible movements will be predominantly in the direction of an increase and therefore unfavorable to the holders of securities.

In conclusion then, the lower the rate of interest, the larger will be the number of owners of assets who will prefer to hold these assets in the form of money for the income period; the demand for money to hold (as distinguished from money to spend, previously considered) or demand for money as an asset is a decreasing function of the rate of interest. Denoting this demand by D_a, we can write

$$D_a = D_a(r)$$

for the schedule of demand for money to hold.

What can we say about the characteristics of this function? It must clearly be a monotonically decreasing function of the rate of interest; in addition, however, it must have, in the author's opinion, two important properties:

In the first place, there must be some value of r, say r', such that $D_a(r) = 0$ for $r \geqq r'$. For there must be, for every individual, some minimum net yield per income period that will induce him to part entirely with money as an asset. Hence, if he can find some type of securities such that by holding them for a given number of income periods he expects to obtain a net yield equal to or larger than the minimum, his demand for money to hold will fall to zero.[11]

---

[11] Let i_0 denote the minimum yield (per income period) at which an individual is ready to hold no assets in the form of money during the period. We may also assume, without being unrealistic, that this minimum yield is the same for each income period. Suppose that the securities which, in his opinion, present the best opportunity are expected by him to produce a net yield (including capital appreciation) i_0', i_1', . . . , i_n' in periods 1, 2, . . . , n. He will be induced to invest provided there is some value of n for which

$$(1 + i_0') \, (1 + i_1') \, \cdots \, (1 + i_n') \geqq (1 + i_0)^n.$$

From M. Timlin's treatment of this subject (*Keynesian Economics*, Chapter III) it would appear that marginal holders should expect any security to yield the same net income, at least during the current period. This however is correct only if the expectations of all dealers about the future short rates of interest agree with the market expectation as shown by the forward rates established in the market. [The forward rate for the nth income period ahead can always

Since this is true for every individual, there must also be some system of interest rates which is sufficient to reduce the aggregate demand to zero.

The second characteristic is more peculiar. Since securities are an "inferior" way of holding assets, it is generally recognized that there must be some minimum rate of interest, say r'', at which nobody will be willing to hold nonphysical assets except in the form of money. When this level is reached, the demand for money to hold becomes "absolute" and the rate of interest cannot fall any lower. Hence, $D'_a(r) = \infty$ for $r \gtreqqless r''$.

6. THE DEMAND FOR MONEY: CONCLUSION

We have so far discussed the demand for money as an asset and the transaction demand for money by individuals; to complete the analysis we must consider the transaction demand by firms. In principle, the same considerations apply here as were stated in connection with individuals' transaction demand. Firms, as well as individuals, have an institutional expenditure-receipt pattern and, given this pattern, the average demand depends on the volume of transactions. We must however recognize that, in the case of firms, generalizations are less meaningful since their expenditure and receipt flows are generally less certain and uniform than for individuals.

Then, too, we must admit that we may have oversimplified the consumers' transaction demand by assuming that individuals have a rigorously defined plan of expenditure at the beginning of the income period. It may very well be that under more realistic conditions they will desire to carry some cash above the amount they plan to spend as a reserve and to avoid ending the period with a zero cash balance. This however does not substantially affect our argument. All we are interested in establishing is that, within an institutional framework, there

_____

be found by comparing the price of riskless securities maturing n periods ahead with those maturing $(n + 1)$ periods ahead.] But if an individual believes this forward rate to be too high he may acquire the security at once even though he may expect that it will yield in the current period less than some other security. For, assuming that he is right, he will be able to realize his capital gain as soon as the market recognizes its error and there is no telling when this will occur. If he should wait until the next income period and hold for the current one the asset that promises to pay a higher yield, he may lose his chance of making the expected capital gain.

must be for any given volume (value) of transactions a certain amount of money that is necessary to carry them out. This amount clearly depends on such institutional factors as the length of the income period and the prevailing customs as to the settlement of current purchases by firms and must therefore be substantially independent of the level of the rate of interest. The level of the rate of interest influences decisions concerning the disposition of assets, and *money needed to carry out transactions planned for the coming income period is not an asset.* In particular, there must be some level of the rate of interest that is sufficient to reduce to zero the demand for money to hold, and hence the total demand to its minimum institutional level which depends on the volume of transactions. As the rate of interest rises above this level, the demand for money will be substantially unaffected and will depend exclusively on the level of money income.

On the basis of these considerations we may, in a first approximation, split the total demand for money into two parts: the demand for money to hold, $D_a(r)$, and the demand for money to spend or for transactions, $D_T(Y)$; and write

(12) $L(r,\ Y) = D_a(r) + D_T(Y) = M.$

This is not really necessary for our argument, but is very useful since it will constantly remind us of the two sources of demand for money and it will permit us to analyze more conveniently the part played by each variable.

With this in mind we shall find it useful to consider the functioning of the money market in which decisions concerning the disposition of nonphysical assets are carried out.

7. The Money Market and The Short-Run Equilibrium Of The Rate Of Interest

There are two ways of looking at this market: (a) in terms of flows (savings and net borrowing) and (b) in terms of stocks. It is from this latter point of view that we shall consider it at this moment.

The supply in this market consists of the stock that is not needed for transactions. On the basis of our first approximation (12), this supply, denoted by S_a, will be

$$S_a = M - D_T\ (Y),$$

and is determined for any value of the money income and the fixed supply of money.

A position of equilibrium in the money market is reached when a system of interest rates is established at which dealers are willing to hold for the income period all the available supply. Or, from a different angle, the system of interest rates is determined by the price (in terms of foregone income) that dealers are willing to pay to hold assets in the form of money for the coming income period.

This can easily be translated into the usual Marshallian supply and demand apparatus, provided we replace the system of interest rates by a single rate r, as shown in Figure 1.

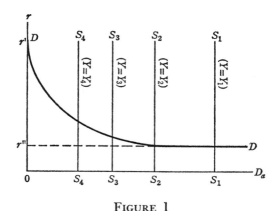

FIGURE 1

DD is the demand curve for money to hold, sloping downward and to the right (when the price, the rate of interest, rises, the demand falls, as in the case of ordinary commodities). The vertical lines are various supply curves corresponding to different values of Y and the fixed value of M. As the income increases, the supply falls: hence

$$Y_4 > Y_3 > Y_2 > \ldots .$$

Since a fall in supply causes a rise in price, the graph shows clearly that equation (1) gives r as an increasing function of Y.

The characteristics of the D_a function described above are shown in the graph. We noted that, for $r \geqq r'$ the demand falls to zero; hence the graph of DD joins the vertical axis and coincides with it.

On the other hand, when the rate of interest falls to the level r'', the demand for money to hold becomes infinitely elastic. Any increase in the supply of money to hold now fails to affect the rate of interest, for the owners of the extra supply will either desire to hold this in the form of cash; or else they will find some owners of securities, who, being just indifferent as to holding cash or securities, will be willing to sell without any necessity for bidding up the price of securities (lowering the rate of interest). Thus, in Figure 1, when the interest rate r'' is reached, the graph of DD becomes parallel to the D_a axis; the income corresponding to r'' cannot be more than Y_2; but if income should fall below Y_2 it would not change the interest rate.[12] This situation that plays such an important role in Keynes's *General Theory* will be referred to as the "Keynesian case."

In the diagram we have assumed that there is a single rate of interest r, instead of a whole system of rates for loans of different duration. While it may be assumed that in principle all the rates tend to move in the same direction, we must bear in mind that the extent to which a change in the supply of money changes the rates on loans of different maturities depends on the character of interest expectations.

A change in the supply will necessarily affect the short rates (unless the short rate has already reached its minimum). But the extent to which it will affect longer rates depends on the relation between the current spot rate and expected future rates.

To denote the relationship between current and expected rates we may again use the Hicksian elasticity of expectation. If this elasticity is unity, expected short rates move in the same direction and in the same proportion as the spot rate; if it is less than unity, a given percentage change in short rates leads to a smaller percentage change in expected rates; and vice versa for elasticity larger than one.

If the expectations about future short rates are based predominantly on the current shorter rates, then the elasticity of

---

[12] From equation (1) we obtain $dr/dY = -L_Y/L_r$, where the subscripts denote partial derivatives. Hence $dr/dY = 0$ if $|L_r| = \infty$.

expectation tends toward one and the whole system of rates moves in close conformity. But if dealers have rigid expectations based on different elements, the elasticity of expectation will be low and a change in short rates will affect longer rates only to the extent that some of the discount rates, which determine the present value of the assets, are changed.

In practice we may expect that this elasticity will be larger than zero and smaller than one and that it will be larger for the rates expected in the near future.[13]

To the extent that this is true there will be two reasons why rates on loans of shorter maturity should move in closer agreement with the very short rate: (a) because they are more affected by a change in the current short rate, (b) because the other future short rates (of which they are an average) are more influenced by such a change.

These necessary qualifications do not alter our previous conclusions concerning the determination of equilibrium in the money market. The equilibrium system of interest rates is determined in each period by the condition that the supply of money to hold, which (given M) depends on the transaction demand for money and hence on income, be equal to the demand for money to hold. We may therefore proceed to draw the graph of equation (1), $M = L(r,Y)$. This is the LL curve of Figure 3. Any point on this curve shows the equilibrium value of r corresponding to a value of Y and the fixed value of M: it shows therefore positions of possible equilibrium in the money market. We must prove next that only one point on this curve is consistent with the long-run equilibrium of the system.

8. SAVING, INVESTMENT, AND THE *IS* FUNCTION

The first part of our system yields a second relationship between interest and income. Making use of equations (2) and (3) and the equilibrium condition (4) we obtain: $I(r, Y) = S(r, Y)$. In order to gain some idea of the shape of this curve we may

---

[13] Denoting by $r_1, r_2, \ldots, r_n$ the short rate of interest anticipated for periods $1, 2, \ldots, n$, we may expect that

$$\frac{\partial r_1}{\partial r_0} > \frac{\partial r_2}{\partial r_0} > \ldots > \frac{\partial r_n}{\partial r_0}.$$

again make use of a graphical method illustrated in Figure 2.

Figure 2-B is the graph of equation (3). Since $\partial S/\partial r$ is usually considered small and of unknown sign we have simplified the drawing by eliminating r. This curve describes the relationship between money income and the proportion of it that people choose not to consume. Its position depends on the value of the fixed money wage rate w_0: given the wage rate, to any level of money income there corresponds a certain real income and price level and, therefore, a certain level of money saving. In this diagram Y_2 denotes the highest money income that can be reached with the money wage rate w_0, and A is the full employment relationship between saving and income.

The straight line beginning at A gives the relationship between money income and money saving once full employment has been reached and the second part of condition (10) replaces the first.[14] We have then what is usually called inflation: real income cannot change but money income can rise to any level. As all prices rise simultaneously the amount of real income saved is unchanged while its money value rises in the same proportion as the price level and money income.[15] The dotted curved line, on the other hand, gives a potential relation between S and I if it were possible to raise the real income above the full employment level.

Figure 2-A is the graph of equation (2). Each curve in this graph shows the amount of investment that would be undertaken at different levels of the rate of interest and for a fixed value of the income. To larger values of Y correspond investment curves higher and to the right.

Since the vertical scale is the same in both Figure 2-A and Figure 2-B, we may use the following method to find the shape of $S(Y) = I(r, Y)$: For any value of Y, say Y_1, the corresponding amount of saving, S_1, can be read from the SS curve. But in

[14] This line is the continuation of the radius vector from the origin to A.

[15] This is strictly correct only if inflation does not provoke any permanent redistribution of income; or if the redistribution does not affect the aggregate propensity to save. Since wages rise with prices we can exclude redistributions from working class to nonworking class. But we cannot exclude redistribution from fixed-income receivers (especially owners of securities) to profits. It is difficult to say whether this will change sensibly the aggregate propensity to save; it is probably a good approximation to assume that the effect will be negligible.

equilibrium $S = I$, hence we can draw a line parallel to the Y axis at height S_1 and prolong it until it intersects the investment

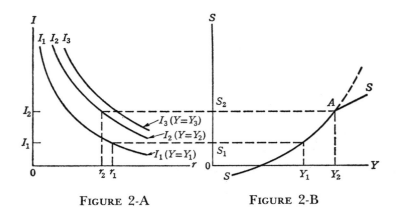

FIGURE 2-A   FIGURE 2-B

curve of Figure 2-A corresponding to the income Y_1. We may thus find the rate of interest r_1 that corresponds to the given income Y_1.

The character of the relationship between r and Y that emerges from this diagram cannot be established a priori as in the case of the LL curve discussed before. For, as Y increases, S in Figure 2-B increases too, but the corresponding value of r in Figure 2-A may increase or decrease. It all depends on the way the change in income affects the position of the investment curves. If the increase in income tends to raise the desire to save more than the desire to invest, the rate of interest will fall; in the opposite case it will rise.[16] This last possibility is, in our opinion, unlikely to occur, but it may materialize when entrepreneurs are highly optimistic and the existing equipment is already working at capacity.

The relationship between r and Y emerging from equations (2) and (3) and the equilibrium condition (4) is shown as the IS curve of Figure 3. In the normal case it will slope downward and to the right as in this diagram, but it is conceivable that, at least in a certain range, it may slope upward to the right. In

[16] From $S(r, Y) = I(r, Y)$ we obtain $dr/dY = (S_Y - I_Y)/(I_r - S_r)$, where the subscripts denote partial derivatives. Since $I_r - S_r$ may be expected to be negative, we have $dr/dY \lesseqgtr 0$ as $S_Y \gtreqless I_Y$.

this case $S_Y < I_Y$ and it is usually assumed that the equilibrium of the system will be unstable (and neutral if $S_Y = I_Y$). We shall see, however, that, with inelastic money supply, the negative slope of the IS curve is a sufficient but not necessary condition for stability.

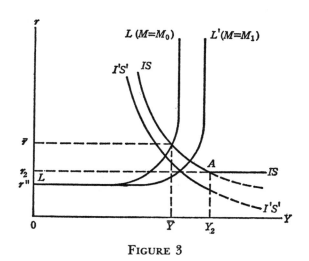

FIGURE 3

The IS curve must also have another important property. In Figure 3, A denotes the equilibrium relationship between full-employment income (Y_2) and rate of interest (r_2). Money income cannot rise above the full-employment level denoted by Y_2 except through inflation, i.e., if wages and prices rise in the same proportion as income. As the stage of inflationary prices and wage increases is reached, the "real" value of investment that it pays to undertake at any interest rate is unchanged since yields and costs change in the same proportion.[17] The money

17 Following the example of Mr. Keynes we may define the marginal efficiency of an asset as the discount rate that makes the sum of the expected marginal discounted yields equal to the marginal cost of the asset. The expected yields need not all be equal since they depend on the expected net physical yield as well as on expected future prices; and neither is necessarily constant in time. But the expected physical yield does not depend on prices; and, owing to our "static assumption" of unit elasticity of expectation, expected prices change in the same proportion as present prices. Therefore the summation of the yields changes in the same proportion as marginal cost and so does the aggregate value of investments having marginal efficiency equal to or larger

value of profitable investments, on the other hand, rises proportionally to prices and money income. As we have seen above, the same will be true of money savings. It follows that inflationary increases in income raise saving and investment in the same proportion and must therefore leave the equilibrium value of the rate of interest unchanged at the full-employment level r_2. It is for this reason that in Figure 3, to the right of A, the IS curve becomes parallel to the income axis. The dotted curved line beyond A is again the hypothetical relationship between r and Y if it were possible to raise real income above the full-employment level (and if the wage rate should remain unchanged at the level w_0).

9. The Money Market and The Determinants of Monetary Equilibrium

We may now finally proceed to consider the process by which the equilibrium of the system is established. For this purpose we must once more revert to the money market which we must, this time, consider in terms of flows rather than in terms of stocks.

In Section 5 we have seen that the rate of interest is established in the money market by the condition that supply of and demand for the stock of money to hold must be equal. This condition is sufficient to determine a position of short-run equilibrium, i.e., a position of equilibrium for the income period. We must now consider under what conditions this level of the rate of interest will also represent a position of long-run equilibrium. As in the textbook analysis of demand and supply, a position of long-run equilibrium is characterized by the fact that neither price nor quantity (demanded and supplied) tend to change any further. In the present case a position of long-run equilibrium will be reached only when the rate of interest does not tend to change from one income period to the other and this in turn is possible only if the stock of money to hold remains constant in time.

Now in each income period people increase their assets by current savings; the money thus saved, since it is not needed for transactions, constitutes an increase in the supply of money

than r_2. Under unit elasticity of expectation a given change in all present prices does not modify entrepreneurs' production plans.

to hold. Borrowing, on the other hand, automatically decreases the supply of money to hold by taking cash out of the money market and putting it into active circulation again, through expenditure on investments. If net saving exceeds net borrowing then, on balance, the supply of money to hold will increase above the level of the previous period, say $D_{a.0}$. But at the old rate of interest (r_0) people will not want to hold the extra supply; they will therefore try to purchase securities and thus will lower the rate of interest. If, on the other hand, at the interest rate r_0 borrowers desire to borrow in the period more than the current amount of money savings, they must induce dealers in the money market to reduce the demand for money as an asset below the previous level $D_{a.0}$; and this is possible only if the rate of interest rises. There are then three possibilities. (The subscripts 0 and 1 denote quantities in periods zero and one, respectively.)

(1) $S_1 > I_1$: then $D_{a.1} > D_{a.0}$ and the rate of interest falls.

(2) $S_1 = I_1$: here $D_{a.1} = D_{a.0}$ and the rate of interest is unchanged.

(3) $S_1 < I_1$: then $D_{a.1} < D_{a.0}$ and the rate of interest rises.

Recalling our definition of long-run equilibrium, we see at once that only situation (2) satisfies it. In equilibrium then, both demand for and supply of the stock of money to hold and demand for and supply of the flow of saving must be equal.[17a] In addition, however, it is necessary that the flows of saving and of borrowing be themselves constant in time. This is possible only if two conditions hold: (a) The borrowing that occurs must be equal to the amount of investment that entrepreneurs wish to undertake at the given rate of interest and income level. The relationship between I_1, r_1, and Y_1 must be described by a point on the corresponding curve of Figure 2-A. (b) The income (and the rate of interest) must be as large as is required to induce people to go on saving an amount S_1. The relationship between Y_1, S_1 and r_1 must be described by a point lying on the curve of Figure 2-B. But if conditions (a) and (b) are satisfied the relationship between Y and r will be described by a point lying on the IS curve of Figure 3. Thus a position of full equilibrium

[17a] The classical example of the level of water in a reservoir fits this case perfectly. The rate of interest, like the level of the water, can be constant only if inflow and outflow are equal.

must be represented by a point lying at the same time on the *LL* curve (denoting equilibrium between demand for and supply of the stock of money to hold) and on the *IS* curve (denoting equality and constancy in time of the inflow and outflow of cash in the money market); hence it must be given by the intersection of these two curves.

This is shown in Figure 3 where the equilibrium values of r and Y, thus determined, are denoted by $\hat{r}$ and $\bar{Y}$. Analytically this corresponds to the simultaneous solution of the two relationships between the income and the rate of interest obtained from equations (1), (2), (3), and (4):

$$M = L(r, Y) \quad \text{and} \quad S(r, Y) = I(r, Y).$$

10. A Dynamic Model of The Keynesian Theory and The Stability of Equilibrium

So far our analysis has apparently been "timeless" [18] since it was based on the system of equations of Section 2, in which time does not appear explicitly. A close examination of the last sections, and especially Sections 7 and 9, will reveal, however, that dynamic elements have gradually slipped into our analysis, thanks to the device of "long- and short-run equilibrium," the oldest and simplest device of developing a dynamic theory with a static apparatus. Actually the criterion that distinguishes short- from long-run equilibrium is essentially a dynamic one: namely, the length of time that is required for certain decisions to be carried out, or, more generally, for certain causes to show their effects.

In our case, the equilibrium of the "money market" is a condition of short-run equilibrium (that determines the rate of interest for each period) because it is the result of decisions that can be carried into effect immediately. The condition saving = investment, on the other hand, is a condition of long-run equilibrium because the equality of *ex ante* saving and investment cannot be brought about instantaneously. This is a different way of stating the familiar proposition that the multiplier takes time to work out its full effect. This well-known fact is in turn

---

[18] The word "timeless" has been used here to avoid confusion since the word "static" has already been used to denote the assumption of homegeneity of the first degree of the "expectations functions."

explained essentially by the existence of a fundamental time lag: the lag between the time when income is earned and the time when it becomes available for expenditure. In the economic systems in which we live, people are usually paid for services already rendered. The income earned (or produced) in a period is the value of services rendered which will be paid for at the end of the normal income period; while the income available for expenditure represents payment for services rendered in the previous period. Decisions as to spending and saving can refer only to the disposable income, and are essentially motivated by it, even though income earned may have some influence.

This explains why the graph of the *IS* curve, unlike the *LL* curve, describes not instantaneous relationships but only possible positions of long-run equilibrium. When the two curves intersect we have a position of full equilibrium since both short- and long-run conditions are satisfied.

It will therefore be useful at this point to give explicit recognition to the dynamic elements that form the basis of our approach. This is the purpose of the following system of difference equations which may be considered as the simplest dynamic model of our theory.

$$
\begin{aligned}
(2.1) \quad & M = L(r_t, Y_{d \cdot t}), \\
(2.2) \quad & I_t = I(r_t, Y_{d \cdot t}), \\
(2.3) \quad & S_t = S(r_t, Y_{d \cdot t}), \\
(2.4) \quad & Y_{d \cdot t} = C_t + S_t, \\
(2.5) \quad & Y_t = C_t + I_t, \\
(2.6) \quad & Y_{d \cdot t} = Y_{t-1}.
\end{aligned}
$$

In this system Y denotes income earned and Y_d income disposable. This is a new variable to which corresponds the new equation (2.6). The remaining equations of the system are unchanged.

By repeated substitution the system reduces to the two equations

$$
\begin{aligned}
& Y_t = Y_{t-1} - S_t + I_t = Y_{t-1} - S(Y_{t-1}, r_t) + I(Y_{t-1}, r_t), \\
& M = L(r_t, Y_{t-1}).
\end{aligned}
$$

Solving the second equation for r_t and substituting in the first, we obtain a single equation of the form: $Y_t = f(Y_{t-1})$ which determines the time path of the income. By similar procedure we obtain the time sequence of the other variables.

If the system is stable, each variable approaches some definite value which it will maintain in time until there occurs some change in the form of the functional relationship or in some parameter (M or w_0). Equation (2.1) is again the "equation of the money market" that determines the value of r for any period; but we have a position of long-run equilibrium only when $r_t = r_{t-1}$. And this implies $Y_t = Y_{d \cdot t} = Y_{t-1}$ and therefore $S_t = I_t$.

The importance of this system is not limited to the fact that it defines rigorously concepts that were loosely used in our previous analysis. It serves also another important purpose: namely it permits us to determine the conditions of stability for the system.

Following the usual method, we proceed to expand equations (2.1) to (2.3) by Taylor series around the equilibrium values neglecting all terms of degree higher than one. We then obtain:

$$0 = L_r \dot{r}_t + L_Y \dot{Y}_{t-1} + \ldots ,$$
$$I_t = I(\bar{r}, \bar{Y}) + I_r \dot{r}_t + I_Y \dot{Y}_{t-1} + \ldots ,$$
$$S_t = S(\bar{r}, \bar{Y}) + S_r \dot{r}_t + I_Y \dot{Y}_{t-1}.$$

Subscripts denote partial derivatives taken around the equilibrium values $(\bar{r}, \bar{Y})$ and $r_t = \dot{r}_t - \bar{r}$, $\dot{Y}_t = Y_t - \bar{Y}$. By making use of (4) and (5) and by repeated substitution we obtain the following linear difference equation with constant coefficients:

$$\dot{Y}_t = \dot{Y}_{t-1} \left[1 + \frac{L_Y}{L_r}(S_r - I_r) + I_Y - S_Y \right].$$

The solution of this equation takes the form:

$$\dot{Y} = \kappa \lambda^t \text{ or } Y = (Y_0 - \bar{Y}) \lambda^t, \text{ since } \dot{Y}_0 = Y_0 - \bar{Y} = \kappa.$$

Y_0 is determined by the initial conditions and

$$\lambda = 1 + \frac{L_Y}{L_r}(S_r - I_r) + I_Y - S_Y.$$

The stability condition is $|\lambda| < 1$; in the present case this reduces to

$$(2.7) \qquad -\frac{L_Y}{L_r} - \frac{2}{S_r - I_r} < \frac{I_Y - S_Y}{S_r - I_r} < -\frac{L_Y}{L_r}.$$

Since the middle term is the slope of the *IS* curve and the right-hand term is the slope of the *LL* curve, the right-hand condition has a very clear graphical meaning. Stability requires that the slope of the *IS* curve be algebraically smaller than the slope of the *LL* curve. The slope of the *LL* curve cannot be negative ($L_Y > 0$, $L_r \geqq 0$). Also general economic considerations suggest that $S_r - I_r > 0$. Hence this condition is necessarily satisfied if $I_Y - S_Y < 0$, i.e., when the *IS* curve falls from left to right. But this is not necessary. Stability is also possible when the *IS* curve rises in the neighborhood of the equilibrium point as long as it cuts the *LL* curve from its concave toward its convex side.[19]

If the stability conditions are satisfied, the variables approach their equilibrium values, which are the same as those obtained by solving the static system of Section 2. In the opposite case they diverge more and more from these values in a process of cumulative contraction or expansion. In the same way, a change in some of the data will lead to a new stable equilibrium if the new functions satisfy the conditions written above.

It is interesting to note that, as long as the money supply is inelastic, the system must always have at least one stable solution since eventually the *LL* curve becomes perpendicular to the horizontal axis and hence its slope must become larger than the slope of the *IS* curve.

11. THE DETERMINANTS OF REAL EQUILIBRIUM

It is now time to consider the role of the second part of the system in the determination of equilibrium. Equations (5), (6), and (7) *explain* the forces that determine the real variables of the system: physical output, employment, real wage rate.[20]

The most important of these equations is (7), which states the conditions of equilibrium in the production of goods

---

[19] It is only as $L_r \to \infty$ (demand for money to hold infinitely elastic, *LL* curve parallel to the horizontal axis) that the condition $I_Y - S_Y < 0$ becomes necessary for equilibrium. This holds equally if the supply of money is infinitely elastic for this has the same effect as $L_r = \infty$.

[20] The price level is also necessary to determine the real wage rate, given the money wage rate W.

whether for consumption or for investment.[21] Production will be extended up to the point at which the given and fixed money wage rate w_0 is equal to the marginal net product of labor, or, if we prefer, up to the point at which price equals marginal labor cost.[22] This assumes that the only variable factor is labor and the quantity of equipment is fixed; a condition that is approximately satisfied in the case we are considering. Eliminating equation (5) by substitution into (7) we can reduce this part of the system to two equations in the two unknowns X and N, where X' is used for dX/dN:

$$W_0 = X'(N) \frac{Y}{X}, \qquad X = X(N).$$

Since the money income is determined exclusively by the *monetary* part of the system, the price level depends only on the amount of output. If, at any given price level, the fixed wage is less than the marginal product of labor, the forces of competition lead to an expansion of employment and output which forces prices down. This lowers the marginal product of labor until it becomes equal to the wage rate. If the wage rate exceeded the marginal product of labor, output and employment would contract, which would force prices up. We see clearly from Figure 3 that the amount of employment thus determined will, in general, not be "full employment"; that is, unless the *LL* curve intersects the *IS* curve at (Y_2, r_2) or to the right of it.

12. UNDEREMPLOYMENT EQUILIBRIUM AND LIQUIDITY PREFERENCE

This last result deserves closer consideration. It is usually considered as one of the most important achievements of the Keynesian theory that it explains the consistency of economic equilibrium with the presence of involuntary unemployment. It is, however, not sufficiently recognized that, except in a limiting case to be considered later, this result is due entirely to

[21] The equilibrium price of each type of physical asset is found by capitalizing a series of expected marginal yields at the current rate of interest. The expected yields of the marginal unit need not be equal in each period.

[22] This is a sufficient condition under assumption of perfect competition; the modifications necessary in the case of monopolies cannot be considered here.

the assumption of "rigid wages" [23] and not to the Keynesian liquidity preference. Systems with rigid wages share the common property that the equilibrium value of the "real" variables is determined essentially by monetary conditions rather than by "real" factors (e.g., quantity and efficiency of existing equipment, relative preference for earning and leisure, etc.). The monetary conditions are sufficient to determine money income and, under fixed wages and given technical conditions, to each money income there corresponds a definite equilibrium level of employment. This equilibrium level does not tend to coincide with full employment except by mere chance, since there is no economic mechanism that insures this coincidence. There may be unemployment in the sense that more people would be willing to work at the current real wage rate than are actually employed; but in a free capitalistic economy production is guided by prices and not by desires and since the money wage rate is rigid, this desire fails to be translated into an economic stimulus.

In order to show more clearly that wage rigidities and not liquidity preference explain underemployment equilibrium we may consider the results to be obtained by giving up the liquidity-preference theory and assuming instead the crudest quantity-of-money theory while keeping the assumption of rigid wages. This can be done by merely replacing equation (1) of our system by the equation

(1a) $$M = kY.$$

Since M and k are constant this equation is sufficient to determine money income. Equations (5), (6), and (7) determine directly physical output and employment as we saw in Section 10. Once more there is no reason to expect that the level of employment thus determined will be "full employment"; and yet the system will be in equilibrium since there will be no tendency for income, employment, and output to change.

It is very interesting to see what part is played under these conditions by equations (2) and (3), the saving and investment equations that have been so much stressed by all the Keynesians. Since the income is determined by equation (1a), equation (2)

[23] The expression "rigid wages" refers to the infinite elasticity of the supply curve of labor when the level of employment is below "full."

reduces to an "orthodox" supply-of-saving schedule, giving saving as a function of the rate of interest. For the same reason, equation (3) reduces to a demand-for-saving schedule. But schedules can be represented in a Marshallian supply and demand diagram as is done in Figure 4. The intersection of these curves, i.e., the equilibrium condition, demand = supply, determines the level of the rate of interest.

Finally let us notice that, in this system also, the rate of interest depends on the quantity of money, or more exactly on the ratio M/W. A change in M (W constant) raises real income and shifts both the SS and II curves to the right. The net result will be a fall in the rate of interest, if the increase in income raises the desire to save more than the desire to invest (normal case); a rise, in the opposite case.

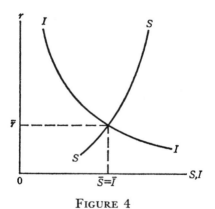

FIGURE 4

In spite of these significant similarities between the present system and the Keynesian system, in which we recognize the existence of liquidity demand for money, there remains one very important difference; this difference is to be found in the role played by the rate of interest in the determination of equilibrium. In both cases the level of employment depends on the quantity of "active" money. But in the Keynesian system this depends on the rate of interest and consequently also on the propensities to save and invest. In the present case the quantity of active money is fixed and independent of the rate of interest. Hence the propensities to save and invest are not a part of the mechanism determining employment; they merely determine the amount of resources devoted to the improvement of the means of production.

We now proceed to consider the determinants of equilibrium in a system in which we do away not only with the liquidity-preference theory but also with the assumption of rigid wages.

13. THE LOGICAL CONSISTENCY OF THE QUANTITY THEORY
OF MONEY AND THE DICHOTOMY OF MONETARY
AND REAL ECONOMICS

In order to discuss the quantity theory of money we substitute equation (1a) for (1) and replace conditions (10) by the identities (11).

It was shown in Section 8 that a given change in prices will change income, investment, and saving in the same proportion. Consequently, after Y in equations (2) and (3) is replaced by the expression given in (5), the saving and investment equations may be written in the form

$$(3.2) \qquad \frac{I}{W} = I\left(r, \frac{P}{W}X\right),$$

$$(3.3) \qquad \frac{S}{W} = S\left(r, \frac{P}{W}X\right).$$

Next we divide both members of equations (4) and (5) by W obtaining

$$(3.4) \qquad \frac{S}{W} = \frac{I}{W},$$

$$(3.5) \qquad \frac{Y}{W} \equiv \frac{P}{W}X,$$

$$(3.6) \qquad X = X(N),$$

$$(3.7) \qquad \frac{W}{P} = X'(N),$$

$$(3.9) \qquad N = F\left(\frac{W}{P}\right),$$

$$(3.8) \qquad \left[\frac{Y}{W} \equiv \frac{I}{W} + \frac{C}{W}\right].$$

Equations (3.2) to (3.7) and (3.9) form a system of 7 equations in the 7 unknowns I/W, S/W, P/W, Y/W, r, X, N. These unknowns are therefore determined. Next we can write equation (1a) in the form $M = kPX = Wk(P/W)X$. But since P/W and X have already been determined, this equation determines the money wage rate and hence the price level, money income, etc. This is essentially the "classical" procedure, and we can only repeat the classical conclusions to the effect that the real parts of the system, namely, employment, *interest rate,* output, or real income, do not depend on the quantity of money. The quantity of money has no other function than to determine the price level.

This result does not, of course, depend on any special feature of our system. It will always follow, provided all the supply and demand functions for commodities [24] and labor are homogeneous of the zero degree; and since we are proceeding under "static" assumptions, all the supply and demand functions must be homogeneous of zero degree, if people behave rationally.[25] *

This conclusion, which is very old indeed, has some interest since it has been recently challenged by Oscar Lange. Of all the recent attacks against the traditional dichotomy of monetary and real economics, Lange's criticism is by far the most serious because it maintains that "the traditional procedure of the theory of money involves a [logical] contradiction." [26] We propose to show, however, that, while Lange's criticism of Say's law cannot be questioned, it does not invalidate the logical consistency of the procedure of the quantity theory of money.

According to Lange, Say's law implies that the amount of cash people desire to hold is always identically equal to the quantity in existence: denoting by D_n and S_n the demand and supply of money respectively, we can write this as $S_n \equiv D_n$. Lange then states that " a proportional change of all prices

[24] "Commodities" are, in this context, all goods except money.
[25] For a proof of this statement see O. Lange, "Say's Law: A Restatement and Criticism," *op. cit.,* pp. 67 and 68. Professor Lange shows that the homogeneity of first degree of all expectation functions is a sufficient condition for all demand and supply equations for "commodities" to be homogeneous of zero degree.
* See postscript, p. 183.
[26] *Ibid.,* p. 65.

does not induce a substitution between different commodities" [27] and concludes that "the demand and supply functions
of commodities are, *when Say's law holds,* homogeneous of zero
degree." [28] But the homogeneity of the supply and demand
functions for commodities does not depend on Say's law: it
depends on the assumption of rationality and the homogeneity
of the expectation functions. Since a proportional change in
all prices does not change the price ratios it also does not change
the marginal rate of substitution, and therefore does not induce a substitution between different commodities.

Let us now consider a system in which there are n goods
($n - 1$ commodities and money). As is well known, there are
only $n - 1$ prices to be determined, the price of money being
unity, and $n - 1$ independent supply and demand equations,
for one follows from the rest. Since the supply and demand
functions for commodities are homogeneous of zero degree, the
quantities demanded of the $n - 1$ commodities are functions
of the $n - 2$ price ratios p_i/p_{n-1} ($i = 1, 2, \ldots, n - 2$), where
p_{n-1} is chosen arbitrarily. [29] At the same time the demand
and supply function to be eliminated is also arbitrary; we may,
if we choose, eliminate one of the $n - 1$ referring to commodities; we are then left with $n - 2$ equations for commodities to
determine the $n - 2$ price ratios. Hence the price ratios are
determined. To determine the actual prices we use the demand
and supply equation for money as was done above. In Lange's
system this is written:

$$k \sum_{i=1}^{n} p_i S_i = M, \quad \text{or also} \quad k p_{n-1} \sum_{i=1}^{n} \frac{p_i}{p_{n-1}} S_i = M,$$

where S_i denotes the equilibrium quantity supplied and demanded of the ith commodity. Since k is a constant this equation determines p_{n-1} and consequently all other prices.

As long as Say's law is not assumed, this procedure is perfectly
legitimate; and we cannot escape the classical conclusion that
money is "neutral," just a "veil." If, however, Say's law holds,
the demand and supply of money are identically equal. The

27 *Ibid.,* p. 63.
28 *Ibid.,* p. 63. Italics ours.
29 In our own system p_{n-1} was arbitrarily chosen as the wage rate.

nth equation is therefore not a genuine equation. Thus we have only $n - 2$ independent equations to determine $n - 1$ prices: the system is not determinate. In Lange's own formulation, the nth equation degenerates into the identity

$$kp_{n-1} \sum_{i=1}^{n} \frac{p_i}{p_{n-1}} S_i \equiv M,$$

which is satisfied by any value of p_{n-1} whatever; the price level is thus indeterminate.[30]

Hence one of Lange's conclusions, namely that "Say's law precludes any monetary theory," [31] is perfectly justified. But Lange goes on to draw a conclusion which does not follow, namely that "the traditional procedure of the theory of money involves a contradiction. Either Say's law is assumed and money prices are indeterminate, or money prices are made determinate—but then *Say's law and hence the neutrality of money* must be abandoned." [32] But the traditional theory of money is not based on Say's law. The necessary condition for money to be neutral is that the $n - 1$ "real" demand and supply equations be homogeneous of order zero and this homogeneity does not "disappear when Say's law is abandoned." [33] Under "static" assumptions money is neutral even without assuming Say's law, if only people are assumed to behave "rationally"; this is all that the classical theory assumes and needs to assume.[34]

The most serious charge against the classical dichotomy can thus be dismissed, as long as we maintain our "static" assumptions.

30 Then k changes in inverse proportion to p_{n-1} instead of being a constant.
31 O. Lange, *op. cit.*, p. 66.
32 *Ibid.*, p. 65. Italics ours.
33 *Ibid.*, p. 66.
34 Lange's result seems due to a failure to distinguish between necessary and sufficient conditions. Say's law is a sufficient condition for the neutrality of money but not a necessary one. Lange asks me to inform the reader that he agrees with my conclusion. This conclusion, however, does not invalidate his result that under Say's law the money prices are indeterminate.

14. LIQUIDITY PREFERENCE AND THE DETERMINANTS OF THE RATE OF INTEREST UNDER THE ASSUMPTION OF FLEXIBLE WAGES [35]

With this in mind we may now proceed to analyze our third system consisting of equations (1) to (7), (9), and identities (11). In this system we recognize that there are two sources of demand for money, the transaction demand and the liquidity demand. But, as in the case just analyzed, we make no restrictive assumptions as to the supply-of-labor equation. The suppliers of labor as well as the suppliers of all other commodities are supposed to behave "rationally." It follows that the only difference between the present case and the case just considered is in equation (1). As in the previous case, the last 7 equations form a determinate system which is sufficient to determine the 7 unknowns it contains, namely *the "real" variables of the system and the rate of interest.*

By use of equation (5) or (3.5) equation (1) takes the form

$$(3.1) \qquad M = L\left(r, \, W\, \frac{P}{W}\, X\right).$$

Since r and P/W are already determined, this equation determines the 8th unknown of the system, the wage rate: and therefore also the price level, money, income, etc.[36]

We thus reach the conclusion that under "static" assumptions and "flexible" wages, *the rate of interest and the level of employment do not depend on the quantity of money.*

Two questions arise at once: (a) what determines the rate of interest and (b) what part do the rate of interest and liquidity demand for money play in the determination of equilibrium.

Strictly speaking, the rate of interest is determined by all the equations of a Walrasian system *except the supply-of-and-demand-for-money equation.* But it is clear that in the first approximation of partial-equilibrium analysis, the determination of the rate of interest must be associated with equations (3.2) and (3.3), the saving and investment schedules. To ex-

---

[35] The expression "flexible wages" is used here and in the following pages for brevity in place of the more exact expression "homogeneity of zero degree of the supply-of-labor function."

[36] Except in the Keynesian case considered later (Section 16).

plain the level of the rate of interest we could use once more Figure 4, changing the variables measured on the horizontal axis from S or I into S/W or I/W. We must add at once, however, that these two schedules should in no way be confused with the schedules of supply of and demand for savings (or supply of and demand for securities) used in the textbook explanation of the determination of the rate of interest.

Equation (3.3) only tells us what part of their real income people wish to devote to increasing their assets rather than to consumption, at different levels of the rate of interest.

In a similar fashion equation (3.2) shows that by devoting output worth I/W to the improvement of the means of production, it is possible to increase real income by an amount (I/W) $(I + r)$ per unit of time. The value of r depends on the given technical conditions, on the quantity I/W and $(P/W)X$ according to the relation expressed by equation (3.2). This shows clearly the fundamental factors that determine the rate of interest. The given technical conditions, expressed by the production function [equation (3.6)], together with *tastes* of people for earning and leisure, expressed by the supply-of-labor function [equation (3.9)], give the level of real income that can be reached.[37] The saving schedule, equation (3.3), tells us what part of this income the community desires to save. The technical conditions (inventions, quantity of capital already in existence, etc.) expressed by the marginal-efficiency-of-investment function (3.2), determine the marginal efficiency of the amount of investment that the giving up of consumption permits undertaking: this is the equilibrium rate of interest.

Let us now examine what part is played by liquidity preference in the present system. On the basis of the given rate of interest determined in the fashion discussed above, people decide what quantity of money they want to hold as an asset. Hence, provided the liquidity demand is finite, the rate of interest, together with the supply of money, determines the quantity of active money and therefore the price level. Thus under "flexible" wages, *the desire to hold assets in liquid form does not determine the rate of interest, but determines the price level*. It follows that any factor that influences the de-

[37] Under flexible wages there is, of course, always full employment under the conditions mentioned in Section 16.

mand for money as an asset, either directly or through the rate of interest, will have a repercussion on the price level, unless it is counteracted by an appropriate change in the quantity of money. This will in particular be the case with changes in the propensities to save and to invest.

15. LIQUIDITY PREFERENCE UNDER RIGID AND FLEXIBLE WAGES—AN EXAMPLE

In order to see clearly the different implications of the liquidity-preference theory under different hypotheses as to the supply of labor we may briefly consider the effects of a shift in the investment schedule [equation (2) or (3.2)].

Suppose that the system is in equilibrium at money income Y_0: the flow of investments is I_0, and its marginal efficiency, r_0, is the equilibrium rate of interest. Now let us assume that for some reason the rate of investment that seems profitable at any level of the rate of interest falls. In particular the marginal efficiency of the rate of investment I_0 falls to the level $r_1 < r_0$. In order for the system to reach a new position of equilibrium, it is necessary that the rate of interest fall to this level. Except under special circumstances, to be considered later, as the rate of interest falls, the demand for money as an asset rises, and a certain amount of current money savings remains in the *money market* to satisfy the increased demand. If the supply of money is not properly increased, this, in turn, implies a fall in money income.

Under the conditions of our last model (flexible wages) the fall is brought about by an all-around reduction in wages and prices. The price level reaches its new equilibrium position when the supply has been increased sufficiently to satisfy the liquidity demand for money associated with the interest rate r_1.[38] The net effect of the shift is then to depress the interest rate, the money income, and money wages without affecting the real variables of the system, employment, output, real wage rate.[39]

[38] The rate of interest must necessarily fall to the level of r_1, for the real income and therefore the amount of real savings will be unchanged, and the marginal efficiency of this amount of real savings is r_1, by hypothesis.

[39] The real wage rate clearly cannot fall. If the real wage rate had fallen, entrepreneurs would try to expand employment while the supply of labor

But if money wages are rigid downward, the reduction in money income, made necessary by the fall in the rate of interest, becomes a reduction in real income and employment as well. The effect of the shift in the investment schedule is now to start a typical process of contraction so frequently described in Keynesian literature. As producers of investment goods make losses, they have no other choice than to dismiss workers, even though their physical productivity is unchanged. This, in turn, reduces the demand for consumption goods and causes unemployment to spread to this sector. Real income falls along with money income (the price level is likely to fall to a smaller extent). The fall in money income increases the supply of money to hold; the fall in real income decreases saving and raises its marginal efficiency above the level r_1.[40] This double set of reactions leads finally to a new equilibrium, with a smaller money and real income, less employment, higher real wages (since the price level falls) and a rate of interest somewhere below r_0 and above the new "full employment interest" r_1.[41] In terms of our graphic apparatus, a decreased marginal efficiency of capital (or increased propensity to save), shifts the IS curve to the left, as shown by the curve $I'S'$, and lowers interest rate and income, money as well as real income.

16.   Two Limiting Cases: (A) The Keynesian Case

There is one case in which the Keynesian theory of liquidity preference is sufficient by itself to explain the existence of underemployment equilibrium without starting out with the assumption of rigid wages. We have seen (Section 5) that, since securities are inferior to money as a form of holding assets, there must be some positive level of the rate of interest (previously denoted by r'') at which the demand for money becomes infinitely elastic or practically so. We have the Keynesian case when the "full-employment equilibrium rate of interest" is less than r''. Whenever this situation materializes, the very

would, if anything, contract. If it had risen, the opposite situation would occur, and neither of these situations is compatible with equilibrium.

[40] Except if the IS curve is not monotonic decreasing, in which case the process of contraction will be more pronounced.

[41] If there was no full employment in the initial situation, then r_1 is simply the rate of interest that would maintain the old level of employment. This conclusion is also subject to the qualification mentioned in footnote 40.

mechanism that tends to bring about full-employment equilibrium in a system with "flexible" wages breaks down, since there is no possible level of the money wage rate and price level that can establish full-employment equilibrium.

From the analytical point of view the situation is characterized by the fact that we must add to our system a new equation, namely $r=r''$. The system is therefore overdetermined since we have 9 equations to determine only 8 unknowns.

Equations (3.2) and (3.3) are sufficient to determine the value of the real income (since r is already determined). But this value will in general not be consistent with the value of the real income determined by the last four equations. More workers would be willing to work at the ruling real wage rate than are employed, but efforts at reducing real wages and increasing employment are bound to fail. For any fall in wages and prices increases the supply of money to hold but cannot lower the rate of interest below the level r'' since the demand for money as an asset is infinitely elastic. As Keynes would say, labor as a whole will not be able to fix its own real wage rate.

It appears clearly that, in this case, equilibrium is determined by those very factors that are stressed in the typical Keynesian analysis. In particular, real income and employment is determined by the position and shape of the saving and investment function, and changes in the propensity to invest or to save change real income without affecting the interest rate.

The price level on the other hand is in neutral equilibrium (at least for a certain range of values). It will tend to fall indefinitely as long as workers attempt to lower money wages in an effort to increase employment; and it can only find a resting place if and when money wages become rigid.

In this case the Keynesian analysis clearly departs from the classical lines and it leads to conclusions that could scarcely have been reached by following the traditional line of approach.

Whether the situation we have characterized as the "Keynesian case" is typical of some or all modern economic systems is a factual question which we cannot attempt to answer here. It is beyond doubt however that its interest is not purely theoretical.[42]

_____

[42] In the *General Theory* Keynes explicitly recognizes that the situation described as the "Keynesian case" does not seem, so far, normally to prevail

(B) THE CLASSICAL CASE

We have the classical case when the equilibrium rate of interest is sufficiently high to make the demand for money to hold zero or negligible. Graphically, the *IS* curve of Figure 3 intersects the *LL* curve in the range in which *LL* is perpendicular to the income axis. Under these conditions changes in the rate of interest (except possibly if they are of considerable size) tend to leave the demand for money unchanged or practically so; $L_r = 0$ or negligible and $M = L(Y)$. The properties of a system satisfying this condition have already been sufficiently analyzed in Sections 11 and 12.[43]

17. PRELIMINARY CONCLUSIONS

This brings to an end the first part of our analysis which aimed principally at distinguishing, as far as possible, to what extent the results of the Keynesian analysis are due to a more refined theoretical approach (liquidity preference) and to what extent to the assumption of rigid wages. We may summarize the results of our inquiry in the following propositions:

I. The liquidity-preference theory is not necessary to explain under-employment equilibrium; it is sufficient only in a limiting case: the "Keynesian case." In the general case it is neither necessary nor sufficient; it can explain this phenomenon only with the additional assumption of rigid wages.

in any economic system. This situation, on the other hand, certainly plays an important part in some phases of the business cycle, when a great feeling of uncertainty and the anticipation of price reductions increase the attractiveness of liquidity and, at the same time, decreases the propensity to invest. Besides, it may also soon become a normal feature of some economies if there should come to prevail a real scarcity of investment outlets that are profitable at rates of interest higher than the institutional minimum. Modifying a well-known statement of Hicks we can say that the Keynesian case is either the Economics of Depression or the Economics of Abundance. (Hicks's original statement: "The General Theory of Employment is the Economics of Depression" is found in "Mr. Keynes and the 'Classics,'" *op. cit.,* p. 155.)

[43] To what extent the "classical case" is met in practice is again a factual question. In our opinion a moderately high rate of interest is sufficient to make it unattractive to hold assets in the form of cash and therefore to induce members of the community to limit their holdings to the amount necessary for transactions (which is determined by the institutional set-up). It is perhaps not unreasonable to expect that under normal conditions a "pure" rate of interest (i.e., net of default risk) in the neighborhood of 5 per cent might be sufficient to reduce the demand for money to hold to negligible proportions.

II. The liquidity-preference theory is neither necessary nor sufficient to explain the dependence of the rate of interest on the quantity of money. This dependence is explained only by the assumption of rigid wages.

III. The result of the liquidity-preference theory is that the quantity of active money depends not only on the total quantity of money but also on the rate of interest and therefore also on the form and position of the propensities to save and to invest. Hence in a system with flexible wages the rate of interest and the propensities to save and to invest are part of the mechanism that determines the price level. And in a system with rigid wages they are part of the mechanism that determines the level of employment and real income.

We proceed now to make use of our results for two purposes: (a) To examine critically, some of the theories that have their logical foundation in the Keynesian analysis. (b) To state some general conclusions about the determinants of the rate of interest.

PART II

18. GENERAL REMARKS ABOUT THE ASSUMPTION OF WAGE RIGIDITY IN THE KEYNESIAN THEORIES

In the *General Theory* Keynes does of course recognize the fundamental importance of the relation between money wages and the quantity of money as is shown by his device of the wage units. This very fact, on the other hand, has had the effect of obscuring the part played by wage rigidities in the determination of economic equilibrium. This can be clearly seen in a large body of literature based on the Keynesian analysis, and will be illustrated with a few examples.

(A) Let us first consider the role of investment.

The statement that unemployment is caused by lack of investment, or that a fall in the propensity to invest or an increase in the propensity to save will decrease employment, has become today almost a commonplace.

As we have seen, however, lack of investment is sufficient to explain underemployment equilibrium only in the "Keynesian case," a situation that is the exception and not the rule.

It is true that a reduced level of employment and a reduced level of investment go together, but this is not, in general, the result of causal relationship. It is true instead that the low level of investment and employment are both the effect of the same cause, namely a basic maladjustment between the quantity of money and the wage rate. It is the fact that money wages are too high relative to the quantity of money that explains why it is unprofitable to expand employment to the "full employment" level. Now to each level of employment and income corresponds a certain distribution of the employment between the production of consumption and investment goods determined by the saving pattern of the community. Hence, when the over-all level of employment is low there will be a reduced level of investment as well as a reduced level of consumption. And the level of investment is low because employment is low and not the other way around.

What is required to improve the situation is an increase in the quantity of money (and not necessarily in the propensity to invest); then employment will increase in every field of production including investment. Again, it is true that, in general, a fall in the propensity to invest (the propensity to save being constant) tends to decrease employment (and that an increase in the same propensity has the opposite effect), but this occurs only because it decreases (or increases) the quantity of money available for transactions relative to the money wage rate and therefore makes it profitable to expand employment. Exactly the same result could be obtained by deflating (or inflating) the quantity of money directly. That a change in the marginal efficiency of investment has no direct influence on aggregate employment can be clearly seen in the "classical case" when the demand for money to hold is zero or negligible. In this case the change mentioned above does not affect employment, but only the rate of interest and therefore, at most, the distribution of the unchanged amount of employment between consumption and investment.

In conclusion, then, the statement that unemployment is caused by lack of investment assumes implicitly that every possible economic system works under the special conditions of the "Keynesian case"; and this is clearly unwarranted. In general the reduced level of employment is not a cause, but just a symptom of unemployment, which in turn is due to essentially monetary disturbances.

This formulation is not only more correct but carries also important implications about the concrete form of economic policies necessary to relieve unemployment.

(B) Another typical result of understressing the assumption of rigid wages is to be found in connection with the concepts of a "natural rate of interest" and of "cumulative inflation" and "deflation" of Wicksellian analysis.[44]

This "natural rate" is the equilibrium (and therefore full-employment) interest rate of a system with flexible wages and not of a Keynesian system with rigid wages. Under "flexible" wages, as we know, the equilibrium rate of interest does not depend on the quantity of money. But, because of the time required for a new position of equilibrium to be reached when some of the conditions change, it will depend on the rate of change of M. Thus the money authority will be able to keep r below (or above) its equilibrium value by increasing (or decreasing) the quantity of money without limit; we thus get a process of cumulative inflation or deflation. Under Keynesian assumptions this ceases to be true; but only because wages are assumed rigid and in this condition, as we have seen, it is in general possible to change the rate of interest with a finite change in the quantity of money.[45]

(C) As a last example, we may quote Lange's "optimum propensity to consume." [46] This concept, outside of its theoretical interest, is only of practical importance if for some reason,

[44] See J. Marschak, "Wicksell's Two Interest Rates," *Social Research*, Vol. 8, November, 1941, pp. 469-478.

[45] The case is more complicated if the relation between Y and r described by the *IS* curve is not monotonic decreasing in the relevant range. It might then appear that an attempt of the money authority at reducing the interest rate will result in a fall in income and employment. This is the result reached by Marschak. Actually as the money authority expands the quantity of money by open-market policy it finds that the rate of interest eventually rises along with income and employment instead of falling. If the money authority insists on keeping the interest rate at the planned level it will have to go on expanding the quantity of money. This will either push the system to some new equilibrium if the planned rate is equal to or larger than the full-employment rate, or it will cause inflation if the planned rate is below this level. But in no event will an initial attempt at lowering r by open-market policy lead to a contraction of income.

[46] Oscar Lange, "The Rate of Interest and the Optimum Propensity to Consume," *Economica*, Vol. 5 (N. S)., February, 1938, pp. 12-32.

money wages and money supply are absolutely inelastic. In general all that is required to increase employment is to expand the quantity of money (or at worst reduce wages) without any necessity for interfering with the propensity to consume.[47]

19. LERNER'S THEORY OF THE RATE OF INTEREST

We proceed now to consider the typically "Keynesian" theory of the rate of interest and money due to A. P. Lerner. We choose Lerner's theory, because its extremism and its clear-cut formulation permit of a useful criticism.

The substance of Lerner's argument, as far as we can make out, is this: The "classical theory" that saving and investment determine the rate of interest must be rejected: saving and investment, being identically equal, cannot determine interest. This is instead determined by the quantity of money according to a demand-for-money function, say $M = f(r)$.[48]

The first argument is clearly unimportant since it is based on definitions. If one accepts the Keynesian definitions then, of course, actual (or *ex post*) saving and investment are identical; and clearly the *ex post* identity, saving $\equiv$ investment, cannot determine either the rate of interest or income. This however does not prove that the propensities to save and to invest are irrelevant to the determination of interest.

We know on the contrary, that, under assumption of flexible wages, neither of Lerner's arguments holds. In this case the rate of interest is independent of the quantity of money and, except in limiting cases, is determined only by the propensities to save and to invest [equations (3.2) and (3.3)].

Let us stress, in order to avoid misunderstandings, that we perfectly agree with Lerner and with all the Keynesians that saving and lending are the result of two independent decisions;

---

[47] If the demand for money is infinitely elastic the propensity to consume plays an important role in the determination of employment. In this case the optimum level of consumption C' would clearly be $C' = Y' - I$ (r'', Y'), where Y' is full-employment income and r'' the critical level of the rate of interest for which $L_r = \infty$.

[48] See especially, "Alternative Formulations of the Theory of Interest," *Economic Journal*, Vol. 48, June, 1938, pp. 211-230; and "Interest Theory—Supply and Demand for Loans or Supply and Demand for Cash?" This latter paper has been recently made available to me by Mr. Lerner in manuscript form; it is to be published in the *Review of Economic Statistics*. The present criticism is also the result of a long personal discussion and correspondence.

our equation (3.3) is a saving schedule and not a schedule of supply of loanable funds. However we cannot agree with Lerner that to treat saving as a "demand-for-securities schedule" is, without qualifications, a serious blunder, or that the classical analysis as to the effect of shifts in the desire to invest or to save is right by pure chance. We must remember that saving and lending coincide when the demand for money to hold is zero or constant. The quantity theory of money starts out with the assumption that the demand for money to hold is identically zero: $D_a'(r) \equiv 0$ or $M = L(Y)$. Now this assumption is unsatisfactory for a general theory, but may be fully justified under certain conditions.

We know that, when the equilibrium rate of interest is sufficiently high, the demand for money to hold does become zero, even if it is not assumed to be identically zero. And, under historically realized conditions, the equilibrium rate of interest may be sufficiently high to make the demand for money to hold so negligible and so scarcely affected by observed changes in the interest rate that this demand can, safely, be neglected. Interest becomes a factor of secondary importance and can be dropped along with many others which certainly do influence the demand for money but are not sufficiently relevant to warrant separate consideration. Under these conditions, the assumption $M = L(Y)$ will give a satisfactory approximation to economic reality.[49] Under changed historical conditions this assumption is no longer justified and it becomes necessary to take into account new factors to avoid oversimplifications.[50]

When we recognize that the demand for money to hold need not be zero (and as long as it is finite), saving and lending coincide only when the demand for money to hold is constant, that is to say, in equilibrium. The equality of money savings

[49] The fact that hoarding and unemployment have always developed in certain phases of the business cycle is not an objection to that. For these are features for a theory of business cycles to explain. Here we are only comparing static theories.

[50] Thus for example, the outcome of a certain physical experiment may be influenced, to a slight extent, by changes in humidity. Then, if the experiment is carried out in a place in which the observed variations in humidity are not sufficient to affect the outcome sensibly, it is perfectly justifiable to neglect it. If the same experiment were conducted somewhere else, where humidity is known to be highly unstable, precautions should be taken in interpreting the results.

and lending becomes an equilibrium condition which, under flexible wages, *determines the price level, not the rate of interest.* And this in turn may explain the traditional lack of attention to the demand for money to hold in connection with the theory of interest.

Thus Lerner's theory cannot explain the rate of interest in a system with "flexible" wages. Let us then see whether it holds within the limits of his (tacit) assumption of rigid wages. We will agree at once that under this assumption the rate of interest depends on the quantity of money, but this is true only in a very special sense. If we look at our "Keynesian" model we find that we have 7 equations in 7 unknowns and two arbitrary quantities or "parameters," M and W_0. The solution of the system gives each of the 7 variables as functions of these arbitrary parameters: $\bar{r} = r(M, W)$, $\bar{Y} = Y(M, W)$, $\bar{N} = N(M, W)$, etc. On the basis of previous considerations these can be written:

$$(5.1) \qquad \bar{r} = r\left(\frac{M}{W}\right), \qquad (5.2) \qquad \bar{Y} = Y\left(\frac{M}{W}\right), \text{ etc.}$$

If this is the sense in which Lerner states that r is a function of M, his statement is formally correct. But in the first place it is not very helpful for understanding the determinants of the rate of interest. In a system with rigid wages practically every economic variable depends on the quantity of money (and the money wage). The rate of interest depends on M as much as the price of shoes or employment in ice-cream manufacturing. In the second place it has nothing to do with Keynes's liquidity preference: r depends on M even if we neglect the liquidity demand for money (see Section 11). Hence if Lerner's equation, $M = f(r)$, corresponds to our equation (5.1), then it is not a demand-for-money schedule, but an empirical relationship obtained by previous solution of a system of equations of which the demand for money itself is one. And his approach certainly throws no light on the determinants of the rate of interest.

The only alternative is to consider Lerner's equation as a true demand for money corresponding to our equation (1): $M = L(r, Y)$. But why has the second variable been omitted? The answer is clear; by concentrating attention on the liquidity preference and the demand for money to hold, sight has been lost of the demand for money to spend. Thus we go from one extreme to the other; instead of neglecting the influence of the rate of interest as in the "quantity theory," we neglect the part played by income in determining the demand for money. The results of this unjustified omission are serious in many respects. The most serious is that it leads to the conclusion (reached by Lerner) that saving and investment play no part in the determination of the rate of interest.[51] Figure 3 shows on the contrary that equations (2) and (3) play as vital a role as the demand-for-money equation. It is clear also that changes in the propensity to save or to invest or in the wage rate, lead directly to changes in the interest rate.

To defend his point Lerner is forced to say that changes in these propensities affect the rate of interest *because* they change the demand for money, i.e., because they shift the graph of $M = f(r)$.[52] But this is true and by definition only if Lerner identifies $M = f(r)$ with our equation (5.1). Since this equation is obtained by previously solving the whole system, it contains the relevant parameters of the functions which determine the rate of interest. A change in any of these parameters changes or shifts the function $r = r(M/W)$ accordingly. But, as we have already seen, equation (5.1) cannot possibly help us in understanding the determinants of the rate of interest.[53]

Another consequence of Lerner's formulation is that it leads to the conclusion that the interest rate can always be lowered by increasing the quantity of money, at least to the point where

[51] In "Alternative Formulations of the Theory of Interest," Lerner writes: "For the first, easy step [from the classical to the modern theory of interest] is the insinuation of Liquidity Preference as a junior partner in the old established one-man firm in the business of interest-determination, and the second . . . step is to put Saving-Investment, the senior partner, to sleep, as a preliminary to kicking him out" (*op. cit.*, p. 221).

[52] That this is Lerner's point of view may be seen for instance in the following passage from a letter written to me in June, 1943. Discussing the effects of an increase in the propensity to invest in the "classical case" (demand for money to hold equals zero) he writes: "Even in that case there must be a fall in income which decreases the need for cash which lowers the rate of interest so that the investors have a signal that they should increase investment, but an infinitesimal decrease in employment is sufficient to bring about any necessary fall in the rate of interest. . . ."

[53] To give another example, we can solve the system to obtain, say, the equilibrium output of shoes (Q) as a function of the quantity of money: $Q = f(M, W)$ or $M = F(Q, W)$. But to say that a change in tastes changes the output *because* it shifts this function is formally correct but perfectly useless as a tool of analysis.

the demand becomes infinitely elastic; while the truth is that no finite change in the quantity of money can hold the interest rate below the full-employment level.[54]

Let us finally note that Lerner's theory is not fully satisfactory even in the "Keynesian case." It is true that in this case saving and investment do not determine the rate of interest, but it is equally clear that the rate of interest does not depend on the quantity of money.

In conclusion, to say that the rate of interest is determined by the schedule $M = f(r)$ is useless and confusing if this schedule is arrived at by previous solution of the entire system; it is an unwarranted simplification, full of serious consequences, if this function is treated as an ordinary demand function. And the statement that the propensity to save and invest plays no part in determining the rate of interest is true only in a limiting case: the Keynesian case.

20.   HICK'S THEORY—THE RATE OF INTEREST AND THE COST OF INVESTING IN SECURITIES

In *Value and Capital* Hicks has developed what is probably the most daring attempt at reducing the rate of interest to a purely monetary phenomenon.

In Hicks's own words the rate of interest is explained by the "imperfect moneyness" of securities. "The imperfect moneyness of those bills which are not money is due to their lack of general acceptability: it is this lack of general acceptability which causes the trouble of investing in them" [55] and it is this trouble, namely "the trouble of making transactions [i.e., of purchasing securities] which explains the short rate of interest." [56] And these same factors also explain the long rate since the long rate is some average of the short rates plus a premium to cover the risk of (unanticipated) movements in the future short rates.[57]

Thus the rate of interest is explained by the fact that securities are not a medium of exchange and is determined essen-

[54] Proper qualifications must be made for the case in which the *IS* curve is not monotonic decreasing.
[55] *Value and Capital*, p. 166.
[56] *Ibid.*, p. 165.
[57] *Ibid.*, Chapter XI.

tially by the cost of making loan transactions. This is certainly an unusual theory of interest and an astonishing one, to say the least; it appears irreconcilable with the theory we have developed throughout this paper.

Hick's theory finds its origin in an attempt to answer a question posed by the Keynesian analysis. The reason that induces people to hold assets in the form of cash rather than securities is that the value of even the safest type of securities is not certain: it is subject to changes due to movements in the rate of interest. Now, as we have seen, this risk decreases as the duration of the loan transaction becomes shorter: and it disappears entirely on loans that last only one "Hicksian week" (or one income period in our model) since by hypothesis the rate of interest cannot change. There must then be some other reason to stop people from holding all of their assets in the form of securities and thus reducing their demand for "money to hold" to zero; this reason can only be the cost of investing in this riskless type of loans. This is Hicks's starting point: and so far there seems to be no difference from our own approach as developed in Section 5. But from these correct premises Hicks draws the wrong conclusion: namely *that it is the cost of investing that explains the rate of interest.* To say that the cost of investing is necessary to explain *why* the demand for money to hold is not always zero and to say that it *explains* the rate of interest are quite different statements. There is a logical gap between the two. Thus, for example, from the correct premise that the cost of automobiles in New York cannot fall to zero because they have to be transported from Detroit, there does not logically follow the conclusion that the cost of cars in New York is explained or determined by the cost of transporting them.

There is a different way of explaining the rate of interest, which is not less satisfactory for the fact of being obvious: namely that for certain categories of people (entrepreneurs as well as spendthrifts) it is worth while to pay a premium to obtain spot cash against a promise to pay cash in the future. This is the course we have followed: and it is clearly all that is necessary to explain the existence of the rate of interest. The cost of investing continues to play an important part in our theory: (a) it explains why the demand for money to hold is not identically zero; (b) it explains why the rate of interest can never fall below a certain level in a free capitalistic economy; and hence it explains the peculiarities of the Keynesian case. But it is clear that it is not necessary to explain the rate of interest.

Our next task is to show that the cost of investing is also not sufficient to explain the nature of interest. To this end we must disprove Hicks's statement that if people were to be "paid in the form of bills . . . there would be no cost of investment and therefore . . . no reason for the bills to fall to a discount," [58] i.e., no rate of interest. It is easy to show that, even if "bills" were to be used as medium of exchange, there would be no reason for the rate of interest to fall to zero.

Let us consider first the case of a "stationary state." It is well known that the stationary state is characterized by the fact that the rate of change of the quantity of capital is zero; the marginal efficiency of the existing quantity of capital is equal to the rate of interest, say r_0, that makes net saving equal to zero. [59] Now it is theoretically conceivable that, in this state, securities might replace money as a medium of exchange; [60] their purchasing power would be objectively determined by their discounted value since, by hypothesis, the future rate of interest is known and constant. Their aggregate value would also be constant but, since individual savings need not be zero, there would be a net flow from dissavers to savers. Under these conditions it is clear that securities would continue to yield the rate of interest r_0, even though they would be performing the function of a medium of exchange. Thus, as far as the stationary state goes, Hicks's conclusion does not follow: the interest rate would be zero only in the special case $r_0 = 0$.

Next let us consider an expanding economy, in which the net level of saving and investment is not zero, and let us assume again that it is technically possible for securities to be accepted as a medium of exchange. [61]

In this economy, if there is to be no inflation, it is necessary

[58] *Ibid.*, p. 165.

[59] For a more detailed description of the conditions that give rise to a stationary state see, for instance, M. Timlin, *Keynesian Economics*, Chapter IV.

[60] See, for instance, *ibid.*, p. 53.

[61] This would require that all people agree at all times on the present value of every security.

that the rate of money investment be not larger than the rate of (*ex ante*) saving. Now there are two possibilities:

(a) There exists some mechanism by which the net increase in outstanding securities cannot exceed net savings. Then the competition of borrowers to obtain loans will automatically determine the level of the rate of interest.

(b) There is no limitation as to the issuance of new securities per unit of time. Then, of course, the rate of interest would be zero, since there would be no necessity for borrowers to compete. But the result would clearly be a situation of unending and progressive inflation. In the first case the stability of the quantity of active money and therefore of the price level is assured by the fact that savers would increase their "hoards" of securities-money, at a rate equal to the net increase in the value of outstanding securities. But in the second case there is nothing to stop the price level from rising indefinitely, except if it so happens that the "full employment" rate of interest is zero or negative.[62]

We may therefore safely conclude that the rate of interest is not explained by the fact that securities are not money. Once we recognize this, the complicated and confusing Hicksian theory about the imperfect moneyness of securities becomes unnecessary and should, in our opinion, be abandoned.

To say that different assets share in different degrees the quality of "moneyness" either has no meaning or it is based on a confusion between liquidity and the properties of a medium of exchange. It is true that different assets have different degrees of liquidity, since the liquidity depends on the perfection of the market in which a good is traded. And it is also true that money is probably, under normal conditions, the most liquid of all assets. But the property of money is that it is accepted (freely or by force of law) as a medium of exchange: and liquidity does not make money out of something that is not money. Whatever one's definition of liquidity, to say that a government bond, a speculative share, a house, are money in different degrees, can at best generate unnecessary confusion. It is true

---

[62] We are well aware of the fact that the excess of money investment over (*ex ante*) saving does not lead to inflation, unless there is full employment to begin with, or until full employment is reached. It remains true however that, except in the case mentioned in the text, a zero rate of interest must eventually lead to inflation.

that money and securities are close substitutes, but this connection is to be found elsewhere than in degrees of moneyness; it depends on the fact that both money and securities are alternative forms of holding assets in nonphysical form. Securities are thus close substitutes for money, but not for money as a medium of exchange, only for money as an asset.

Having shown that the cost of investment neither explains nor determines the rate of interest, we will agree with Hicks that "the level of that [short] rate of interest measures the trouble involved in investing funds . . . to the marginal lender." [63] One cannot disagree with this statement any more than with the statement that the price of butter measures the marginal utility of butter to each member of the community.[64] Both statements are either tautologies or definitions of rational behavior. They are tautologies if they mean that all those who found it convenient to perform a certain transaction have done so. They are definitions of rational economic behavior if they state the conditions under which economic agents will maximize their satisfaction.[65] But it is clear that whether these statements are tautologies or definitions they are not sufficient to explain either the price of butter or the level of the rate of interest.

To conclude then we agree with Hicks that the rate of interest is at least equal to the cost of investing to the marginal lender, but this statement is not very helpful for understanding the rate of interest. But the Hicksian theory that the rate of interest is determined or simply explained by the imperfect moneyness of securities must be discarded as faulty.

21. SAVING AND INVESTMENT OR SUPPLY OF AND DEMAND FOR CASH?—CONCLUSIONS

It will now be useful, in concluding this paper, to restate in brief form the general theory of interest and money that emerges from our analysis.

We believe that the best way of achieving this aim is to show

---

[63] *Op. cit.*, p. 165.

[64] More exactly: the ratio of the price of butter to that of any other commodity measures the ratio of their respective marginal utilities.

[65] If anything, Hicks's statement is less illuminating, since there is, at least theoretically, the possibility that the rate of interest may exceed the cost of lending idle funds to the marginal lender: it is this very possibility that gives rise to the "classical case."

how, by means of our theory, we can answer the controversial question that has caused so much discussion in recent economic literature.

Is the rate of interest determined by the demand for and supply of cash? Or is it determined by those "real factors," psychological and technological, that can be subsumed under the concepts of propensity to save and marginal efficiency of investment?

We consider it to be a distinct advantage of our theory that we can answer both questions affirmatively. We do not have to choose between these two alternatives any more than between the following two: Is the price of fish determined by the daily demand and the daily supply; or is it determined by the average yearly demand and the cost of fishing?

Since we have maintained throughout this paper that, in general, saving and lending are independent decisions, we must clearly agree that the "daily" rate of interest is determined by the demand for and supply of money to hold (or, for that matter, by demand for and supply of loanable funds).[66] It is this very principle that has formed the base of our analysis of the money market (Section 7). But we cannot stop at this recognition and think that this is sufficient for a general theory of the rate of interest.

To come back to our example, it is certainly true that the daily price of fish is entirely explained by the daily catch of fish. But if we want to understand why the daily price fluctuates around a certain level and not around a level ten times as high, we must look for something more fundamental than the good or bad luck of the fishermen on a particular day. We shall then discover that the number of fishermen and the amount of equipment used does not change daily but is determined by the condition that the average returns, through good and bad days, must be sufficiently high to make the occupation of fishing (and investment in fishing equipment) as attractive as alternative ones.

What is obviously true for the price of fish must also hold

[66] In this respect we have nothing to add to the arguments developed by Hicks in Chapter XII of *Value and Capital*. There are enough equations to determine all the prices on each Monday and it makes no difference which equation is eliminated.

for the price of loans. The statement that the "daily" rate is determined by the "daily" demand for and supply of money (or, more exactly, of money to hold) does not greatly advance us in the understanding of the true determinants of the rate of interest. This theory by itself is insufficient to explain, for instance, why in countries well-equipped and of great saving capacity, like England or the United States, the system of rates of interest fluctuates around low levels (2 or 3 per cent for the pure long rate and much less for short rates); while it fluctuates around much higher levels (5 or 6 per cent or more for the long rate) in countries poor in savings or rich but scarcely developed. Is that because in the last-mentioned countries the supply of cash is insufficient? Clearly not. The explanation for this difference can only run in terms of those more fundamental factors, technological and psychological, that are included in the propensity to save and the marginal efficiency of investment.

As we have shown in our model the equality of demand and supply of loanable funds is the equilibrium condition for the week (or for our income period) and determines the equilibrium rate of interest (or system of rates) for the week. It corresponds to the short-run equilibrium condition of the Marshallian demand and supply analysis: price equals marginal cost. But the stock of money to hold (the supply) tends itself to change and thus push the "daily" rate toward the level at which the flow of money saving equals the flow of money investment. The condition, (ex ante) saving = (ex ante) investment, corresponds to the long-run Marshallian condition (under perfect competition): price = average cost including rent.

The first condition is satisfied even in the short period since it is the result of decisions that can be carried out instantaneously (see Section 5). The second is a long-run condition and therefore may actually never be satisfied: but it is necessary to explain the level toward which the weekly rate tends (even though this level may never be reached since the long-run equilibrium rate of interest itself changes).

Thus, to complete our theory, we must be able to explain what determines the level of long-run equilibrium. At this point we find that our answer is not unique since it depends on the assumptions concerning the form of the supply-of-labor schedule.

I. As long as wages are flexible, the long-run equilibrium rate of interest is determined exclusively by real factors, that is to say, essentially by the propensity to save and the marginal efficiency of investment. The condition, money saving = money investment, determines the price level and not the rate of interest.

II. If wages are rigid it is still true that the long-run equilibrium rate of interest is determined by the propensities to save and to invest but the situation is now more complicated; for these propensities depend also on money income and therefore on the quantity of active money which in turn depends itself on the level of the rate of interest. Thus, unless wages are perfectly flexible or the supply of money is always so adjusted as to assure the maintenance of full employment, the long-run equilibrium rate of interest depends also on the quantity of money and it is determined, together with money income, by equations (1), (2), and (3) of our model. We want however to stress again that the dependence of the rate of interest on the quantity of money does not depend on liquidity preference. In a system with rigid wages not only interest but also almost every economic variable depends on the quantity of money.

III. Finally our theory of the rate of interest becomes even less uniform when we take into account the "Keynesian case." In this case clearly the long-run equilibrium rate of interest is the rate which makes the demand for money to hold infinitely elastic. The economic theorist here is forced to recognize that under certain conditions the rate of interest is determined exclusively by institutional factors.

Postscript

I want to take the opportunity offered by this reprinting to warn the reader that the latter part of section 13, beginning with the second paragraph on page 160, contains several errors which vitiate the argument—though the main conclusion can be salvaged. These errors and their implications were first pointed out by D. Patinkin, in "Relative prices, Say's Law and the Demand for Money," *Econometrica*, April 1948, and elaborated in *Money Interest and Prices*, Row, Peterson, 1956, appendix to Chapter 8. While it is not possible in this postscript to provide a rigorous restatement, we offer a brief sketch of the correct formulation.

In the first place, in line with the model used throughout the rest of the paper, one must add to the $n - 1$ commodities and money mentioned on page 161, an $n + 1$ good, namely bonds, a good whose quantity may be positive (credits) or negative (debts). Also, when credits and debts are taken into account, the homogeneity of zero degree in prices of the *individual* demand functions for commodities no longer logically follows from rational behavior. Nor can homogeneity be introduced as a plausible, ad hoc, behavior assumption.

On the other hand it can be verified that, provided (a) the given money supply consists entirely of bank money which is offset by the debt of the private sector to the banking system, and (b) all existing bonds represent claims on, or liabilities to, the private sector (including banks), then *aggregate* private real wealth will be invariant under a proportional change of all prices (no Pigou effect exists). Under these conditions it is both permissible and justifiable to postulate that (c) the *market* demand for each commodity is homogeneous of zero degree and the *market* demand for money is homogeneous of first degree, in all commodity prices. Indeed (c) is then equivalent to assuming that the aggregate demand for each commodity and for money is unaffected by a mere redistribution of wealth. Such an assumption does not seem unreasonable, at least as a convenient first approximation. (It follows of course from assumptions (a) to (c) that the net demand for bonds by household and banks combined is not homogeneous in prices, as can be verified from the budget equation of individuals plus banks).

Under assumptions (a) to (c) the argument in the rest of the paper remains valid. That the bond market is, at times, not given explicit treatment, is accounted for by the fact that, through the so-called Walras Law, one of the markets is necessarily cleared when the remaining ones are cleared, and hence need not be explicitly exhibited.

January 1960.

IX

BENJAMIN M. ANDERSON was born in 1886 and died in 1949. He took his doctor's degree in economics, philosophy, and sociology at Columbia University in 1911. Between 1911 and 1918 he was on the economic faculties of Columbia and Harvard universities. He became economist of the Chase National Bank in 1920. His chief works are *Social Value* (1911), *The Value of Money* (1917: reprinted 1922, 1926, and 1936), and *Economics and the Public Welfare* (1949). The following essay, "Digression on Keynes," appeared as Chapter 60 of *Economics and the Public Welfare*.[1] It had already appeared in substance, however, in a symposium published by the Twentieth Century Fund in 1945, in their publication entitled *Financing American Prosperity*, as an appendix to Anderson's contribution, under the title: "A Refutation of Keynes' Attack on the Doctrine that Aggregate Supply Creates Aggregate Demand —Basic Fallacies in the Keynesian System."

DIGRESSION ON KEYNES

BENJAMIN M. ANDERSON

1. A REFUTATION OF KEYNES'S ATTACK ON THE DOCTRINE THAT AGGREGATE SUPPLY CREATES AGGREGATE DEMAND

The central theoretical issue involved in the problem of postwar economic readjustment, and in the problem of full employment in the postwar period, is the issue between the equilibrium doctrine and the purchasing power doctrine.

[1] Published by D. Van Nostrand Co., Inc., Princeton, N. J.

Those who advocate vast governmental expenditures and deficit fianancing after the war as the only means of getting full employment, separate production and purchasing power sharply. Purchasing power must be kept above production if production is to expand, in their view. If purchasing power falls off, production will fall off.

The prevailing view among economists, on the other hand, has long been that purchasing power grows out of production. The great producing countries are the great consuming countries. The twentieth century world consumes vastly more than the eighteenth century world because it produces vastly more. Supply of wheat gives rise to demand for automobiles, silks, shoes, cotton goods, and other things that the wheat producer wants. Supply of shoes gives rise to demand for wheat, for silks, for automobiles and for other things that the shoe producer wants. Supply and demand in the aggregate are thus not merely equal, but they are identical, since every commodity may be looked upon either as supply of its own kind or as demand for other things. But this doctrine is subject to the great qualification that the proportions must be right; that there must be equilibrium.

On the equilibrium theory occasional periods of readjustment are inevitable and are useful. An active boom almost inevitably generates disequilibria. The story in the present volume of the boom of 1919-1920 and the crisis of 1920-1921 gives a classical illustration. The period of readjustment may be relatively short and need not be severe, but a period of shakedown, a period in which overexpanded industries are contracted and opportunities made for under-developed industries to expand, a period in which prices and costs come into equilibrium, a period in which weak spots in the credit situation are cleaned up, a period in which excessive debts are liquidated—such periods we must have from time to time. The effort to prevent adjustment and liquidation by the pouring out of artificial purchasing power is, from the standpoint of the equilibrium doctrine, an utterly futile and wasteful and dangerous performance. Once a reëquilibration is accomplished, moreover, the equilibrium doctrine would regard pouring out new artificial purchasing power as wholly unnecessary and further as dangerous, since it would tend to create new disequilibria.

The late Lord Keynes was the leading advocate of the purchasing power doctrine, and the leading opponent of the doctrine that supply creates its own demand. The present chapter is concerned with Keynes's attack on the doctrine that supply creates its own demand.

Keynes was a dangerously unsound thinker.[1] His influence in the Roosevelt Administration was very great. His influence upon most of the economists in the employ of the Government is incredibly great. There has arisen a volume of theoretical literature regarding Keynes almost equal to that which has arisen around Karl Marx.[2] His followers are satisfied that he has destroyed the long accepted economic doctrine that aggregate supply and aggregate demand grow together. It seems necessary to analyze Keynes's argument with respect to this point.

Keynes Ignores the Essential Point in the Doctrine He Attacks. Keynes presents his argument in his *The General Theory of Employment, Interest and Money,* published in 1936. But he nowhere in the book takes account of the law of equilibrium among the industries, which has always been recognized as an essential part of the doctrine that supply creates its own demand. He takes as his target a seemingly crude statement from J. S. Mill's *Principles of Political Economy* (Book III, chap. 14, par. 2) which follows:

What constitutes the means of payment for commodities is simply commodities. Each person's means of paying for the productions of other people consist of those which he himself possesses. All sellers are inevitably, and by the meaning of the word, buyers. Could we suddenly double the productive powers of the country, we should double the supply of commodities in every market; but we should, by the same stroke, double the purchasing power. Everybody would bring a double demand as well as supply: everybody would be able to buy twice as much, because every one would have twice as much to offer in exchange.

Now this passage by itself does not present the essentials of the doctrine. If we doubled the productive power of the coun-

[1] Lord Keynes was a man of genius. He had great abilities and great personal charm.

[2] I have not read much of this elaborate literature. Keynes himself I have studied with care. I think it probable that other critics have anticipated many of the points I make here, and I would gladly give them credit if I knew.

try, we should not double the supply of commodities in every market, and if we did, we should not clear the markets of the double supply in every market. If we doubled the supply in the salt market, for example, we should have an appalling glut of salt. The great increases would come in the items where demand is elastic. We should change very radically the proportions in which we produced commodities.

But it is unfair to Mill to take this brief passage out of its context and present it as if it represented the heart of the doctrine. If Keynes had quoted only the three sentences immediately following, he would have introduced us to the conception of balance and proportion and equilibrium which is the heart of the doctrine—a notion which Keynes nowhere considers in this book. Mill's next few lines, immediately following the passage torn from its context, quoted above, are as follows:

It is probable, indeed, that there would now be a superfluity of certain things. Although the community would willingly double its aggregate consumption, it may already have as much as it desires of some commodities, and it may prefer to do more than double its consumption of others, or to exercise its increased purchasing power on some new thing. If so, the supply will adapt itself accordingly, and the values of things will continue to conform to their cost of production.

Keynes, furthermore, ignores entirely the rich, fine work done by such writers as J. B. Clark and the Austrian School, who elaborated the laws of proportionality and equilibrium.

The doctrine that supply creates its own demand, as presented by John Stuart Mill, assumes a proper equilibrium among the different kinds of production, assumes proper terms of exchange (*i.e.*, price relationships) among different kinds of products, assumes proper relations between prices and costs. And the doctrine expects competition and free markets to be the instrumentality by means of which these proportions and price relations will be brought about. The modern version of the doctrine [3] would make explicit certain additional factors. There must be a proper balance in the international balance sheet. If foreign debts are excessive in relation to the volume of

[3] See the *Chase Economic Bulletin*, Vol. XI, No. 3, June 12, 1931.

foreign trade, grave disorders can come. Moreover, the money and capital markets must be in a state of balance. When there is an excess of bank credit used as a substitute for savings, when bank credit goes in undue amounts into capital uses and speculative uses, impairing the liquidity of bank assets, or when the total volume of money and credit is expanded far beyond the growth of production and trade, disequilibria arise, and, above all, the *quality* of credit is impaired. Confidence may be suddenly shaken and a countermovement may set in.

With respect to all these points, automatic market forces tend to restore equilibrium in the absence of overwhelming governmental interference.

Keynes has nothing to say in his attack upon the doctrine that supply creates its own demand, in the volume referred to, with respect to these matters.

Indeed, far from considering the intricacies of the interrelations of markets, prices and different kinds of production, Keynes prefers to look at things in block. He says:

In dealing with the theory of employment I propose, therefore, to make use of only two fundamental units of quantity, namely, quantities of money-value and quantities of employment. The first of these is strictly homogeneous, and the second can be made so. For, in so far as different grades and kinds of labor and salaried assistance enjoy a more or less fixed relative remuneration, the quantity of employment can be sufficiently defined for our purpose by taking an hour's employment of ordinary labor as our unit *and weighing an hour's employment of special labor in proportion to its remuneration; i.e., an hour of special labor remunerated at double ordinary rates will count as two units.* [Italics mine.] [4] . . .

It is my belief that much unnecessary perplexity can be avoided if we limit ourselves strictly to the two units, money and labor, when we are dealing with the behavior of the economic system as a whole . . .[5]

Procedure of this kind is empty and tells us nothing about economic life. How empty it is becomes apparent when we observe that these two supposedly independent units of quantity, namely, "quantities of money value" and "quantities of employment," are both merely quantities of money value. If

[4] *The General Theory of Employment, Interest and Money*, p. 41.
[5] *Ibid.*, p. 43.

ten laborers working for $2 a day are dismissed and two laborers
working for $10 a day are taken on, there is no change in the
volume of employment, by Keynes's method of reckoning, as
is obvious from the italicized portion of the quotation above.
His "quantity of employment" is not a quantity of employment. It is a quantity of money received by laborers who are
employed.[6]

Throughout Keynes's analysis he is working with aggregate,
block concepts. He has an aggregate supply function and an
aggregate demand function.[7] But nowhere is there any discussion of the interrelationships of the elements in these vast
aggregates, or of elements in one aggregate with elements in
another. Nowhere is there a recognition that different elements
in the aggregate supply give rise to the demand for other elements in the aggregate supply. In Keynes's discussion, purchasing power and production are sharply sundered.

The Function of Prices. It is part of the equilibrium doctrine
that prices tend to equate supply and demand in various markets: commodities, labor, capital, and so on. If prices go down
in particular markets this constitutes a signal for producers
to produce less, and a signal for consumers to consume more.
In the markets, on the other hand, where prices are rising we
have a signal for producers to produce more, for consumers
to consume less, and a signal for men in fields where prices
are less satisfactory to shift their labor and, to the extent that
this is possible, to shift their capital to the more productive
field. Free prices, telling the truth about supply and demand,
thus constitute the great equilibrating factor.

The Function of the Rate of Interest. Among these prices
is the rate of interest. The traditional doctrine is that the rate
of interest equates supply and demand in the capital market and
equates saving and investment. Interest is looked upon as
reward for saving and as inducement to saving. The old doctrine which looked upon consumer's thrift as the primary source
of capital is inadequate. It must be broadened to include
producer's thrift, and especially corporate thrift, and direct

[6] See my criticism of the analogous procedure by Irving Fisher in his "Equation of Exchange," in my *Value of Money,* New York, 1917 and 1936, pp. 158-
162.
  [7] *Ibid.,* p. 29.

capitalization, as when the farmer uses his spare time in building fences and putting other improvements on his farm, or when the farmer lets his flocks and herds increase instead of selling off the whole of the annual increase, and so forth. It must include governmental thrift, as when government taxes to pay down public debt or when government taxes for capital purposes instead of borrowing—historically very important! The doctrine needs a major qualification, moreover, with respect to the use of bank credit for capital purposes.[8]

Keynes's Attack on the Interest Rate as Equilibrator. It is with respect to the interest rate as the equilibrating factor that Keynes has made his most vigorous assault upon prevailing views. Where economists generally have held that saving and avoiding unnecessary debt and paying off debt where possible are good things, Keynes holds that they are bad things. He deprecates depreciation reserves for business corporations. He deprecates amortization of public debt by municipalities. He deprecates additions to corporate surpluses out of earnings. His philosophy is responsible for the ill-fated undistributed profits tax which we adopted in 1936 and which we abandoned with a great sigh of relief, over the President's plaintive protest, in 1938.

Keynes gives two reasons for his rejection of prevailing ideas with respect to interest and savings, and the equilibrating function of the rate of interest. The first will be found on pages 110 and 111 of his *General Theory*. He says:

The influence of changes in the rate of interest on the amount actually saved is of paramount importance, but is *in the opposite direction* to that usually supposed. For even if the attraction of the larger future income to be earned from a higher rate of interest has the effect of diminishing the propensity to consume, nevertheless we can be certain that a rise in the rate of interest will have the effect of reducing the amount actually saved. For aggregate saving is governed by aggregate investment; a rise in the rate of interest *(unless it is offset by a corresponding change in the demand-*

8 See my *Value of Money*, New York, 1917 and 1936, pages 484, n; 484-489; ch. XXIV; my address before the Indiana Bankers Association, published in *The Chase*, the house organ of the Chase National Bank, November, 1920; the *Chase Economic Bulletin*, November, 1926, and May, 1936. See also my article on "The Future of Interest Rates" in the *Commercial & Financial Chronicle* of Aug. 26, 1943.

schedule for investment) [italics mine] will diminish investment; hence a rise in the rate of interest must have the effect of reducing incomes to a level at which saving is decreased in the same measure as investment. Since incomes will decrease by a greater absolute amount than investment, it is, indeed, true that, when the rate of interest rises, the rate of consumption will decrease. But this does not mean that there will be a wider margin for saving. On the contrary, saving and spending will both decrease.[9]

This is an extraordinarily superficial argument. The whole case is given away by the parenthetical passage, "(unless it is offset by a corresponding change in the demand-schedule for investment)." The usual *cause* of an increase in the rate of interest is a *rise* in the demand-schedule for investment. Interest usually rises because of an increased demand for capital on the part of those who wish to increase their investments, of businesses which wish to expand, of speculators for the rise, of home-builders, and so on. Usually, when the interest rate rises, it rises because investment is increasing, and the increased savings which rising interest rates induce are promptly invested. Indeed, investment often *precedes* saving [10] in such a situation, through an expansion of bank credit, also induced by the rising rate of interest.

Keynes is assuming an *uncaused* rise in the rate of interest, and he has very little difficulty in disposing of this. But economic phenomena do not occur without *causes*.

Keynes's second argument against the prevailing doctrine will be found in his Chapter 14 (*ibid.*) called "The Classical Theory of the Rate of Interest." Here (with a diagram on page 180) he complains that the static theory of interest has not taken account of the possibility of changes in the level of in-

---

[9] Harold G. Moulton, whose book, *The Formation of Capital*, was published at about the same time that Keynes's book appeared, independently presents essentially the same argument, which Moulton calls "The Dilemma of Savings." I have discussed Moulton's view in the *Chase Economic Bulletin*, Vol. XVI, No. 2, May 12, 1936, "Eating the Seed Corn," and in my discussion of the undistributed profits tax in the present volume.

[10] The Keynesian reader will observe that I am using the word "savings" in the ordinary sense, and not in Keynes's peculiar sense. I am under no obligation to use Keynes's terminology, since Keynes himself, as shown in the first sentence of the passage quoted above, is discussing the usual view of the relation of the rate of interest to savings. To the extent that there is any shift in the meaning of the terms in the course of the argument, it is done by Keynes and not by me. I use the word "savings" in the ordinary sense throughout.

come, or the possibility that the level of income is actually a function of the rate of investment.

Now it may be observed that Keynes is here introducing dynamic considerations into a static analysis. By this device one may equally destroy the law of supply and demand, the law of cost of production, the capitalization theory, or any other of the standard working tools of the static analysis. Thus the static law of supply and demand is that a decrease in price will lead to an increase in the amount demanded. But with a sudden, violent general fall in prices the tendency is for buyers to hold off and wait until they see where prices are going to settle.

The static economist has known all this almost from the beginning. He has been aware that he was making abstractions. He has protected himself in general by the well-known phrase, *"ceteris paribus"* (other things equal), and the general level of income has been among those other things assumed to be unchanged. Moreover, the static economist has concerned himself with delicate marginal adjustments, and with infinitesimal variations in the region of the margin, a device which Keynes is very glad to borrow from static economics in his conception of the "marginal propensity to consume" and in his initial conception of the "marginal efficiency of capital."

The Multiplier. Rejecting the function of the interest rate as the equilibrator of saving and investment, Keynes is so impressed with the danger of thrift that he finally convinces himself in one of his major doctrines that *no part* of an increase in income which is not consumed is invested; *that all of the unconsumed increase in income is hoarded.* This major doctrine is the much-praised Keynesian "investment multiplier theory." [11] If an investment is made it gives a certain amount of employment, but that is not the end of the story. Investment tends to multiply itself in subsequent stages of spending. The recipients of the proceeds of the investment spend at least part of it, and the recipients of their spending spend part of what they get, and so on. How many times does the original investment multiply itself? Keynes gives a definite mathematical answer in which his investment multiplier rests solely on what he calls "the marginal propensity to consume." The multiplier figure rests on the assumption that the subsequent spending

[11] *Ibid.,* pp. 113-119.

consists entirely of purchases for consumption. None of the unconsumed increase in income is invested. If any of the recipients of the proceeds of the investment should add to their expenditures for consumption any investment at all, the mathematics of the Keynes multiplier would be upset, and the multiplier would be increased. It is a source of satisfaction to find this view in agreement with that of Professor James W. Angell on this point.[12]

The multiplier concept is an unfruitful notion. In times when the business cycle is moving upward, particulary in the early stages of revival, increased expenditure, whether for investment or consumption, tends to multiply itself many fold, as Wesley Mitchell [13] has shown.

In times of business reaction there may be very little multiplication. The soldiers' bonus payments by the Government under Mr. Hoover made no difference in the business picture. On the other hand, the soldiers' bonus payments under Mr. Roosevelt in 1936, at a time when the business curve was moving upward sharply, appear to have intensified the movement.

The Relation of Savings to Investment. The preoccupation with the varying relationship of saving to investment is superficial. Investment tends to equal saving in a reasonably good business situation, when bank credit is not expanding. In a strong upward move, when bank credit is readily obtainable, investment tends to exceed saving because men borrow at the banks and because expanding bank credit facilitates the issue of new securities. In a crisis and in the liquidation that follows a crisis, saving exceeds investment. Men and businesses are saving to pay down debts and especially to repay bank loans—a necessary preliminary to a subsequent revival of business. But the *reasons* for these changes in the relation of saving to investment are the all-important things. The relation of saving to investment is itself a very superficial thing. The *reasons* lie in the factors which govern the prospects of profits, including the price and cost equilibrium, the industrial equilibrium, and the *quality* of credit.

Keynes strives desperately to rule out bank credit as a factor

---

[12] James W. Angell, *Investment and Business Cycles,* New York, 1941, pp. 190-191.

[13] *Business Cycles,* University of California Press, 1913, pp. 453-454.

in the relation of savings to investment. At one point he does it very simply indeed:

> We have, indeed, to adjust for the creation and discharge of debts (including changes in the quantity of credit or money); but since for the community as a whole the increase or decrease of the aggregate creditor position is always exactly equal to the increase or decrease of the aggregate debtor position, this complication also cancels out when we are dealing with aggregate investment.[14]

But bank credit is not so easily canceled out as a factor in the volume of money available for investment. The borrower at the bank is, of course, both debtor to and creditor of the bank when he gets his loan. But his debt is an obligation which is *not* money, and his credit is a demand deposit, which *is* money. When he uses this money for investment, he is making an investment in addition to the investment which comes from savings.

On pages 81 to 85 of the same book, Keynes engages in a very confused further argument on this point.

> It is supposed that a depositor and his bank can somehow contrive between them to perform an operation by which savings can disappear into the banking system so that they are lost to investment, or, contrariwise, that the banking system can make it possible for investment to occur, to which no saving corresponds. But no one can save without acquiring an asset, whether it be cash or a debt or capital-goods; and no one can acquire an asset which he did not previously possess, unless *either* an asset of equal value is newly produced *or* someone else parts with an asset of that value which he previously had. In the first alternative there is a corresponding new investment: in the second alternative someone else must be dissaving an equal sum. For his loss of wealth must be due to his consumption exceeding his income. . . .

But the assumption that a man who parts with an asset for cash is losing wealth, and that this must be due to his consumption exceeding his income, is purely gratuitous. The man who sells an asset for cash may hold his cash or he may reinvest it in something else. It is not "dis-saving" unless he spends it for current consumption, and he does not have to do that unless he wants to. Indeed on the next page (page 83) the man who

[14] *General Theory*, etc., p 75.

holds the additional money corresponding to the new bank-credit is said to be *saving*. "Moreover the savings which result from this decision are just as genuine as any other savings. No one can be compelled to own the additional money corresponding to the new bank-credit, unless he deliberately prefers to hold more money rather than some other form of wealth."

Keynes's confusion here could be interpreted as due to his effort to carry out a puckish joke on the Keynesians. He had got them excited in his earlier writings about the relation between savings and investment. Then, in his *General Theory*, he propounds the doctrine that savings are always equal to investment.[15] This makes the theology harder for the devout follower to understand, and calls, moreover, for a miracle by which the disturbing factor of bank credit may be abolished. This miracle Keynes attempts in the pages cited above, with indifferent success.

One must here protest against the dangerous identification of bank expansion with savings, which is part of the Keynesian doctrine. This fallacy is discussed at length in the chapters dealing with the expansion of bank credit in the 1920's and the discussion of the doctrine of oversaving in connection with the undistributed profits tax. This doctrine is particularly dangerous today, when we find our vast increase in money and bank deposits growing out of war finance described as "savings," just because somebody happens to hold them at a given moment of time. On this doctrine, the greater the inflation, the greater the savings! The alleged excess of savings over investment in the period, 1924-1929, was merely a failure to invest *all* of the rapidly expanding bank credit. All of the real savings of this period was invested, and far too much new bank credit in addition.

The Wage-rate as Equilibrator of the Supply and Demand of Labor. Keynes also tries to destroy the accepted doctrine regarding the rate of wages as the equilibrating factor between the supply and demand of labor. He attempts at various places to suggest that a reduction in money wages "may be" ineffective in increasing the demand for labor (*e.g., ibid.*, p. 13), but he nowhere, so far as I can find, positively states this. He does suggest (p. 264) that a fall in wages would mean a fall in prices,

---

[15] *Ibid.*, pp. 61-65.

and that this could lead to embarrassment and insolvency to entrepreneurs who are heavily indebted, and to an increase in the real burden of the national debt. On this point it is sufficient to say that the fall in wages in a depression usually follows, and does not precede, the fall in prices, and that it is usually more moderate than the fall in prices. It does not need to be so great as the fall in prices in order to bring about a reëquilibration, since wages are only part of cost of production, and since the efficiency of labor increases in such a situation.

Keynes accuses other economists of reasoning regarding the demand schedule for labor on the basis of a single industry, and then, without substantial modification, making a simple extension of the argument to industry as a whole (pp. 258-259). But this is merely additional evidence that he has ignored John Bates Clark's *Distribution of Wealth*, and the theory of costs of the Austrian School, for whom the law of costs, including wages, is merely the law of the leveling of values among the different industries. Moreover, the studies of Paul Douglas, dealing with the elasticity of the demand for labor as a whole, constitute a sufficient answer to Keynes on this point. Douglas holds that the demand for labor is highly elastic; so much so that a 1% decline in wages can mean a 3% or 4% increase in employment, when wages are held above the marginal product of labor.[16]

But the practical issue does not usually relate to wages as a whole. The wages of nonunion labor, and especially agricultural labor, usually recede promptly and sometimes to extremes, in a depression, The issue usually relates to union wage scales held so high in particular industries that employment falls off very heavily in these industries, and that the industries constitue bottlenecks.[17]

But Keynes does not come to the theoretical conclusion that a reduction in money wages could not bring about an increase in employment. He rather reaches the practical conclusion that this is not the best way to do it. Instead, he would prefer in a closed economy, *i.e.*, one without foreign trade, to make such readjustments as are necessary by manipulations of money, and

[16] Paul H. Douglas, *The Theory of Wages*, New York, 1934, pp. 113-158 and 501-502.

[17] See the figures showing the wide disparities of wage reductions as among different groups, in 1931, in the *Chase Economic Bulletin*, Vol. XI, No. 3.

for an open economy, *i.e.,* one with large foreign trade, to accomplish it by letting the foreign exchanges fluctuate (p. 279).

The fact seems to be that Keynes entertains a settled prejudice against any reduction in money wages. He is opposed to flexibility downward in wage scales. He has, however, no such prejudice against flexibility upward. On the contrary, in the Keynes plan for an International Clearing Union of April 8, 1943, Keynes proposes, as a means of maintaining stability in foreign exchange rates, that a member state in the Clearing Union whose credit balance is increasing unduly, shall encourage an increase in money rates of earnings (meaning wages).[18] This would increase the cost of its goods in foreign trade, and consequently reduce its exports, and consequently hold down its credit balance. But Keynes makes no corresponding demand on the country whose *debit* in the Clearing Union is increasing unduly that it should encourage a *decrease* in money rates of earnings.

II. KEYNES'S CONSTRUCTIVE THEORY

The foregoing discussion of Keynes's doctrines has been primarily concerned with refuting his attack upon the long-established view that, given equilibrium, aggregate supply creates aggregate demand, that consumption keeps pace with production, and that the power to consume grows out of production. Now, however, it is planned to go further and to demonstrate that Keynes's constructive substitute for prevailing economic doctrine is essentially fallacious. Keynes builds his positive doctrine around three central notions: (1) the propensity to consume, (2) the schedule of the marginal efficiency of capital, and (3) the rate of interest. These three Keynes regards as independent variables. These three independent variables govern the dependent variables, namely, the volume of employment, and national income measured in "wage-units." [19]

There are two main criticisms of this scheme, either of which would invalidate it. (1) Keynes does not adhere to fixed meanings for his terms in the case of the rate of interest or in the case of the marginal efficiency of capital. (2) The three inde-

[18] *Op. cit.,* (9) (b)
[19] *General Theory of Employment,* p. 245.

pendent variables are not independent of one another, either in fact or on Keynes's own showing.

Keynes's Terms Lack Fixed Meanings. Let us consider first Keynes's failure to adhere to fixed meanings for his terms.

Keynes at times uses the rate of interest to mean a rate of discount, measuring the premium on present goods over future goods. This is implied in his initial definition of the marginal efficiency of capital, to which later reference is made on page 135 of this book. It is, moreover, made explicit by Keynes on page 93 of his book, where he says that, as an approximation, we can identify the rate of time-discounting, *i.e.*, the ratio of exchange between present goods and future goods, with the rate of interest. Later, however, Keynes gives us a radically different theory of interest. He makes the rate of interest depend on liquidity preference and the quantity of money. And he holds that interest is not paid for the purpose of inducing men *to save* but for the purpose of inducing men *not to hoard*. He holds that if money is made sufficiently abundant so that it can satiate liquidity preference, it will pull down, not merely the short time rate of interest or the short time money rates, but also the whole complex of interest rates, long and short.[20] The whole complex of interest rates (with a given liquidity preference scale) can be governed, and is governed, in his system, by the abundance or scarcity of money. Interest becomes a phenomenon of money *par excellence*. Strangely enough, however, we find Keynes playing with the notion of commodity rates of interest, or "own rates of interest," the rate between future wheat and present wheat, and designating this rate as the "wheat rate of interest." Every commodity can have its own rate of interest in terms of itself, and Keynes says that there is no reason why the wheat rate of interest should be equal to the copper rate of interest, because the relation between the spot and future contracts as quoted in the markets is notoriously different for different commodities.[21] The reader will find whatever he pleases in Keynes about the rates of interest, though his formal theory is the doctrine that the quantity of money, taken in conjunction with liquidity preference, governs the rate of interest.

[20] *Ibid.*, p. 167 and note 2.
[21] *Ibid.*, pp. 223-224.

But Keynes does not adhere long to his own theory of interest. In the same volume, 29 pages later, he has abandoned it. After saying, on pages 167-168, that the supply of money in relation to liquidity preference will govern the whole complex of interest rates, long and short, on page 197 he critizes the Federal Reserve banks for their open market policy, 1933-1934, on the ground that they purchased only short term securities, the effect of which "may, of course, be mainly confined to the very short term rate of interest and have little reaction on the much more important long term rates of interest." And he calls upon the central banks to regulate all rates of interest by having fixed rates at which they will buy obligations of differing maturities, long and short.[22]

There is no consistency in Keynes's use of the term "rate of interest" in this volume.

The conception of "the marginal efficiency of capital" has an even more extraordinary history in this volume. His initial definition of the marginal efficiency of capital (pp. 135-136) appears in the following passage:

> Over against the prospective yield of the investment we have the *supply price* of the capital-asset, meaning by this, not the market-price at which an asset of the type in question can be purchased in the market, but the price which would just induce a manufacturer newly to produce an additional unit of such assets, *i.e.,* what is sometimes called its *replacement cost.* The relation between the prospective yield of one more unit of that type of capital and the cost of producing that unit, furnishes us with the *marginal efficiency of capital* of that type. More precisely, *I define the marginal efficiency of capital as being equal to that rate of discount which would make the present value of the series of annuities given by the returns expected from the capital-asset during its life just equal to its supply price.* [Italics in this sentence are mine.] This gives us the marginal efficiencies of particular types of capital-assets. The greatest of these marginal efficiencies can then be regarded as the marginal efficiency of capital in general.

The reader should note that the marginal efficiency of capital is here defined in terms of the *expectation* of yield and of the *current* supply price of the capital-asset. It depends on the rate of return expected to be obtainable on money if it were invested in a *newly* produced asset; not on the historical result of what an investment has yielded on its original cost if we look back on its record after its life is over. . . .

For each type of capital we can build up a schedule, showing by how much investment in it will have to increase within the period, in order that its marginal efficiency should fall to any given figure. We can then aggregate these schedules for all the different types of capital, so as to provide a schedule relating the rate of aggregate investment to the corresponding marginal efficiency of capital in general which that rate of investment will establish. We shall call this the investment demand-schedule; or, alternatively, the schedule of the marginal efficiency of capital.

Keynes seems here to be talking about the calculation which an entrepreneur would make in deciding whether or not to buy a machine or other productive capital instrument. This impression is intensified when he states that the definition which he has given is fairly close to what Marshall intended to mean by the term, Marshall's phrase being the "marginal net efficiency" of a factor of production, or alternatively, the "marginal utility of capital," and by the passage which he quotes from Marshall's *Principles,* from which the following is taken:

"There may be machinery which the trade would have refused to dispense with if the *rate of interest* had been 20 per cent per annum. If the rate had been 10 per cent, more would have been used; if it had been 6 per cent, still more; if 4 per cent, still more; and finally, the rate being 3 per cent, they use more still. When they have this amount, the *marginal utility of the machinery, i.e.,* the utility of that machinery which it is only just worth their while to employ, is measured by 3 per cent.[23] [Italics mine.]

We seem, in the initial definition, to have the marginal efficiency of capital tied up with specific instruments of production, and the "expectation" regarding the future to be tied up with the anticipated returns from these specific instruments of production. These are familiar notions of static economics. But Keynes, before he has finished this chapter, gives us a warning against static economics, and indicates that the notion of the marginal efficiency of capital is going to be a dynamic concept, much more so even than the rate of interest, which is a *current* phenomenon.

In what follows in his volume, the marginal efficiency of

[23] *Ibid.,* pp. 139-140.

capital becomes dynamic by ceasing to be a fixed notion. It goes through more metamorphoses than even Ovid knew about! In Chapter 12 of the book, dealing with "The State of Long-Term Expectation," the expectation factor becomes everything and the efficiency of specific capital goods is forgotten, except for one footnote later to be quoted. This chapter develops a fantastic economic theory based on the somewhat less fantastic behavior of the New York stock market in 1928 and 1929. Expectation comes to mean expectations regarding expectations, and expectations regarding the reactions of different buyers and sellers of securities who are anticipating future expectations. It would seem that this, at best, could explain the selling prices of securities representing industries with a great variety of physical capital assets, rather than the marginal efficiency of specific capital-goods. Keynes, however, does not hesitate to identify the two. He says in a footnote on page 151 of that chapter, ". . . a high quotation for existing equities involves an increase in the marginal efficiency of the corresponding type of capital. . . ."

At times the marginal efficiency of capital means simply expectation regarding business profits, which may be due to entrepreneurial efficiency or to labor efficiency, quite as much as to the efficiency of capital instruments, or which may be due to maladjustments in the proportions of the industries, or between prices and costs, or to a war or war scare. On page 149 he makes "the state of confidence" one of the major factors governing the marginal efficiency of capital, and here he is clearly making the marginal efficiency of capital mean business profits rather than the specific return to a specific instrument of production. On page 315, talking about the business cycle, he suggests that "a more typical, and often the predominant, explanation of the crisis, is, not primarily a rise in the rate of interest, but a sudden collapse in the marginal efficiency of capital." Here, clearly, marginal efficiency of capital means anticipations regarding business profits rather than any specific return to specific capital instruments.

Keynes's doctrine that the schedule of the marginal efficiency of capital is today, and presumably for the future, much lower than it was in the nineteenth century (pages 307-309) seems to rest primarily on the view that employers were strong enough in the nineteenth century to prevent wages from rising much faster than the efficiency of labor, whereas they are not strong enough to do this today or presumably in the future. Here the "marginal efficiency of capital" would seem to depend on the relation between wages and the marginal efficiency of labor.

Finally, on page 207, the marginal efficiency of capital, "(especially of stocks of liquid goods)," comes to mean the speculative money profits which a man can anticipate from holding goods in a wild inflation, under the expectation of an ever greater fall in the value of money.

The maker of a new system of economics may be expected to adhere more closely than Keynes does to the meanings of his terms if he is to be taken seriously. Lumping all the causes of changes in anticipations regarding business profits under the one term, "marginal efficiency of capital," does not represent progress in the economic analysis of cause and effect.

Keynes's "Independent Variables" Not Independent. We come now to the second main criticism of Keynes's constructive system. As shown above, he takes as his three independent variables (1) the propensity to consume, (2) the schedule of the marginal efficiency of capital, and (3) the rate of interest. Now, these supposedly independent variables are in fact dependent on one another, and are even dependent on Keynes's own showing.

The schedule of *the marginal efficiency of capital* is said, on page 136, to be the equivalent of *the investment demand schedule.* But on page 106 we have been told that every weakening in the propensity to consume, regarded as a permanent habit, must weaken the demand for capital. On Keynes's own showing, the schedule of the marginal efficiency of capital is, in part, dependent on the propensity to consume.

The propensity to consume is, in part, dependent upon the rate of interest. From the standpoint of the old analysis, the rate of interest, the propensity to consume, and the propensity to save are all three *interdependent* variables. The rate of interest is, indeed, the equilibrating factor which brings savings and consumption into balance. Human nature being more concerned with present consumption than with future consumption,[24] there is need for an inducement to make men save. The

[24] Keynes does not believe this, but offers no evidence against it.

future looks smaller than the present. The pressure to consume today is great. Human wants of specific kinds are often satiable, but human wants in general are not. As old wants are satisfied, new wants spring up. The pressure to consume is insistent. Men must be induced to save for the future by a reward, and that reward is interest.

When savings are large and capital increases, the rate of interest goes down. When interest is high because accumulated capital is scarce, men are forced to make savings that they would not otherwise make, or are induced to make savings that they would not otherwise make. The farmer who can borrow at 4% to buy additional capital goods for his farm, will have a higher propensity to consume than the farmer who must pay 10%. If he can borrow at 4%, he will let his wife have a new dress and his family buy a new automobile. If he must pay 10%, the new dress and the new automobile are not bought and new savings go into fertilizer, harrows, and combines. The propensity to consume is definitely dependent on the rate of interest.

The interdependence of the rate of interest, savings, and the propensity to consume, Keynes escapes formally, in part, by giving us the new theory of interest stated above. He makes the rate of interest dependent, not on the necessity of paying interest to induce men *to save,* but rather on the necessity to induce them *not to hoard* what they save. Interest rates are governed (given the scale of liquidity preference) by the quantity of money. We have seen above that he adheres to this theory for 29 pages.

But even this emancipation of the rate of interest from time preference does not emancipate the propensity to consume from interest rates. If interest rates are high, whether from scarcity of money of from scarcity of real savings, men will be forced or induced to save more than would otherwise be the case, and the propensity to consume will be lower. The independence of the interest rate would still leave the propensity to consume dependent upon interest rates.

It has been shown above that, on Keynes's own showing, his schedule of marginal efficiency of capital, as initially defined, is dependent upon the propensity to consume. In the later meanings of the marginal efficiency of capital, however, it becomes dependent upon both the other variables. When marginal effi-

ciency of capital comes to mean speculative profits in the stock
market, or general business profits, it is clear that changes in
the rate of interest, or in the propensity to consume, can radically alter the schedule of the marginal efficiency of capital.
Keynes's three great independent variables are not independent.

3. STATIC ECONOMIC THEORY AND THE BUSINESS CYCLE

One reason why Keynes has found inadequate resistance
among the younger economists to his casual throwing aside
of the sound and subtle work of the great masters of static economic theory is that increasingly in the last two or three decades
economists have been interested in the laws of the business
cycle, in the ups and downs of business, and too many of them
have felt that they could get very little help in the study of the
business cycle from the generalizations of static economics.

The economic theorist has indeed devoted himself much too
exclusively to the laws of completed equilibrium, to theory
concerned with what prices and costs, and the proportions of
the productive forces, would be if markets were fluid and if
industry were in perfect balance. Students of the business cycle,
on the other hand, have been concerned much too exclusively
with the sequence and flow of events, losing sight of the goal in
watching the motions of the runners.

It must be apparent, however, that in ignoring the static conceptions, the business forecaster is throwing away a most valuable aid. Static theory does describe underlying economic
forces. If it tells nothing about the *rate* at which they will move,
it does at least indicate the *directions* in which they move. It
indicates their relative power and it indicates their relations
inter se. The student of change who knows the goal toward
which his forces are tending is certainly much better informed
than the man who does not know what the goal is, but merely
knows that change is taking place and that some things change
first and others later.

Wesley C. Mitchell's *Business Cycles* could not have been
written by a man who was not deeply learned in static theory
and the equilibrium notion. Mitchell objects to the expression
"the static state," but his interpretation of the business cycle
constantly employs equilibrium notions. The later stages of
prosperity generate abnormalities, stresses, and strains. Costs

rise faster than prices. There are inequalities in the rise of costs and prices. Other abnormalities occur, such as shortages of particular kinds of raw materials, with excess industrial equipment in some lines and inadequate equipment in others. A crisis comes and corrects these abnormalities, restoring equilibrium—not a previous equilibrium, but a new equilibrium—roughly and approximately. Then revival comes.

Mitchell's analysis makes business profits and the prospect of business profits the dynamo in the ups and downs of business. When the outlook for profits is good, business expands. When profits are cut, business contracts. The analysis runs in highly realistic terms, taking account of labor costs, rentals, and raw material costs as well as interest charges, taking account of rigidities and fluidities, of rigid prices and flexible prices.

There is no more startling instance of deterioration in a great science than the recent trends, largely influenced by Keynes, to turn away from an analysis that takes account of *all* the changing factors in economic life, and to concentrate attention almost exclusively upon monetary and budgetary phenomena, in explaining the business cycle and in formulating public policy with respect to prosperity and employment.

The present writer's testimony, after a quarter of a century devoted very largely to the study of markets and the ups and downs of business, would be to the effect that the equilibrium notion is the most useful tool of thought to be found. When economic forces are working toward balance, we may trust the situation. When they are obviously working toward unbalance, we should grow increasingly concerned. From theoretical concepts of the Keynesian type we receive no help at all.

X

PHILIP CORTNEY, a life-long student of economics, is president of Coty, Inc., and of Coty International. He was graduated as an electrical engineer from the University of Nancy, France, and began his career in the steel business. He has been decorated as an officer of the French Legion of Honor and has been president of the United States Council of the International Chamber of Commerce. The following excerpt is taken from two articles which originally appeared in the *Commercial and Financial Chronicle* (New York) of February 8 and 15, 1945, and were later reprinted in his book, *The Economic Munich,* 1949.

THE PHILOSOPHY OF LORD KEYNES

PHILIP CORTNEY

It is essential to study the philosophy of Lord Keynes if we want to explain and understand his attitude toward gold. It is not the presupposed tyranny exercised by gold on men and economy which has led him to espouse his philosophy, but it is this last which determined his attitude regarding gold.

First of all, what does Lord Keynes think about human nature? The answer to this question seems of primary importance for it is impossible without it to have a workable political philosophy and also because economic phenomena are determined, to a large extent, by psychological factors. Men seem to him to have natural inclinations toward cruelty as well as a desire for personal power. Lord Keynes also admits that man has a passion for money. He even feels that it is better for humanity that man's desire for power be directed towards increasing his bank account. Lord Keynes does not believe that we can change human nature, but he is of the opinion that we can "direct" it. (I am indeed very much afraid that if we push too far our control of money and economy, we will be obliged to direct human nature . . . with the help of a knout.) For what purpose should we educate human nature? The ruling class, answers Lord Keynes, should be trained to be satisfied with smaller returns than in the past in order to allow a more equitable distribution of revenue.

To the question of whether what Lord Keynes calls an equitable distribution of revenue is not going to decrease savings, he answers with satisfaction in the affirmative, since for him there is not only too much saving, but this latter is practically a sin. Too much saving and not enough consumption and investments, these are the source of all our evils, according to the diagnosis of Lord Keynes. He maintains that the needs for capital are too moderate and that interest rates on savings should tend toward zero. He is in favor of "the euthanasia of the rentier" and he predicts their eventual disappearance . . . when they will have finished their job (?). On the other hand, only last September, the "Economist" published a series of articles asserting that the increase of productivity of English industry—without which increase England is facing serious dangers—depends on savings, and, furthermore, that the investment of these savings will be governed by the possibility of realizing profits in proportion to the risks involved. Lord Keynes is fighting against savings maintained in the form of money and bank deposits. He has even declared himself in favor of "melting money" as recommended by a German, Silvio Gesell. This consists of a penalty on money not used which should be proportionate to the time it has not been utilized. One may recall that in France a former Prime Minister endorsed, in 1935, "melting money" as a remedy for the depression from which she was then suffering. But, may I ask, with such theories on saving and the functions of money, what part can gold well play?

Assuming that the national needs of well-to-do countries are satisfied, could the excess savings not be invested in those countries which need to be developed and equipped industrially?

The development of backward countries was in 1933 not only the last and least of Lord Keynes' worries but he frankly declared himself as being opposed to the export of capital. In the article published under his signature in the American publication, "Yale Review" (1933) entitled "National Self-Sufficiency," he states: "above all, let finance be primarily national." Perhaps in none of his other writings is the philosophy of Lord Keynes as clearly expounded as in this article. He herein states that he detests "individualistic and decadent capitalism" and he adds that he is beginning to be contemptuous of it. But does not economic liberalism contribute to the maintenance of peace through commerce and international division of labor? On the contrary! says Lord Keynes; it stimulates the struggle for markets between nations; it fosters the progress of economic imperialism and it necessitates the defense of investments abroad. One is certainly not misinterpreting his thought in attributing to him the conviction that the war of 1914 was due to economic internationalism. What is more, he can only see advantage from a national point of view that capital be prevented from emigrating. In reading Lord Keynes, one cannot help discovering a sort of aversion towards competition, the cornerstone of economic liberalism. For him, the Stock Exchange is only a casino for gambling! Summing up, Lord Keynes in 1933, was advocating the adoption of a form of economic nationalism (national self-sufficiency) which might lend itself for "experiments" in accordance with his doctrines and in order to bring about the realization of an "ideal social republic." One may wonder what could well be the role of gold in such an "ideal social republic" and how should one be surprised at the pride Lord Keynes takes in having called gold "a barbarous relic"?

During the last few years, Lord Keynes has been defending exchange instability and disparity in national price levels in the name of the "full employment" dogma. He has published in the British magazine, "The Economic Journal" (September, 1943) a curious and rather obscure article in which he rejects stability of prices as a desirable objective of monetary policy. He justifies his position with the argument that politically it would not be expedient or possible to prevent the constant rise of wage rates, or rather what he calls "efficiency wages."

Furthermore, Lord Keynes thinks that the quantity of money available should not be an obstacle to the "natural" rise of wages. If I understand him correctly, he now declares himself against exchange stability in the name of the "full-employment" doctrine which has as a corollary a constant rise of nominal salaries, which rise would be difficult or impossible to control. It is clear, however, that exchange instability is defended presently by Lord Keynes for political rather than economic reasons. Lord Keynes also makes (innocently or facetiously?) the remark that a communist country is in a position to be very successful in preserving stability of internal prices and efficiency wages. Nazi Germany has demonstrated to the world by what means this double objective can be attained. They are simple and obvious: dictatorship, suppression of liberty and of labor unions, and last but not least, exchange control.

The political and economic-social philosophy of Keynes would suffice alone to explain his animosity towards gold and exchange stability which have been the excellent servants of liberalism and economic internationalism.

THE ANGLO-AMERICAN ECONOMIC RIVALRY

Another reason, however, for his position against the gold standard is the fact that after 1918 England lost her industrial and financial supremacy. It can be proven that the ideas, leanings and prejudices of many economists are often determined by the problems with which their era or their particular country is confronted. The struggle involving the gold standard is fundamentally only an aspect of the economic-financial rivalry between Englishmen and Americans. The extraordinary rise of American industrial power after 1918 and the switch of the financial center of gravity of the world from London to New York, explain, to a great extent, Lord Keynes' hostility, as well as that of other English economists, towards the gold standard. Among these latter, we must mention Paul Einzig, one of the influential editors of the newspaper "Financial News," and also author of the "Daily Express" article to which we have already referred. He has the merit of speaking in plain terms of the economic-financial rivalry between the Anglo-Saxon cousins. For several years he has been campaigning against the gold standard. After reading what he has to say on it at present, we cannot help but wonder if he has ever read the book, "The Future of Gold," written by Paul Einzig in 1935 in which he himself states that if the gold standard did not exist, it would have to be invented.

There is still another reason which should incite us to listen with a critical mind to the ideas and opinions of Lord Keynes. He is the author of several new monetary theories, of which the most important is the one which deals with the influence of low rates of interest on investments and economic activity. It often happens that philosophers who have a system of their own, or economists who believe they have discovered the philosopher's stone, suffer from a particular blindness which prevents them from being objective; they become prisoners and sometimes victims of their own theories. To the extent that Lord Keynes' position against the gold standard is influenced by consideration of monetary doctrines, it is due to his theory concerning interest rates.

XI

R. Gordon Wasson was born in Great Falls, Montana, in 1898. He was instructor of English at Columbia College in 1921 and 1922, a financial reporter for the *New York Herald-Tribune* from 1925 to 1928, and became vice-president of the banking firm of J. P. Morgan and Company in 1943. He is the author of *The Hall Carbine Affair: A Study in Contemporary Folklore,* 1941, a carefully documented study which refutes the allegation that the elder Morgan, founder of the banking house, sold to the government some condemned arms at a profit that would have been exorbitant for first-class weapons.

The following article appeared in the summer issue of the *Harvard Business Review* for 1945, pages 507-518. While it does not deal directly with Keynes, it does deal brilliantly with the "full employment policy" inspired by the Keynesian theories.

BEVERIDGE'S "FULL EMPLOYMENT IN A FREE SOCIETY"

R. GORDON WASSON

Sir William Beveridge's new book,[1] which could be accurately subtitled *A Brief for a Planned Economy,* captivates the reader by its kindliness and tone of sweet reasonableness. In the United States and also on the Continent controversy over

[1] *Full Employment in a Free Society* (New York, W. W. Norton & Company, Inc., 1945).

212

the system of free enterprise slips easily into violence, verbal if not physical. Not so Beveridge. He is that winning person, a radical free of rancor. With the gentlest bedside manner, he administers strong medicine. His argument deflects the lightning of passion, insulates itself from the thunder of controversy. The reader feels that this book is the integral expression of a distinguished personality, a natural fruit of the humane aspect of the English genius.

Like Keynes, Beveridge has been an influence in Washington. What he says in England is likely to reach us here, after a sea-change, through the mouths of our own "intellectuals." It behooves us all to know what he is saying.

FULL EMPLOYMENT

Beveridge proposes a program that he thinks will end the ravages of unemployment in Britain. When he speaks of "full employment," he means "having always more vacant jobs than unemployed men, not slightly fewer jobs." The market for labor is to be always—always, mind you—a seller's market. There are to be no more cyclical fluctuations, no more periods of chronic unemployment. We are to plan "for continuous steady expansion."

The author is eloquent in describing the blight of unemployment. He points out the moral difference between a buyer's and a seller's market for labor:

A person who has difficulty in buying the labor that he wants suffers inconvenience or reduction of profits. A person who cannot sell his labor is in effect told that he is of no use. The first difficulty causes annoyance or loss. The other is a personal catastrophe.

And again:

. . . the continuance of a system [of employment] which relies mainly on personal application, that is to say on the hawking of labour from door to door, is an anachronism which is socially indefensible.

The benevolence that suffuses these sentences tends to hide the fallacies in them. Of course employment offices should be available to help workers place themselves; but, as British experience in particular has shown, many workers find they can do better for themselves by hawking their labor than by relying on official employment agencies. Furthermore, the man "who cannot sell his labor" is not told that he is of no use. He may well find an outlet for his capacities in a different field. Beveridge himself shows how easily labor shifts from one occupation to another.

Let us recognize, however, the glow of high endeavor that often irradiates the author's style, as when he says that full employment

. . . is an adventure, because it has never been accomplished in the past. It is an adventure, because the State in this field is not wholly master of events so long as it desires to preserve the freedom of individuals, and so long as it must adjust its actions to the actions of other communities. It is an adventure which must be undertaken if free society is to survive. It is an adventure which can be undertaken with confidence of ultimate success. Success, however, will come not by following any rigid formula but by adapting action to circumstances which may change continually. The adventure of full employment in a free society is not like the directed flight of an aircraft on a beam. It is a voyage among shifting and dangerous currents. All that can be done is to see that the craft is well found, and that the pilot has all the necessary controls, and instruments to guide his use of them.

Essential Liberties

Beveridge thinks his program will safeguard what he calls "the essential liberties which are more precious than full employment itself." These liberties are: (1) freedom of worship, speech, writing, study, and teaching; (2) freedom of assembly and of association for political and other purposes, including the bringing about of a peaceful change of the governing authority; (3) freedom in choice of occupation; and (4) freedom in the management of a personal income.

Beveridge takes pains to declare that the essential liberties as he conceives them do "not include liberty of a private citizen to own means of production and to employ other citizens in operating them at a wage." And further, "private ownership of means of production . . . must be judged as a device. It is not an essential citizen liberty in Britain, because it is not and never has been enjoyed by more than a very small proportion of the British people."

That few achieve such ownership may be true. But what Beveridge is ready to sacrifice is far more than he admits. If private ownership of means of production ends, this will mean the end of the *hope* of ownership among a vast number—the hope that has inspired many men's endeavors and added much to life's value. And if private ownership of means of production ends, this also will mean for millions the end of the right to choose among employers. To all employees that right is above price, and a wholesome restraining influence on the arbitrary impulses of employers. The state as an employer can be as tyrannical as anyone else. Beveridge's willingness to sacrifice the right of many workers to choose among employers illustrates how cruel a kind man can unwittingly be.

TRADE CYCLES

Much of the book deals with statistics of unemployment in Britain. Beveridge unravels this intricate evidence with masterly assurance. He traces the fluctuations of unemployment back through the decades, its distribution by industries and by areas and by age groups, and the extent to which unemployment is concentrated among persons long out of work; and he skillfully interrelates these separate chains of facts. He points up the arid data with his interpretative comments, which sometimes run counter to common belief. For example, he establishes beyond challenge, I believe, that the mobility of British labor from industry to industry has been high: "Men move freely from occupation to occupation in response to demand. They move less freely but substantially from place to place." The high quality of these passages dealing with unemployment data is in curious contrast, as we shall see, with the faulty, yes, muddled structure of the book as a whole.

Beveridge believes that he has an important contribution to make to our knowledge of the trade cycle. He has discovered a statistical series that pushes back our record of trade cycles in Great Britain to 1785—far earlier than any previous study. And this series, he thinks, establishes "the identity of the trade cycle over all the whole period of one hundred and fifty years." Furthermore, by an ingenious breakdown of the component parts of the trade cycle, a colleague of his seems to have discovered that the source of depressions has always lain in agricultural areas and among the primary producers. His evidence leads Beveridge to observe: "It must be taken as highly probable, though not finally established, that the trade cycle has an agricultural root."

Now these two discoveries give rise to an extraordinary non sequitur in Beveridge's argument, for after setting them forth he straightway says that "the trade cycle . . . is the common scourge of all advanced industrial countries with an unplanned economy." He has just shown that the trade cycle as we know it today afflicted Britain back in the days when industry was in a foetal stage and before the "unplanned market economy" had triumphed. He has just indicated that the epicenter of the recurrent disturbance is "probably" in the farming and mining areas. How willful it is for him, then, to identify this scourge with modern industry! But by thus saddling industry with a peculiar responsibility for mass unemployment, he lays the groundwork for his plea that we modify profoundly our economic system.

GIANT EVILS

This brings us to a further non sequitur.

We must, Beveridge says, "destroy the giant social evils of Want, Disease, Squalor, and Ignorance," and "reduce also the evil of Inequality" in the distribution of material resources. And he proceeds to give the impression that these Giant Evils are also rooted, like the trade cycle, in modern industrialism; that they are, so to speak, the pervasive occupational infirmities of our era. Yet Beveridge himself says, "There had been a rising return to labour throughout the nineteenth century and this continued [into the twentieth]." The same thought recurs elsewhere. In short, Beveridge is himself authority for the statement that the material welfare of the human species has been rising steadily in our modern industrial era, under what he calls repeatedly and critically our "unplanned market economy." Let us now examine more closely those four Giant Evils—really three since squalor overlaps want and is redundant.

Want was worse before our "unplanned market economy" took wings into the industrial revolution. Where does one turn to find squalor at its worst? To lands like China, of course, where industry is still primitive.

As for disease, we need only recall the trend of life expectancy over the past 150 years, and the scourges like smallpox and diphtheria that have been conquered, to see that under our "unplanned market economy" we have achieved miracles in the field of disease, largely as the fruit of our scientific advances. And just as our industrial progress is still gaining momentum, so are our advances in medicine and public health. The "unplanned market economy" has yielded breath-taking dividends in health to us all.

Finally, there is "ignorance." Now the past century and a half has seen the virtual elimination of illiteracy in every "modern industrial community." Never was so much education available to so many as today, under our "unplanned market economy." Perhaps we have not made the most of our opportunities, and certainly the quality of our education leaves much to be desired. Our educators may have let us down. But the fault does not lie in our "unplanned market economy."

Beveridge mentions a fifth Evil, the unequal distribution of material goods. But if the floor of human welfare is rising constantly, what is the basis for complaint? Beveridge never meets the question whether big fortunes—which individually have no assurance of long duration—are not a price, and a cheap price, that we pay for lifting the floor of well-being for the whole population.

In short, the biggest foe of the Giant Evils is the self-same unplanned market economy that Beveridge would sweep away. It has done more to achieve Beveridge's ends than any other economy in the history of mankind.

PLANNING

Beveridge's prescription for Great Britain is a planned economy, and the key to full employment is spending, or "outlay" as he prefers to call it:

The first condition of full employment is that total outlay should always be high enough to set up a demand for products of industry which cannot be satisfied without using the whole manpower of the country: only so can the number of vacant jobs be always as high as or higher than the number of men looking for jobs.

And again:

It must be a function of the State in future to ensure adequate total outlay and by consequence to protect its citizens against mass unemployment, as definitely as it is now the function of the State to defend the citizens against attack from abroad and against robbery and violence at home. Acceptance of this new responsibility of the State . . . marks the line which we must cross in order to pass from the old Britain of mass unemployment and jealousy and fear to the new Britain of opportunity and service for all.

Then he points out the logical conclusion to be drawn from this premise, viz., that "the State cannot undertake the responsibility for full employment without full powers." What are these powers and where do they lead us?

Beveridge recognizes that through the attainment of his goal of "full employment" labor will be in a perpetual seller's market, and its bargaining power will be vastly increased. But the state is not to invade the bargaining rights of labor. The perils of spiraling wages are to be avoided by the "sense of citizenship and responsibility" of labor, which "justify the expectation that it will evolve, in its own manner, the machinery by which a better co-ordinated wage policy can be carried through." Even in Britain such optimism seems extreme; in the United States today it would be even less justified. To make the task easier for labor leadership, Beveridge would maintain *permanent* price controls.

But this is only the beginning of the story. Driven by the logic of his premise, Beveridge would have the state "plan the rate of national investment as a whole, both privately and publicly financed." There is to be a new kind of national budget, which takes as its datum "the man-power of the country," not money. It is, we are told, to be a "human budget." The total outlay of the nation, public and private, is to be sufficient to give work to all. A National Investment Board is to decide on all capital expenditures, according to social priorities. Private entrepreneurs must win the approval of the National Investment Board before undertaking anything; otherwise investment might be diverted into projects low on the official list of priorities. Of the total national investment, "probably not more than 25%" would be accounted for by private manufacturing industry.

The government is to "coordinate and steady the activities of business men." It is to control the location of industry and organize the mobility of labor—of course, all for the general welfare. With the passing of unemployment, Beveridge hoped that labor would relinquish restrictive practices.

There must be government "planned marketing and production of primary products, both agricultural and mineral," in order to make possible a stable wage policy and reduce cyclical fluctuations. The sector of industry directly controlled by the government is to expand, but remain only a sector. (Incidentally, the commercial banks are *not* to be nationalized.) All movements of capital in and out of the country are to be controlled, and this means, says Beveridge, "a general system of control over all exchange transactions, though this need not involve a postal censorship." But how could the control be effective without postal censorship?

In short, under Beveridge's planned economy, "the allocation of resources would be in accord with the natural desires of the citizens, as interpreted by the planners." Note the phrase: "as interpreted by the planners." Just as in Germany the objective of a planned economy "involved some distortion of ordinary human desires," so in Britain Beveridge wants to impose on consumers some curbing of their desires. He sees a danger that the spending power of the citizens might not be wisely directed. If left free, it might disregard the quality and location of available labor, or flow into forms of consumption "which were not most desirable," or leave unmet certain crying needs for social improvement. For these reasons consumers will be free to spend their money as they please only after a minimum for all citizens has been provided. One gets the impression from Beveridge that his proposals would drastically reduce the citizen's "disposable income," i.e., what he has left after taxes; and that thus the consumer's right to choose among goods would be only a sliver of what it is today. It is a pity that Beveridge never tells us how much "disposable income" his planners might relinquish to the population.

At no point in Beveridge's long book does he discuss the difficulty, not to say impossibility, of finding "planners" wise enough and good enough to make the decisions that shape the destinies of the British people. Under the "unplanned market economy" of the past two centuries, men who sometimes were regarded at first by their contemporaries as crackpots have created the industries that today enrich the lives of us all. Beveridge's planners would pass upon the merits of such proposals in the embryonic stage. Their veto power would be absolute. Of course the official planners would favor their own plans and innovations, mostly of a humanitarian bent no doubt. What sympathy would they have for the explosive dreams of industrial geniuses?

Nor does Beveridge deal with the danger to his "essential liberties" from encroachments by wicked planners, by arrogant planners, by ambitious and monstrous individuals who might by one means or another get control of the planning. Being himself humane, Beveridge overlooks the danger of tyranny.

ADVENTURE

Time and again Beveridge takes pains to explain that he does not ask for the complete abolition of private enterprise, at least at present. He is willing to give it another try, under a suspended sentence of death.

Not once in this whole book does he explore the secret of our dynamic economy; not once does he acknowledge the role played by private initiative and the profit motive in the achievements of western civilization in the last century. He dwells on the unemployment that has afflicted the industrial world, but never mentions the gifts bestowed on us by the economy of the "unplanned market." He would launch us all on "the adventure of full employment"—an anemic sort of adventure, indeed, for a people who have led in the adventure of building an empire and the industrial world.

Beveridge's conception of "adventure" is planning a society in which there will be no risk, no adventure. He invites us to undertake the adventure to end all adventures. His specific program of priorities may arouse fire in him and a few others, but how static and dull it will seem to venturers in the great historic line! There is to be social security, and socialized medicine, and scientific nutrition for all, and a large program of public outlay for more education, and fuel for all, and vigorous town planning, and country planning as well, and let us not forget housing and transport improvements.

But Beveridge's imagination remains curiously unmoved by the stupendous adventure of industrial progress, with its repercussions in pure science, in multiplying life's satisfactions, in raising our living standards, in the miracles of applied medicine, and in education. He does not argue this whole subject. He ignores it, like one who is denied the use of his senses over a wide area of experience. He does not know what makes the Western World go round.

For a man of Beveridge's background, concerned as he has been all his life with the problem of unemployment, the culminating ambition of his personal world is naturally the permanent elimination of unemployment. There lies his heaven. In his mind's eye he sees unemployment dissolving like mist against the background of an ever-expanding, prosperous economy, managed by all-wise, all-virtuous planners. It is a pleasant dream, in its unexciting way.

But others will be aware, as he is not, of the stirring even if disturbing appeal of another dream—a world of spiritual adventure in which economic expansion takes place according to no predictable program, as pioneering thinkers make their discoveries and practical men apply those discoveries to human problems. The work of these leaders cannot be plotted in advance, for by definition the realm for discovery is still undiscovered. The adventure of discovery is the great adventure. Its appeal is to the individual and to small teams of individuals. Most of them discover nothing for their pains, and get no reward. Yet the big rewards that go to the successful are the lure that attracts adventurous spirits into the contest.

At one point in Beveridge's book we come across a surprising phrase in which he says that "clearly no attempt should be made to stop technical progress"—surprising because that pallid reference seems to express all of the author's thinking on the subject. In a lengthy book advocating a new kind of economy, one looks to the author for a discussion of the bearing his program would have on industrial and scientific progress. Beveridge seems to assume that technical progress can be taken for granted, unless we deliberately arrest it. And this, he roundly says, we should not attempt!

Shortly after the Beveridge book appeared, Prime Minister Churchill gave voice to a different vision, one shot through with adventure in the high tradition of the men of his breed who risked much to win much:

> Controls under the pretext of war or its aftermath which are, in fact, designed to favor the accomplishment of wayside totalitarian systems, however innocently designed, whatever guise they assume, whatever liveries they wear, whatever slogans they mouth, are a fraud which should be mercilessly exposed to the British public.
>
> At the head of our mainmast we, like the United States, fly the flag of free enterprise. We are determined that the native genius and spirit of adventure, of risk-taking in peace as in war, shall bear our fortunes forward, finding profitable work and profitable trade for our people, and also we are determined that good and thrifty housekeeping, both national and private, shall sustain our economy.[2]

To thrive and thus make good its promise, private enterprise must have air to breathe and room to move in. Beveridge refrains from declaring himself a socialist, and declares repeatedly that his program by-passes the controversy between socialism and capitalism. But he consigns private enterprise to a reserved area of our economy where it will lack oxygen and water and heat and light and room, all of them. He would confine private enterprise to a cage, cut its hamstrings, and then admonish the creature to give a good performance, under threat of death. "The necessity of socialism . . . has not yet been demonstrated," he says. Note the phrase, "not yet." And then:

> If . . . it should be shown by experience or by argument that abolition of private property in the means of production was necessary for full employment, this abolition would have to be undertaken.

Let the reader remember that "full employment," with Beveridge, means a perpetual excess of jobs over workers in a perpetually expanding economy. One slump, and, under Beveridge, the day of "private property in the means of production" is over. And note the author's willingness to rely, in shaping the weightiest public policies, on what is shown by experience *or* by argument—argument presumably unsupported by experience!

[2] Address before the annual conference of the Conservative party, March 15, 1945; text from *The Times* (London), March 16, 1945.

If in the reduced sector of the economy in which private business would survive there should be fluctuations in activity that cause unemployment, then instability "can be reduced by extension of the public sector of business investment." Beveridge never asks the question whether his whole program will not, of itself, discourage or "stop technical progress." For him, private ownership of the means of production is merely a device to be judged by its results. Apparently only once in the whole book are profits mentioned as an incentive, and then in a lukewarm, negative way by his colleague, Professor Kaldor, the author of Appendix C.

What does Beveridge think of competition in the business world? It is not to be encouraged:

> As a general principle it may be laid down that business competition must be free, not forced. If in any industry a strong tendency develops towards collaboration between independent units or towards their amalgamation, the part of the State should be, not to try vainly to stop that tendency, but to bring it under control.

Beveridge claims to have devised a program assuring full employment without the sacrifice of private initiative in production. It is hard to avoid the conclusion that his program would doom private initiative to a lingering and inglorious end, at a cost to Britain in industrial leadership that Beveridge never stops to weigh.

SPENDING

Keynes's spending thesis is the basis for Beveridge's solution to the problem of unemployment. It is therefore the more surprising that he argues the merits of the Keynes thesis so briefly, since, if Keynes is mistaken, Beveridge collapses. The whole structure of the book depends on Keynes, and Keynes is taken for granted. Beveridge cites the appearance of Keynes's *General Theory* in 1936 as marking the start of a "new era" in economic thought, summarizes it in a few paragraphs, and then, as to its chief points, asserts that "the analysis is probably now accepted by all persons qualified to judge." This is a cavalier way of meeting disagreement on fundamentals. Beveridge goes to great pains elsewhere in the book, as we have seen, to expand the frontiers of our knowledge concerning the trade cycle, which constitutes only a part of the unemployment problem. But when he comes to the capstone of his argument, he shoves it into place with unseemly haste. Those who disagree with Keynes are ruled out of court in advance as probably "not qualified to judge." The skeptical reader may well feel that Keynes's theory is simply used as an indispensable rationalization for Beveridge's whole program, and not be satisfied with the crude way it is grafted into Beveridge's argument.

Beveridge never comes to close quarters with the relationship between spending and employment. He takes for granted that the two are intimately associated, subject to the one qualification that spending may mean higher prices rather than more employment. To avoid that danger he advocates, as we have seen, permanent price controls and other restrictions. His excellent analysis of the labor market suggests that many kinds of unemployment will not respond readily to spending; and the two parts of the book are never tied together.

The Keynes theory says in Beveridge's words:

> Employment depends on spending, which is of two kinds—for consumption and for investment; what people spend on consumption gives employment. What they save, i.e., do not spend on consumption, gives employment only if it is invested, which means not the buying of bonds or shares but expenditure in adding to capital equipment. . . .

Beveridge himself seems to admit the present inadequacy of certain data needed to establish the Keynes hypothesis. We must still depend in part on "general impressions"!

Nowhere in the book does Beveridge discuss Keynes's concept of the "multiplier," or the acceleration principle. He does not face the experience of our federal deficits in the 1930's, which suggested that the "multiplier" can be less than 1, when a government expenditure discourages a greater expenditure by private spenders.

The Minister of National Finance in Beveridge's vision of the future has to make each year one cardinal decision: after estimating how much, with full employment assumed and under the taxation that he proposes, private citizens may be expected to lay out on consumption and private investment, he must propose for that year public outlay sufficient, with this estimated private outlay, to employ the whole manpower of the country. We must abandon once and for all, he says, the old-fashioned goal of keeping down government expenses to a minimum and of balancing the budget.

Beveridge deals with none of the ticklish difficulties that his Minister of National Finance would face in practice. Figures for consumption and investment in the immediate past are only estimates with a wide margin of uncertainty; those for the short-term future would be guesses. Day-to-day developments affect individual action in these matters, and events which cannot be calculated in advance, such as the stock market collapse of 1929 and 1937, would upset the forecasts completely from one day to another. Furthermore, Beveridge fails to deal with the influence, favorable or unfavorable, on private consumption and investment of the government's intended outlays.

Under the new system there are to be three rules of national finance: (1) total outlay at all times must be sufficient for full employment; (2) outlay should be directed by regard to social priorities ordained for the welfare of the people by the planners; and (3) it is better to provide the means for outlay by taxing than by borrowing; but Beveridge adds that this third rule "is of an altogether minor order of importance." Beveridge goes on to say:

> The State in matters of finance is in a different position from any private citizen or association of private citizens; it is able to control money in place of being controlled by it. Many of the mistakes of the past have arisen through failure to make this fundamental distinction.

A continuous expansion of the national debt on a large scale over the coming decades can be viewed with equanimity, says Beveridge, and he quotes with approval certain calculations of Professor Kaldor, leading to this conclusion:

> . . . taking into account prospective changes in population, in productivity, and in working hours, as well as foreseeable changes of Government expenditure on pensions, education, etc., and assuming an average rate of interest of 2 per cent, the National Debt could be expanded at the rate of not less than £775 millions a year from 1948 (taken as the beginning of the reconstruction period) to 1970, without involving on that account any increase

of tax rates to meet the additional charge for interest. This is a rate of borrowing far in excess of anything that would be needed to sustain full employment in peace time. A policy of continuous borrowing, on a more reasonable scale adequate for all possible requirements, is consistent with a steady reduction of the burden of the debt on the taxpayer.

The principal reason for raising funds by taxation rather than borrowing, says Beveridge, is to avoid increasing the number and wealth of rentiers. We ought to levy taxes as high as possible without stifling "desirable" enterprise and also to reduce the rate of interest "continually" until the "euthanasia of the rentier" is accomplished. (This last phrase is Keynes's, quoted by Beveridge.) Another argument for taxation, it seems, is that borrowing too freely would encourage "general political bribery." Taxation in the future is to be looked upon as a means of reducing private expenditure on consumption, and to be considered generally for its bearing on "priorities," that is to say, on social and economic policy.

Why should the government issue interest-bearing debt rather than print paper money to meet its outlays? In a passage that reveals with notable candor his ways of thinking, Beveridge discusses this issue. It is worth quoting in full:

It might well be asked why the Government should not decide right away that the best rate of interest is a zero rate and proceed to finance all its deficits by the "creation" of new cash or bank money through "Ways and Means Advances." This question is a pertinent one. It does not raise, as many of the so-called monetary reformers seem to think it raises, an issue of principle. The difference between printing paper which is a claim to cash in ten years and carries an appreciable rate of interest and printing paper which is a claim to cash on demand and carries an insignificant rate of interest is merely a difference of degree, not one of substance. Equally, there is no difference of substance between "creating" cash and printing, say, short-term bills carrying 1 per cent interest. If it is demanded, therefore, that the Government should cease to borrow at interest and simply cover its deficits by creating cash, this, in effect, amounts to demanding that governmental monetary policy should reduce the basic rate of interest, that is, the rate on paper, which carries no private risk, not gradually, but suddenly and to zero. It would have to be shown that a sudden reduction is preferable to a gradual one. Can this be shown?

There are at least two objections against it. First, a sudden reduction in the rate of interest produces a sudden appreciation in the capital value of all outstanding long-term money claims and all durable capital assets, such as land, houses, industrial property and so forth. An appreciation of these values—particularly a sudden one—which means windfall profits to their owners, may induce them to increase their luxury expenditure on an appreciable scale. While this, of course, would create additional employment, it would do so for purposes of small social value and might create social tensions that are wholly undesirable. Second, there are innumerable financial and other institutions, whose activities depend upon their being able to convert cash into interest-bearing paper that carries no appreciable private risk. If there is no further supply of gilt-edged Government paper, an important foundation of their activity crumbles away, and special arrangements are necessary to maintain them in being. This applies not only to insurance companies and banks, but also to pension funds, charitable organizations, research endowments, and so forth. These two objections lose their force when applied to a gradual and long-term policy of reducing the rate of interest; but they would appear to have considerable weight against a policy of sudden changes.

A policy of gradual reduction gives time for adjustment. The speed with which it proceeds can be adjusted to circumstances. If the long-term rate of interest is reduced by one-tenth of 1 per cent every two years, a total reduction from the present level of 3 per cent to a new level of 2 per cent is effected in twenty years. This rate of reduction may be considered too slow; it can hardly be considered too fast. If through conversions of the existing national debt, it could be spread over the total of that debt, it would allow the annual amount of interest payable on the national debt to remain stationary in spite of an annual budget deficit of £400 millions. This calculation alone should dispose of the argument of those who claim that annual budget deficits would impose an unmanageable "transfer burden" upon society.

The method that might be applied for the gradual reduction in the rate of interest on long-term bonds is the following: The length of the bonds offered "on tap" is increased every month at a stable rate of interest. After a while, the length of the bond is reduced, and the rate of interest offered on the shorter bond is also reduced. This can be repeated over and over again, giving a perfectly smooth transition. As long as the method of issuing bills and bonds "on tap" is maintained, the rate of interest is controllable without any difficulty whatever.

One cannot lay at Beveridge's door any cheap-jack "semantic" evasions. This high-minded man is here proposing, without a trace of self-consciousness, a program and technique by which the state would gradually cheat its creditors. As with the sharpster's thimble trick, one gasps with admiration at the smoothness of it all. If the managers of a private enterprise engaged in such plottings, imagine the outcry from "liberals"! In private business, schemings against creditors of this kind might bring a man into court, and one recalls with uneasiness that sentence of Beveridge's, already quoted, in which he says that "the State in matters of finance is in a different position from any private citizen." It is disturbing to see a liberal expounding the philosophy of a double moral standard for the state.

UNITED STATES

Beveridge describes his book as "first and foremost a Report for Britain," and says expressly that the details for a full employment policy in the United States might be different. Then he adds:

But the principle of the proposals is applicable to the United States as to Britain, that it must become the responsibility of the supreme organ of the community, the National Government, to ensure at all times outlay adequate for full employment. This is consistent with leaving the actual conduct of production and the giving of employment mainly or wholly to private enterprise, that is to say in the hands of undertakings working for profit, and tested by their success in yielding profit.

And again:

Full employment . . . can be attained while leaving the actual conduct of industry in private hands, if that course commends itself. Full employment, finally, is attainable by several different routes. The route suggested for Britain in this Report is not likely to be that which would best suit the United States, with her sparser population, her higher standard of capital equipment, and her different structure of Government.

Moreover, while disclaiming any specific intention to recommend a program for the United States, Beveridge is nevertheless outspoken in expressing his misgivings about our future. We have the "strongest and most productive national economy in the world," but also "the least stable." Listen to this:

So far as the United States is concerned, there is no reason for confidence or even for hope that the economic system which produced this depression, if left to itself, will fail to reproduce similar depressions in the future.

That the ideas in the Beveridge book already have some advocates in the United States is evident. President Roosevelt's last Budget Message, submitted on January 9, 1945, included figures estimating "the Nation's Budget" along the lines of the new comprehensive kind of national budget that Beveridge describes. But the fullest expression of Beveridge's philosophy is incorporated in Senate Bill 380, introduced by Senator Murray, and known as the Murray Full Employment Bill. Not only does it provide for the regular preparation of a "National Budget" of the kind envisaged by Beveridge; following his views, it would clothe our government with responsibility for full employment.

The Murray Bill, however, parts company with Beveridge in the emphasis it places on private initiative. It starts by declaring:

It is the policy of the United States to foster free competitive enterprise and the investment of private capital in trade and commerce and in the development of the natural resources of the United States.

It goes on to say that

. . . it is the responsibility of the Federal Government to pursue such consistent and openly arrived at economic policies and programs as will stimulate and encourage the highest feasible levels of employment opportunities through private and other non-Federal investment and expenditures.

Furthermore, any deficiency in private expenditures that the government makes up in order to assure employment is to be designed "to stimulate increased employment opportunities by private enterprise."

The Murray Bill in reality consists, first, of a declaration of policy and, secondly, of a mechanism for generating the new kind of budget.

That policy means the assumption by the Federal Government of responsibility for maintaining full employment. But already the government, if it so chooses, can take responsibility for employment without being formally committed by legislative declaration to do so. Faced with unemployment it can recommend the steps that in its wisdom are best aimed at meeting the problem. The formal declaration by Congress of responsibility for eliminating unemployment might carry with it a compulsion to spend, at the first appearance of abnormal unemployment, that in practice would forestall the other more wholesome alternative solutions. And hasty and ill-considered spending could easily make the patient worse, aggravating the illness while providing purely symptomatic relief. In the light of our conspicuous political weaknesses, such a declaration of policy might make our government "trigger-happy" when it comes to spending. If men with no understanding of, or sympathy with, free enterprise were seeking to graft the Beveridge program on our economy, what strategy could be simpler than to permeate their bill with professions of allegiance to private initiative, at the same time setting up the mechanism that would insure its failure?

The mechanism, the elaborate statistical apparatus, could be created also without legislation—and its practicality tested, before being put to use, by trial and error against actualities. The inability of the United States Treasury to predict its own revenues and expenditures for a year in advance has been notorious. How calculations infinitely more abstruse, involving far greater, and more important, unknown quantities, can be made with sufficient accuracy to be useful is hard to see.

The community must do all it can to avoid unemployment and to alleviate its hardships. Let us not forget that there are limits to human wisdom for which statutory declarations are not a substitute. As long as the world is convulsed by recurring wars and as long as the fiscal authorities commit blunders (however unintentional these may be), the economic repercussions will surely include employment dislocations. Furthermore, let us always keep in mind that the unemployment problem has been a major preoccupation of the modern industrial world only in recent times. For upwards of a century mankind has been reaping fabulous rewards from industrial progress wherever the competitive, profit economy has been functioning. If we lift our eyes from our immediate concern with unemployment and view our situation in the perspective of a longer past, how foolish becomes the proposal that we scrap the competitive, profit economy because, forsooth, we do not yet find ourselves in Elysian meadows blooming with asphodel.

XII

GARET GARRETT was born in Illinois and brought up in Iowa. At the age of 25 he became a staff writer for the *New York Sun,* and then successively for *The New York Times, The Wall Street Journal,* and *New York Evening Post.* In 1912 he became the first editor of *The New York Times Annalist,* a weekly magazine of finance and economics. He later became executive editor of the *New York Tribune.* At 38 he retired from the newspaper business and between 1920 and 1932 wrote eight books and numerous articles. In 1940 he became chief editorial writer for *The Saturday Evening Post,* and from 1944 to 1950 he was editor of the quarterly *American Affairs.* The following article by him appeared in the July, 1946, issue of *American Affairs,* pages 203-204, published by the National Industrial Conference Board. Among Garrett's books were *Where the Money Grows,* 1911; *The American Omen,* 1929; *The Wild Wheel,* 1952; *The People's Pottage,* 1953; and *The American Story,* 1955.

JOHN MAYNARD KEYNES

GARET GARRETT

The work cumbersomely entitled, "The General Theory of Employment, Interest and Money," now commonly abbreviated as "The General Theory," was published in 1936. It was therefore only ten years old when the author, John Maynard Keynes, died last April. Probably no other book has ever produced in so little time a comparable effect. It has tinctured, modified and conditioned economic thinking in the whole world. Upon it has been founded a new economic church, completely furnished with all the properties proper to a church, such as a revelation of its own, a rigid doctrine, a symbolic language, a propaganda, a priestcraft and a demonology. The revelation, although brilliantly written, was nevertheless obscure and hard to read, but where one might have expected this fact to hinder the spread of the doctrine, it had a contrary result and served the ends of publicity by giving rise to schools of exegesis and to controversies that were interminable because nothing could be settled. There was no existing state of society in which the theory could be either proved or disproved by demonstration— nor is there one yet.

The moment of the book was most fortunate. For the planned society they were talking about the Socialists were desperately in need of a scientific formula. Government at the same time was in need of a rationalization for deficit spending. The idea of welfare government that had been rising both here and in Great Britain—here under the sign of the New Deal— was in trouble. It had no answer for those who kept asking, "Where will the money come from?" It was true that government had got control of money as a social instrument and that the restraining tyranny of gold had been overthrown, but the fetish of solvency survived and threatened to frustrate great social intentions.

Just at this historic crisis of experimental politics, with the Socialists lost in a wilderness lying somewhere between Utopia and totalitarianism, and with governments adrift on a sea of managed currency, afraid to go on and unable to turn back, the appearance of the Keynes theory was like an answer to prayer. Its feat was twofold. To the Socialist planners it offered a set of algebraic tools, which, if used according to the manual of instructions, were guaranteed to produce full employment, economic equilibrium, and a redistribution of wealth with justice, all three at once and with a kind of slide-rule precision—provided only that society really wanted to be saved. And the same theory by virtue of its logical implications delivered welfare government from the threat of insolvency. That word—insolvency—was to have no longer any meaning for a sovereign government. The balanced budget was a capitalist bogey. Deficit spending was not what it seemed. It was in fact *investment;* and the use of it was to fill an investment void—a void created by the chronic and incorrigible propensity of people to save too much. "There has been," he said, "a chronic tendency throughout history for the propensity to save to be stronger than the inducement to invest. The weakness of the inducement to invest has been at all times the key to the economic problem." By investment he was supposed to mean the use of capital in the spirit of adventure.

This idea was the very base of the theory. From oversaving and underinvestment came unemployment. And when from this cause unemployment appeared, as it was bound to do, first periodically and then as a permanent evil, the only cure was for government to spend the money. Among the algebraic tools was the famous *multiplier* by use of which the experts would be able to determine precisely how much the government would have to spend to create full employment.

Briefly therefore the theory was that when people were not investing enough in their own future to keep themselves all at work the government must do it for them. Where and how would the government get the money? Well, partly by taxing the rich, who notoriously saved too much; partly by borrowing from the rich, and, if necessary as a last resort, by printing it— and everything was bound to come out all right because from full employment society at large would grow always richer and richer. Ultimately the economic satisfactions of life would become dirt cheap, the interest rate would fall to zero, and the sequel would be the painless extinction of the rentier class, meaning those who live by interest and, produce nothing.

If I am right [he said] in supposing it to be comparatively easy to make capital goods so abundant that the marginal efficiency of capital is zero, this may be the most sensible way of gradually getting rid of many of the objectionable features of capitalism. For a little reflection will show what enormous social changes would result from a gradual disappearance of a rate of return on accumulated wealth. A man would still be free to accumulate his earned income with a view to spending it at a later date. But his accumulation would not grow. He would simply be in the position of Pope's father, who, when he retired from business, carried a chest of guineas with him to his villa at Twickenham and met his household expenses from it as required.

And what would the government spend the money for? Preferably of course for the creation of productive works, that is, means to further production of the things that satisfy human wants; but such was the importance of keeping everybody fully employed that it were better to invest the money in monuments and pyramids than not to spend it at all.

Ancient Egypt [he said] was doubly fortunate, and doubtless owed to this its fabled wealth, in that it possessed *two* activities, namely, pyramid building as well as the search for the precious metals, the fruits of which, since they could not serve the needs of man by being consumed, did not stale with abundance. The Middle Ages built cathedrals and sang dirges. Two pyramids, two masses for the dead, are twice as good as one; but not so two railways from London to York. Thus we are so sensible, have schooled ourselves to so close a semblance of prudent financiers, taking careful thought before we add to the *financial* burdens of posterity by building them houses to live in, that we have no such easy escape from the sufferings of unemployment. We have to accept them as an inevitable result of applying to the conduct of the State the maxims which are best calculated to enrich an individual by enabling him to pile up claims to enjoyment which he does not intend to exercise at any definite time.

This passage is seldom referred to by the Keynesians, perhaps because they have never been sure that he meant it to be taken seriously. It might very well be Keynes in one of his impish moods.

It is significant to recall that the first definite and conscious application of the theory was made by the New Deal; and when in the third year Mr. Roosevelt began to say that the government's deficit spending must be regarded as an *investment* in the country's future, he was taking the word directly from the Keynes theory. The promised results did not follow; unemployment was not cured. This disappointment, say the believers, was owing to no fault of the theory but simply and only to the fact that the deficit spending did not go far enough. The deficits should have been courageously greater.

It is perhaps even more significant that in his own country he was regarded as a dangerous luminary and that the British

Government was unable to avail itself of his genius until the time came when it found itself in a very difficult money position. It had already divorced the gold standard, pretending to make a moral of it; and then, as the British mentality changed from that of a creditor to that of a debtor country, what the Treasury needed was someone who could clothe the bareness of financial heresy with a plausible nontransparent drapery and at the same time give to the managed pound sterling a glitter to replace the lost luster of the gold pound. And so it happened that Mr. Keynes was taken into the British Treasury as its principal advisor, seated on the board of the Bank of England and elevated to the peerage as Baron Keynes of Tilton.

All planners take Keynes for their prophet. But in the one great test of his prophetic powers he failed historically. He had represented the British Treasury at the making of the Versailles Treaty. Soon after, he resigned his post in order to attack the treaty and wrote a book entitled "The Economic Consequences of the Peace," the political effect of which, regarding it now in retrospect, was disastrous. His argument was that Germany could never pay the reparations that were demanded of her, and that even if she could afford to pay them her creditors could not manage to receive them. In view of what Germany was able to do in preparation for World War II, it was nonsense to say that she couldn't pay reparations on account of World War I, and if she had not been let off, World War II might not have been, or at least not yet.

The literature founded on Keynes is dogmatic. Keynes himself was not. At the end of his book he suddenly wondered if it would work. Were his ideas "a visionary hope?" Were they properly rooted "in the motives which govern the evolution of political society?" Were "the interests which they will thwart stronger and more obvious than those which they will serve?" He made no attempt to answer his own questions. It would take another book, he said, to indicate the answers even in outline.

XIII

Jacques Rueff was born in Paris in 1896, and studied at the École Polytechnique. In 1927 he joined the League of Nations Secretariat as a member of the economic and financial section. In the following years he served as financial attaché to the French Embassy in London, as professor of economics at the École libre des Sciences politiques, as assistant director in the Ministry of Finance, and finally, in 1936, as head of the French Treasury. From 1939 to 1940 he was vice-governor of the Bank of France. He has since occupied many official positions for the French government and, under President de Gaulle, was the head of a commission appointed by Finance Minister Pinay which drew up the famous Rueff Plan for fiscal and economic reform. He is at present a judge at the Court of Justice of the European Coal and Steel Community. His works include: *Des Sciences physiques aux Sciences morales*, 1922; *Théorie des Phénomènes monétaires*, 1927; *L'Assurance-chômage*, 1931; *L'Ordre social* (in two volumes), 1945; and *Epître aux dirigistes*, 1949.

The following article appeared in *The Quarterly Journal of Economics* for May, 1947, pages 343-367, published by Harvard University Press.

THE FALLACIES OF LORD KEYNES' GENERAL THEORY

JACQUES RUEFF

Lord Keynes' theory, as expounded in his *General Theory of Employment, Interest, and Money,* dominates the economic thought of our time. Its author does not hesitate to declare that it demonstrates the futility of the classical theory and is destined to replace it:

> I shall argue that the postulates of the classical theory are appli-cable to a special case only and not to the general case, the situa-tion which it assumes being a limiting point of the possible positions of equilibrium. Moreover, the characteristics of the spe-cial case assumed by the classical theory happen not to be those of the economic society in which we actually live, with the result that its teaching is misleading and disastrous if we attempt to apply it to the facts of experience.

But the new theory has not merely a philosophical signifi-cance. It leads to rules of action, notably in the struggle against the chief malady of modern society—chronic unemployment. Indeed, it is this aspect of it—the doctrine of "full employment" —that has been most influential. Explaining the evil and pro-viding the means of curing it, it has brought great comfort to the world.

As a remedy for unemployment, it quickly expanded beyond economic science to become an instrument of government. It has led to the publication of white papers in England and Canada and to a proposed law in the United States, the Murray Full-Employment Bill, which undertake to bind governments to its prescriptions. The new French constitution obliges the government to present each year "a national economic plan de-signed to provide full employment of labor and the rational utilization of material resources." The Economic Committee of the United Nations is called "Committee on Economic Ques-tions and Employment." Finally, the International Conference which is to deal with the problem of international trade and whose first session was held in London in October-November, 1946, is the Conference on Commerce and Employment.

The Keynesian philosophy is unquestionably the basis of a world policy today; and if the spectre of "under-employment" appears again in the world tomorrow, as is probable, it will be the universal recourse of peoples and governments. If it is true, it will be the salvation of the world; if it is false, it may lead to catastrophe by turning the world to ineffective remedies which may make the evil much worse.

For all those concerned with the future of human society there are, therefore, no questions more important at the present time than those raised by Lord Keynes' theory, and no duty more pressing than that of passing judgment on the value of the explanations which it offers and the efficacy of the remedies which it suggests. This is the task which I am undertaking here.

In formulating the criticisms which seem to me to apply to the Keynesian theory, it is a source of great regret that I must do so after the author's death. Fortunately, however, his supporters are so numerous, so active, and so powerful, that my scruples on this point are somewhat relieved. Moreover, I have already had the honor of a polemic with Lord Keynes. Far from avoiding discussion, he opened the columns of the Economic Journal to me for an article entitled, "The Ideas of Mr. Keynes on the Transfer Problem." [1]

1. THE KEYNESIAN THEORY

To avoid any possibility of misrepresenting the General Theory, I quote the résumé of its doctrine given in the work itself:

The outline of our theory can be expressed as follows. When employment increases, aggregate real income is increased. The psychology of the community is such that when aggregate real income is increased aggregate consumption is increased, but not by so much as income. Hence employers would make a loss if the whole of the increased employment were to be devoted to satisfying the increased demand for immediate consumption. Thus, to justify any given amount of employment there must be an amount of current investment sufficient to absorb the excess of total output over what the

[1] Economic Journal, September, 1929, Revue d'Economie Politique, July-August, 1929.

community chooses to consume when employment is at the given level. For unless there is this amount of investment, the receipts of the entrepreneurs will be less than is required to induce them to offer the given amount of employment. It follows, therefore, that, given what we shall call the community's propensity to consume, the equilibrium level of employment, i.e., the level at which there is no inducement to employers as a whole either to expand or to contract employment, will depend on the amount of current investment.

Thus, given the propensity to consume and the rate of new investment, there will be only one level of employment consistent with equilibrium. But there is no reason in general for expecting it to be *equal* to full employment . . . *the economic system may find itself in stable equilibrium with N at a level below full employment.* (Pages 27-30. Italics mine.)

Such is the fundamental basis of the whole Keynesian system, the explanation of "the remarkable inability of the classical theory to serve for scientific prediction," and the demonstration of the baselessness of the "famous optimism of the traditional theory . . . founded on failure to recognize the obstacle to prosperity which may be raised by lack of effective demand."

It is a question, then, of a revolution in economic theory and a profound modification of the rules of action suggested by it. The classical theory holds that no permanent equilibrium can exist as long as there is unemployment. The Keynesian theory, on the contrary, claims that a society can continue indefinitely with large numbers of unemployed, and on this basis offers itself as an explanation of this new phenomenon in the world— chronic unemployment.

The whole Keynesian analysis is based entirely on a psychological hypothesis, the producers' insufficient propensity to consume. On this hypothesis the increase of income which might be produced by an increase of employment would not increase the demand for consumers' goods in the same proportion.

With income not giving rise to demand for consumers' goods, and in the absence of government initiatives stimulating investment expenditures of the same amount, the increment of production resulting from the increase in employment could not find a market. Lacking a market, the corresponding production would cease, and with it would disappear the increment of income which it might have engendered. Thus would be established, by the simultaneous limitation of production and of the income making possible its acquisition, the state of under-employment equilibrium whose explanation is given as the great discovery and the essential significance of the Keynesian theory.

There is one element in this explanation which will surprise all those familiar with the analyses of the classical economics: the idea that an economic society in which an unabsorbed offer of labor exists at all times can be, without expressly assuming any fixing of prices, a state of equilibrium.

But if this is the case, it is because it is impossible in the Keynesian hypothesis that this offer of labor should be accepted, because it does not give rise in any direction whatever to any demand capable of absorbing it. Unemployment, then, is the only solution offered to the workers from which it emanates. For anyone wishing to judge the General Theory, therefore, the question is, is it possible that an offer actually appearing in the market should not give rise to any demand of the same volume? If so, Keynes' theory can explain equilibrium with under-employment, therefore chronic unemployment, and provide the means to deal with it. If not, the explanation which it offers needs to be reconsidered.

For Lord Keynes, the steps in the reasoning appear to be as follows. As a result of their insufficient propensity to consume, the workers able to take advantage of an increase in employment are not disposed to increase their expenditures on consumption in proportion to the additional income which they could obtain. Moreover, since they have no propensity to invest, they will therefore demand nothing for all the increment of resources which they do not devote to additional expenditures. I maintain that this analysis involves a serious error.

If there is really under-employment, it is not that certain workers *can* do more work, but that under the conditions offered by the market they *wish* to do more work. If they actually offer an increment of labor on the market, and if they do not intend to divert to consumption expenditure or investment the whole of the increment of income which an increment of labor makes possible, it is because they intend to increase their cash holdings by an amount equal to the increment of income which they do not spend. In proportion as they offer labor without demanding consumers' goods or investment goods, they are, and must be, demanders of money. This is a fundamental conclusion whose necessity must be carefully understood; for we shall see that if it is admitted, it upsets the whole Keynesian construction.

If there is under-employment, it means that laborers desire to do more work. If they offer labor on the market, it is because they desire to obtain an increment of remuneration; and if they do not wish to devote their increment of resources to an increase of their expenditures on consumption or investment, it is because they intend to increase the amount of money which they keep on hand. If this were not so, their offer of labor would be purely platonic. There might be a possibility of more work, but there would be no desire for it, and there would not be under-employment.

This being so, I maintain that the demand for additional cash holdings is equivalent in its economic effects to demand for consumption goods or investment goods and, consequently, that it is able to provide a market for the labor forces offered, on the same conditions as the demand for such goods. To show this, I shall be obliged to study in detail the effect of the demand for money. This will be the purpose of the following section. It may perhaps seem out of proportion with the minor practical importance of the case with which it deals. There is no doubt that the increase of individual cash holdings could never amount to more than a limited sum, and that as soon as individuals have reached the limit of the holdings which they wish to have, they will divert any increment of resources to increasing their demand for consumers' goods or investment goods. But since the hypothesis of the non-employment of this increment of resources in response to a corresponding demand is the very center of the Keynesian argument, it is indispensable, in order to judge the latter, to study the former with care.

2. The Effects of the Demand for Cash Balances

I maintain that Lord Keynes is mistaken in claiming that incomes which do not give rise to a demand for consumption goods or investment goods, that is, which give rise to a demand for additional cash balances, will be permanently lost to the mass of incomes required for the absorption of the production associated with them and consequently will create a permanent under-employment equilibrium. To show this simply, I shall first assume a regime where money is entirely metallic. Following that, I shall consider the general case.

If a worker enjoying an increase of employment increases his cash holdings, all other conditions, including the amount of cash holdings desired by the other members of the society, remaining unchanged, the increase in cash holdings realized by the owners of the incomes increased but not spent will necessarily have as a consequence a decrease in the cash holdings of other members of the society below the level of the holdings which they desire to maintain. To restore their cash holdings to the level desired, the latter will have no recourse but to offer without demanding. This will tend to bring about a fall in the whole system of prices.[2]

One price, however, remains stable amidst all these falling prices: the price of gold, automatically maintained at the legal parity by the purchases of the coinage authority. Hence the fall in the system of prices tends to bring about the transfer of productive resources from the products whose prices have fallen to the product whose price has not changed, a diminution in the production of the former and an increase in the production of gold. But the Bank of Issue buys all of the yellow metal offered and not demanded, and consequently supplies, by monetizing the increased production of metal, the additional cash holdings desired.

Since the fall of prices and the consequent transfer of productive resources continue as long as the cause which produced them persists—that is, the insufficiency of actual cash holdings relatively to those desired—this double movement cannot but result in bringing the former to the level of the latter by increasing the quantity of monetized metal and at the same time establishing between the price of gold, stabilized at the legal parity, and the other prices in the market the relations which formerly obtained.

Thus, the demand for additional cash holdings will have had the effect of diverting the labor forces offered in an increase in

---

[2] I have analyzed in detail, in Chapter 4 of my L'Ordre Social, the mechanism by which this fall is brought about.

employment from the production of consumers' goods or investment goods which would not have been wanted to the production of metal destined for monetization, and consequently
providing the increases in cash holdings desired.

It is therefore impossible to accept Lord Keynes' conclusion
that, in the case assumed, the insufficiency of demand for consumers' goods or investment goods constitutes an obstacle to
the increase of employment. If there is really an offer of an increment of employment on the market, and if only increases in
cash holdings are desired by the persons for whom the increase
of employment will provide an increase of income, the labor
forces offered will find themselves spontaneously but inevitably
directed by the force of the price mechanism alone towards the
production of the additional cash holdings desired. Thus, the
increment of production associated with an increase of employment will not have lacked a market, since it will have taken the
form in which the owners of the additional incomes wished to
absorb it.

It is therefore not true that the limitation of the propensity
to consume, if it is not compensated by investment expenditures
of an appropriate amount, is the cause of a limitation of employment. It is still less true that it leads to an equilibrium
with under-employment, since the forces spontaneously brought
into being by every increase in labor offered tend to adapt the
economic structure to the utilization which the newly employed
workers wish to make of their additional income. An economic
state in process of adaptation, whatever it is, cannot be a state of
equilibrium. A theory which neglects the influences tending to
produce these adaptations cannot be a general theory, still less
a true theory.

The Keynesian faithful will, it is true, object that the preceding analysis is purely theoretical. They will point out, first of
all, that it is solely by movements of prices that the adaptation
required for the absorption of an increment of production tends
to be stimulated, and that in the absence of these movements
or in the absence of action by price movements on the structure
of the productive system, no increase of employment could be
expected. Therefore, in such a case, one would, in fact, be in a
state of under-employment equilibrium.

This is true, but it is no less true that, in fact, in most of the economic systems which existed before the war, spontaneous movements of prices were able to develop, and that they effectively brought about the allocation of the factors of production. The considerable variations in the rate of gold production between periods of boom and periods of depression clearly showed the sensitiveness of the productive apparatus to price movements.

I shall consider in a later section the effects of price stabilization measures and the immobilization of the factors of production. But in no part of the General Theory are stabilization of prices and immobilization of the factors of production expressly indicated as fundamental conditions of under-employment equilibrium. If they were the fundamental conditions, it would have been indispensable that this be pointed out, for among the possible remedies it would have been necessary to count, alongside the interventions suggested by Lord Keynes, the suppression of the causes of economic rigidity. Even if this had been pointed out, however, a theory based upon such special hypotheses could not have been considered a "general theory."

In any case, even in economies not very sensitive to the forces which tend to upset economic equilibria, these forces, as long as prices are not strictly stabilized, exist, and make it impossible to consider an economic structure subject to influences which tend to modify it a state of equilibrium.

It may be noted, however, that the preceding reasoning holds only so far as workable mines of gold exist in the society under consideration. However, the absence of accessible deposits only modifies the form of the regulatory apparatus; it does not destroy it, and it eliminates none of its consequences. The fall of prices brought about by the state of under-employment, if not checked by the absorption of the under-employed into the industries producing the yellow metal, tends to divert them to the production of goods capable of being marketed abroad.[3] In this way it tends to bring about a favorable balance of payments for the country under consideration. It gives rise, as in the preceding case, to additional offers of metal on the market and consequently to additional monetizations. These latter furnish the additional cash holdings desired by the newly employed work-

[3] This mechanism, too, is analyzed in detail in Volume 1 of my L'Ordre Social (p. 383).

ers who do not apply their increments of income to consumption goods or investment goods.

Thus, in this case also, the fact that the workers available for an increment of employment are not disposed to devote more than a fraction of their increments of income to demand for consumers' goods or investment goods does not create a lack of markets for the increments of production which these workers can supply. It merely diverts a part of the additional production to foreign markets, where it will procure, by way of exchange, the increments of metal which provide the additional cash holdings desired by the newly employed workers. In this case, again, the additional production will have been subjected to forces tending to provide it with a market. As long as prices and factors of production have not been stabilized, no state of under-employment equilibrium can exist.

The preceding analysis applies, it is true, only to a special case—that of a society using metallic money only. This leaves us with the general case of a society using inconvertible money or money which can be obtained both by the monetization of metal and the discount of commercial paper.

As in the preceding case, the non-utilization of a part of the increment of income arising from the increase of employment will lead the beneficiaries of the increments of income not utilized to increase their cash holdings. As a result, all other conditions remaining the same, the cash holdings of certain members of the society under consideration will prove to be less than they desire to hold. To bring their cash holdings back to the level they desire, they will have no other solution except to offer without demanding. It is the existence of these uncompensated offers which sets in motion a regulatory mechanism analogous in principle, if not in form, to that revealed by our study of a purely metallic regime.

The increment of offers may react either upon wealth in the strict sense or upon credit instruments. In the first case, it leads to a fall in prices; in the second, to an increase of money rates. If it affects wealth in the strict sense and credit instruments in the same proportion in which these enter into total offerings, the excess of offers resulting from the non-utilization of an increment of income will produce a fall in prices and a rise in money rates simultaneously. This preliminary statement shows the close relation which must exist between the two opposite movements. I shall next show—and this is essential for the argument—that they are inseparably bound together.

If the offer without demand reacts solely upon wealth in the strict sense, it' affects cash markets to the exclusion of credit markets, since its object is the procurement of immediate increments of cash holdings. It therefore brings about a fall in cash prices. The fall in cash prices leads speculators to buy for cash with a view to sale on credit, obtaining by way of discount of the commercial paper derived from the second transaction the resources required to settle the first. The increase of the demand for discount brings about a rise in rates on the money market, a rise which does not come to an end until the general level of prices stops falling.[4] Conversely, every increase in money rates leads speculators, other things remaining the same, to sell for cash with the intention of buying back on credit, investing in the market the funds derived from the first transaction until the settlement of the second. It therefore leads to a fall in the general level of cash prices.

The preceding analysis shows that the excess of offers resulting from the existence of non-utilized incomes gives rise in all cases, and simultaneously, to a fall in the general level of prices and a rise in money rates.

I know that the statement that such a relation exists will surprise certain readers who know that periods of boom, that is, periods of rising prices, are periods of high interest rates. However, the rise of money rates which has usually accompanied periods of boom in the past was caused by the increases in the discount rate decreed by the monetary authorities, almost always as a result of fears inspired by the decrease of their metallic reserves. In fact, in every country of the world, the periods of rising prices resulting from the budget deficits of recent years have been periods of very low money rates. Be it noted that in the absence of the relation stated above the functioning of an inconvertible monetary system would be simply inconceivable, since the need for cash holdings could not lead to the issue of

[4] The rate does not depend upon the absolute level of prices, but only on variations in it. Mathematicians would say that it is a function of the derivative of the general level of prices with respect to time. (L'Ordre Social, Vol. I, p. 61.)

new money. Moreover, and this seems to me the essential argument, the possibility that every excess of offers may react as well upon credit instruments as upon wealth in the strict sense suffices to make of this statement, which at first seems paradoxical, a truth of common sense.

If, in the light of this proposition, we follow the unfolding of the phenomena which result from the insufficiency of cash holdings, we observe that in the first phase the fall in the general level of prices furnishes, by reducing the cash holdings required for the carrying on of transactions, the increments of cash holdings desired.

Now the rate of discount of the bank of issue is always very close to the market rate. When the rising market rate reaches the rate of discount, it stops increasing, since at this rate the bank accepts all paper offered and not demanded. From this moment on, all the excess of offers above the demand for short-term paper is diverted from the market to the bank of issue. The latter monetizes the paper which it has bought, and in this way supplies the increments of cash holdings desired. Commercial paper, however, is representative of wealth of the same value, wealth which is either stored up or, more generally, on its way through the process of production.

Everything goes on, therefore, as if the rights which contained this wealth, instead of being thrown upon the market, were disposed of outside the market in the assets of the bank of issue, the latter clothing them in the monetary garb which makes them reappear in the form of additional cash holdings.

Thus, in a regime of inconvertible money, as in a metallic regime, the non-ultilization of certain incomes does not give rise to a lack of markets. Wealth of the same value as that not demanded is spontaneously diverted from the market to the bank of issue. There it is ultilized for the manufacture of the increments of cash holdings demanded by the owners of the additional incomes which were not consumed and not invested. Thus, as long as the increase in cash holdings continues, the increments of production will find a market. The abstinence of the owners of the additional incomes will not have brought about under-employment.

The preceding analysis shows that in a regime of inconvertible money the process is analogous in principle, if not in form, to that characteristic of a metallic regime; but as a result of the great flexibility of interest rates, the first process is evidently more sensitive than the second. It will therefore act more easily and more promptly. In this way, it will assure a smoother adaptation of the productive apparatus to the opportunities offered it by the market. In a mixed regime—where money is obtainable both by the coinage of gold and by the monetization of commercial paper, the two processes may act simultaneously. The conclusion, from the point of view which interests us here, is not modified.

There is a case, however, where money and credit instruments do not represent wealth of equal value: when they are issued against engagements which draw their value only from a governmental act, obliging the bank of issue to buy them at a nominal rate entirely different from that at which they could be sold in the market—the situation characteristic of every regime with a deficit financed by recourse to the bank of issue. In such a case, however, the rights which contain the false credits are added, when their owners wish to turn them into real wealth, to those from which the wealth offered on the market has been derived. The demand is increased in proportion. It is impossible, therefore, to imagine that the purchasing power impinging upon the market should not be sufficient to absorb the wealth offered there.

The preceding analysis shows that in all cases the demand for liquidity implies a demand for wealth of equal value. This wealth can, according to circumstances, be metal or credits, themselves representatives of goods stored or sold on credit. We are therefore not entitled to conclude that "liquidity preference" diminishes proportionately the purchasing power impinging on the market. This always remains determined, everything remaining the same, by the value of the production offered there. The demand for liquidity—like every demand, whatever its nature—simply sets forces in motion which tend to stimulate in the productive apparatus the adaptation capable of satisfying it.

To demand money is not, as Lord Keynes believes, to demand nothing. It is to demand wealth capable of being monetized within the framework of the existing monetary system. Hence, the preference for liquidity offers, like any other demand, an outlet for the labor forces offered on the market. Contrary to the Keynesian conclusion, it cannot be, at least so far as prices and the factors of production are not entirely immobilized, a cause of under-employment in the society which it affects.

3.   THE ORIGINS OF THE KEYNESIAN ERROR

The Keynesian theory of permanent under-employment equilibrium rests, then, essentially on an erroneous idea—the idea that all income not spent on consumers' goods or investment goods involves an inadequate absorption of the production of which it is the result. This idea is itself the consequence of two fundamental errors which characterize Lord Keynes' thought in the monetary sphere.

The first is based on the over-simplified idea that money and credit instruments are nothing but empty symbols with no value. This, one might say, is the effect of a monetary nominalism with which the General Theory is thoroughly impregnated. The most characteristic passage from this point of view is the one dealing with financial provisions:

> But when the financial provision *exceeds* the actual expenditure on current upkeep, the practical results of this in its effect on employment are not always appreciated. For the amount of this excess neither directly gives rise to current investment nor is available to pay for consumption.
> Thus sinking funds, etc., are apt to withdraw spending power from the consumer long before the demand for expenditure on replacements (which such provisions are anticipating) comes into play; i.e. they diminish the current effective demand and only increase it in the year in which the replacement is actually made. (Pages 99, 100.)

Nothing shows more clearly that, for Lord Keynes, to accumulate reserves—that is to say, to accumulate money or short-term credit instruments—involves a proportionate diminution in the effective current demand, and therefore, the creation of under-employment.

The fallacy of this thesis appears immediately when the accumulation is in the form of metal. I have shown in the preceding section that the process characteristic of a circulation made up entirely of gold is general, and that the Keynesian thesis is just as untenable when the holdings consist of inconvertible money or short-term credit instruments.

At the beginning of Chapter 16, Sundry Observations on the Nature of Capital, our author presents the thesis even more clearly:

An act of individual saving means—so to speak—a decision not to have dinner today. But it does *not* necessitate a decision to have dinner or to buy a pair of boots a week hence or a year hence or to consume any specified thing at any specified date. Thus it depresses the business of preparing today's dinner without stimulating the business of making ready for some future act of consumption. It is not a substitution of future consumption-demand for present consumption-demand—it is a net diminution of such demand.

Here there is no question that, for Lord Keynes, to save is to demand nothing. He does not realize that to accumulate money or credit instruments is to demand the values of which the money or credit instruments are a representation, and that to diminish one's cash holdings is to liberate the same values, causing them to be offered on the market.

The regulatory process thus neglected is, however, an essential one, indispensable to a comprehension of the monetary mechanism. If it is not granted, it goes without saying that, as Keynes believes, preference for liquidity, that is to say, the accumulation of monetary reserves, tends to destroy the equilibrium of the market by inadequacy of demand, just as their utilization destroys it by excess. Every variation in reserves and holdings would, therefore, preclude the maintenance of economic equilibrium.

If, on the contrary, we grant it, the increase of reserves and holdings tends merely to divert to the fabrication of money the productive forces previously devoted to the production of the goods which are no longer demanded, while the utilization of these holdings tends to free the productive forces which were utilized for the production of the wealth represented by the money and orient them towards the production of the newly demanded goods.

I believe, moreover, that the process of monetary regulation, if it is generally admitted so far as metallic money is concerned—though not always very conscientiously—is ignored by most monetary theorists, so far as inconvertible monetary systems are concerned. For my part, I have found it difficult to disentangle it and to show its generality.[5] I now believe it to be unquestionably established, and I believe, moreover, that it is the keystone of the whole theory of money.

In particular, I cannot see how one could explain the bond which must exist between the total amount of individual cash holdings and the quantity of money in circulation without making use of the theory of regulation. Every individual fixes freely, more or less consciously, the amount of his cash holdings. He generally ignores the existence of the procedures by which money can be created, and yet, in order that his desire for cash holdings may be satisfied, it is necessary that he be able by his decision to bring about variations in the quantity of money in circulation, in a regime of inconvertible money as well as a regime of metallic money. Only the theory of monetary regulation, based upon the mechanism which I have analyzed above, seems to me able to furnish the indispensable explanation and to show how each individual, in fixing the amount of his own cash holdings, helps to determine the total amount of money issued.

The problem of the bond between the amount of individual cash holdings and the total amount of money in circulation did not escape Lord Keynes, but since he ignores and denies the process of monetary regulation, he elaborates, to resolve it, an obscure explanation of the mechanism by which

. . . the liberty, which every individual possesses, to change, whenever he chooses, the amount of money he holds [is harmonized] with the necessity for the total amount of money, which individual balances add up to, to be exactly equal to the amount of cash *which the banking system has created.* (Page 84. Italics mine.)

Thus, for Keynes, the quantity of money which the banking system has created is a datum. The total amount of individual cash holdings has to be adapted to it. I am convinced, on the contrary, that it is the total of cash holdings desired by individuals which, thanks to the mechanism of regulation, determines the quantity of money in circulation. But I have also shown that the mechanism of regulation, if we admit that it

[5] L'Ordre Social, Vol. I, Chs. 17-20.

exists, excludes the possibility of equilibrium with under-employment and, consequently, destroys the foundation of the Keynesian theory.

It is not only the paragraphs which I have cited but the whole General Theory which leads to the conclusion that Lord Keynes' position is entirely dominated by the idea that the quantity of money in circulation is a datum arbitrarily fixed by the monetary authorities, upon which the market demand exercises no influence. His theory of interest (Chapter 13) in particular, rests upon this foundation:

It is the "price" which equilibrates the desire to hold wealth in the form of cash with the available quantity of cash—
And the quantity of money is not determined by the public. All that the propensity of the public towards hoarding can achieve is to determine the rate of interest at which the aggregate desire to hoard becomes equal to the available cash.

Furthermore, Lord Keynes believes that the monetary authorities can cause the quantity of money in circulation to vary. "If we have to govern the activity of the economic system by *varying* the quantity of money," he writes. Can a more outmoded and over-simplified conception be imagined? Among men who have reflected on monetary questions, are there any considerable number today who believe that a bank of issue fixes the quantity of money in circulation? All those who, from near or far, have participated with their eyes open in the management of a bank of issue are well aware that the open market can modify the cover of the outstanding circulation, can substitute to the great profit of the bank, treasury bills for an advance to the state, and lower the rate of interest, but cannot directly modify the quantity of money in circulation.

As Directeur du Mouvement General des Fonds, I have known periods of equal deficit where the circulation increased and others where it decreased, without the monetary authorities having taken any action to bring about these changes and in spite of everything they could do to prevent them. As Deputy Governor of the Bank of France, I witnessed the vain attempts of the central bank to resist the increase of note issue.

Thus, the quantity of money in circulation, contrary to popular belief, is not fixed by the authorities of the market, and the fundamental error of Lord Keynes seems to me to result from the wholly superficial views which he holds concerning the monetary mechanism.

If we admit the existence of the mechanism of monetary regulation which I think I have demonstrated, under-employment cannot be a permanent state of equilibrium, since the mechanism of regulation tends to bring about those very transfers of the factors of production which are capable of making it disappear, even in the case where, as a result of liquidity preference, the demand of workers newly employed is exercised only in part upon consumers' goods and investment goods. Thus, either the quantity of money in circulation is a datum—and the theory of Keynes can be true—or the quantity of money is fixed by the size of the cash balances which the users of money desire to hold, and the Keynesian explanation of permanent under-employment equilibrium falls to pieces.

4.   THE GENERAL THEORY, IMPERFECT PHILOSOPHY OF UNSPECIFIED RIGIDITY

It will be pointed out, to be sure, that the tendencies resulting from an increase of unutilized incomes, i.e., neither consumed nor invested, will not prevent unemployment unless they effectively divert productive forces from the production of wealth in the strict sense to wealth susceptible of being monetized, gold or commerical paper. Until the transfer has occurred, new production will throw upon the market wealth not demanded, and in this way will condemn to unemployment those who were disposed to devote themselves to such production. Under-employment will simply be the expression of the refusal of the owners of incomes to accept what they do not want.

Thus, at the moment when the increase of employment takes place, if it is not directed into a channel which permits it to furnish the increments of money desired by the beneficiaries of the unspent increments of income, the situation may be that envisaged in, and explained by, the Keynesian theory. The only difference will be that while Keynes considers this situation a position of under-employment equilibrium, I regard it as a temporary state which the forces arising from the mechanism of regulation tend to modify.

If the action of these forces were rendered ineffective, however, if they were incapable of diverting factors of production, Keynes' theory could then be considered a faithful explanation of reality. Thus, the theory of employment which Keynes calls "general" is valid only for very special cases, for economies which are entirely insensitive to movements of prices and of interest rates.

Moreover, in this case, if the theory is really to take account of reality, it would have to be the object of a profound generalization. If permanent unemployment can exist in an entirely rigid economy, it is not merely because the demand for investment goods may not be sufficient to offset the excess of a given increment of income above the increment of consumption which it is capable of causing, but because it might happen in various ways that the increase of production which an increase of employment might make possible in the channels where it is practically feasible would not consist of products which the beneficiaries of corresponding increases of incomes would wish to obtain.

An example will make my thought clearer. I assume a state of general under-employment; in other words, a state in which important segments of the labor force are either unemployed or employed less than they would like to be. Keynes says that in the absence of a systematic increase in investment this state might be a permanent state of equilibrium, because if employment increased, a part of the increments of income associated with the new production would not give rise to any demand, as a consequence of the psychological disposition of individuals to devote only a part—varying with their propensity to consume—of their increments of income to increased consumption.

I have shown that in such a case individuals who do not consume demand money, and that the increments of cash holdings which their attitude leads them, consciously or not, to desire could be furnished them only by a suitable orientation of production—an orientation which the mechanism of monetary regulation tends to bring about. Hence, under the assumption which implicitly underlies Keynes' theory—a rigid economy and a propensity to consume not offset by an increase of investment—under-employment is permanent only because, while the owners of increments of income are not disposed to accept anything but increments of cash holdings, the increments of production which an increase of employment might afford them are only wealth in the strict sense—consumers' goods or investment goods.

Let the unemployed laborers apply themselves to the production of what is demanded, namely, gold in a country capable of producing it, exportable goods in a country possessing no gold deposits, or goods capable of being absorbed in a process giving rise to commercial paper, and employment can increase. Thus, in the Keynesian hypothesis, unemployment will result only from the incapacity of the productive apparatus to adapt itself to the market demand.

But this defect of adaptation—essentially temporary, since no one, it seems obvious, is disposed to hoard increments of income indefinitely—is only a very special and very exceptional form of the defects of adaptation possible. Under-employment is not caused only by an insufficient propensity to consume. It also results from every divergence between the increments of production which an increment of employment might supply and the increments of demand which the corresponding increment of incomes could give rise to.

Let us suppose, for example, that the situation in which Keynes sees the essential cause of under-employment does not exist, every owner of increments of income being disposed to demand consumers' goods for the totality of his new resources. Now in such a situation, where the propensity to consume would be 100 per cent, any increase in employment would be impossible if the workers capable of being newly employed were adapted only to the manufacture of investment goods or consumers' goods other than those which the owners of increments of income desired. The state of under-employment would exist despite a total propensity to consume.

Conversely, in a society where the unemployed workers were not ready to produce anything except consumers' goods—the case, in particular, of unemployed workers specialized in agricultural production—every demand for investment goods, however important, would have no effect upon employment. The Keynesian remedy would be wholly ineffective.

Thus, Lord Keynes has taken account, among all possible

causes of under-employment attributable to economic rigidity, only one very special case, that of unemployment due to incapacity of the economic organism to furnish the increments of cash holdings or of short-term credit instruments which are temporarily demanded of it. He has given to this cause of under-employment an importance which it does not in general deserve, since unemployment can result from any defect of adaptation between production and the demand capable of absorbing it, and can last until this adaptation has been effected. He has, furthermore, failed to note that the complete economic rigidity required, if his theory is to be partially true, is not a general characteristic of economic societies but, on the contrary, a very exceptional state, which only special measures of immobilization or control could engender.

The omission in the general theory of the essential effects of economic rigidity is evidently an extremely serious matter, since it conceals the true character of the Keynesian explanation and brushes aside some of the remedies for under-employment which it should have suggested.

The considerations developed in the present section lead to a general view of the mechanism of unemployment. Contrary to Keynes' view, it does not result from an insufficiency of income. Income is never insufficient to absorb existing production; for, apart from special circumstances which I cannot consider in detail here, it is engendered by this production and its amount at every period is identically equal to the value of the said production.[6]

On the other hand, if the products offered are not those desired by the market, their value may be reduced to zero at the same time as the income of the producers to whose activity they are due. Thus the total income is not rendered incapable of absorbing the production, for the value of the latter is reduced in the same degree as the total of the former. But if the production of unwanted goods comes to an end, the state of unemployment to which it gave rise is not a state of equilibrium, for it engenders forces which tend to modify it with a view to restoring to the factors of production their normal productivity. It is only when these forces are system-

[6] L'Ordre Social—Ch. 10.

atically paralyzed that under-employment can become a permanent characteristic of the society in question.

5.   THE POLITICAL CONSEQUENCES OF THE GENERAL THEORY

The preceding analysis will enable us to form an opinon concerning the efficacy and probable consequences of the remedies for unemployment which the Keynesian theory suggests.

These remedies all rest upon the central idea that under-employment is due to an inadequate propensity to consume. To increase employment, therefore, it is sufficient either to increase the propensity to consume or to offset the inadequacy of the demand for consumption goods by a systematic increase of investment. In order to increase the propensity to consume, Lord Keynes recommends a redistribution of income designed to discourage the deplorable instinct to save:

> Thus our argument leads towards the conclusion that in contemporary conditions the growth of wealth, so far from being dependent on the abstinence of the rich, as is commonly supposed, is more likely to be impeded by it. (Page 373.)

He also contemplates appropriate fiscal and interest-rate policies. If the level of investment is fixed, total income depends entirely on the propensity to consume, therefore on measures tending to develop it. "So long as the marginal propensity to consume out of wages is greater than that out of profits," says one of his disciples, "any rise in wage rates at the expense of profits will raise the aggregate marginal propensity to consume . . . thus raising the level of income that can be supported by a given level of investment and federal expenditure." (Econometrica, July, 1946, p. 227.)

The preceding analysis shows that these remedies cannot have any permanent effect on the level of employment, which is indifferent to the utilization made of the incomes to which it gives rise. It also shows that the corresponding interventions will reduce the temporary unemployment arising from economic rigidity only in the exact degree to which the increase in the propensity to consume arouses demand for the goods which the under-employed labor forces are capable of producing. If the latter are unable or unwilling to offer anything but investment goods, the increase in the propensity to consume will leave them unemployed. In any event, their adaptation to the new markets afforded them by a given increase in the propensity to consume would be neither less difficult nor less painful than that which would have made possible the absorption of unemployment by adaptation to the utilization which the owners of incomes intended to make of them, whether it responds to a desire to save or a desire to hoard.

But the fundamental and quasi-universal remedy of the Keynesian theory is the investment expenditure undertaken by the state with a view to warding off the alleged inadequacy of private demand. For each level of investment there is supposed to be a corresponding level of income, and hence of employment. If employment declines, it is because the volume of investment required to sustain the existing employment has not been achieved. To do away with unemployment, it is necessary and sufficient that the state assume the investment expenditures which private initiative is unwilling to undertake.

The whole preceding analysis shows that this conclusion is false. The level of investment expenditures, whether public or private, does not define the level of employment, since with every level of employment there is associated an income capable of absorbing the corresponding production, under the one condition that the latter be adapted, in its nature, to the effective demand of the owners of incomes. Even if we admit "as a permanent characteristic of human nature" the existence of a consumption function analogous to that assumed in the Keynesian analysis, it does not lead to the conclusion that investment expenditures are necessary in order to insure full employment; for every demand which is not exercised upon the market for consumers' goods will reappear in the form of demand for investment goods or for hoarding.

It should be noted further that a demand for additional cash holdings will always be of limited amount, and that when it is satisfied, the corresponding demand will reappear upon the market for investment goods or consumers' goods.

It is true, however, that investment expenditures can bring relief to a temporary unemployment crisis, though only to a limited extent. They can furnish a market for unemployed labor forces available for the production of the investment goods for which they produce the demand. Every increment of investment expenditure can increase employment in the investment industries and in these alone. Moreover, we should not consider the investment industries as a whole. It is only the factors of production specialized in the industries which benefit from the additional demand which will be afforded an additional market by the investment expenditures, relieving them from the unemployment which would have led them to make the adjustment required by the conditions of market demand.

However, though investment expenditures can in this way reduce temporary unemployment in the industries affected by them, they entail secondary effects which must be taken into account if we wish to arrive at a decision on balance concerning the consequences which the full-employment policy will bring in its train when it becomes the object of generalized application. These secondary effects will vary according to whether the investment expenditures are achieved within the framework of a treasury in equilibrium or with a deficit; in other words, according to whether they are financed by taxes and loans or by the issue of treasury bills rendered eligible for discount because the market has not of its own accord assured the absorption of them.

In the first case, there is a levy on the society of the resources devoted to the financing of the investment program. If the purchasing power thus taken away from individuals is that which they intended to spend on wealth not offered in the market (for example, in the Keynesian hypothesis, additional cash holdings), and if the increment of demand arising from the investment program impinges on wealth which the unemployed factors of production are capable of producing, the investment program will increase employment, but it need not turn out this way. It is probable that in large measure the demand for articles not produced—for example, increments of cash holdings—will persist and that the levies accomplished will, to the extent of an important fraction of their total, reduce the demands which were impinging upon the other segments of the market.

Consequently, the program will have augmented the amplitude of the adjustments required for spontaneous reabsorption of the unemployed and delayed the moment when the latter will be able to come to pass. Under the (improbable) assumption that the public investment program has absorbed all the unemployed productive resources—that is, to the degree in which it has achieved its purpose—it would have brought about the disappearance of every force capable of assuring an ultimate spontaneous recovery of the market.

But, furthermore, if the investment expenditures imply the utilization of raw materials or goods demanded in the market, they will, by increasing the demand and hence the price of these goods, help to reduce the outlets spontaneously afforded them by the market. So far as they have served to absorb this wealth, the investment expenditures will not have helped to increase the employment in the market. Finally, so far as the investment program diverts means of production from the areas where they are more desired to less useful employments, it will reduce the standard of living of the society.

However, it is unlikely that a large investment program following a period when economic depression has seriously reduced government revenues should ever be financed within the framework of a balanced budget. In the majority of cases, if not in all, resources will be obtained by the issue of treasury bills eligible for discount.

In the situation foreseen by the Keynesian hypothesis—a depression caused by the refusal of certain workers to utilize the increment of income afforded them by an increment of employment—inflation can supply them with the increments of cash holdings which they wish to obtain. In this way, so far as the offer of employment is accepted by the under-employed workers, whether it corresponds to their previous specialization or they accept the modifications in activity which it implies, an investment program financed by inflation can bring about an increase of employment.

However, individuals, other things remaining the same so far as prices go, cannot be supposed to increase their cash holdings indefinitely. The moment will necessarily arrive when the newly issued monetary tokens will not be wanted. Then they will produce, along with a rise in the general level of prices, all the economic and social disorders associated with inflation. If we wish to avoid the latter without abandoning the investment program which has given rise to them, there will be no other solution but to limit demand by a system of general rationing.

Thus, the inauguration of a vast program of public works, if it is carried out over a prolonged period, will revive in the world an economic regime invented by Hitler, from which victory was supposed to free us. We shall see the restraints progressively tightening and expanding, and the steady unfolding of the familiar process of inflation will again bring about the suppression of all human liberties. In this way it will be demonstrated once more that the governments of human societies have a choice between only two solutions: to allow the apparatus of production to adapt itself to the structure which, by the movements of prices, the will of the consumers tends to impose upon it, or to adapt the desires of consumers by authoritative regulation to the structure of the productive apparatus which we do not propose to change.

The preceding analysis illuminates the phenomena which we have observed during the past decade and explains why the development of war industries caused unemployment to disappear, while investment plans applied in peace time seem incapable of accomplishing it. The war-time programs created a practically unlimited demand. They reabsorbed unemployment because the workers available were transferred, voluntarily or under compulsion, into the employments which this demand brought into being. As for financing, it was assured, so far as it was not covered by taxation or by loans, by recourse to the bank of issue. The inflation thus engendered was in large measure neutralized by rationing, that is, by the suppression of the freedom of the demanders in the utilization of their purchasing power.

The new activities obviously restricted the previous production by the utilizations of material and of energy which they implied, but no one thought of complaining about it, because at the same time taxation, borrowing, and rationing restricted the power of buying.

Can the same result—unsatisfactory as it is, since it implies and requires the suppression of all economic liberty—be hoped for in time of peace? I do not think so. In the first place, it is improbable that the administrative authorities will be able to impose in time of peace the transfers of labor power which such a program implies. These transfers will probably be neither less extensive nor less painful than those which would have assured the spontaneous reabsorption of the under-employed; and since the latter are considered unacceptable, it is improbable that the former would be any more acceptable, even if the public authorities had a mind to impose them. Moreover, the inauguration of a large investment program will appreciably diminish, by the utilization of raw materials and of energy which it requires, the production of articles really demanded. Public opinion will be reluctant to give up what it wants for the production of what it does not want.

The privations which the investment program will cause will be much more appreciable than in time of war, for it will not be possible to raise the tax revenues to the level which they had attained during hostilities, or to obtain voluntary loans of such large amounts, or to impose, by means of rationing, a sufficient neutralizing of purchasing power. For all these reasons, an unsatisfied demand will persist in the market and this will give rise more or less rapidly, according to its relative magnitude, to all the troubles of inflation.

In spite of these prospects, it is probable that the next period of depression will see a general application in the world of the policy suggested by Lord Keynes. I am confident that this policy will not reduce unemployment, except to a very limited extent, but that it will have profound consequences upon the evolution of the countries in which it is applied. Through the economic disorders to which it will give rise, it will re-establish in the world a regime of general planning analogous to the regime of war time and based upon the suppression of all individual liberty. Thus, the next economic crisis seems likely to be the occasion for profound political changes, welcome to some people, dreaded by others. In any event, being based on a false theory, the remedies, which will be adopted will give rise to repercussions very different from those they were designed to produce. Their ineffectiveness will be, for a great part of public opinion, one more reason for urging the suppression of a regime which, by denying itself, will have destroyed itself.

Whom Jupiter wishes to destroy, he first makes mad.

XIV

John H. Williams, born in Wales in 1887, took his master's degree in 1916 and his doctor's degree in 1919 at Harvard University. He was assistant professor of economics at Harvard from 1921 to 1925, associate professor from 1925 to 1929, and full professor from 1929 to 1933. He has been Nathaniel Ropes professor of political economy at Harvard since 1933. He was also vice-president of the Federal Reserve Bank of New York from 1936 to 1947 and has been economic adviser since 1933. In 1951 he was president of the American Economic Association.

The following article appeared in the *American Economic Review* for May, 1948, pages 273-290.

AN APPRAISAL OF KEYNESIAN ECONOMICS

JOHN H. WILLIAMS

I

The topic assigned to me is, I am afraid, much too ambitious. I cannot do more than select some questions that seem to me important for an appraisal of Keynesian economics. I shall in part be going over ground I have already tried to explore at some of our earlier meetings and elsewhere, but I do hope to make some further progress.

Keynes's greatest virtue, I have always felt, was his interest in economic policy. Economic theorizing seems to me pointless unless it is aimed at what to do. All the great theorists, I think, have had policy as their central interest, even if their policy was merely laissez faire. If, nevertheless, I have been skeptical of theory, in its traditional form, it is because of its pretension to universality. Economic theory is an exercise in logic, involving abstraction from what the theorist regards as nonessential. Added to the simplifications of selection and emphasis is that involved in the one-thing-at-a-time method of analysis. Our dilemma is, and has always been, that, as Keynes said, without theory we are "lost in the woods." Without hypotheses for testing, we have no basis for economic inquiry. But one can reject with Bagehot what he long ago called the "All-Case" method of the German historical school, while questioning, as he did, the range of validity of what he called the "Single-Case" method of English political economy.[1] This is the kind of question that has chiefly interested me with regard to Keynesian, as well as classical, economics.

As the reference to Bagehot indicates, Keynes was not the first great English critic of classical enconomics. As a graduate student, nothing interested me more than the writings of the heretics. I found no more penetrating discussion of the relativity of economic concepts than Bagehot's *The Postulates of English Political Economy;* and I returned repeatedly to ponder over Cliffe Leslie's savage outcry against "generalizations . . . which have passed with a certain school of English economists for economic laws . . . generalizations which were once useful and meritorious as first attempts to discover causes and sequence among economic phenomena, but which have long since ceased to afford either light or fruit, and become part of the solemn humbug of 'economic orthodoxy.' "[2] The weakness of such men, from the standpoint of the impression they made on later generations of economists or their own, was that they set up no rival system.[3] By the nature of their objections they could not, and had no interest in trying. The strength of Keynes, again from the standpoint of the impression he has made, stems

---

[1] Walter Bagehot, "The Postulates of English Political Economy," in *The Works of Walter Bagehot* (Hartford, Conn., 1889), Vol. V, pp. 249, 253.

[2] Thomas Edward Cliffe Leslie, "The Movements of Agricultural Wages in Europe," *Essays in Political Economy* (Dublin, 1888), p. 379.

[3] How they affected my own thinking about international trade theory I tried to show in my old paper, "The Theory of International Trade Reconsidered," *Economic Journal*, June, 1929. Reprinted as Chapter 12 in my book, *Postwar Monetary Plans and Other Essays* (3rd ed., New York, 1947).

from the fact that he did set up a rival system, for which, like his classical predecessors, he claimed universal validity. To reduce classical economics to the status of a "special" case under his "general" theory, as he so dramatically did in his single-page first chapter, was to stake out his claim on what he undoubtedly regarded as the highest conceivable level; it probably has no parallel in economic literature. But the questions remain: how valid is his system as a picture of reality, what is the range of its application, how useful is it as a guide to economic policy?

In one of the most interesting essays in *The New Economics,* Arthur Smithies, whom I have always considered a good Keynesian, says that Keynes's theory must be regarded as the beginning rather than the end, and calls upon us to construct a really "general" theory, in which Keynes's theory would be a "special" case.[4] This is welcome evidence—and one could cite much besides in the recent work of men who have been ardent Keynesians—of a willingness to appraise Keynesian economics more critically than was apparent in the first wave of enthusiasm that greeted the appearance of *The General Theory* in the thirties. Perhaps it will help us to get away from the tendency to classify everyone as Keynesian or anti-Keynesian. That never seemed to me a helpful starting point for considering objectively either what Keynes's contribution has been or what its limitations are. I doubt, however, whether "dynamizing" Keynes's static equilibrium analysis, which is what Smithies, Klein, and other mathematical economists seem to have in view, will remove the limitations. To my mind, they are inherent in the nature of equilibrium analysis, especially when applied to income as a whole.[5]

4 "Effective Demand and Employment," in *The New Economics: Keynes' Influence on Theory and Public Policy* (New York, 1947), Ch. XXXIX.

5 The limitations of mathematical economic theory were never better expressed than by Keynes himself: "It is a great fault of symbolic pseudo-mathematical methods of formalising a system of economic analysis . . . that they expressly assume strict independence between the factors involved and lose all their cogency and authority if this hypothesis is disallowed; whereas, in ordinary discourse, where we are not blindly manipulating but know all the time what we are doing and what the words mean, we can keep 'at the back of our heads' the necessary reserves and qualifications and the adjustments which we shall have to make later on, in a way in which we cannot keep complicated partial differentials 'at the back' of several pages of algebra which assume that

II

Keynes leaves no room for doubt that, in his view, his principle of effective demand revolutionized traditional economic theory. In the preface to *The General Theory* he speaks of "treading along unfamiliar paths," and of his long "struggle of escape." It is clear, too, that he regarded his contribution as monetary. The evolution of his thinking covered the greater part of the interwar period, and the stages in it were marked by the *Tract on Monetary Reform* (1923), the *Treatise on Money* (1930), and *The General Theory* (1936). It is clear all the way through that he was intensely concerned with the problems of his day, and particularly with those of England. In this sense all his books are dated. The first deals with the monetary disturbances of the early twenties, with a large emphasis on international monetary policy; it is dedicated to the "Governors and Court of the Bank of England, who now and for the future have a much more difficult and anxious task than in former days." [6] The second is a monumental work—analytical, statistical, historical—whose central theme is a monetary theory of the business cycle (mainly on closed economy lines) and a policy of control of the cycle by the central bank. There is no evidence as yet of preoccupation with unemployment as a chronic tendency, booms are emphasized quite as much as depressions (nothing interested him more than our stock market boom), underconsumption and oversaving theories are given only passing reference.

In a famous passage of *The General Theory*, every sentence of which has a special revelance for his own theory, Keynes refers to "the completeness of the Ricardian victory" as "due to a complex of suitabilities in the doctrine to the environment into which it was projected." [7] It was, I have always felt, a similar complex of suitabilities that accounted not only for the great impression made by Keynes's theory but also for its

---

they all vanish. Too large a proportion of recent 'mathematical' economics are mere concoctions, as imprecise as the initial assumptions they rest on, which allow the author to lose sight of the complexities and interdependencies of the real world in a maze of pretentious and unhelpful symbols." *The General Theory of Employment, Interest and Money* (London, 1936), pp. 297-298.

[6] Preface, p. vi.

[7] Pp. 32-33.

origin. It was not a coincidence, or a misinterpretation of Keynes, that the first great development of the theory by his disciples was the stagnation thesis, that the war was regarded as a superlative demonstration of what could be accomplished to sustain employment by a really adequate volume of effective demand, and that the weight of expectation of Keynesian economists was that we would relapse after the war into mass unemployment unless vigorous antideflation measures were pursued. There is no better short statement of the stagnation thesis than that given by Keynes: "The richer the community, the wider will tend to be the gap between its actual and its potential production; and therefore the more obvious and outrageous the defects of the economic system. . . . Not only is the marginal propensity to consume weaker in a wealthy community, but, owing to its accumulation of capital being already larger, the opportunities for further investment are less attractive." [8] In an article in the *New Republic* which I have often quoted, Keynes concluded: "It appears to be politically impossible for a capitalistic democracy to organize expenditure on the scale necessary to make the great experiment which would prove my case . . . except in war conditions." [9]

I find it increasingly suggested that we should distinguish between Keynes's "personal opinions" and his "theory." I agree there is often a real point in the distinction between what Keynes says and what his theory says. The book contains many obiter dicta which do not fit into the skeleton of his theory, and indeed provide in some cases valid grounds for objection to it. But it has been my belief that the stagnation thesis constitutes the essential content of the theory, and that as we move away from the circumstances that thesis envisaged the difficulties for the determinancy of the theory are increased and its force as a formula for economic policy is decreased. I have, however, been skeptical of the stagnation thesis, and some of my reservations about Keynes's theory date back to that phase of the discussion.

[8] P. 31.
[9] July 29, 1940.

III

Keynes's main interest was in monetary theory and policy. The development of his thinking was directed toward "pushing monetary theory back toward becoming a theory of output as a whole." [10] His progress can be traced in the transition from $MV = PT$ to $I + C = Y$. There is the question in each case of distinguishing between the truism and the theory. In the traditional quantity theory (which Keynes endorsed without reservation in the *Tract*),[11] V and T were assumed constant, or independently determined, though in the later writings on the subject this is qualified by such statements as "normally," "except in transition periods," "apart from the business cycle." On these assumptions M affected only P (though some thought the connection often ran the other way), which was a complete demonstration that money was merely a *numéraire* and could be ignored in real analysis.

The main concern of business cycle theory, whether monetary or non-monetary, has been with fluctuations of income, output, and employment. In this sense, we had half a century and more of "macro-economics" before *The General Theory* appeared. But there have been formal difficulties with both sides of the quantity equation. In Keynes's *Treatise,* so far as the "fundamental equations" were concerned, the effects of monetary changes were registered exclusively in P. As he later said, the equations "were an instantaneous picture taken on the assumption of a given output." [12] Moreover, as his critics pointed out, they were identities, his excess of investment over saving (via the quantity of money and the interest rate), his windfall profit rise, and his price rise being the same thing, with no causal relationship disclosed, so far as the equations

10 *The General Theory,* Preface, p. vi.
11 P. 81: "This theory is fundamental. Its correspondence with fact is not open to question." But in the accompanying footnote he quotes with approval a statement by Pigou which seems to me to raise rather than settle the essential question: "The Quantity Theory is often defended and opposed as though it were a definite set of propositions that must be either true or false. But in fact the formulae employed in the exposition of that theory are merely devices for enabling us to bring together in an orderly way the principal causes by which the value of money is determined."
12 *The General Theory,* Preface, p. vii.

270 THE CRITICS OF KEYNESIAN ECONOMICS

were concerned.[13] There has been difficulty also in the business cycle literature with MV. V has often been treated as a constant (whatever the writer may have said about it in chapters outside his formal theory), or as reinforcing the effects of changes in money quantity. But there is also discussion of demand for money as a factor to be offset by control of the supply, and of the concept of the natural rate of interest as the equator of saving and investment. All these versions, I think, appear in the *Treatise,* though the last undoubtedly interested Keynes most and constitutes a main theme of the book. But the chief emphasis is on business deposits. Regarding income deposits, so crucial for his later theory, his statement in the *Treatise* is: "I incline to the opinion that the short-period fluctuations of V^1 (velocity of income deposits) are inconsiderable," which appears to mean that consumers' demand for money is not a determinant of prices or output (consumers spend what—or in proportion to what—they get), and contains no hint of the later marginal-propensity-to-consume analysis.[14]

In *The General Theory,* $MV = PT$ is replaced by $I + C = Y$, but one can readily see the old equation underneath. Y is PT. Investment and consumption are the components of income through which monetary changes register their effects. Though not in the equation, the quantity of money (together with

---

[13] I agree with Lawrence Klein's statement (*The Keynesian Revolution* [New York, 1947], p. 17), though it comes oddly from a mathematician, that there is more to the *Treatise* than the equations. In my own review (*Quarterly Journal of Economics,* August, 1931), I referred only briefly to them, though pointing out their truistic nature, and dealt chiefly with the responsiveness of investment and the price level to the interest rate (which seemed to me the core of the book), his monetary analysis, and my reasons for doubting the effectiveness of his central bank policy.

[14] *Treatise,* Ch. 15, p. 246. It is not possible to find a consistent monetary analysis in the *Treatise.* Sometimes he speaks of business deposits A as interacting with income deposits, as though it were merely the quantity of the former (in response to the central-bank-determined interest rate) that mattered; at other times the main emphasis is on business deposits B (a part of the financial circulation); at other times, and particularly in the statistical and historical chapters, it is on transfers between "cash deposits" and "savings deposits," a part of the analysis that always seemed to me particularly oversimplified and unrealistic; see my review above. In the "bear position" there is some anticipation of liquidity preference, but, as Keynes pointed out, they are by no means the same thing (*The General Theory,* p. 173). For an interesting and suggestive interpretation of the extent to which the *Treatise* foreshadowed *The General Theory* (as Keynes thought it did), see John Lintner, "The Theory of Money and Prices," *The New Economics,* pp. 515-526.

"liquidity preference") determines the interest rate, which (in relation to the expected profit rate—"the marginal efficiency of capital") determines the volume of investment. The demand for money is broken down into the three strands that had been implicit in the analysis since Marshall. Velocity becomes the multiplier, command-over-consumption-units becomes the propensity to consume, and the distinction between the decision to save and the decision to invest becomes liquidity preference. The identity equation $I + C = Y$ becomes the causal equation $I + C(Y) = Y$. It is the development of the analysis of demand for money which constitutes, I think, the chief innovation of *The General Theory*, and upon it, and the use Keynes makes of it, mainly turns the answer to the question whether he has succeeded in "pushing back the theory of money to becoming a theory of output as a whole." But a question hardly secondary is what has become in the new theory of P. In the *Treatise*, as I have said, T was constant; in the new theory it is P that has become constant, or neutral.

Having shown the development of Keynes's income equation out of the quantity equation, I must add a brief statement of the theory in his own terms. As he sums it up on page 29, "the essence of *The General Theory*" is that "the volume of employment in equilibrium depends on (i) the aggregate supply function, (ii) the propensity to consume, and (iii) the volume of investment." The supply function is the supply price of total output, measured in unit labor costs, assumed (up to full employment) to be constant or neutral. With the cost-price level thus stabilized, changes in effective demand are registered in output and employment. Of the two components of effective demand, the schedule of the relation of consumption to income is a stable function (which may, however, have a characteristic cyclical pattern) determined by the "psychological law" of the "marginal propensity to consume," which is that as income rises a part of the increment is saved. It follows that for every point on the schedule a multiplier can be computed. With consumption and the multiplier thus given, changes in investment (the "autonomous" factor), together with their multiplied effect, determine changes in the level of output and employment, which may settle at any point (up to full employment as the limiting case) determined by the quantity of effective demand. Thus, the lower the marginal propensity to consume, at a full-employment level of income, the greater will need to be the volume of investment if that level of income and employment is to be maintained. As a society grows richer, its marginal propensity to consume grows "weaker . . . but, owing to its accumulation of capital being already larger, the opportunities for further investment are less attractive." Therefore, the state must intervene, through monetary and fiscal policy, to compensate for the widening "gap between actual and potential production" and maintain a full employment level of effective demand.

IV

I have stated the theory baldly because that, I think, is the only way to get at its logic. After that has been done, the rigor of the assumptions may be relaxed, but this is a process of relaxing also the conclusions, and leads back to the questions I asked earlier about the validity of the theory as a picture of reality and a basis for policy.

The paradox of the book (and one of its chief weaknesses) is that while its central thesis is long run, its formal analysis is short run, not in the business cycle sense (to which Keynes devoted only a chapter of "Notes"), but, as Hicks pointed out, in the sense of Marshall's short-run equilibrium. It is in this sense a special rather than a general theory, and a theory more static than the classical theory it was intended to supplant. Moreover, as has been shown by various writers,[15] some of the more novel features of Keynes's interest and wage theory rest on special assumptions, and are less damaging to classical theory (on the appropriate "level of abstraction") than he supposed. In this sense, too, he falls short of presenting an acceptable general theory.

But much of the formal wage and interest theory seems to me secondary. Keynes's main concern was monetary, and it was the quantity equation, and particularly his long meditation over the Marshallian K (plus the impact upon him of the Great Depression), that led him to formulate his income equation and his income theory. Having done so, he worked out the interest theory that seemed to him appropriate, took over such

[15] E.g., Schumpeter, Hicks, Lange, Leontief, Tobin, Modigliani.

parts of traditional wage theory as seemed to fit and rejected those that seemed not to fit. His great contribution was in focusing attention upon income and in challenging on monetary grounds the assumption, implicit in classical economics, of a full employment level of income automatically sustained. But the important question to ask, I think, is not how much his theory differs in its formal logic from classical economics but how much it differs from business cycle theory, the relation of which to classical equilibrium theory had been becoming increasingly tenuous for at least half a century; and whether in attempting to push the analysis of economic fluctuations back into an abstract framework of equilibrium theory he has done economics a service or a disservice.

As I said earlier, the study of economic fluctuations had of course been concerned all along with "macro-economics." But the main emphasis had been placed on fluctuations in investment. To this Keynes adds little that is conceptually new, unless it is the emphasis on expectations, which comes oddly in a book that is otherwise not only static, with constant technique, but very short run. The emphasis on declining investment opportunities, though part of his central thesis, is certainly not new; it had made its appearance in each preceding major depression. As a practical problem it seems remote today, as it has in each previous period of renewed expansion.[16] Yet as a statement of a long-run tendency (wars apart) it has seemed to me not only plausible but desirable that new investment should become a decreasing part of total income in an advancing society, with qualitative technological change taking over more of the role of progress on the side of supply, and the benefits going increasingly to consumption on the side of demand. But Keynes himself did not discuss technology, and in any case the real seat of his pessimism and the core of his theory lie in his views about consumption. It is here, too, that his theory differs fundamentally from business cycle theory.

[16] The reader is doubtless familiar with the literature of the controversy over declining opportunities for investment. In addition to the references elsewhere in the paper, I should mention (among others) Terborgh, *The Bogey of Economic Maturity* (Chicago, 1945), and Wright, "The Future of Keynesian Economics," *American Economic Review,* June, 1945, and " 'The Great Guessing Game': Terborgh versus Hansen," *Review of Economic Statistics,* February, 1946.

V

Keynes's law of the propensity to consume is the important novel feature of his theory. It has been also the most controversial. It was the main question raised by my paper on "Deficit Spending" at our meeting in 1940,[17] by Kuznets' review of Hansen's *Fiscal Policy and Business Cycles* in 1942,[18] and (along with his attack on equilibrium economics generally) by Burns's recent papers on Keynesian economics.[19]

As a first statement, apart from the business cycle or other special circumstances, Keynes's "law" that as income rises consumption rises by less than unity is a plausible hypothesis; but it does not mean, necessarily, that consumption is the "passive" factor or that the consumption function is stable. These two assumptions—(1) that consumption is dependent on income and (2) that there is a "regular" or "stable" or "normal" relation between them, such that the consumption function can be derived as a given datum of the system and used as a basis of policy and prediction—constitute the essence of Keynesian economics. They bear a striking resemblance to the basic assumption of the quantity theory, that demand for money could be treated as a given factor, with the difference that, whereas that assumption was used to support the classical conclusion of full-employment equilibrium (apart from the business cycle), the new law of demand for money becomes the basis of the new equilibrium theory in which full employment is merely the limiting case. The whole structure rests upon the validity of the new law of the demand for money.

Historically, there seem to me to be ample grounds for doubting both the assumptions I have stated. They do not, for example, account for the effect of the rise of the automobile, a consumption good—or of new products generally—upon the growth of national income, where we have had a dynamic response of consumption and investment, each to the other. The application of an investment "multiplier" to consumption

17 *American Economic Review*, February, 1941; see my *Postwar Monetary Plans, op. cit.*, Ch. 9.

18 *Review of Economic Statistics*, February, 1942, pp. 31-36.

19 Arthur F. Burns, *Economic Research and the Keynesian Thinking of Our Times* (New York, 1946), and also his paper on "Keynesian Economics Once Again," *Review of Economic Statistics*, November, 1947, pp. 252-267.

as a passive, given factor in order to account for such changes seems wholly unrealistic. Nor would, I think, any "dynamizing" of Keynes's technique by mathematical methods get us much further. Keynes's proposition that autonomous changes in investment determine changes in income, and hence in consumption (according to the "law"), is probably no better than its opposite, that spontaneous changes in consumption determine changes in income, and in investment. The *interdependence* of consumption and investment, each responding to the other—and both responding (spontaneously rather than systematically) to changing ideas, methods, resources—seems to me to be the essence of economic progress. But it does not lend itself readily to equilibrium analysis, which is probably the reason why it has been the concern of the historians and the more imaginative kind of statisticians rather than of the pure theorists. As between Keynesian and classical economics, however, the latter provides, in many respects, a more realistic point of departure for a study of progress.

The rise of consumer durable goods has been the outstanding economic phenomenon of our times. From the standpoint both of long-run growth and of business cycle behavior it raises serious questions for Keynesian analysis. Between the two wars expenditures on such goods were fully as large as those on capital goods, and their fluctuations fully as great; nor can we make any clear generalization as to which played the greater role in initiating cyclical changes. As "outlets for saving" they played as large a role, and the same kind of role, as new investment; nor is there any more reason for applying a "multiplier" to the one kind of expenditure than to the other. They make the Keynesian statements about "oversaving," or "institutional factors which retard the growth of consumption," or consumption as the "passive" factor, seem much less realistic than they might otherwise.

Historically, however, the growth of consumer durable goods accounts only in part for the rise in real consumption. Kuznets' paper on "Capital Formation, 1879-1938," at the University of Pennsylvania Bicentennial Conference constitutes an important landmark in the modification of Keynesian theory.[20] He dem-

[20] *Studies in Economics and Industrial Relations* (Philadelphia, 1941), pp. 53-78.

onstrated that, while national income rose greatly during that period, standards of living rose correspondingly, and the great bulk of the increase in income went into consumption. Saving, as measured by real investment, remained a constant fraction of income, with an apparent moderate tendency in the twenties (on which he does not insist) for consumption to increase relative to income.[21] In England before the war, according to Colin Clark's data, saving had been a diminishing fraction of a growing national income for at least a generation.[22] Since Kuznets' paper, the "secular upward drift" of the consumption function, to which no reference is made in Keynes,[23] has become a standard part of the statement of the consumption function. Its practical effect has been to bring the plane of discussion (the possible "gap between actual and potential production") back pretty much to where it had been before Keynes wrote, by disposing of the more serious version of his law and the one which I think he himself believed—that consumption, as a society grew richer, became a diminishing fraction of income—and limiting the stagnation thesis to a discussion of declining opportunities for investment.

But while the "secular upward drift" is now regularly included in consumption function formulae, its implications for the analysis have not been sufficiently examined. One thing it means, I think, is the point mentioned earlier, the dynamic interaction of consumption and investment. No application of the growth of investment and a multiplier to the consumption existing at the beginning of Kuznets' period, on the assump-

[21] Had residential housing been counted as consumption rather than investment, the upward tendency of consumption would have been more marked.

[22] His figures on net investment as a percentage of national income show a decline from 12.2 per cent in 1907 to 8.1 per cent in 1924, 7.2 per cent in 1929, and 6.9 per cent in 1935. His conclusion was: "I believe the facts have destroyed the view up till now generally prevalent, that the rate of economic growth was primarily dependent upon the rate at which capital could be accumulated. The very rapid expansion at the present time [before the war] is taking place at a time of heavily diminishing capital accumulation. What is more remarkable, practically none of the capital which is being saved is being put into productive industry proper." *National Income and Outlay* (New York, 1938), p. 270.

[23] Hansen's *Fiscal Policy and Business Cycles* (New York, 1941), Ch. 11, p. 233, contains, so far as I know, his first reference to it. It is accompanied by a footnote referring to Kuznets' forthcoming data (the paper mentioned above); they were both present at the Pennsylvania Conference.

tion of passivity (in the way that was so commonly being done in the thirties) could ever account for the income-consumption relation at the end; and if instead we take a historical regression of the previous relation and project it forward, we are merely begging the question.

Another part of the explanation, without doubt, has been the cost reducing function of investment, with which, because it is too short run, Keynes's analysis does not deal. As I tried to show in an earlier paper, investment is significant, not primarily because of the money income and the employment provided by the capital-goods industries themselves, but because of the fact that by producing consumer goods in more efficient, and therefore cheaper, ways it releases consumer income for expenditure on other goods and services, and by increasing productivity per worker makes possible upward adjustments of income and increased voluntary leisure. This has been the heart of the productive process under the free-enterprise system. It points to the importance of price-wage-profits relationships which in the Keynesian system become submerged, and to the inadequacies in these directions of the Keynesian monetary and fiscal policies as the means of sustaining full employment in an advancing society.[24]

VI

Since the war Keynesian economics has undergone a number of significant shifts. Faced with a condition of inflation as alarming, and seemingly as intractable, as the deflation Keynes faced when he wrote his book, the stagnation thesis has receded into the background of the theory. This is mainly what is meant by distinguishing between Keynes's opinions and his theory. But, as I said earlier, the difficulties for the determinacy of the theory have been increased by the new conditions, and its applicability to policy has become less clear cut. One

[24] "Free Enterprise and Full Employment," in *Financing American Prosperity* (New York: Twentieth Century Fund, 1945), pp. 360-373; see also William Fellner, "The Technological Argument of the Stagnation Thesis," *Quarterly Journal of Economics,* August, 1941; and E. D. Domar, "The Prospect for Economic Growth," *American Economic Review,* March, 1947. This is a point I have emphasized in virtually all my papers on Keynesian economics since my review of the *Treatise, op. cit.,* pp. 554-555.

of the new questions is the relative importance of monetary and fiscal policies—control over the broad aggregates of the income equation—as against more specific (including direct control) policies. Is Beveridge's program for full employment,[25] and that of the six Oxford economists,[26] a logical following out of Keynesian theory (as they assume) or a contradiction of it? Keynes did not favor a planned or regimented economy (except in war), and regarded his theory as a defense against it. Another important set of questions relates to the cost-price effects of monetary expansion, which seemed secondary in deep depression when there were large unemployed resources. Another relates to the longer-run relations of costs, prices, profits, productivity which Keynes's analysis ignores, but which seem to me more important for stability and progress than the short-run monetary factors which his theory selects for emphasis.

Most interesting has been the postwar development of the consumption function. Keynes's book, despite his distrust of mathematics, has undoubtedly given a great impetus to the study of econometrics, and the consumption function in particular has given the mathematicians, whether Keynesian or non-Keynesian, an ideal concept for building models of national income and making forecasts. Thus far, the forecasts have been almost uniformly bad. Though I am quite incompetent to judge, my suspicion has been that the explanation is twofold: first the stagnation bias carried over from prewar Keynesian economics; second, the fact that in the depressed thirties the income-consumption relation (as well as investment) was abnormally low, reflecting consumers' insecurity and pessimistic expectations. In any event, it does seem significant that the chief error made in the forecasts has not been in the estimates of postwar investment but in the consumption function, the one element theoretically derivable from within the Keynesian system.

After the appearance of the "secular upward drift," the emphasis was on the assumed short-run stability of the consumption function. But postwar experience has cast doubt also on this. It seems now to be agreed among econometricians that

[25] Lord Beveridge, *Full Employment in a Free Society* (London, 1944).
[26] *The Economics of Full Employment* (Oxford: Oxford Institute of Statistics, 1944).

the "simple relation" between income and consumption, as Keynes stated it, is unstable. In searching for a more complex relation which may have some promise of greater stability, hypotheses have been introduced which contradict Keynes's own theory. For example, liquidity is now commonly accepted as a factor affecting consumption, whereas in Keynes's theory liquidity affected only investment. Such a change strikes at Keynes's whole structure of demand for money, with its elaborately worked out separation into the three distinct strands I discussed earlier. Instead of the simple relation between current income and current consumption on which Keynes built his theory, we are today working with various hypotheses, including saving out of past income, liquid assets, capital gains, the last highest income reached in a boom, expectations of future income, and other possible factors affecting the income-consumption relation. That expectation should be brought in to explain consumption, whereas with Keynes it affected only investment, is surely a major departure. But it seems unnecessary, and even misleading, to pick out any particular points of difference. The broad fact seems to me to be that we have nothing left of this basic concept of the Keynesian theory other than that consumption is an important component of income and deserves all the study we can give it. The same is of course true of investment, the other component of income. That this is not now being studied with equal intensity by the econometricians is doubtless due to the fact that the changes in it are not derivable from within the system and do not lend themselves as readily to mathematical manipulation.[27]

[27] Lawrence Klein has recognized that for a true equilibrium system both investment and consumption should be determinable from within the system, see "A Post-Mortem on Transition Predictions of National Product," *Journal of Political Economy*, August, 1946, pp. 302-303. He lists the relations we must know before we can make good forecasts: "A principal failure of the customary models is that they are not sufficiently detailed. There are too many variables which are classified as autonomous when they are actually induced . . . The surplus of autonomous variables results from a failure to discover all the appropriate relationships constituting the system. In addition to the consumption function, we should have the investment function, the inventory function, the housing function, the price-formation equations, etc." In *Econometrica*, April, 1947, he made his own forecast for the fiscal year 1947, and said that if he were wrong the reason would probably be his failure to take account of the further rise of prices. (Why should not prices be predictable from within the

Scarcely less significant among the postwar developments is the growing recognition of Keynes's underemphasis on the price aspect of monetary changes. As I said earlier, in deep depression this could be ignored, but the practical problem that confronts us, except in that unique condition, is that a volume of effective demand that is adequate for full employment appears to have cost-price effects which not only expand money income at the expense of real income but create a highly unstable economic situation. In other words, Keynes's stable equilibrium (even if we could concede it on other grounds) would seem not to include full employment as the limiting case, but something substantially short of that. This seems to me our most serious practical dilemma. It has both short- and long-run aspects. It presents a question whether we have to make a choice between allowing for a certain amount of slack (and fluctuation) in our use of resources, in a free-market system, or, if we insist on continuous full employment, recognizing the need for more specific controls. But this leads on to the question, not only of our scheme of values (political and social as well as economic), but also of the vitality of the system, whether in a more planned and controlled system we would not weaken the dynamic forces which promote growth and which might, with further study, be directed toward the achievement, not of stable equilibrium in any exact sense, but of a less unstable economy than we have had hitherto. Much, I think, could be accomplished through the further study of price-wage-profit practices and policies. As I said in an earlier paper, though these relations have long been a main concern of (classical) economic theory they have been overlaid in recent years by preoccupation with monetary and fiscal analysis, and the tendency has been to regard price-cost behavior as a kind of *force majeure* to be "offset" rather than corrected. It is surprising how little we know, and can agree upon, with regard to these relationships, and what course to steer in order to avoid merely (a) letting them take their course, (b) compensat-

---

system?) The actual price level was not significantly different from the one he chose to use; his estimate of investment was too high (though not seriously); but his forecast of national product was too low because he underestimated the consumption function.

ing for them by monetary and fiscal manipulation, or (c) subjecting them to direct control.[28]

Chapter 21, on "The Theory of Prices," is for me one of the high spots of *The General Theory*. One of Keynes's characteristics was that while he was as sharp as anyone could wish in seeing possible qualifications and objections to his theory, he never permitted them to interfere with his conclusions. Chapter 21 (in which occurs the passage on mathematical economics) is an excellent discussion of the reasons why before full employment is reached, monetary expansion affects prices and costs as well as output and employment. It is interesting that the chapter runs in terms of the quantity theory of money, which suggests again that his own theory is a recast version of the quantity theory.

If there is perfectly elastic supply so long as there is unemployment, and perfectly inelastic supply so soon as full employment is reached, and if effective demand changes in the same proportion as the quantity of money, the quantity theory of money can be enunciated as follows: "So long as there is unemployment, *employment* will change in the same proportion as the quantity of money; and when there is full employment, *prices* will change in the same proportion as the quantity of money." [29]

Inserting Keynes's new concept of demand for money, this is not a bad statement of his own theory. But he goes on to introduce five qualifications: effective demand will not change in exact proportion to the quantity of money; resources are not (a) homogeneous, and (b) interchangeable, so that their supply elasticities vary; the money wage-unit will tend to rise before full employment; the remuneration of the factors entering into marginal cost will not all change in the same proportion. I cannot reproduce the discussion here. It contains references to bottlenecks, collective bargaining, boom and depression psychology, and other factors. One would need nothing more than this chapter to explain not only the kind of dilemma that confronts us today, but the inflationary conditions

[28] See my statement on "The Employment Act of 1946" before the Joint Congressional Committee on the President's Economic Report, July 2, 1947, reprinted in my book, *Postwar Monetary Plans, op. cit.,* Appendix 1, p. 240.
[29] Pp. 295-296.

of 1936-37 on a comparatively low level of employment.[30] But so far as I can see, Keynes does nothing to resolve the dilemma, and this chapter has no place in either the logic of his theory or his policy prescription. It is on a par with similar qualifications of his fundamental equations in the *Treatise,* which he said did not "affect in any way the rigor or validity of our conclusions." [31] In distinguishing between what Keynes says and what his theory says, it is this kind of difference that seems to me significant. I can offer no explanation of it except that it is what equilibrium analysis seems to do to us. The key, I think, lies in what Keynes says about the rise of money wage rates before full employment (he might equally have said it of any of the other qualifications): "They have . . . a good deal of historical importance. But they do not readily lend themselves to theoretical generalizations." [32]

VII

I am afraid I am outrunning the space assigned to me, but some other topics must be briefly mentioned. Keynes's claim to having put monetary analysis into real terms depends largely on his assumption of constant prices; price and wage changes would affect the consumption function, liquidity preference, and investment. He overstated his point (with which I have long sympathized) that the interest rate does not determine saving. He was wrong in saying that investment does not affect the interest rate but is only affected by it, though we had a striking demonstration during the war of how far an easy money policy can go in freezing the rate at a low level. His point that there is a minimum rate below which liquidity preference will not permit the rate to be driven is valid but needs elaboration. So far as the time risk is concerned, our experience with a frozen pattern of rates demonstrated that

[30] One of the peculiarities of an inflationary volume of effective demand is, apparently, that the slope of the consumption function is no longer necessarily less than unity. For a discussion of this and other aspects of the behavior of the consumption function under war and postwar conditions, see a forthcoming paper, "Use of the Consumption Function in Economic Forecasting," by Robert V. Ross.

[31] See my review, *op. cit.,* pp. 556-558.

[32] *The General Theory,* p. 302.

rates on long-term governments would fall progressively toward the shortest. But so far as the income risk is concerned, an easy money policy widens the gaps in the interest-rate structure and suggests the need of other methods of attack. An all-out easy money policy, such as some Keynesians have favored, designed to saturate liquidity preference, carries both short-run inflationary dangers (as we are now recognizing) and longer-run dangers of undermining the whole fabric of the private capitalistic economy.[33]

Keynes's emphasis on wages as income and on the downward rigidity of money wage rates and his insistence that unemployment could not be cured by a policy directed primarily at cutting wage rates are among his most important contributions from a practical standpoint, whatever their theoretical merits on some abstract level. But as related to monetary business cycle analysis they have always seemed to me less novel than he supposed. Monetary policy had not run primarily in terms of wage cuts but in terms of compensating for wage and price rigidities. His conclusion, moreover, is subject to two large reservations: the effect of cost reduction on investment and its effect (which he recognized) on foreign trade. Moreover, from a purely economic standpoint, there is no reason why cost-reduction policies should not be combined with monetary policies of expansion, as Sweden and Australia did with notable success in the Great Depression.

One of the points most commonly agreed upon, even by Keynesians, is that the aggregates of the income equation must

[33] In my last talk with Keynes, a few months before his death, it was clear that he had got far away from his "euthanasia of the rentier." He complained that the easy money policy was being pushed too far, both in England and here, and emphasized interest as an element of income, and its basic importance in the structure and functioning of private capitalism. He was amused by my remark that it was time to write another book because the all-out easy money policy was being preached in his name, and replied that he did think he ought to keep one jump ahead.

How greatly Keynesian fiscal policy (and war finance) have complicated the problem of varying the interest rate as an instrument of cyclical control (because of the public debt), we are only now beginning to recognize fully.

For a discussion of these and other aspects of the interest-rate problem, see my paper, "Implications of Fiscal Policy for Monetary Policy and the Banking System," *American Economic Review*, March Sup., 1942, reprinted as Ch. 10 in my book, *Postwar Monetary Plans, op. cit.*; see also H. C. Wallich, "The Changing Significance of the Interest Rate," *American Economic Review*, December, 1946.

be broken down. A point that has especially interested me is the need of breaking down the saving function to differentiate between business and consumers' saving. I have never understood how Samuelson's findings could be offered in verification either of Keynes's propensity to consume or of Hansen's chapter to which they are appended. His analysis yielded the striking conclusion that consumers in the aggregate spent virtually all their increases in money income and that any additional saving accompanying rising income almost wholly took the form of business saving.[34] The implications of such a conclusion for economic policy are of course very great.

Finally, there is the now familiar point that the Keynesian saving-investment concept (like so much else in the analysis) has tended to submerge the study of the *process* of economic change. We have again, as in the *Treatise,* "instantaneous pictures." How saving and investment must always be equal in real terms, and yet how sometimes the equality denotes equilibrium and sometimes it does not, has caused endless confusion. We can make some headway by differentiating between a "normal" income-saving relation and a process of adjustment to the normal relation. But Keynes does not discuss process, and "normal" saving begs the questions I raised earlier. For a study of change the Swedish *ex ante, ex post,* or Robertson's time-period analysis seems much more realistic.[35]

VIII

As I look back over my paper, my appraisal of Keynesian economics seems to be mostly critical. The most difficult thing to appraise is one's own bias. No doubt my appraisal has in it some element of unfavorable reaction, both to Keynes's own

[34] See Alvin H. Hansen, *Fiscal Policy and Business Cycles, op. cit.,* Ch. 11, Appendix, pp. 250-260, by Paul A. Samuelson.

Samuelson's analysis is based on Kuznets' data (1919-35). For consumers he finds a marginal propensity to consume of 0.97, and for business enterprises a marginal propensity to save of 0.49. "This [business saving] accounts for most of the leakages incident upon net investment: as far as these data go, the leakages incident upon household savings are much smaller and possibly negative" (p. 257). In his conclusion (p. 260) he again emphasizes "the very sensitive relation of consumption to aggregate income payments."

[35] See, among recent discussions of this point, David M. Wright, *The Economics of Disturbance* (New York, 1947), Ch. II.

showmanship and his tendency to oversimplify and overstate his case, and to the sheer mass and exuberance of the claims made by his followers in his behalf. I admit all this has been working on me for a long time. Economic instability is equaled only by the instability of economists; what we need most, and often seem to have little of, is perspective. While I have no fondness for prediction, I do believe that the wave of enthusiasm for the "new economics" will, in the longer perspective, seem to us extravagant. And perhaps it will be only then that we shall be able to appraise objectively Keynes's contribution.

Beyond question it was very great. No one in our time has shaken up economists as much or been as influential in bringing economic analysis to bear on public policy. What he has given us, in particular, is a much stronger sense than we had before of the need for consumption analysis. It was the combination of the man and the times that did it. But I do have to insist again that it was policy, in Keynes's case, that led to theory, and that the weakness (as well as the strength of the impression made) lies in the overgeneralization. What we shall probably find ourselves doing is bringing back the things he temporarily submerged, the study of the processes of short- and long-run change, the emphasis on productivity, and on price-cost-profit relationships. If the conditions to which his theory was mainly directed should reappear, we shall probably find ourselves swept far beyond the kinds of remedies he favored, and forced into things he thought his theory and policies would avoid. But if we can maintain reasonable stability and, by the study of forces and relationships he largely ignored, continue to promote growth, his policies should play an effective role in a more rounded economic policy. I have sympathized all along with the idea of a cyclically unbalanced budget and with tax policies designed to promote stability and growth. But these, for Keynesians, at least before the war, were relatively mild objectives. Moreover, these are not exclusively Keynesian policies, but have been quite as popular with economists in Sweden, for example (where Keynesian economics has never really taken hold), as anywhere else.

What I find increasingly said, as the stagnation thesis recedes into the background, and the postwar questions about the consumption function, the price effects, and the like cast further doubts upon the theory as Keynes stated it, is that (and here the analogy with the quantity equation is striking) he has arranged the elements affecting the income equation in a useful form. This, I think, is true, with all the qualifications I have made. Undoubtedly, his formulation has greatly intensified the study of national income and its composition, though it is interesting that, as I indicated earlier, men like Kuznets and Colin Clark, who have pioneered such studies, dissented from his theory.

What it comes down to is that Keynes's analysis would appeal to me more if he had not claimed too much for it. As with his predecessors, it is the pretension to universality, and the equilibrium technique, that offend me, with the further point that in his case the defect seems to me worse. There is a legitimate and important role in economics for partial equilibrium analysis but the analogy with it of the Keynesian type of total equilibrium analysis seems to me most imperfect, because in the nature of the case the "other things equal" condition is invalid. Consumption, investment, total income interact, and they comprise all the "other things." Until, at least, the econometricians make more headway in deriving them (and their parts) from "within the system," this will be the nature of my skepticism.

XV

L. ALBERT HAHN, born at Frankfort-am-Main in 1889, is a German banker and economist whose theories anticipated those of J. M. Keynes. He had abandoned these theories before the *General Theory* was published, and has himself declared that: "All that is wrong and exaggerated in Keynes I said much earlier and more clearly." His books include *Geld und Kredit,* 1924 (his pre-Keynes "Keynesian" volume); *The Economics of Illusion,* 1949, a collection of essays and articles analyzing the Keynesian fallacies; and *Common Sense Economics,* 1956, a constructive exposition of the economic process on neo-classical as opposed to Keynesian lines.

The following article is Chapter 16 from *The Economics of Illusion,* published by the Squier Publishing Company and distributed by the New York Institute of Finance.

CONTINENTAL EUROPEAN PRE-KEYNESIANISM

L. ALBERT HAHN

In contrast to most of his followers, Keynes was well aware that his ideas were not entirely original. Every age has brought forth a crop of books on "easy money," having in common the thesis that economic disturbances, especially unemployment, are caused largely by monetary maladjustments and can be corrected by monetary measures. Keynes himself points out in his *General Theory* the merits of the Mercantilists.

When a young man I read with great interest a book called *The Gold Craze*,[1] written by an American living in Germany, which anticipated the arguments in favor of a domestic easy-money policy and of external devaluation. It was considered the product of a crank and went more or less unnoticed by economists.

Another precursor of Keynes was the "unduly neglected prophet, Silvio Gesell," [2] the proponent of *Schwundgeld* (vanishing money). Gesell's book, *Die Verstaatlichung des Geldes* (1891), was well known in continental Europe, especially in Switzerland. But despite wide propaganda by clubs formed to spread his theories, it was not taken seriously either. The proposition that depressions could be postponed indefinitely by keeping money rolling through fear of its depreciation rather than by correcting maladjustments seemed too absurd.

Keynes could have discovered an even closer spiritual relative in his contemporary, Gottfried Feder, who promised full employment through *Breaking the Slavery of Interest*.[3] The Nazis, before they came to power, used his theories in their campaign against democracy and the free enterprise system, but afterwards threw him out of his high office, recognizing that, if put into practice, his theories would immediately ruin the Reich's currency and credit.

Furthermore, my own *Volkswirtschaftliche Theorie des Bankkredits,* containing essential parts of Keynes' ideas, appeared as long ago as 1920. Influenced by it, a whole crop of easy-money books sprouted on the Continent. However, the counterarguments advanced during the next decade [4] were so convincing that in my third edition I modified my theory in essential respects.

As I think it rather important to show that the arguments against my theory apply also to Keynes', I have tried to demonstrate that the basic ideas of my *Volkswirtschaftliche Theorie des Bankkredits* were in substance, if not in form, very similar to those of his *General Theory*. To this end I have summarized what I consider essential and common to the two

[1] W. Lincoln Hausmann, *Der Goldwahn*, Berlin, 1905.
[2] Keynes, *General Theory*, p. 353.
[3] *Das Manifest zur Brechung der Zinsknecktschaft des Geldes,* 1932.
[4] This literature was reviewed in the preface to the third edition, 1930.

theories, supplementing each statement by quotations of some characteristic passages from the two books. Many other passages that show similarities can, incidentally, be found in the two books.

The Consumption Deficit

1. Employment and production are dependent upon demand, but demand is not automatically created by production or employment. A consumption deficit threatens when employment increases, because part of the larger income is saved (Keynes' "psychological law").

Hahn, p. 148:

The smaller consumption has its origin in the psychological attitude of the member of the economy: a worker, an industrialist, a business man is not inclined to spend more just because he earns more. The conservatism inherent in all his social activities, and above all, in his living standard, keeps his consumption constant within certain limits. A man does not consume more simply because he produces more. He does not, to be sure, forego remuneration for his activity but he demands it in another form, namely, in the form of means for future spending. The desire for consumer goods to raise the current living standard is replaced by the desire for means of hoarding and saving to ensure the future living standard. As soon as their wants are covered to a certain extent, people begin to feel, so to speak, mercantilistic rather than physiocratic.

Keynes, p. 97:

But, apart from short-period *changes* in the level of income, it is also obvious that a higher absolute level of income will tend, as a rule, to widen the gap between income and consumption. For the satisfaction of the immediate primary needs of a man and his family is usually a stronger motive than the motives towards accumulation, which only acquire effective sway when a margin of comfort has been attained. These reasons will lead, as a rule, to a greater *proportion* of income being saved as real income increases. But whether or not a greater proportion is saved, we take it as a fundamental psychological rule of any modern community that, when its real income is increased, it will not increase its consumption by an equal *absolute* amount, so that a greater absolute amount must be saved, unless a large and unusual change is occurring at the same time in other factors.

p. 98:

This simple principle leads, it will be seen, to the same conclusion as before, namely, that employment can only increase *pari passu* with an increase in investment; unless, indeed, there is a change in the propensity to consume.

2. An increase in income leads to an absolute increase not only in saving but also in the proportion of the income saved, i.e., in the saving-income ratio (Keynes' "psychological law" in its stronger form).

Hahn, pp. 153-54:

Credit expansion accelerates as well as increases the building up of savings accounts. . . . Credit expansion not only builds bigger savings accounts but builds them faster.

Keynes, p. 127:

. . . the marginal propensity to consume falls off steadily as we approach full employment.

THE INVESTMENT GAP

1. The consumption deficit can be harmful because the purchasing power withdrawn by saving does not necessarily come into the hands of entrepreneurs seeking funds to invest.

Hahn, p. 147:

The argument that every production leads automatically to a corresponding consumption appears incorrect if the producers of consumer goods save their purchasing power and if the resulting purchasing power deficit is not always automatically made up by the granting of new credits by banks.

If, concerning the reasons for depressions and crises, we return to Malthus' ideas, we see that the stagnation on the market for goods that occurs in the course of the boom phase of a business cycle is due to the fact that the purchasing power of working individuals, which normally comes back to the entrepreneur in the form of demand, no longer finds its way back to him. Checking accounts are transformed into savings accounts, are "consolidated," and no longer cause demand on the markets for goods.

Keynes, p. 165:

But the notion that the rate of interest is the balancing factor which brings the demand for saving in the shape of new investment forthcoming at a given rate of interest into equality with the supply of saving which results at that rate of interest from the community's psychological propensity to save, breaks down as soon as we perceive that it is impossible to deduce the rate of interest merely from a knowledge of these two factors.

2. Certain preclassicists, especially Malthus, deserve praise because they saw much better than Ricardo and other classicists that savings can interrupt the flow of demand.

Hahn, p. 147, note 138:

It is astonishing how clearly Malthus recognized these interrelations. His opponents argued that every saving automatically increases the demand for producer goods: against them Malthus asserted that their chief error lay in the assumption that accumulation automatically creates demand (*Principles of Political Economy*, Ch. 7, 3d par.). The same holds true today for those who, with the prevailing opinion, assume an absolute dependence of investment on saving.

Keynes, p. 362:

. . . in the later phase of Malthus the notion of the insufficiency of effective demand takes a definite place as a scientific explanation of unemployment.

p. 364:

. . . Ricardo, however, was stone-deaf to what Malthus was saying.

INTEREST AND LIQUIDITY

1. Savings are not automatically absorbed by investments because money is essential also as a means of liquidity. Interest must therefore be considered as the price for acquiring and the compensation for parting with liquidity. As lending money entails risks, interest can also be considered as a compensation for taking risks.

In discussing interest and liquidity, Keynes' argument is phrased almost exactly like mine, except that he attributes the supply of credit to the liquidity preference of individuals, whereas I attribute it to the liquidity preference of banks, for the simple reason that banks are the marginal lenders in an economy.

Hahn, p. 102:

If the amount of the credit advanced by banks is dependent on their individual liquidity, interest, i.e., the price that has to be paid for the credit, is merely the reward for the loss of liquidity caused by the granting of the credit. From the viewpoint of the bank, interest is the reward for running the risk.

Keynes, pp. 166-67:

It should be obvious that the rate of interest cannot be a return to saving or waiting as such. For if a man hoards his savings in cash, he earns no interest, though he saves just as much as before. On the contrary, the mere definition of the rate of interest tells us in so many words that the rate of interest is the reward for parting with liquidity for a specified period. For the rate of interest is, in itself, nothing more than the inverse proportion between a sum of money and what can be obtained for parting with control over the money in exchange for a debt for a stated period of time.

p. 182:

The mistake originates from regarding interest as the reward for waiting as such, instead of as the reward for not-hoarding; just as the rates of return on loans or investments involving different degrees of risk, are quite properly regarded as the reward, not of waiting as such, but of running the risk. There is, in truth, no sharp line between these and the so-called "pure" rate of interest, all of them being the reward for running the risk of uncertainty of one kind or another. Only in the event of money being used solely for transactions and never as a store of value, would a different theory become appropriate.

2. Liquidity requirements are a highly subjective matter, depending upon confidence and speculation.

Hahn, pp. 59-60:

. . . the means of banks are determined by the latter's liquidity. The creation of claims against a bank leads in fact only to the one important consequence that its balance sheet is lengthened and its liquidity impaired.

However, the actual state of liquidity or non-liquidity is merely a center around which the considerations of the individual bank manager oscillate. For opinions about liquidity are in highest degree subjective. With more or less strong confidence in the future, a higher or lower degree of liquidity will be deemed adequate. The supply of credit offered by banks, which, as shown above, constitutes fundamentally a supply of confidence, depends upon the strength of the prevailing confidence.

Keynes, pp. 196-97:

In normal circumstances the amount of money required to satisfy the transactions-motive and the precautionary-motive is mainly a resultant of the general activity of the economic system and of the level of money-income. But it is by playing on the speculative-motive that monetary management (or, in the absence of management, chance changes in the quantity of money) is brought to bear on the economic system.

p. 148:

The state of long-term expectation, upon which our decisions are based, does not solely depend, therefore, on the most probable forecast we can make. It also depends on the *confidence* with which we make this forecast—on how highly we rate the likelihood of our best forecast turning out quite wrong.

3. Interest rates are in large degree determined conventionally.

Hahn, p. 104:

The owners of checking and deposit accounts owe their income to historical chance rather than economic necessity. Unlike every other payment in economic life, payment of interest does not serve to stimulate supply. For the owners of checking and deposit accounts would—as the example of England teaches—leave their funds, which they need as a means of payment, in banks even if interest were not paid.

Keynes, p. 203:

It might be more accurate, perhaps, to say that the rate of interest is a highly conventional, rather than a highly psychological phenomenon.

4. The liquidity of even long-term investments can be improved by creating what I have called "indirect liquidity."

Hahn, pp. 94, 95, 96:

. . . a special technique of credit granting was gradually developed with the aim of lessening the dangers of illiquidity inherent in investments. It makes investments, so to speak, artificially liquid by granting them what we would like to call an "indirect liquidity."
. . . The illiquidity of the investment disappears as soon as the assets of the bank need no longer be turned into cash by withdrawal but can be liquidated by sale.

The chief example of such an indirectly liquid investment is the ordinary commercial bill. . . . Other examples are all transactions that lead to the creation of stocks and bonds.

Keynes, pp. 150-51:

Decisions to invest in private business of the old-fashioned type were, however, decisions largely irrevocable, not only for the community as a whole, but also for the individual. With the separation between ownership and management which prevails today and with the development of organized investment markets, a new factor of great importance has entered in, which sometimes facilitates investment but sometimes adds greatly to the instability of the system.

p. 153:

Investments which are "fixed" for the community are thus made "liquid" for the individual.

Interest and Employment

1. If lack of investment—caused by interest rates too high to guarantee that investments will absorb savings—makes for a deficiency of effective demand, and thereby unemployment, a reduction in interest rates must bring about employment. This is contrary to the classicists' view; they thought that a reduction in interest rates leads at best to inflation.

Hahn, p. 132:

Reducing interest rates . . . causes, as will be shown, also increase of production. Thus the argument of the quantity theorists must be wrong; namely, that the lower interest rates achieved by increasing the quantity of money could never raise industrial employment, because more goods could not be bought as prices would be higher.

Keynes, p. 292:

If we reflect on what we are being taught and try to rationalise it, in the simpler discussions it seems that the elasticity of supply must have become zero and demand proportional to the quantity of money.

Hahn, pp. 140-41:

. . . the opinion of the quantity theorists, shared by nearly all interest, credit, and capital theorists, that money and credit expansion do not increase production, is not only inexact but entirely wrong. By altering distribution, every expansion of credit increases the quantity of goods. Credit creates goods out of the nothingness in which they would have remained unproduced.

p. 149, note 142:

Herein lies a further reason why the quantity theory is to be considered merely a quite rough solution of the problem of the relation between the quantity of money and the prices of goods, and why the banking theory, which assumed the automatic elimination of additional and superfluous money, contained a correct kernel. . . . It shows too the invalidity of the assumption that the level of incomes determines the level of prices. It would be much more correct to say that the level of expenditures is the determinant.

Keynes, p. 375:

. . . the extent of effective saving is necessarily determined by the scale of investment and . . . the scale of investment is promoted by a *low* rate of interest, provided that we do not attempt to stimulate it in this way beyond the point which corresponds to full employment. Thus it is to our best advantage to reduce the rate of interest to that point relatively to the schedule of the marginal efficiency of capital at which there is full employment.

2. The reason a reduction in interest rates must bring about employment is that it alters the distribution of income in favor of entrepreneurs, enabling them to use additional labor profitably despite its diminishing marginal productivity. The change in the income distribution takes place at the cost of the rentier class.

According to Keynes, the worker too bears a part of the cost, because he can buy less with his wages when prices rise following the credit expansion that takes place after interest rates are reduced. This argument is, to my mind, unrealistic.

Hahn, p. 137:

As shown above, the expansion of credit has the consequence that through competition of enterprises, expanded in the wake of interest reductions, wages begin to rise. . . .

To those who have been unwilling to work . . . the value of the wage now appears higher than the value of leisure. They change from "marginal non-workers" to "marginal workers" because the fundamental facts of their valuations have changed. The remuneration offered for work has become greater. And this is really the case and does not depend merely upon a kind of self-deception on the part of the worker due to the nominal increase in wages. To be sure, the increase in labor's earnings causes the prices of consumer goods to rise because of the larger demand. Nevertheless, the increase in wages is not only nominal but real; for the prices of goods always tend, because of the competition of entrepreneurs, to equal the costs. But as the latter have risen to compensate only for the additional outlays for wages, not for capital, the prices of goods have risen only to this degree, that is, less than wages. There thus remains a real increase in the remuneration paid labor which appears the more important for economic calculation the more one considers that compensation of other participants, although nominally still the same, has been devaluated through the rise in the prices of goods.

Keynes, p. 290:

Since that part of his profit which the entrepreneur has to hand on to the rentier is fixed in terms of money, rising prices, even though unaccompanied by any change in output, will redistribute incomes to the advantage of the entrepreneur and to the disadvantage of the rentier. . . .

p. 8:

. . . The supply of labor is not a function of real wages.

p. 284:

. . . if the classical assumption does not hold good, it will be possible to increase employment by increasing expenditure in terms of money until real wages have fallen to equality with the marginal disutility of labor, at which point there will, by definition, be full employment.

3. The limit to increasing employment by reducing interest rates is reached when the labor supply cannot be augmented by further wage increases.

Hahn, p. 145:

Credit expansion as a means of raising production and consumption, and thereby the well-being of the nation, is effective . . . up to the point where new credit is no longer able to induce new labor forces to enter production, when through wage increases the last reserves have been tapped.

Keynes, p. 289:

Consequently, as effective demand increases, employment increases, though at a real wage equal to or less than the existing one, until a point comes at which there is no surplus of labour available at the then existing real wage; *i.e.* no more men (or hours of labour) available unless money-wages rise (from this point onwards) *faster* than prices. The next problem is to consider what will happen if, when this point has been reached, expenditure still continues to increase.

Up to this point the decreasing return from applying more labour to a given capital equipment has been offset by the acquiescence of labour in a diminishing real wage. But after this point a unit of labour would require the inducement of the equivalent of an increased quantity of product, whereas the yield from applying a further unit would be a diminished quantity of product.

4. The net effect of an increase in effective demand following an expansion of credit is in general twofold: on prices, on the one hand; on production, on the other. For the unutilized reserves of workers give elasticity to modern economy

Hahn, pp. 135-36:

. . . in the modern economy . . . the increase in the demand for goods and labor on the part of enterprises whose purchasing power has been augmented by an expansion in credit leads to a rise not only in prices but also in production, to prosperity. . . . One reason is the enormous progress in the techniques of production, especially in the greater use of machines. . . . The other reason is that the modern economy, as a result of this progress in techniques, possesses—in the persons of rentiers, women, and workers willing to work overtime—a tremendous reserve of unoccupied, half occupied, and workers who can be induced to work harder. From this labor reserve the relatively small amount of labor necessary to step up production can easily be won. The two factors together cause the phenomenon that can best be called the "elasticity" of the modern economy.

Keynes, p. 285:

Effective demand spends itself, partly in affecting output and partly in affecting price, according to this law.

p. 296:

. . . and the increase in effective demand will, generally speaking, spend itself partly in increasing the quantity of employment and partly in raising the level of prices. Thus instead of constant prices in conditions of unemployment, and of prices rising in proportion to the quantity of money in conditions of full employment, we have in fact a condition of prices rising gradually as employment increases.

General Recommendations to Combat Unemployment

1. Technological progress tends to reduce prices directly or through the pressure it exerts on wages through labor-saving machinery. To counteract these undesirable by-effects of technological progress, credit expansion is recommended.

Hahn, pp. 139-40:

In the modern economy, as far as credit is not expanded, a certain number of workers are thrown out of work each year because labor-saving methods of production are constantly being adopted. Furthermore, the urban population is still growing today in modern industrial countries. As the possibilities for work, as such, do not grow as fast as the population, a certain part of the addition to the population becomes unemployed. The excess supply of labor thus created tends to press on wages and thereby also on the prices of goods until, on the one hand, the supply of labor contracts through the elimination of those for whom the lower wages no longer seem an equivalent for leisure; in other words, until "marginal workers" become "marginal non-workers." . . . Here credit expansion steps in as a corrective and an eminently social factor. It increases the demand for labor, thereby preventing the decline of wages and the prices of goods, and putting to work new strata of workers who, with static credit, would have to remain outside the production process. It thus prevents the raising of the capitalist's share that would otherwise follow from falling prices.

Keynes, p. 271:

In the long period, on the other hand, we are still left with the choice between a policy of allowing prices to fall slowly with the progress of technique and equipment whilst keeping wages stable, or of allowing wages to rise slowly whilst keeping prices stable. On the whole my preference is for the latter alternative, on account of the fact that it is easier with an expectation of higher wages in future to keep the actual level of employment within a given range of full employment than with an expectation of lower wages in future, and on account also of the social advantages of gradually diminishing the burden of debt, the greater ease of adjustment from decaying to growing industries, and the psychological encouragement likely to be felt from a moderate tendency for money-wages to increase.

2. Employment can be increased either by lowering wages or by expanding credit. In the general case the latter is to be preferred. My statement was, however, much more cautious than Keynes'.

Hahn, p. 141:

Every expansion of credit increases the quantity of goods. But whether for this reason an expansion of credit is always a boon for a country is not decided thereby. Moreover, whether expropriation of money owners and rentiers is not too high a price for a larger total output can be decided only from certain non-economic viewpoints. The problem, seemingly theoretical, is in reality political.

Keynes, p. 268:

Having regard to human nature and our institutions, it can only be a foolish person who would prefer a flexible wage policy to a flexible money policy, unless he can point to advantages from the former which are not obtainable from the latter.

RECOMMENDATIONS TO COMBAT CYCLICAL DEPRESSIONS: AN EASY-MONEY POLICY AND GOVERNMENT SPENDING

1. As booms end when demand becomes deficient, new demand must be created. This can be done by making new in-

vestments profitable by lowering interest rates, i.e., through an easy-money policy.

Interest rates should be reduced at the top of the boom instead of raised in the traditional way long before the peak; by such a method the boom can be protracted indefinitely.

This is the statement I regret most and the one that aroused most opposition when my book was published.

Hahn, p. 150:

Since production is hindered by the stagnation of consumption . . . is it possible to induce the entrepreneur to continue production even when he cannot sell goods, so that he produces for stock rather than for consumption?

Such possibilities exist, at least in theory. One possibility is to grant larger and, above all, cheaper credit, the moment consumption begins to stagnate, so that entrepreneurs will be spurred to continue producing.

Keynes, p. 164:

. . . we are still entitled to return to the latter [i.e., the interest rate] as exercising, at any rate, in normal circumstances, a great, though not a decisive, influence on the rate of investment. Only experience, however, can show how far management of the rate of interest is capable of continuously stimulating the appropriate volume of investment.

p. 322:

Thus the remedy for the boom is not a higher rate of interest but a lower rate of interest! For that may enable the so-called boom to last. The right remedy for the trade cycle is not to be found in abolishing booms and thus keeping us permanently in a semi-slump: but in abolishing slumps and thus keeping us permanently in a quasi-boom.

2. If, despite lower interest rates, demand is not created, the government must and can replace private demand by public spending.

Hahn, p. 151:

The other way to continue production in an economy and have its results stored, despite lack of consumption, is to have the results of production that are ready for consumption taken over by a large scale buyer. This way, however, is open only if the buyer, who would of course need immense amounts of credit, enjoys the privilege of not having to pay interest. Otherwise he would be unable to "hold" the goods.

Such a privileged debtor exists in every economy in the person of the government. For although the state has to pay interest on its loans, it can transfer the burden to the taxpayer, so that it practically enjoys credit without charge; and, in any case, does not have to calculate the interest burden as a cost in the way an "economic" subject must.

Hahn, p. 136, note 125:

Had houses, means of transportation, and labor-saving machinery been built, with the same methods of financing, instead of war materials, the golden age would have dawned through the ensuing abundant satisfaction of every demand.

Keynes, p. 164:

I expect to see the State, which is in a position to calculate the marginal efficiency of capital-goods on long views and on the basis of the general social advantage, taking an ever greater responsibility for directly organising investment; since it seems likely that the fluctuations in the market estimation of the marginal efficiency of different types of capital, calculated on the principles I have described above, will be too great to be offset by any practicable changes in the rate of interest.

RECEPTION AND INFLUENCE OF MY BOOK IN CONTINENTAL EUROPE

The reader may not feel that Keynes' and my theories coincide as closely as I feel they do. To me, the similarities evident in the above quotations are amazing, especially in view of the fact that my book was written sixteen years before Keynes', in another tongue, in another economic environment, and before the demand supply-curve language was as entrenched as it is today. One is struck by the similarity of the gist of the two books. Consider, for example, that the *leitmotif* of Keynesianism—that it is better to produce nonsense than nothing—which led him to praise pyramid-building; [5] can be found in my book where it is expressed as follows: "The time that passes without

---

[5] Keynes, *op. cit.*, p. 131.

production and is thus unused can never be recouped," and "The saying 'time is money' is applicable also to the wealth of nations." [6]

Incidentally I have never been able to understand why Keynes did not quote my work in his *General Theory* although there is no doubt he knew it, for he quotes me in the German translation of his *Treatise on Money* [7] when he refers to the approach of German scholars to the savings-investment problem.

As mentioned above, my theories were widely discussed in business and academic circles. A second edition of my *Volkswirtschaftliche Theorie des Bankkredits* had to be published in 1924, and a third in 1930. As in the case of Keynes' *General Theory*, opinions about my book went to extremes of approval and disapproval. Some critics, especially older men, dubbed it the height of scientific nonsense, cynicism, and carelessness; in short, just a bluff. The great economist and statistician Bortkiewicz, for example, was very hostile. Others, especially younger students, looked upon it as an entirely new discovery of immense theoretical and economic-political importance. To my followers—for instance to Hans Honegger, author of *Der schöpferische Kredit,* 1929—there seemed no limit to what credit and monetary expansion could achieve. When their publications came to my notice, I wrote, paraphrasing the exclamation from Schiller's *Wallenstein* that I quoted in an early chapter of this book: "God defend me from my friends; from my enemies, I can defend myself!" Compared with what some of Keynes' followers in this country advocate, however, these recommendations seem highly conservative and orthodox.

I am now of the opinion that my ideas, as expressed in the first and second editions of my book—and consequently also the corresponding ideas of Keynes—are bad economic theory, leading to fatal economic policy, mainly for the reasons developed in the preceding chapters in this book. To a certain degree I had already taken them into account in my third edition.

The development of money and credit theory on the Continent during the 'thirties might be summarized as follows:

[6] Hahn, *Volkswirtschaftliche Theorie des Bankkredits,* p. 148.
[7] Munich and Leipzig, 1932, p. 140, note 2.

Theory at first turned away from the classical concept of a more or less inelastic economy to a concept that emphasized strongly the possibility of stimulating production and avoiding depression by monetary manipulations. The pendulum had swung back to an almost preclassic Mercantilistic concept. However, after a short time the exaggerations were recognized and the pendulum swung back, though only part way. A sort of synthesis of classical and pre- and post-classical theory was reached: a synthesis that avoided the undeniable inadequacies of classical theories as well as the mistakes of Mercantilist, free-money, vanishing-money, easy-money theorists and monetary illusionists in general.

XVI

Ludwig von Mises was born in Lemberg, in what was then Austria-Hungary, in 1881. He studied law and economics, the latter partly under the great Böhm-Bawerk, at the University of Vienna, and in 1906 that university conferred upon him the degree of Doctor of Law and Social Sciences. He was professor of economics at the University of Vienna from 1913 to 1938, and during part of the same period, from 1926 to 1938, he was acting vice-president of the Austrian Institute of Business Cycle Research in Vienna. When Hitler came into power in Germany, Mises foresaw that he would eventually take over and dominate Austria, and in 1934 he left for Geneva, Switzerland, to become professor of international economic relations at the Graduate Institute of International Studies there. He came to the United States in 1940 and was naturalized in 1946. He was visiting professor at the National University of Mexico in 1942 and has been visiting professor of economics at New York University since 1946.

His earlier volumes were originally published in German and later translated, but his later volumes were written in English. His most important works are: *The Theory of Money and Credit* (Munich, 1912, 1924; London, 1934; New Haven, 1953); *Socialism: An Economic and Sociological Analysis* (Jena, 1922, 1932; London, 1936; New Haven, 1951); and *Human Action* (Geneva, 1940; revised American edition, New Haven, 1949). Mises' book on *Money and Credit* has been a standard text for years; his analysis of Socialism stands unrivaled, except for Böhm-Bawerk's work, as the most devastating that has ever appeared; and his *Human Action* is not only a profound analysis of the economic process, but the most uncompromising and the most rigorously reasoned statement in existence of the case for capitalism.

The first of the two articles that follow appeared in *Plain Talk* of March, 1948, and is reprinted here by permission of Isaac Don Levine, editor of *Plain Talk*. The second appeared in *The Freeman* of October 30, 1950. They have been published as chapters in Dr. Mises' book, *Planning for Freedom*, 1952.

STONES INTO BREAD, THE KEYNESIAN MIRACLE

LUDWIG VON MISES

I

The stock-in-trade of all Socialist authors is the idea that there is potential plenty and that the subsitution of socialism for capitalism would make it possible to give to everybody "according to his needs." Other authors want to bring about this paradise by a reform of the monetary and credit system. As they see it, all that is lacking is more money and credit. They consider that the rate of interest is a phenomenon artificially created by the man-made scarcity of the "means of payment." In hundreds, even thousands, of books and pamphlets they passionately blame the "orthodox" economists for their reluctance to admit that inflationist and expansionist doctrines are sound. All evils, they repeat again and again, are caused by the erroneous teachings of the "dismal science" of economics and the "credit monopoly" of the bankers and usurers. To unchain money from the fetters of "restrictionism," to create free money (*Freigeld*, in the terminology of Silvio Gesell) and to grant cheap or even gratuitous credit, is the main plank in their political platform.

Such ideas appeal to the uninformed masses. And they are very popular with governments committed to a policy of increasing the quantity both of money in circulation and of deposits subject to check. However, the inflationist governments and parties have not been ready to admit openly their endorsement of the tenets of the inflationists. While most countries embarked upon inflation and on a policy of easy money, the literary champions of inflationism were still spurned as "monetary cranks." Their doctrines were not taught at the universities.

John Maynard Keynes, late economic adviser to the British Government, is the new prophet of inflationism. The "Keynesian Revolution" consisted in the fact that he openly espoused the doctrines of Silvio Gesell. As the foremost of the British Gesellians, Lord Keynes adopted also the peculiar messianic jargon of inflationist literature and introduced it into official documents. Credit expansion, says the *Paper of the British Experts* of April 8, 1943, performs the "miracle . . . of turning a stone into bread." The author of this document was, of course, Keynes. Great Britain has indeed traveled a long way to this statement from Hume's and Mill's views on miracles.

II

Keynes entered the political scene in 1920 with his book, *The Economic Consequences of the Peace*. He tried to prove that the sums demanded for reparations were far in excess of what Germany could afford to pay and to "transfer." The success of the book was overwhelming. The propaganda machine of the German nationalists, well-entrenched in every country, was busily representing Keynes as the world's most eminent economist and Great Britain's wisest statesman.

Yet it would be a mistake to blame Keynes for the suicidal foreign policy that Great Britain followed in the interwar period. Other forces, especially the adoption of the Marxian doctrine of imperialism and "capitalist warmongering," were of incomparably greater importance in the rise of appeasement. With the exception of a small number of keensighted men, all Britons supported the policy which finally made it possible for the Nazis to start the second World War.

A highly gifted French economist, Étienne Mantoux, has analyzed Keynes' famous book point for point. The result of his very careful and conscientious study is devastating for Keynes the economist and statistician, as well as Keynes the statesman. The friends of Keynes are at a loss to find any substantial rejoinder. The only argument that his friend and biographer, Professor E. A. G. Robinson, could advance is that this powerful indictment of Keynes' position came "as might have been expected, from a Frenchman." (*Economic Journal,* Vol. LVII, p. 23.) As if the disastrous effects of appeasement and defeatism had not affected Great Britain also!

Étienne Mantoux, son of the famous historian, Paul Mantoux, was the most distinguished of the younger French economists. He had already made valuable contributions to economic theory—among them a keen critique of Keynes' *General Theory,* published in 1937 in the *Revue d'Economie Politique*—before he began his *The Carthaginian Peace or the Economic Consequences of Mr. Keynes* (Oxford University Press, 1946). He did not live to see his book published. As an officer in the French forces he was killed on active service during the last days of the war. His premature death was a heavy blow to France, which is today badly in need of sound and courageous economists.

III

It would be a mistake, also, to blame Keynes for the faults and failures of contemporary British economic and financial policies. When he began to write, Britain had long since abandoned the principle of *laissez-faire.* That was the achievement of such men as Thomas Carlyle and John Ruskin and, especially, of the Fabians. Those born in the eighties of the nineteenth century and later were merely epigones of the university and parlor Socialists of the late Victorian period. They were no critics of the ruling system, as their predecessors had been, but apologists of government and pressure group policies whose inadequacy, futility and perniciousness became more and more evident.

Professor Seymour E. Harris has just published a stout volume of collected essays by various academic and bureaucratic authors dealing with Keynes' doctrines as developed in his *General Theory of Employment, Interest and Money,* published in 1936. The title of the volume is *The New Economics, Keynes' Influence on Theory and Public Policy* (Alfred A. Knopf, New York, 1947). Whether Keynesianism has a fair claim to the appellation "*new* economics" or whether it is not, rather, a rehash of often-refuted Mercantilist fallacies, and of the syllogisms of the innumerable authors who wanted to make everybody prosperous by fiat money, is unimportant. What matters is not whether a doctrine is new, but whether it is sound.

The remarkable thing about this symposium is that it does not even attempt to refute the *substantiated* objections raised against Keynes by serious economists. The editor seems to be unable to conceive that any honest and uncorrupted man could disagree with Keynes. As he sees it, opposition to Keynes comes from "the vested interests of scholars in the older theory" and "the preponderant influence of press, radio, finance and subsidized research." In his eyes, non-Keynesians are just a bunch of bribed sycophants, unworthy of attention. Professor Harris thus adopts the methods of the Marxians and the Nazis, who preferred to smear their critics and to question their motives instead of refuting their theses.

A few of the contributions are written in dignified language and are reserved, even critical, in their appraisal of Keynes' achievements. Others are simply dithyrambic outbursts. Thus Professor Paul E. Samuelson tells us: "To have been born as an economist before 1936 was a boon—yes. But not to have been born too long before!" And he proceeds to quote Wordsworth:

> "Bliss was it in that dawn to be alive,
> But to be young was very heaven!"

Descending from the lofty heights of Parnassus into the prosaic valleys of quantitative science, Professor Samuelson provides us with exact information about the susceptibility of economists to the Keynesian gospel of 1936. Those under the age of 35 fully grasped its meaning after some time; those beyond 50 turned out to be quite immune, while economists in-between were divided. After thus serving us a warmed-over version of Mussolini's *giovanezza* theme, he offers more of the outworn slogans of fascism, e.g., the "wave of the future." However, on

LUDWIG VON MISES   309

this point another contributor, Mr. Paul M. Sweezy, disagrees. In his eyes Keynes, tainted by "the short-comings of bourgeois thought" as he was, is not the savior of mankind, but only the forerunner whose historical mission it is to prepare the British mind for the acceptance of pure Marxism and to make Great Britain ideologically ripe for full socialism.

IV

In resorting to the method of innuendo and trying to make their adversaries suspect by referring to them in ambiguous terms allowing of various interpretations, the camp-followers of Lord Keynes are imitating their idol's own procedures. For what many people have admiringly called Keynes' "brilliance of style" and "mastery of language" were, in fact, cheap rhetorical tricks.

Ricardo, says Keynes, "conquered England as completely as the Holy Inquisition conquered Spain." This is as vicious as any comparison could be. The Inquisition, aided by armed constables and executioners, beat the Spanish people into submission. Ricardo's theories were accepted as correct by British intellectuals without any pressure or compulsion being exercised in their favor. But in comparing the two entirely different things, Keynes obliquely hints that there was something shameful in the success of Ricardo's teachings and that those who disapprove of them are as heroic, noble and fearless champions of freedom as were those who fought the horrors of the Inquisition.

The most famous of Keynes' *aperçus* is: "Two pyramids, two masses for the dead, are twice as good as one; but not so two railways from London to York." It is obvious that this sally, worthy of a character in a play by Oscar Wilde or Bernard Shaw, does not in any way prove the thesis that digging holes in the ground and paying for them out of savings "will increase the real national dividend of useful goods and services." But it puts the adversary in the awkard position of either leaving an apparent argument unanswered or of employing the tools of logic and discursive reasoning against sparkling wit.

Another instance of Keynes' technique is provided by his malicious description of the Paris Peace Conference. Keynes disagreed with Clemenceau's ideas. Thus, he tried to ridicule his adversary by broadly expatiating upon his clothing and appearance which, it seems, did not meet with the standard set by London outfitters. It is hard to discover any connection with the German reparations problem in the fact that Clemenceau's boots "were of thick black leather, very good, but of a country style, and sometimes fastened in front, curiously, by a buckle instead of laces." After 15 million human beings had perished in the war, the foremost statesmen of the world were assembled to give mankind a new international order and lasting peace . . . and the British Empire's financial expert was amused by the rustic style of the French Prime Minister's footwear.

Fourteen years later there was another international conference. This time Keynes was not a subordinate adviser, as in 1919, but one of the main figures. Concerning this London World Economic Conference of 1933, Professor Robinson observes: "Many economists the world over will remember . . . the performance in 1933 at Covent Garden in honour of the Delegates of the World Economic Conference, which owed its conception and organization very much to Maynard Keynes."

Those economists who were not in the service of one of the lamentably inept governments of 1933 and therefore were not Delegates and did not attend the delightful ballet evening, will remember the London Conference for other reasons. It marked the most spectacular failure in the history of international affairs of those policies of neo-Mercantilism which Keynes backed. Compared with this fiasco of 1933, the Paris Conference of 1919 appears to have been a highly successful affair. But Keynes did not publish any sarcastic comments on the coats, boots and gloves of the Delegates of 1933.

V

Although Keynes looked upon "the strange, unduly neglected prophet Silvio Gesell" as a forerunner, his own teachings differ considerably from those of Gesell. What Keynes borrowed from Gesell as well as from the host of other pro-inflation propagandists was not the content of their doctrine, but their practical conclusions and the tactics they applied to undermine their opponents' prestige. These stratagems are:

(a) All adversaries, that is, all those who do not consider credit expansion as the panacea, are lumped together and called *orthodox*. It is implied that there are no differences between them.

(b) It is assumed that the evolution of economic science culminated in Alfred Marshall and ended with him. The findings of modern subjective economics are disregarded.

(c) All that economists from David Hume on down to our time have done to clarify the results of changes in the quantity of money and money-substitutes is simply ignored. Keynes never embarked upon the hopeless task of refuting these teachings by ratiocination.

In all these respects the contributors to the symposium adopt their master's technique. Their critique aims at a body of doctrine created by their own illusions, which has no resemblance to the theories expounded by serious economists. They pass over in silence all that economists have said about the inevitable outcome of credit expansion. It seems as if they have never heard anything about the monetary theory of the trade cycle.

For a correct appraisal of the success which Keynes' *General Theory* found in academic circles, one must consider the conditions prevailing in university economics during the period between the two world wars.

Among the men who occupied chairs of economics in the last few decades, there have been only a few genuine economists, i.e., men fully conversant with the theories developed by modern subjective economics. The ideas of the old classical economists, as well as those of the modern economists, were caricatured in the textbooks and in the classrooms; they were called such names as old-fashioned, orthodox, reactionary, bourgeois or Wall Street economics. The teachers prided themselves on having refuted for all time the abstract doctrines of Manchesterism and *laissez-faire*.

The antagonism between the two schools of thought had its practical focus in the treatment of the labor union problem. Those economists disparaged as orthodox taught that a permanent rise in wage rates for all people eager to earn wages is possible only to the extent that the per capita quota of capital invested and the productivity of labor increases. If—

whether by government decree or by labor union pressure—minimum wage rates are fixed at a higher level than that at which the unhampered market would have fixed them, unemployment results as a permanent mass phenomenon.

Almost all professors of the fashionable universities sharply attacked this theory. As these self-styled "unorthodox" doctrinaries interpreted the economic history of the last two hundred years, the unprecedented rise in real wage rates and standards of living was caused by labor unionism and government pro-labor legislation. Labor unionism was, in their opinion, highly beneficial to the true interests of all wage-earners and of the whole nation. Only dishonest apologists of the manifestly unfair interests of callous exploiters could find fault with the violent acts of the unions, they maintained. The foremost concern of popular government, they said, should be to encourage the unions as much as possible and to give them all the assistance they needed to combat the intrigues of the employers and to fix wage rates higher and higher.

But as soon as the governments and legislatures had vested the unions with all the powers they needed to enforce their minimum wage rates, the consequences appeared which the "orthodox" economists had predicted; unemployment of a considerable part of the potential labor force was prolonged year after year.

The "unorthodox" doctrinaires were perplexed. The only argument they had advanced against the "orthodox" theory was the appeal to their own fallacious interpretation of experience. But now events developed precisely as the "abstract school" had predicted. There was confusion among the "unorthodox."

It was at this moment that Keynes published his *General Theory*. What a comfort for the embarrassed "progressives"! Here, at last, they had something to oppose to the "orthodox" view. The cause of unemployment was not the inappropriate labor policies, but the shortcomings of the monetary and credit system. No need to worry any longer about the insufficiency of savings and capital accumulation and about deficits in the public household. On the contrary. The only method to do away with unemployment was to increase "effective demand" through public spending financed by credit expansion and inflation.

The policies which the *General Theory* recommended were precisely those which the "monetary cranks" had advanced long before and which most governments had espoused in the depression of 1929 and the following years. Some people believe that Keynes' earlier writings played an important part in the process which converted the world's most powerful governments to the doctrines of reckless spending, credit expansion and inflation. We may leave this minor issue undecided. At any rate it cannot be denied that the governments and peoples did not wait for the *General Theory* to embark upon these "Keynesian"—or more correctly, Gesellian, policies.

VI

Keynes' *General Theory* of 1936 did not inaugurate a new age of economic policies; rather it marked the end of a period. The policies which Keynes recommended were already then very close to the time when their inevitable consequences would be apparent and their continuation would be impossible. Even the most fanatical Keynesians do not dare to say that present-day England's distress is an effect of too much saving and insufficient spending. The essence of the much glorified "progressive" economic policies of the last decades was to expropriate ever-increasing parts of the higher incomes and to employ the funds thus raised for financing public waste and for subsidizing the members of the most powerful pressure groups. In the eyes of the "unorthodox," every kind of policy, however manifest its inadequacy may have been, was justified as a means of bringing about more equality. Now this process has reached its end. With the present tax rates and the methods applied in the control of prices, profits and interest rates, the system has liquidated itself. Even the confiscation of every penny earned above 1,000 pounds a year will not provide any perceptible increase to Great Britain's public revenue. The most bigoted Fabians cannot fail to realize that henceforth funds for public spending must be taken from the same people who are supposed to profit from it. Great Britain has reached the limit both of monetary expansionism and of spending.

Conditions in this country are not essentially different. The Keynesian recipe to make wage rates soar no longer works. Credit expansion, on an unprecedented scale engineered by the New Deal, for a short time delayed the consequences of inappropriate labor policies. During this interval the Administration and the union bosses could boast of the "social gains" they had secured for the "common man." But now the inevitable consequences of the increase in the quantity of money and deposits have become visible; prices are rising higher and higher. What is going on today in the United States is the final failure of Keynesianism.

There is no doubt that the American public is moving away from the Keynesian notions and slogans. Their prestige is dwindling. Only a few years ago politicians were naively discussing the extent of national income in dollars without taking into account the changes which government-made inflation had brought about in the dollar's purchasing power. Demagogues specified the level to which they wanted to bring the national (dollar) income. Today this form of reasoning is no longer popular. At last the "common man" has learned that increasing the quantity of dollars does not make America richer. Professor Harris still praises the Roosevelt Administration for having raised dollar incomes. But such Keynesian consistency is found today only in classrooms.

There are still teachers who tell their students that "an economy can lift itself by its own bootstraps" and that "we can spend our way into prosperity." [1] But the Keynesian miracle fails to materialize; the stones do not turn into bread. The panegyrics of the learned authors who cooperated in the production of the present volume merely confirm the editor's introductory statement that "Keynes could awaken in his disciples an almost religious fervor for his economics, which could be effectively harnessed for the dissemination of the new economics." And Professor Harris goes on to say, "Keynes indeed had the Revelation."

There is no use in arguing with people who are driven by "an almost religious fervor" and believe that their master "had the Revelation." It is one of the tasks of economics to analyze carefully each of the inflationist plans, those of Keynes

[1] Cf. Lorie Tarshis, *The Elements of Economics*, New York 1947, p. 565.

and Gesell no less than those of their innumerable predecessors from John Law down to Major Douglas. Yet, no one should expect that any logical argument or any experience could ever shake the almost religious fervor of those who believe in salvation through spending and credit expansion.

LORD KEYNES AND SAY'S LAW

I

Lord Keynes's main contribution did not lie in the development of new ideas but "in escaping from the old ones," as he himself declared at the end of the Preface to his "General Theory." The Keynesians tell us that his immortal achievement consists in the entire refutation of what has come to be known as Say's Law of Markets. The rejection of this law, they declare, is the gist of all Keynes's teachings; all other propositions of his doctrine follow with logical necessity from this fundamental insight and must collapse if the futility of his attack on Say's Law can be demonstrated.[1]

Now it is important to realize that what is called Say's Law was in the first instance designed as a refutation of doctrines popularly held in the ages preceding the development of economics as a branch of human knowledge. It was not an integral part of the new science of economics as taught by the Classical economists. It was rather a preliminary—the exposure and removal of garbled and untenable ideas which dimmed people's minds and were a serious obstacle to a reasonable analysis of conditions.

Whenever business turned bad, the average merchant had two explanations at hand: the evil was caused by a scarcity of money and by general overproduction. Adam Smith, in a famous passage in "The Wealth of Nations," exploded the first of these myths. Say devoted himself predominantly to a thorough refutation of the second.

As long as a definite thing is still an economic good and not

[1] P. M. Sweezy in *The New Economics,* Ed. by S. E. Harris, New York, 1947, p. 105.

a "free good," its supply is not, of course, *absolutely* abundant. There are still unsatisfied needs which a larger supply of the good concerned could satisfy. There are still people who would be glad to get more of this good than they are really getting. With regard to economic goods there can never be *absolute* overproduction. (And economics deals only with economic goods, not with free goods such as air which are no object of purposive human action, are therefore not produced, and with regard to which the employment of terms like underproduction and overproduction is simply nonsensical.)

With regard to economic goods there can be only *relative* overproduction. While the consumers are asking for definite quantities of shirts and of shoes, business has produced, say, a larger quantity of shoes and a smaller quantity of shirts. This is not general overproduction of all commodities. To the overproduction of shoes corresponds an underproduction of shirts. Consequently the result can not be a general depression of all branches of business. The outcome is a change in the exchange ratio between shoes and shirts. If, for instance, previously one pair of shoes could buy four shirts, it now buys only three shirts. While business is bad for the shoemakers, it is good for the shirtmakers. The attempts to explain the general depression of trade by referring to an allegedly general overproduction are therefore fallacious.

Commodities, says Say, are ultimately paid for not by money, but by other commodities. Money is merely the commonly used medium of exchange; it plays only an intermediary role. What the seller wants ultimately to receive in exchange for the commodities sold is other commodities. Every commodity produced is therefore a price, as it were, for other commodities produced. The situation of the producer of any commodity is improved by any increase in the production of other commodities. What may hurt the interests of the producer of a definite commodity is his failure to anticipate correctly the state of the market. He has overrated the public's demand for his commodity and underrated its demand for other commodities. Consumers have no use for such a bungling entrepreneur; they buy his products only at prices which make him incur losses, and they force him, if he does not in time correct his mistakes, to go out of business. On the other hand, those entrepreneurs who have better succeeded in anticipating the public demand earn profits and are in a position to expand their business activities. This, says Say, is the truth behind the confused assertions of businessmen that the main difficulty is not in producing but in selling. It would be more appropriate to declare that the first and main problem of business is to produce in the best and cheapest way those commodities which will satisfy the most urgent of the not yet satisfied needs of the public.

Thus Smith and Say demolished the oldest and most naïve explanation of the trade cycle as provided by the popular effusions of inefficient traders. True, their achievement was merely negative. They exploded the belief that the recurrence of periods of bad business was caused by a scarcity of money and by a general overproduction. But they did not give us an elaborated theory of the trade cycle. The first explanation of this phenomenon was provided much later by the British Currency School.

The important contributions of Smith and Say were not entirely new and original. The history of economic thought can trace back some essential points of their reasoning to older authors. This in no way detracts from the merits of Smith and Say. They were the first to deal with the issue in a systematic way and to apply their conclusions to the problem of economic depressions. They were therefore also the first against whom the supporters of the spurious popular doctrine directed their violent attacks. Sismondi and Malthus chose Say as the target of passionate volleys when they tried—in vain—to salvage the discredited popular prejudices.

II

Say emerged victoriously from his polemics with Malthus and Sismondi. He proved his case, while his adversaries could not prove theirs. Henceforth, during the whole rest of the nineteenth century, the acknowledgment of the truth contained in Say's Law was the distinctive mark of an economist. Those authors and politicians who made the alleged scarcity of money responsible for all ills and advocated inflation as the panacea were no longer considered economists but "monetary cranks."

The struggle between the champions of sound money and the inflationists went on for many decades. But it was no longer considered a controversy between various schools of economists. It was viewed as a conflict between economists and anti-economists, between reasonable men and ignorant zealots. When all civilized countries had adopted the gold standard or the gold-exchange standard, the cause of inflation seemed to be lost forever.

Economics did not content itself with what Smith and Say had taught about the problems involved. It developed an integrated system of theorems which cogently demonstrated the absurdity of the inflationist sophisms. It depicted in detail the inevitable consequences of an increase in the quantity of money in circulation and of credit expansion. It elaborated the monetary or circulation credit theory of the business cycle which clearly showed how the recurrence of depressions of trade is caused by the repeated attempts to "stimulate" business through credit expansion. Thus it conclusively proved that the slump, whose appearance the inflationists attributed to an insufficiency of the supply of money, is on the contrary the necessary outcome of attempts to remove such an alleged scarcity of money through credit expansion.

The economists did not contest the fact that a credit expansion in its initial stage makes business boom. But they pointed out how such a contrived boom must inevitably collapse after a while and produce a general depression. This demonstration could appeal to statesmen intent on promoting the enduring well-being of their nation. It could not influence demagogues who care for nothing but success in the impending election campaign and are not in the least troubled about what will happen the day after tomorrow. But it is precisely such people who have become supreme in the political life of this age of wars and revolutions. In defiance of all the teachings of the economists, inflation and credit expansion have been elevated to the dignity of the first principle of economic policy. Nearly all governments are now committed to reckless spending, and finance their deficits by issuing additional quantities of irredeemable paper money and by boundless credit expansion.

The great economists were harbingers of new ideas. The

economic policies they recommended were at variance with the policies practiced by contemporary governments and political parties. As a rule many years, even decades, passed before public opinion accepted the new ideas as propagated by the economists, and before the required corresponding changes in policies were effected.

It was different with the "new economics" of Lord Keynes. The policies he advocated were precisely those which almost all governments, including the British, had already adopted many years before his "General Theory" was published. Keynes was not an innovator and champion of new methods of managing economic affairs. His contribution consisted rather in providing an apparent justification for the policies which were popular with those in power in spite of the fact that all economists viewed them as disastrous. His achievement was a rationalization of the policies already practiced. He was not a "revolutionary," as some of his adepts called him. The "Keynesian revolution" took place long before Keynes approved of it and fabricated a pseudo-scientific justification for it. What he really did was to write an apology for the prevailing policies of governments.

This explains the quick success of his book. It was greeted enthusiastically by the governments and the ruling political parties. Especially enraptured were a new type of intellectuals, the "government economists." They had had a bad conscience. They were aware of the fact that they were carrying out policies which all economists condemned as contrary to purpose and disastrous. Now they felt relieved. The "new economics" reestablished their moral equilibrium. Today they are no longer ashamed of being the handymen of bad policies. They glorify themselves. They are the prophets of the new creed.

III

The exuberant epithets which these admirers have bestowed upon his work cannot obscure the fact that Keynes did not refute Say's Law. He rejected it emotionally, but he did not advance a single tenable argument to invalidate its rationale.

Neither did Keynes try to refute by discursive reasoning the teachings of modern economics. He chose to ignore them, that was all. He never found any word of serious criticism against the theorem that increasing the quantity of money cannot effect anything else than, on the one hand, to favor some groups at the expense of other groups, and, on the other hand, to foster capital malinvestment and capital decumulation. He was at a complete loss when it came to advancing any sound argument to demolish the monetary theory of the trade cycle. All he did was to revive the self-contradictory dogmas of the various sects of inflationism. He did not add any thing to the empty presumptions of his predecessors, from the old Birmingham School of Little Shilling Men down to Silvio Gesell. He merely translated their sophisms—a hundred times refuted—into the questionable language of mathematical economics. He passed over in silence all the objections which such men as Jevons, Walras and Wicksell—to name only a few—opposed to the effusions of the inflationists.

It is the same with his disciples. They think that calling "those who fail to be moved to admiration of Keynes's genius" such names as "dullard" or "narrow-minded fanatic"[2] is a substitute for sound economic reasoning. They believe that they have proved their case by dismissing their adversaries as "orthodox" or "neo-classical." They reveal the utmost ignorance in thinking that their doctrine is correct because it is new.

In fact, inflationism is the oldest of all fallacies. It was very popular long before the days of Smith, Say and Ricardo, against whose teachings the Keynesians cannot advance any other objection than that they are old.

IV

The unprecedented success of Keynesianism is due to the fact that it provides an apparent justification for the "deficit spending" policies of contemporary governments. It is the pseudo-philosophy of those who can think of nothing else than to dissipate the capital accumulated by previous generations.

Yet no effusions of authors however brilliant and sophisticated can alter the perennial economics laws. They are and work and take care of themselves. Notwithstanding all the passionate fulminations of the spokesmen of governments, the

2 Professor G. Haberler, *Opus cit.*, p. 161.

inevitable consequences of inflationism and expansionism as depicted by the "orthodox" economists are coming to pass. And then, very late indeed, even simple people will discover that Keynes did not teach us how to perform the "miracle . . . of turning a stone into bread," [3] but the not at all miraculous procedure of eating the seed corn.

[3] Keynes, *Opus cit.*, p. 332.

XVII

Joseph Stagg Lawrence was born in Budapest, Austria-Hungary, in 1896. He was brought to the United States in 1903, attended high school in Buffalo, served as a private in the U. S. Army in France, was discharged as a first lieutenant, became a student at the University of Grenoble in France for a few months in 1919, and graduated from Princeton University in 1923. He taught at Princeton from 1924 to 1926, and at New York University from 1927 to 1929. When he went into business he became a director in several corporations and vice-president of the Empire Trust Company of New York.

The following originally appeared in two issues of the Empire Trust Letter (January 1 and February 1, 1950). It is one of the most hard-hitting as well as one of the least technical criticisms of Keynesian economics and policy.

LORD KEYNES AND THE FINANCIAL COMMUNITY

JOSEPH STAGG LAWRENCE

I

The New Deal, the Fair Deal, the English Labor Government, and economic liberalism throughout the world derive their philosophic inspiration from the mind and works of a single Englishman, the late Lord Keynes. The full measure of American official dependence upon Keynesian dogma is not apparent in this country today only because it still enjoys boom prosperity. Employment is still high. Public documents and the character of present leadership leave little doubt that expedients derived from the creed of this scholar will be applied at the first onset of economic decline in the United States.

The following propositions are taken directly from the works of Keynes or are clearly implicit in his thinking. They provide in the aggregate the key to American policy tomorrow. Some of this thinking has already been applied in pump-priming, deficit financing, and a currency severed from gold and managed by a group of "competent and responsible men." These propositions constitute the matrix of high level political, labor, and liberal thought in this country at the mid-point of the twentieth century.

NEW ORDER APHORISMS

1. A wealthy community is more unstable than a poor community.
2. The thrift of the wealthy aggravates the distress of the poor.
3. The apparent victory of a free economy during the 19th and early 20th centuries was due to historic accident.
4. Digging holes and filling them again can be more useful socially than the private accumulation of wealth.
5. Building useless pryamids can be more desirable socially than building a railroad.
6. The desire for liquidity is a silly fetish and is anti-social.
7. The hoarding of money is anti-social.
8. Legitimate long term investment is so difficult "as to be scarcely practical."
9. The long term investor who considers the public interest comes in for the most criticism from banks and investment committees.
10. "It is better to fail conventionally than to succeed unconventionally."
11. Wall Street is a gambling casino and should be made inaccessible to the public.
12. Speculation is the black art of forecasting the psychology of the market.

13. A heavy transfer tax should be imposed on all stock market transactions to discourage trading.
14. A real investment should be "permanent and indissoluble, like marriage."
15. Individuals should be ordered by the state to devote all their income to consumption or investment in a "specific capital-asset."
16. Important business decisions are more often the result of "animal spirits" and "spontaneous optimism" than "careful calculation."
17. "An act of individual saving means . . . a decision not to have dinner today."
18. The source of all real value is labor.
19. The prices of all goods should be proportioned to the labor embodied in them.
20. The efficiency of capital is determined "by the uncontrollable and disobedient psychology of the business world."
21. "The rate of interest is the reward for parting with liquidity for a specified period."
22. The payment of interest serves no useful purpose and should (within a generation) be eliminated altogether.
23. The theory of negative interest, where a man pays for the privilege of spending his money in the future, is sound.
24. Full employment can be achieved provided the government spends enough money.
25. Until we have full employment, the spending of money by the government cannot lead to inflation.
26. The government should control and direct all investment.
27. Speculation, promotion, business judgment, have all been greatly overrated.
28. It is the duty of the state to reduce inequality of wealth and income.
29. The government should control the location and mobility of labor.
30. Gold is an impediment in a socially desirable currency system.

The Substance of Neo-Liberalism

"We owe it to ourselves. No country can ever go bankrupt by operating on a deficit. Since the obligation runs to itself the size of the public debt is of no great moment."

Fiscal Sleight of Hand

This is not the exact language, though it is the fair substance of a statement by Marriner Eccles, the present Vice Chairman of the Board of Governors of the Federal Reserve System. It was made at a recent private gathering in New York City during which a number of the solid burghers present had expressed concern over the theory of innocuous deficit financing and the continuous rise of the public debt.

Eccles ridiculed these fears. He did so by offering the group one of the most tenacious, plausible and mischievous sophistries in the propaganda repertoire of the welfare state.

Although his audience, consisting of businessmen and bankers, found the views of Marriner Eccles preposterous and exasperating, it must be remembered that they are not the unique aberration of Mr. Eccles. He is an intelligent public servant who agrees with and reflects theories of public finance which are expounded today in many of our universities. In fact, two of the leading research agencies of the country, the Committee for Economic Development and the Twentieth Century Fund, largely supported by the donations of the very men who find the views of Eccles so irritating, seem to approve and promote a fiscal philosophy which flies in the face of the most elementary common sense.

The notion that the debt of the state is of no consequence so long as it is owed to its own citizens is not an original discovery of the Federal Reserve Board. It was rationalized in its modern form by John Maynard Keynes, a brilliant thinker in the field of monetary theory.

A Prescription for Economic Senility

He noted the hardening of England's economic arteries in the early thirties and realized that the free economy theories of Adam Smith no longer suited the position and prospects of his country. After carefully examining his conscience, he decided that he was an Englishman first and an economist secondly.

Thereupon he devised an abstruse body of dogma which suited the needs of a declining England. Its central premise is economic stagnation, its conclusive remedy economic planning. Among its major features are the control of investment volume, a managed currency, and a public debt that is all horsepower and no brakes.

To argue that the state can disregard the requirement, operating on all the rest of us, to live within our financial means, calls for a repudiation of instinct and reason so violent that it can be accepted only after the most careful groundwork. The rule that we must make ends meet whether we be governments, corporations, institutions, or individuals, together with the corollary that we should save a part of our incomes, is embedded so deeply in the mores and mind of western civilization that its attempted dislodgement a generation ago would have been held fantastic. To do so would require prodigies in semantics and sophistry which did not then, in the twenties, seem possible.

The Great Casuist

Nevertheless, precisely this feat has been accomplished. To the dismay of those who believed in the old rules, whose virtues had been apparently fully attested during centuries of human experience, whose validity had been expounded by some of the ablest thinkers of the race, a body of plausible dogma has appeared which challenges the foundations of orthodox thought in the field of economics and finance. Marriner Eccles, John Snyder, and Harry Truman illustrate the force and appeal which the new doctrines exercise.

The fallacy of the proposition that a nation may prosper, that it may achieve stability, only through the continued use of red ink cannot be understood or refuted unless the sources of error are examined. The great casuist who led the assault on the ramparts of common sense is John Maynard Keynes. Until his *General Theory of Employment, Interest and Money* appeared statesmen nibbled cautiously at the toxic sweetmeat of inflation. Finance Ministers who could say: "No," were still esteemed. Abandonment of a commodity money standard, the use of credit by the state to pay its bills in time of peace were still accompanied by apologies and a vow to return to fiscal virtue.

Helped By Circumstances

It is no easy matter for any polemist, however able, to engage such giants as David Ricardo, John Stuart Mill, Jeremy Bentham, and Alfred Marshall, discredit them, and sever the hold which their reasoning had on the minds of men for over a century. Yet that is precisely what Keynes has done. Of course, this has not been achieved solely through the power and plausibility of his logic. His victory was aided by two other circumstances.

Classical economic thinking assigns a passive role to the economist. It teaches that men pursuing their own interests—properly limited to protect society—will in the long run promote progress more effectively than any direction of community energies by a master intelligence, i.e., by the political sovereign.

It teaches that recurring maladjustments in the form of depression or unemployment can best be cured by leaving the individual to his own devices. The state has a moral duty to prevent extreme hardship and may provide minimum necessities for individuals while they reorient themselves preparatory to another forward move.

In the exposition of such a function for the state, the economist can hope for little authority and a minimum of influence. He is in the position of an honest physician who is compelled to admit that his patient is more likely to recover if nature takes its course than if he submits to medical treatment. This may be sound therapy but promises little income for the doctor.

Assume now that a new theory of healing is expounded which preaches active medication, the frequent use of the surgeon's knife, and a minimum recourse to nature's automatic healing. The doctor now becomes an important member of the community. Life, we are assured, is impossible without him. The door to wealth and influence opens. This is precisely what planning and full employment have done for the economist. He is the important technician seated at the right of the policy-maker. Laws must not be passed, funds may not be appropriated, without first consulting the economist.

He would hardly be human if he failed to respond warmly to a doctrine which seemed to prove the absolute need for state intervention, in which the economist must determine where, and how, the intervention shall take place. Obviously, he will give such a doctrine the benefit of every doubt.

It is little wonder that the executive departments of the government and the faculties of our universities are filled with men who worship at the feet of Keynes. Scholars and bureaucrats also have vested interests.

A Boon To Statesmen

Enthusiastic as was the welcome which his professional colleagues gave to Keynes, it hardly matched the ardor with which he was embraced by statesmen. Here was blessing on an august plane for practices which had always in the past been considered reprehensible. Good deeds could now be underwritten by drafts on the Treasury. The harsh precepts of finance no longer governed the practices of the exchequer. That loose lady of the Fisc, the budget deficit, was touched with the wand of a refreshing philosophy and made respectable.

Keynes was elevated to the nobility. He was accorded honors that formerly went to other great heroes of England—to a Nelson, a Marlborough. He had rationalized the decadence of Great Britain in flattering terms and devised a creed which was no less useful in Downing Street than it proved to be in the White House. That his revolutionary concepts in the field of economic thought imposed a great strain on Keynes himself is indicated by his remark at the outset of his *General Theory* that it was "a long struggle of escape—a struggle of escape from habitual modes of thought and expression."

A Self-Evident Axiom

Keynes starts by challenging one of the most self-evident premises of classical economics, i.e., that every act of production creates the means for the purchase of the product. This is best illustrated by the simplified income statement of the X company which, in a given period, produces a thousand cars sold at the plant for a thousand dollars each. The statement for the period looks as follows:

PROFIT AND LOSS STATEMENT

Income		*Expenses*	
Production	$1,000,000	Raw material	$ 300,000
		Labor	500,000
		Depreciation	100,000
		Overhead	50,000
		Profit	50,000
Total	$1,000,000	Total	$1,000,000

Every item on the outgo side of this statement represents buying power to the recipient and the items in the aggregate equal precisely the value of the product to be sold. Mathematically there cannot be any failure of buying power. This applies not alone to the X company but to the economy as a whole.

In fact Keynes admits the foregoing. He quotes Marshall.

The whole of a man's income is expended in the purchase of services and of commodities . . . it is a familiar economic axiom that a man purchases labour and commodities with that portion of his income which he saves just as much as he does with that he is said to spend. He is said to spend when he seeks to obtain present enjoyment from the services and commodities which he purchases. He is said to save when he causes the labour and commodies which he purchases to be devoted to the production of wealth from which he expects to derive the means of enjoyment in the future.

Keynes states that the proposition inherent in this observation by Marshall "is indubitable, namely, that the income derived in the aggregate by all the elements in the community concerned in a productive activity necessarily has a value exactly equal to the *value* of the output."

A KEYNESIAN DISTINCTION

This seems sufficiently obvious to dispose of the contention that buying power in a community fails because wage payments are not high enough, or that consuming power in the aggregate is too low to absorb the products of industry, or that the state must intervene with pump-priming injections into the economic stream to sustain buying power and full employment.

Keynes says the fallacy in this apparent axiom lies in timing.

The items of depreciation and profit in the statement of the X company may or may not be spent in the period in which the finished cars are offered for sale. The aggregate of these two items, namely $150,000, may be deposited in a bank account.

To be sure, he recognizes the complex osmosis by which this $150,000, even when deposited in an inactive bank account, may become available for investment. But, argues Keynes, *the act of saving and the act of investment are two entirely different and unrelated activities.* The mere fact that one man saves a thousand dollars does not mean that another man will invest a thousand dollars at the same time.

Those who think so "are fallaciously supposing that there is a nexus which unites decisions to abstain from present consumption with decisions to provide for future consumption; whereas the motives which determine the latter are not linked in any simple way with the motives which determine the former."

Wealth and Thrift Take A Beating

It is this preoccupation with the failure of effective demand in a capitalistic community which gives rise to some of the most startling deductions applicable to practical government policy.

The first, of course, is the need of the state to compensate for the failure of investment to match savings. This is the basic justification of deficit financing and the concept of a cyclically balanced rather than an annually balanced budget. Out of it grows full employment as the test of effective budgetary policy since full employment is the putative real test of effective demand.

There are other startling corollaries. Accepting the Keynesian premise that cyclical instability is due to a lack of coordination between savings and investment, it is an easy step to the proposition that investment should be directed actively by the government and that the entire savings functions should pass from individuals to the state. Nationalized savings may make social security practicable.

A Text for the Demagogue

The stark bias against wealth and material success present in the soap box exhortations of every rabble-rouser finds in Keynes a wholly detached support.

*. . . the richer the community, the wider will tend to be the gap
between its actual and its potential production; and therefore the
more obvious and outrageous the defects of the economic system.
For a poor community will be prone to consume by far the greater
part of its output, so that a very modest measure of investment
will be sufficient to provide full employment; whereas a wealthy
community will have to discover much ampler opportunities for
investment if the saving propensities of its wealthier members are
to be compatible with the employment of its poorer members. . . .
This analysis supplies us with an explanation of the paradox of
poverty in the midst of plenty.*

A better text for the demagogue could hardly be found. It is
little wonder that the English government regards the elimination of high incomes as a duty and the confiscation of wealth
by way of taxes as a salutary prelude to stabilization.

*There is little room in Keynesian theory for personal incen-
tive or private initiative.*

The Multiplier

In his chapter on the "marginal propensity to consume"
Keynes develops his famous concept of the multiplier. This
holds, briefly, that the consuming power of a given group of
workers has a stimulating effect on the economy equal to their
wages at the moment of full employment. Below full employment a given total of worker incomes gives the economy a boost
much greater than the aggregate of those incomes.

The manner in which this stimulant varies is calculated by a
mathematical formula. Let's use his own illustration. Ten
million jobs constitutes full employment in the Keynes example. Employment has dropped to 5,200,000. At that point, according to his formula, "If . . . an additional 100,000 men are
employed on public works, total employment will rise to 6,400,-
000. . . . Thus public works even of doubtful utility may pay
for themselves over and over again at a time of severe unemployment . . ." Here we have the genesis of leaf-raking. A
hundred thousand PWA workers indirectly provide jobs for
1,100,000 other workers.

Keynes chides the conservative for trying to find some useful
form of employment for the jobless during periods of unem-

ployment, for trying to operate relief on "business principles."
He suggests seriously:

If the Treasury were to fill old bottles with banknotes, bury them
at suitable depths in disused coal mines which are then filled up
to the surface with town rubbish, and leave it to private enterprise
on well tried principles of *laissez faire* to dig the notes up again
(the right to do so being obtained, of course, by tendering for
leases of the note-bearing territory), there need be no more unemployment and, with the help of the repercussions, the real income
of the community, and its capital wealth also, would probably become a good deal greater than it actually is. . . .

HOLES IN THE GROUND AND PROSPERITY

The analogy between this expedient and the gold mines of the
real world is complete. At periods when gold is available at suitable depths experience shows that the real wealth of the world
increases rapidly; and when but little of it is so available, our
wealth suffers stagnation or decline. Thus gold mines are of the
greatest value and importance to civilization. Just as wars have
been the only form of large-scale loan expenditure which statesmen
have thought justifiable, so gold mining is the only pretext for
digging holes in the ground which has recommended itself to
bankers as sound finance; and each of these activities has played
its part in progress—failing something better.

Here is the origin of the cosmic-jest interpretation of the gold
standard so highly relished by the advocates of a managed currency. It also opens the door to the dynamic direction of our
economy by "competent and responsible men" under which the
surplus energies of the unemployed are applied to useful projects. How this sensible procedure contrasts with the silly sub-
terfuges, such as digging holes for gold, under a *laissez faire*
economy!

It is precisely because Ancient Egypt had an effective equivalent for modern shovel leaning that it became so wealthy and
suffered so rarely from unemployment.

Ancient Egypt was doubly fortunate, and doubtless owed to this
its fabled wealth, in that it possessed *two* activities, namely, pyramid-building as well as the search for the precious metals, the fruits
of which, since they could not serve the needs of man by being
consumed, did not stale with abundance. The Middle Ages built

cathedrals and sang dirges. Two pyramids, two masses for the dead, are twice as good as one; but not so two railways from London to York.

According to Keynes we try too much to act like "prudent financiers." We think too long and carefully about adding "to the financial burdens of posterity." We try too hard to apply to the conduct of the state those "maxims which are best calculated to enrich an individual by enabling him to pile up claims to enjoyment which he does not intend to exercise at any definite time." Here is a dignified rationalization of the conduct of the drunken sailor and the fabled grasshopper to be applied by a government seeking full employment and cyclical stabilization.

A Low Opinion of the Businessman

Lord Keynes has a low opinion of the average businessman and seems particularly incensed over the role which business confidence plays in the decisions to invest or not to invest. According to Keynes, the "positive activities" of men depend upon a "spontaneous optimism" and not on "mathematical calculation." Thus, decisions are taken as a result of "animal spirits" and

. . . not as the outcome of a weighted average of quantitative benefits multiplied by quantitative probabilities.

Thus if the animal spirits are dimmed and the spontaneous optimism falters, leaving us to depend on nothing but a mathematical expectation, enterprise will fade and die. . . . This means, unfortunately, not only that slumps and depressions are exaggerated in degree, but that economic prosperity is excessively dependent on a political and social atmosphere which is congenial to the average business man. If the fear of a Labour Government or a New Deal depresses enterprise, this need not be the result either of a reasonable calculation or of a plot with political intent; . . . it is the mere consequence of upsetting the delicate balance of spontaneous optimism. In estimating the prospects of investment, we must have regard, therefore, to the nerves and hysteria and even the digestions and reactions to the weather of those upon whose spontaneous activity it largely depends.

What Keynes is saying in effect is that capital is notoriously timid. Since its owners must necessarily reach into an apaque future where the shape of things can only be guessed and rarely discerned, they may respond strongly to such irrelevant considerations as the character of the government. These owners may interpret the conduct of that government as a threat to the future safety of their accumulations and may hunt for havens instead of applying their funds boldly to new enterprises.

This means that government must so conduct itself as to win and hold the confidence of the men who have accumulated the investment funds of the community. Such subservience to pusillanimous plutocrats may hamstring the capacity of the government for good deeds. This is an intolerable brake upon progress and a sure guarantee of cyclical instability.

The Speculator—An Unsavory Character

Keynes disparages the functions of security markets and the practices of professional investors. The speculator represents a low order in the human scale. It is in *The General Theory* that we find the rational base for much of the hostility in official quarters toward orthodox financial practices and established financial institutions.

Of the maxims of orthodox finance none, surely, is more antisocial than the fetish of liquidity, the doctrine that it is a positive virtue on the part of investment institutions to concentrate their resources upon the holding of liquid securities. . . . The social object of skilled investment should be to defeat the dark forces of time and ignorance which envelop our future.

Actually, says Keynes, the object of most investment is to beat the crowd and it is for this reason alone that liquidity is so highly esteemed.

Investment based on genuine long-term expectation is so difficult to-day as to be scarcely practicable. . . . There is no clear evidence from experience that the investment policy which is socially advantageous coincides with that which is most profitable. . . . It is rare, . . . for an American to invest, as many Englishmen still do, for income; and he will not readily purchase an investment except in the hope of capital appreciation. This is only another way of saying that . . . the American . . . is . . . a speculator.

Speculators may do no harm as bubbles on a steady stream of enterprise. But the position is serious when enterprise becomes the bubble on a whirlpool of speculation. *When the capital development of a country becomes a by-product of the activities of a casino, the job is likely to be ill-done.* (Our italics). . . . These tendencies are a scarcely avoidable outcome of our having successfully organized "liquid" investment markets. It is usually agreed that casinos should, in the public interest, be inaccessible and expensive. And perhaps the same is true of Stock Exchanges. That the sins of the London Stock Exchange are less than those of Wall Street may be due, not so much to differences in national character, as to the fact that to the average Englishman Throgmorton Street, is, compared with Wall Street to the average American, inaccessible and very expensive.

The Cure

Keynes has some definite ideas on how to abate the speculative faults of American security markets.

The introduction of a substantial Government transfer tax on all transactions might prove the most serviceable reform available, with a view to mitigating the predominance of speculation over enterprise in the United States. . . . The spectacle of modern investment markets has sometimes moved me towards the conclusion that to make the purchase of an investment permanent and indissoluble, like marriage, except by reason of death or other grave cause, might be a useful remedy for our contemporary evils.

This suggests that some educational foundation should select as a research project the personal experience of liberals hellbent on reforming the financial community. We know of at least three characters, two of them still alive, who became active reformers of the American social system after their luck in the stock market had turned on them. One of these characters had run a shoe string in the twenties up to a paper fortune exceeding a million dollars. When the market collapsed he was engaged in an attempt to add still more to the substantial fund which an unbridled acquisitive lust and speculative luck had already accumulated. In his period of postspeculative penitence he became one of the active authors of the security legislation which now governs the stock market.

He Includes A Blackjack

Continuing his prescription for reform, Keynes proposes:

The only radical cure for the crises of confidence which afflict the economic life of the modern world would be to allow the individual no choice between consuming his income and ordering the production of the specific capital asset which, even though it be on precarious evidence, impresses him as the most promising investment available to him. It might be that, at times when he was more than usually assailed by doubts concerning the future, he would turn in his perplexity towards more consumption and less new investment. But that would avoid the disastrous, cumulative and far-reaching repercussions of its being open to him, when thus assailed by doubts, to spend his income neither on the one nor on the other. . . . Those who have emphasized the social dangers of the hoarding of money have, of course, had something similar to the above in mind.

All of this leads to tighter markets in securities, to the deliberate discouragement of trading, to a limitation of liquidity which is likely in this country, as in others, to discover its first application to government bonds, to forced savings with the government resolving the doubts of the thrifty by compelling them to buy its own bonds.

Labor the Source of Value

Throughout *The General Theory* Keynes disparages the role of the promoter, the banker, the speculator, the entrepreneur, the security market and business management as factors of any consequence in economic progress. In fact it is a fair conclusion that Keynes on balance believes that all these factors combined do the community more harm than good. So far has his thinking gone in this direction that he revives the medieval theory of labor as the ultimate source of all value.

I sympathise, therefore, with the pre-classical doctrine that everything is *produced* by *labour,* aided by what used to be called art and is now called technique, by natural resources which are free or cost a rent according to their scarcity or abundance, and by the results of past labour, embodied in assets, which also command a price according to their scarcity or abundance. It is preferable to regard labour, including, of course, the personal services of the entrepreneur and his assistants, as the sole factor of production, operating in a given environment of technique, natural resources, capital equipment and effective demand.

Out of this philosophic nubbin we can derive the condemnation of promotional profits like those derived from the recent organization of Texas Eastern Transmission or the denial of reward for the risk that discovers a new oil field. If "everything is produced by labour" it will become difficult to justify any jackpot profits. By the same token it will become relatively easy to recapture all excess income by taxation and limit personal earnings, as the English now are doing, to ten or twelve thousand dollars a year.

No Justification for Interest

This disparagement of finance, management and promotion leads Keynes, as it did the thinkers of the Middle Ages, to the proposition that there is no economic justification for interest. In the book of Keynes the interest rate often interferes with that optimum rate of investment which might insure full employment. Watch him now as he goes to work on the concept of interest and the fate of the coupon clipper. All this in a chapter entitled: *"Observations On The Nature Of Capital."*

Let us assume that steps are taken to ensure that the rate of interest is consistent with the rate of investment which corresponds to full employment. Let us assume, further, that State action enters in as a balancing factor to provide that the growth of capital equipment shall be such as to approach saturation-point at a rate which does not put a disproportionate burden on the standard of life of the present generation.

On such assumptions . . . *a properly run community* equipped with modern technical resources . . . ought to be able to bring down the marginal efficiency of capital . . . approximately *to zero within a single generation.* (Our italics.)

This will create a situation in which, according to Keynes, "The products of capital" should be

. . . selling at a price proportioned to the labour . . . embodied in them on just the same principles as govern the prices of consumption-goods into which capital-charges enter in an insignificant degree. . . . This may be the most sensible way of gradually getting rid of many of the objectionable features of capitalism.

The entire gas industry in this country is currently agitated by the attempt of the Federal Power Commission to limit the price of gas at the well to a figure which will just afford a "fair rate of return" on the cost of drilling the well and installing the facilities necessary to make this gas available to the consumer. While the power which the F. P. C. claims rests on a disputed interpretation of a Supreme Court decision, the philosophy traces directly to the Keynesian admonition that "the products of capital" should be "selling at a price proportioned to the labour . . . embodied in them . . ."

NEGATIVE INTEREST

Keynes continues with his discussion of the "rentier," the coupon clipper, the owner of savings bonds.

For a little reflection will show what enormous social changes would result from a gradual disappearance of a rate of return on accumulated wealth. A man would still be free to accumulate his *earned income* (our italics) with a view to spending it at a later date. But his accumulation would not grow. He would simply be in the position of Pope's father, who, when he retired from business, carried a chest of guineas with him to his villa at Twickenham and met his household expenses from it as required.

Keynes disinters a vagrant thinker named Sylvio Gesell who flourished at the turn of the century and had considerable vogue among advanced thinkers. At one point in his career he served for a brief period in 1919 as the Minister of Finance in the Soviet cabinet of Bavaria. Gesell believed that the growth of real capital was held back by the interest charge. If this brake on capital were removed it would grow so rapidly that "a zero money-rate of interest would probably be justified . . . within a comparatively short period of time."

It was Gesell who originated the concept of stamped money under which the holder of cash would be charged according to to the length of time he held his money. In other words, he would be subject to a negative rate of interest. It was an idea picked up by Irving Fisher and became one of the many proferred "solutions" for the great depression. Says Keynes: "The idea behind stamped money is sound. It is, indeed, possible that means might be found to apply it in practice on a modest scale."

EUTHANASIA OF THE RENTIER

Keynes believed that investment determined the rate of savings and not the other way around as most ordinary people hold. A low rate of interest would stimulate investment and therefore saving.

I feel sure that the demand for capital is strictly limited in the sense that it would not be difficult to increase the stock of capital up to a point where its marginal efficiency had fallen to a very low figure. This would mean that the use of capital instruments would cost almost nothing. . . . In short, the aggregate return from durable goods in the course of their life would, as in the case of short-lived goods, just cover their labour-costs of production *plus* an allowance for risk and the costs of skill and supervision.

Now, though this state of affairs would be quite compatible with some measure of individualism, yet it would mean the euthanasia of the rentier, and, consequently, the euthanasia of the cumulative oppressive power of the capitalist to exploit the scarcity-value of capital. Interest to-day rewards no genuine sacrifice any more than does the rent of land. The owner of capital can obtain interest because capital is scarce, just as the owner of land can obtain rent because land is scarce.

If there is any "intrinsic reason" for the scarcity of capital

. . . it will still be possible for communal saving through the agency of the State to be maintained at a level which will allow the growth of capital up to the point where it ceases to be scarce.

INFLUENCE OF KEYNES

The revolutionary heresies embodied in *The General Theory* of Keynes found a swift and sympathetic response both in this country and in England. Before this work appeared he had been consulted by our own government. Many of the startling innovations of the thirties are attributable to the personal advice of Keynes. The most notable were pump-priming and deficit financing. It was his thinking that justified the New Deal concept of limited personal income, of vast river valley development by the government, of taxation to absorb unexpended personal income, of punitive taxes upon undistributed corporate earnings.

Even before the advent of the labor government, England submitted its policies to the novel criteria evolved by Keynes. The *Report on Social Insurance and Allied Services* submitted by Sir William Beveridge to the government in November, 1942 rested its basic thinking on Keynesian theory. Beveridge acknowledges his intellectual debt to Keynes in *Full Employment in a Free Society* which appeared in 1945.

In paraphrasing the Keynesian prescription for full employment, Beveridge says:

Employment depends on spending, which is of two kinds—for consumption and for investment; what people spend on consumption gives employment. What they save, i.e., do not spend on consumption, gives employment only if it is invested, which means not the buying of bonds or shares but expenditure in adding to capital equipment, such as factories, machinery, or ships, or in increasing stocks of raw material. . . . Adequate total demand for labour in an unplanned market economy cannot be taken for granted.

Re-stating the theory that savings depend on investment, Beveridge quotes a passage from Keynes:

Thus our argument leads toward the conclusion that in contemporary conditions the growth of wealth so far from being dependent on the abstinence of the rich as is commonly supposed, is more likely to be impeded by it. One of the chief social justifications of great inequality of wealth is therefore removed.

Continuing, he asserts that

for Britain and for the United States alike, the savings that tend to produce depression are the undistributed profits of companies and the large surpluses of a very limited class of owners of great wealth.

ADVICE TO ENGLISH GOVERNMENT

Beveridge leaves no doubt as to what should be done to insure full employment and who should do it. Three conditions are necessary:

1. Adequate total outlay at all times.
2. The controlled location of industry.
3. The controlled mobility of labour.

It is the recognition of these three conditions, implicit in the policy of the present Labor Government, which accounts for the determination to nationalize industry. To the extent that they have been accepted as the premises of official thinking in our own government—and we believe they have to a substantial degree—they forecast a similar urge toward nationalization when unemployment becomes an intractable problem as un-economic wage levels and high unemployment relief are sure to make it.

The fact that "controlled" location of industry and "controlled" mobility of labour imply limitations upon personal freedom hardly compatible with democracy does not disturb Beveridge. A similar club is thinly concealed in his statement:

> The central proposition of this *Report* is that the responsibility of ensuring at all times outlay sufficient in total to employ all the available manpower in Britain should formally be placed by the people of Britain upon the State. . . . Adoption of a national policy of full employment means a revolution in national finance—a new type of budget introduced by a Minister who, whether or not he continues to be called Chancellor of the Exchequer, is a Minister of National Finance.

Debts Without Burden

In urging that a "policy of cheap money should be regarded as an integral part of any plan for full employment," Beveridge discusses the fallacious inhibitions of orthodox finance.

> The State in matters of finance is in a different position from any private citizen . . . ; it is able to control money instead of being controlled by it. . . . Spending in excess of current income and borrowing have altogether different implications for the State than for private citizens. . . . An internal national debt increases the incomes of some citizens by just as much as the taxation necessary to pay interest and sinking fund on the debt decreases the incomes of other citizens; it does not and cannot reduce the total wealth of the community.

Nor is it likely, says Beveridge, that an increase in the debt in time of peace will ever force an increase in taxes. He thereupon presents a calculation which purports to show that Great Britain could expand its National Debt each year, starting with 1948, by 775 million pounds "without involving on that account any increase of tax rates to meet the additional charge for interest."

Applying this calculation to the United States would permit an annual increase of $26 billion in the national debt without requiring any increase in taxes to meet the service charges.

This is where Marriner Eccles comes in. If he has any doubts regarding the validity of English debt doctrine or the soundness of the logic which supports it, he can find a Harvard professor who has already demonstrated that our national debt could be increased to $4,000 billion without any increase in burden. In fact one academic calculation has already raised the figure to $10,000 billion. He can refer to such a popular treatment of the subject as the Stuart Chase study for the Twentieth Century Fund, *Where's the Money Coming From?*

BANKRUPTCY IMPOSSIBLE

Says this gifted writer:

If the national debt is all internal, as ours is, the nation can hardly go bankrupt. The American people are on both sides of the balance sheet. Nations do not hand themselves over to outsiders in settlement of internal debts. . . . The idea of national bankruptcy in the modern world is a verbal bugaboo.

Chase "proves" *a la* Beveridge that the interest charge on the debt cannot be a national burden.

The complete capitulation of a large segment of high level American thinking to the Keynesian thesis is illustrated by the following from Professor Alvin Hansen. Under certain assumptions of continued growth and technical efficiency, says Hansen,

. . . it can be shown mathematically that if the government continued to borrow indefinitely on the average 10 per cent each year of the national income, and if the rate of growth of increase was 2.5 per cent, (of the national income), and if the average rate of interest on government obligations continued at 2 per cent, then the interest charges would never exceed 8 per cent of the national income. In other words, the government could continue to borrow, on the average, 10 per cent of the national income indefinitely without the tax burden, caused by the public debt, ever rising above 8 per cent of the national income.

In fairness to Hansen, it should be pointed out that he is not advocating such an increase but merely saying that it could be done without leading to bankruptcy or even an increase in the tax burden.

TRUE ONLY UNDER COMPLETE COMMUNISM

What precisely is the fallacy in the we-owe-it-to-ourselves-and-cannot-go-bankrupt argument? It rests on a communal conception of rights and obligations which in fact does not—yet—have a counterpart in the reality of a free society. *The duties of an individual toward his government are never bulked with similar duties of other citizens.* He has an obligation to fight for his country in time of war. This is a specific, personal obligation. Whether he does in fact serve in the armed forces depends upon *his* age, *his* physical condition, *his* occupation, *his* sex. Whether this citizen pays taxes and how much he pays depends upon *his* income and *his* family status. Whether he holds any of the securities of his government depends upon *his* means and *his* judgment.

The obligation to fight for country, to pay taxes and the decision to buy government bonds are not determined by any impersonal count of heads—that is not yet. There is no uniform distribution of these duties owed by a citizen to his government. They can become uniform and generalized only in a communist society.

The government does not owe its debt to all the citizens. It owes that debt to particular citizens, with the obligation to each precisely defined. It is not a general debt to all the citizens. To say that we owe it to ourselves is to ignore all those careful demarcations between individual citizens, between such citizens and the institutions which serve them, between such citizens and their government. It has been the chief burden of civilized jurisprudence to define and protect these distinctions. The meticulous boundaries between the rights and duties of citizens within a community are the true test of whether that community is free or is the fief of a totalitarian master.

It would be just as logical for Marriner Eccles, or William Beveridge, or Stuart Chase to argue that a tax could never be burdensome since we pay in our capacity as citizens to our instrument, the government, which in turn pays it right back to us. Therefore whether the tax is high or low is irrelevant. In fact, with this brand of logic we may argue that there is no point in paying any taxes at all, since we merely take them out of one pocket as citizens and put them in another. Why not leave them there in the first place and save all the cost and friction of collection and disbursement?

ANOTHER DEFINITION OF BANKRUPTCY

Can a government go bankrupt? If it appears not to go bankrupt it is due solely to its power as the sovereign. However, bankruptcy in the sense in which the word is used by the aforementioned Keynesians refers primarily to a limited legal procedure following bankruptcy under which the assets of the bankrupt are formally seized to satisfy the claims of creditors.

Bankruptcy of the sovereign occurs in fact when he uses his authority to evade the penalties visited upon the private debtor who fails to meet the terms of his obligations. Considerate euphemisms have been contrived to describe various forms of sovereign bankruptcy. An irredeemable paper currency is such a euphemism. A pegged bond market is another.

Every paper dollar is defined by law as 13.71 grains of pure gold. The American sovereign has long since welshed on this obligation and persists in his welshing although he has more gold on hand now than he ever had before.

Every time a government, which has repudiated this currency covenant with its citizens, issues additional I O Us under circumstances in which those citizens cannot assert their rights as creditors, it is compounding its bankruptcy.

The fact that it has not been haled before a court by a sheriff is not proof of its financial strength, as Eccles implies, but merely proves that all the instruments of justice so quickly applied to the offending private debtor are subservient to the state and cannot impose upon it the penalties which they apply to other similar transgressors.

The fact that a public sale of assets does not take place when the government welshes on its obligations hardly affects the end result. In both cases the creditor loses out. The French government has not confessed its bankruptcy and it is not likely that it will ever do so. Such action can hardly affect the position of the French citizen who bought a bond in 1939 and now finds that it has lost 98 per cent of its real value. Here is a creditor of the state who can now realize, in real terms, only two per cent on his claims. What difference can a formal confession of bankruptcy make?

The debt fallacies of Keynesian dogma are probably among its less serious features. It is a perfect Pandora's box of mischievous incitement to the statesman seeking a degree of power which the legitimate framework of an authentic democracy and a free society does not permit.

II

A MISCHIEVOUS ASSAULT

Actually *The General Theory of Employment, Interest and Money* constitutes the most subtle and mischievous assault on orthodox capitalism and free enterprise that has appeared in the English language. Where Marxian communism proceeds with bludgeon and meat cleaver, Lord Keynes uses a sharp rapier. Where Marx claims capitalism is unjust, Keynes "proves" it cannot work. Where Marx threatens capital with violent overthrow by the miserable and exploited working classes, Keynes assures it of collapse through self-frustration. Where Marx calls for seizure of all the instruments of production and individual egalitarianism, Keynes believes that many of the vital functions of capitalism can be performed more efficiently collectively without the incentive of private gain. He proposes semi-autonomous bodies for this purpose not subject to popular vote or constitutional restrictions, like the TVA or the Bank of England.

Consider the strategic scheme. Thrift breaks the circuit of income and spending because the decision to save and the decision to invest are separate decisions. They are made by different parties with entirely distinct motives. Booms are caused by the optimism of the businessman, the promoter, the investment banker, the speculator. Depressions are caused by their pessimism. In the former they over-invest; in the latter they under-invest.

Their decisions to invest or not to invest, moreover, are generally irrational. They are the result of "animal spirits" and not "careful mathematical calculation." These fellows are motivated by private profit and not by public welfare. The incentives to risk the funds which promoters and businessmen control, namely, the prospect of personal gain, are unnecessary and socially undesirable.

This is where the theory that all value traces to labor, that all value, even of capital goods, should be measured by labor input, comes in. If this is the source and measure of value, then the promoter, the speculator, the businessman, are entitled to no special rewards that cannot be fixed by the test of labor performance.

Finally, the fellow who saves money, who withdraws his dollars from the "firing line of the economy" should be glad to have the right to spend it at some future date without extracting from the community a charge called interest. This involves no labor beyond clipping coupons or opening the mail. The fellow who lives on interest—a dignified and stuffy parasite called the rentier—should be eliminated gradually but painlessly through a form of financial euthanasia.

A NEAT SYLLOGISM

This all adds up to a neat syllogism. Economic stability depends upon the complete and simultaneous expenditure of all the proceeds of production. The governing variable is the volume of investment. This vital function has so far been left in private hands which have been extravagantly compensated.

Moreover they have proved themselves incompetent and venal. Since the volume of desirable investment is a matter of mathematical calculation and since the government has the necessary prescience and probity, such investment should be a government function.

Savings similarly should be nationalized.

The accumulation of great wealth is not only immoral. It is also uneconomic.

If labor be the measure of reward, then great wealth and unequal incomes are the result of larcenous acquisitive lusts. They should be curbed by the ruthless surgery of progressive income and inheritance taxes. Better still, the opportunity to acquire great wealth and receive high incomes should be eliminated.

The nationalization of industry and the funneling of thrift and investment through government departments have obvious corollaries. Life insurance companies and savings banks would become superfluous. Security markets would become obsolete institutions and stock brokers unnecessary parasites. Investment bankers and promoters would have to go to work. The fate of the economy would no longer depend on the haphazard hunches of ulcerous old tories who "distrusted the policies of the government." The new era would be marked by a succession of national programs, the result of "careful mathematical calculation" by "competent and responsible" public officials. These might even be known as "Five Year Plans."

Let's look at some of the basic premises.

THIS IS THE KEYSTONE

In terms of theory and the gravity of ultimate effect, the most important postulate of Keynes is his distinction between the act of saving and the act of investment. Classical theory, no less than common sense, assumes that something must first be saved out of current income to make possible the construction of shelter or manufacture of tools, to subsidize periods of experimentation and invention, to underwrite losses in ventures which fail in order that a small fraction may succeed.

... it is natural to suppose [says Keynes] that the act of an individual, by which he enriches himself without apparently taking anything from anyone else, must also enrich the community as a whole; so that ... an act of individual saving inevitably leads to a parallel act of investment. ...

Those who think in this way are deceived, nevertheless, by an optical illusion, which makes two essentially different activities appear to be the same. They are fallaciously supposing that there is a nexus which unites decisions to abstain from present consumption with decisions to provide for future consumption; whereas the motives which determine the latter are not linked in any simple way with the motives which determine the former.

It is, then, the assumption of equality between the demand price of output as a whole and its supply price which is to be regarded as the classical theory's "axiom of parallels." Granted this, all the rest follows—the social advantages of private and national thrift, the traditional attitude toward the rate of interest, the classical theory of unemployment, the quantity theory of money, the unqualified advantages of *laissez-faire* in respect of foreign trade and much else which we shall have to question.

THE REST OF THE ARCH

In other words, if the "nexus which unites decisions to abstain from present consumption with decisions to provide for future consumption" does not exist, then "private and national thrift" may not have any social advantages; interest may not be the premium for waiting or a first claim against profits or the equalizer of savings and investment; unemployment may not be the result of excessive wages; the value of money may not be the result of its supply; and *laissez-faire* in foreign trade must yield to government trade.

Out of the philosophic matrix, arising from the discovery that the motives for saving and for investment have nothing in common, we develop the corollaries that thrift itself has questionable social merit in the first place; that it should be socialized; that the payment of interest interferes with that volume of effective demand which insures full employment; that full employment depends upon the complete expenditure of all income at the time it is received; that full employment does not depend upon wage costs per unit of output; that the quantity theory of money must be substantially qualified; that quotas, licenses, bilateral deals, currency controls in foreign trade, and barriers against the movement of capital all constitute sound devices in promoting an optimum economy.

This is an enormous burden upon the single tenuous distinction between the motives of the saver and the motives of the investor. Let's examine the validity of this distinction.

It would seem to the layman that a premise so pregnant with revolution must be carefully supported by a convincing array of inductive evidence which had hitherto been ignored, or by a test of such evidence with logic that had previously not been applied. The assertion of the Keynesian distinction between the motives of the saver and the motives of the investor is just that, i.e., an assertion. It is solemnly repeated over and over again, as though it were a self-evident truth, that it should be accepted on the plane of exalted revelation and not prosaic demonstration.

GENERALIZATION WITHOUT EVIDENCE

In a world which abounds with precise and approximate measurements of almost every conceivable form of economic activity, in which a rich store of quantitative evidence, contemporary and historical, is available to the student, Keynes in his *General Theory* uses no such evidence at all. (In 384 pages of text there are two pages of references to statistical studies by Colin Clark and Simon Kuznets.)

The broad principles, the premises on which they rest, the elaborate details and the revolutionary implications of Keynesian theory derive from heroic deductions which are completely innocent of any contact with the measurable realities of the world in which we live. It is difficult, in fact, to discover a single concrete example in which any of his prodigious propositions are given a living form. Even More's *Utopia* and Plato's *Republic, Das Kapital* of Karl Marx, and *Progress and Poverty* of Henry George reveal a regard for the inductive method which is singularly absent in *The General Theory*.

The *Federal Reserve Bulletin,* the *National Income Supplement of the Survey of Current Business,* and occasional studies of private research agencies, such as *Social Security and the Economics of Saving* of the National Industrial Conference Board, provide continuing figures on both savings and investments. Furthermore, these figures are analyzed to a degree which permits fairly valid conclusions regarding the issues of theory raised by Keynes. There is nothing in the phenomena of savings that warrants its analysis on a purely deductive level— unless it be an apprehension that the facts cannot be reconciled with the theory.

WHO SAVES AND WHO INVESTS

During the year 1948 net personal savings amounted to $12 billion out of total disposable income of $190.8 billion. Corporations saved another $11.1 billion, making a total of $23.1 billion. Since national income before taxes amounted to $211.9 billion, the aggregate of corporate and personal savings amounted to 10.9 per cent of the national income.

Bear in mind now the Keynesian emphasis on the fallacious "nexus" between savings and investment. Of the total savings

—$23.1 billion—$11.1 billion, or 48 per cent, was accounted for by corporations. In the aggregate, these savings were reinvested by the very managements which made them in the first place.

Can anyone say that these savings did not serve, directly and immediately, the purpose for which they were made? If there was any distinction in motives it could have been no greater than the distinction between the decision to order a steak and the decision to eat it.

In 1948 business savings accounted for almost one-half the total of savings. In 1947 they accounted for more than two-thirds. Obviously, the distinction which Keynes makes between the motives governing savings and those governing investment—if it has any validity whatsoever—shrinks in importance to the extent that savings and investment are made by the same party.

SAVINGS NOT INVESTED BY THE SAVERS

Within the area of individual savings, amounting to $12 billion in 1948, or 5.3 per cent of the national income, we have substantial quantitative adjustments which further limit the area to which the Keynesian distinction may be applied. Roughly a quarter of personal savings are accounted for by social security contributions which are promptly spent by the government and covered in the trust funds by its own I O Us. Another quarter is represented by purchase of U. S. Savings Bonds and savings and loan association shares.

A little less than half of the total of liquid institutional savings is represented by an increase in life insurance reserves and time deposits. Insofar as banks utilize savings, they are limited to legal investments determined by the states within which they operate. The investments of life insurance companies are in the hands of professionals. The decisions to invest on the part of savings banks and insurance companies, though they represent a purpose distinct from that which induced the individual to save, are competent decisions.

Now, having granted that one-quarter of total net savings (less than 3 per cent of the national income in 1948) is converted into investments by institutions which are partly guided by law and partly by the judgment of competent professionals, what horrendous conclusions can this support? There can hardly be any doubt in the mind of a layman, whose horse sense has not been overcome by ponderous dogma, that the individual who saves and entrusts his funds to a savings bank or an insurance company is much better off than if he were compelled, as Keynes suggests, to spend all his income for consumption or invest his surplus income in some "specific capital asset."

It might be interesting to speculate on the type of capital asset which a vested bureaucracy might specify for such compulsory investment. In all the countries of the world where the *dirigisme,* toward which Keynesian thinking inevitably leads, is in effect, the investment which absorbs savings must be in government bonds.

A Vain Distinction

The distinction which Keynes laboriously distills between the motives of saving and investment lacks substance. It applies in any event to only a small fraction of all savings—those made by individuals in the lower income brackets, who are interested primarily in the rainy day purpose of thrift. Without the benefit of more exalted advice, these individuals take only a passive interest in the ultimate application of their savings and wisely entrust them to institutions which, in the course of time, have evolved to serve this particular function.

The great bulk of savings—those by business and individuals in the upper fifth of income brackets—is usually invested directly. In these instances there is definitely "a nexus which unites decisions to abstain from present consumption with decisions to provide for future consumption."

Year by year this probably covers no less than three-quarters of all savings.

The Long View

Keynes established, for his purposes and to his satisfaction, the distinction between savings and investments. He propounds this distinction at the very opening of his *General Theory* with all the startled elation of Archimedes discovering the principle of displacement. Thereafter he proceeds to cut down the intelligence, competence, and social solicitude of all those who perform the investment function.

In the first place, the professional investor—and this applies particularly to the American—is disinclined and unable to take the long view. He is interested primarily in the quick turn, in outguessing the crowd.

The social object of skilled investment should be to defeat the dark forces of time and ignorance which envelop our future. The actual, private object of the most skilled investment today is "to beat the gun," as the Americans so well express it, to outwit the crowd, and to pass the bad, or depreciating, half crown to the other fellow.

This battle of wits to anticipate the basis of conventional valuation a few months hence, rather than the prospective yield of an investment over a long term of years, does not even require gulls among the public to feed the maws of the professional; . . . it can be played by professionals amongst themselves. Nor is it necessary that anyone should keep his simple faith in the conventional basis of valuation having any genuine long term validity. For it is, so to speak, a game of Snap, of Old Maid, of Musical Chairs—a pastime in which he is victor who says *Snap* neither too soon nor too late, who passes the Old Maid to his neighbor before the game is over, who secures a chair for himself when the music stops. These games can be played with zest and enjoyment, though all the players know that it is the Old Maid which is circulating, or that when the music stops some of the players will find themselves unseated.

NOBODY LOVES THE LONG VIEW

The boys who take the long view, says Keynes, have a rough time of it.

Investment based on long-term expectation is so difficult today as to be scarcely practicable. He who attempts it must surely lead much more laborious days and run greater risks than he who tries to guess better than the crowd how the crowd will behave; and, given equal intelligence, he may make more disastrous mistakes. There is no clear evidence from experience that the investment policy which is socially advantageous coincides with that which is most profitable. It needs *more* intelligence to defeat the forces of time and our ignorance of the future than to beat the gun. . . . Finally it is the long-term investor, he who most promotes the public interest, who will in practice come in for the most criticism, wherever investment funds are managed by committees or boards or banks. For it is the essence of his behaviour that he should be eccentric, unconventional and rash in the eyes of average opinion. If he is successful, that will only confirm the general belief in his rashness; and if in the short run he is unsuccessful, which is very likely, he will not receive much mercy.

Keynes qualifies this harsh judgment by admitting that speculative motives do not always govern investment, but

In one of the greatest investment markets in the world, namely, New York, the influence of speculation (in the above sense) is enormous. Even outside the field of finance, Americans are apt to be unduly interested in discovering what average opinion believes average opinion to be; and this national weakness finds its nemesis in the stock market. It is rare, one is told, for an American to invest, as many Englishmen still do, "for income"; and he will not readily purchase an investment except in the hope of capital appreciation.

THE SHORT TERM TRADER

It is difficult to find anywhere in economic literature a more distorted, ill-informed account of the motives and the procedures of the American financial community. In a country as rich as the United States, with highly organized markets in which shares are traded daily, with highly efficient and severely competitive sources of up-to-the-minute information, there is bound to be a fringe of traders constantly striving to determine "what average opinion believes average opinion to be."

However short term their views may be, these traders serve a useful function in providing volume and fluidity to a security market. Without these traders to absorb the short term shocks of the market, it would be difficult to float issues either for private corporate or government account without greater friction and more risk. It is these "reprehensible" speculators, the "bubbles on a steady stream of enterprise," who facilitate the application of savings to productive "long term" purposes by helping to provide a ready market.

INVESTMENT FOR INCOME

Americans, Keynes avers, rarely invest for income and "will not readily purchase an investment except in the hope of capital appreciation." This is both naive and contradictory. It is naive because it fails to note the effect of the income tax on investment "for income." A capital gain is subject to an extreme tax of 25 per cent, while income in its final personal increments in the upper brackets is subject to a tax of 82 per cent. No investment decision is made today without a careful appraisal of tax incidence on the investor.

However, there is a broad category of investment in which income is the dominant motive. This is true of all charitable, religious, and educational foundations where income is not subject to tax. It is true of all investment trusts which pay out not less than 90 per cent of their income. It is true of the thousands of small trusts managed by banks for beneficiaries who must subsist on income.

CAPITAL APPRECIATION AND THE LONG VIEW

The Keynesian argument here is contradictory because, having just demonstrated that the American investor is prone to "jump the gun" and is disinclined to take the "long view," the same argument now holds that this American investor looks for capital appreciation rather than income.

The only thing that this argument really proves is that Keynes did not know what he was talking about. For it is precisely the hope of capital appreciation which calls for the long view *ahead*. Generally speaking, securities are bought for income only after they have demonstrated a stable earning power and a capacity for regular dividends. In other words, such companies are more likely to be matured, established enterprises with their greatest period of growth *behind* them.

On the other hand, the situations which offer the greatest promise of capital gains are those which are young, whose earning power remains to be established. Still more significant in terms of Keynesian concern for full employment, it is the younger enterprises, those offering the brightest prospect for capital gains, which also offer the greatest opportunities for new and additional employment *in the future*.

It may be something of an exaggeration—though certainly no greater than those found in *The General Theory*—that investment for capital gains looks *ahead*, while investment for yield looks *behind*.

MISINFORMED

Keynes holds that the investment manager, particularly the man who must work with bank, insurance, and investment company committees has a rough time of it when he tries to take the long view; that he is regarded as eccentric; that he is damned if he fails and similarly damned if he succeeds.

The Englishman could not be more mistaken in his facts. The average investment committee, managing a portfolio for a bank, an insurance company, or investment trust, usually, at least in this country, consists of mature men who have almost invariably been successful in the management of their own affairs; who, by nature, training, and experience are disposed to prefer the long over the short view.

In any number of instances, within an extended period of personal experience, in the course of discussion and investment, the suggestion that a short-term profit might be made in guessing what "the average opinion of the average opinion" might be has been deplored. There has been a correlative willingness to sustain short-term fluctuations, even when adverse, in order to make the longer commitment in what was felt to be—usually after careful study—the more promising prospect.

In fact, the shrewdest investors and the best paid professionals are men who operate on the assumption that the crowd is usually wrong. Whenever they find their views coincide with the popular opinion they become uneasy.

AN INTEGRATED TEXT

The Keynesian analysis of the motives and procedures of the financial community are all part of an integrated text. Their purpose is to indict the competence of the financial professional, undermine public confidence in financial institutions, and prepare the way for governmental assumption of all those vital functions now performed by investment banking, security markets, and the private management of capital.

In addition to the charge that investment decisions are generally capricious and short-sighted, that they depend on irrational moods, on "animal spirits" and not on "careful calculation," there is added the further charge that long-term social interest and private profit rarely coincide; that in any event it is only private profit and not the social interest which actuates the businessman and the financier.

This particular current of thought was already forming in the mind of Keynes at least ten years before he wrote *The General Theory*. In 1926 he brought out a short volume entitled *Laissez-Faire and Communism* under the imprint of the *New Republic*. In a literary sense it shows Keynes at his best, for it is a superb example of writing in the field of philosophic economics. It is also a trenchant assault on individualism and *laissez-faire*.

Let us clear from the ground the metaphysical or general principles upon which, from time to time, *laissez-faire* has been founded. It is *not* true that individuals possess a prescriptive "natural liberty" in their economic activities. There is *no* "compact" conferring perpetual rights on those who Have and those who Acquire. The world is *not* so governed from above that private and social interest always coincide. It is *not* a correct deduction from the Principles of Economics that enlightened self-interest always operates in the public interest. Nor is it true that self-interest generally *is* enlightened; more often individuals acting separately to promote their own ends are too ignorant or too weak to attain even these. Experience does *not* show that individuals, when they make up a social unit, are always less clear-sighted than when they act separately.

THE SOLUTION

The foregoing appears at the beginning of a chapter on the future organization of society. More clearly and succinctly than in his later works, in which he too frequently involves himself in fancy reasoning and incomprehensible abstractions, he tells us what our trouble is and what we ought to do about it.

Many of the greatest economic evils of our time are the fruits of risk, uncertainty and ignorance. It is because particular individuals, fortunate in situation or in abilities, are able to take advantage of uncertainty and ignorance, and also because for the same reason big business is often a lottery, that great inequalities of wealth come about; and these same factors are also the cause of Unemployment of Labour, or the disappointment of reasonable business expectations, and of the impairment of efficiency and production. Yet the cure lies outside the operations of individuals; it may even be to the interest of individuals to aggravate the disease. I believe that the cure for these things is partly to be sought in the deliberate control of the currency and of credit by a central institution, and partly in the collection and dissemination on a great scale of data relating to the business situation, including the full publicity, by law if necessary, of all business facts which it is useful to know.

My second example relates to Savings and Investment. I believe that some co-ordinated act of intelligent judgment is required as to the scale on which it is desirable that the community as a whole should save, the scale on which these savings should go abroad in the form of foreign investments, and whether the present organization of the investment market distributes savings along the most nationally productive channels. I do not think that these matters should be left entirely to the chances of private judgment and private profits, as they are at present.

My third example concerns Population. The time has already come when each country needs a considered national policy about what size of Population, whether larger or smaller than at present or the same, is most expedient. And having settled this policy, we must take steps to carry it into operation. The time may arrive a little later when the community as a whole must pay attention to the innate quality as well as to the mere numbers of its future members.

THE PROFIT MOTIVE

With a surface appearance of moderation and sweet detachment, Keynesian economics aims the poniard of its cunning casuistry at the vitals of private enterprise. The general context of his material, together with innumerable specific statements, leave with the reader the strong impression that business leadership is incompetent, ignorant, selfish, and—most damning of all—unenlightened. After re-reading the pertinent passages in *The General Theory* and in *Laissez-Faire and Communism,* there remains the conviction that profits and the profit motive are not only *occasionally* incompatible with the public welfare but that this is *generally* the case. The business world, according to Keynes, is a jungle without the salutary discipline of that higher regard for the public interest which neo-liberals consider imperative. In this jungle each businessman is a wolf prepared to destroy his competitor, to ravish his customer, to expose his community to calamity.

As in almost every other position taken by Keynes during the generation before his death, he had neglected to consult the record. The strong inference that private profit and the public interest are in conflict, if true, could readily be supported by particular example and general statistics. Keynes carefully avoids the deductive, judicial approach. Let's look at a typical example of private profit.

During 1948 the General Motors Corporation turned out, among other products, 1,634,000 passenger cars and 508,000 trucks. These were badly needed by the American economy and by scores of other countries striving for recovery. Was this contrary to public interest?

In producing these vehicles the company provided jobs for 380,000 workers at peak peacetime wage levels. Was this incompatible with the general welfare?

For doing this the company earned $801,418,000 in gross profits. Out of these profits $360,970,000 or 45 per cent went to the government in taxes, $210, 774, 000 or 26.3 per cent went to the owners of the company in the form of dividends, and $229,674,000 or 28.7 per cent was reinvested in the business to improve plant, to underwrite research and experimentation for the purpose of getting a better product at a lower cost. Was this unenlightened?

The Arrogance of the Planner

This is the sensible, the fair approach to an analysis of profits. To the ideological prosecutor who knows beforehand that business is guilty, such an examination of the evidence has no appeal. If an inductive study of profit evidence fails to sustain the charge of conflict with social interest, on the criteria here suggested, what then do Keynes and the legion of sycophantic satellites who gather about his intellectual star mean by their indictment of profit?

They mean that if the major lines of business policy could be laid down by the ivory tower torchbearers of a new Utopia the nation would be much better off. If all the important decisions affecting the conduct of business could be made by men free from those acquisitive lusts which quench the pure zeal for social welfare, we could readily eliminate unemployment, the violent spasms of the business cycle, and lift human happiness several notches toward the terrestrial peak of mundane paradise to which all bleeding hearts aspire.

What Keynes really means is that he and his company of zealots could manage our affairs through national planning to much better effect than they are in fact being managed by private parties who are unable to work in concert, whose judgments moreover are corrupted by the fatal poison of self-interest.

These fellows are convinced that the risks which private management must always take in planning for the future, on the limited scale necessary within their own field of company responsibility—risks which sometimes go awry—would invariably be sound and successful if taken on a national scale by men imbued with a unique concern for the general welfare.

They mean that the information, which is at present sometimes inadequate and frequently leads private judgment astray, would be adequate under a scheme of national planning; that, in contrast with private decisions, national decisions by a public spirited departmental head would invariably be correct.

They mean in short that planning on a national scale by official intelligence could do a much better job in terms of a stable economy and rising living standards than planning on a local scale by men whose zeal is limited by the harsh requirements of double entry accounting. That is what they mean when they speak of the incompatibility of private profit and social interest.

AN APPLICANT WITHOUT REFERENCES

Before asking for such a revolutionary transfer of power from those who have acquired it, under the rugged rules of private enterprise and open competition, it would seem that some evidence of competence and success should be submitted by the aspirants for this power.

In this the proponents of Keynesian prosperity are understandably coy. In Russia the corrupting lust of private profit has been thoroughly exorcized. During the thirty years in which this has taken place, personal liberty has vanished and living standards have declined at least 40 per cent. The Russian worker must labor for 1 hour for a heavy loaf of bread and $104\frac{1}{2}$ hours for a pair of shoes. The American gets the same loaf of bread for $\frac{1}{4}$ hour of effort and the pair of shoes for $7\frac{1}{4}$ hours of effort.

England under a Labor Government has experienced a succession of crises since the end of the war. The Empire is disintegrating. Private savings have practically ceased. Britain has been subsisting on the fat accumulated by her rugged individualists during a century in which they were spurred on by the lure of private reward. On such fat, and on aid from her imperial offspring.

It is not to be inferred that the distress of England and the stark reaction in Russia are due to national planning alone. Yet when Keynes says: "Experience does *not* show that individuals, when they make up a social unit, are always less clear sighted than when they act separately," one may reply: "No, but the evidence is persuasive."

Personally Keynes presents a series of paradoxes which cannot help but confuse not only his opponents, but, even more so, his own followers. Here is a man who once made what we regard as one of the best statements which we have ever seen in defense of the gold standard. Yet he proceeded to develop a system of managed currency the end result of which must inevitably be the demonetization of gold.

In a single page of his *General Theory* he exposes the fallacy and futility of a mathematical presentation of economic theory. Yet in this same volume he resorts to mathematical symbols and procedures which bar comprehension for all but the specially trained professional.

Finally, after several volumes of brilliant but specious reasoning, designed apparently to undermine the basis of a free competitive society, he ends in the "Concluding Notes" of *The General Theory* with this comment on "the traditional advantages of individualism."

The "Advantages of Individualism"

Let us stop for a moment to remind ourselves what these advantages are. They are partly advantages of efficiency—the advantages of decentralization and of the play of self-interest. The advantage to efficiency of the decentralization of decisions and of individual responsibility is even greater, perhaps, than the nineteenth century supposed; and the reaction against the appeal to self-interest may have gone too far. But, above all, individualism, if it can be purged of its defects and its abuses, is the best safeguard of personal liberty in the sense that, compared with any other system, it greatly widens the field for the exercise of personal choice. It is also the best safeguard for the variety of life, which emerges precisely from this extended field of personal choice, and the loss of which is the greatest of all the losses of the homogeneous or totalitarian state. For this variety preserves the traditions which embody the most secure and successful choices of former generations; it colours the present with the diversification of its fancy; and, being the handmaid of experiment as well as of tradition and of fancy, it is the most powerful instrument to better the future.

XVIII

Wilhelm Röpke was born near Hamburg, Germany, in 1899. He taught at the universities of Jena and Marburg in Germany, of Graz in Austria, and of Istanbul in Turkey. From 1926 to 1927 he visited the United States as a professor sponsored by the Rockefeller Foundation. In 1933 he was one of the first German professors dismissed by Hitler for his liberal convictions. In 1937 he accepted the chair for international economics, which he still occupies, at the Graduate Institute of International Studies at Geneva. Professor Röpke served as economic adviser to the Brüning Government of Germany from 1930 to 1932 and has been serving the Adenauer Administration in the same capacity since 1949. Columbia University conferred an honorary degree upon him in 1954.

Among his most important works are: *Crises and Cycles,* 1936; *International Economic Disintegration,* 1942; *Civitas Humana,* 1948; and *The Social Crisis of Our Time,* 1950.

The following appeared as a pamphlet published by the American Enterprise Association in January, 1952. It is not directly an analysis of Keynes's *General Theory,* but of the United Nations Report on National and International Measures for Full Employment. Like R. Gordon Wasson's article, however, it analyzes "full employment policies" based on Keynesian assumptions.

THE ECONOMICS OF FULL EMPLOYMENT

WILHELM RÖPKE

I

BACKGROUND AND SUMMARY OF THE U. N. REPORT

No single economic issue in our time has been responsible for so much confusion, passion and acrimonious discussion as the one which goes under the glib heading of "full employment." And, because of the terminology used, there is no other economic issue which appears so attractive and yet may be so dangerous as the one based on this misleading and bitterly discussed concept.

When, as at the present time, the main concern of the Western World is not to find jobs but rather workers, and when we are faced with a condition not of deflation but of inflation, it might appear that the question of "full employment"—in the sense of a continuous absence of any amount of "involuntary" unemployment guaranteed by government action and monetary manipulation—is no longer topical.

Such an impression, however, is illusory. For apart from the fact that the enormous tensions and difficulties of the present rearmament boom are the direct consequences of "full employment policies" being practiced everywhere, onto which new "military inflation" is now being grafted, we also have two other factors to face in the present situation. One is that in some countries "full employment" has become the slogan to justify almost every action of the government. Thus the ideology has become so ingrained, and the corresponding policy so immovable, that in spite of high inflationary pressure and dangerous over-full employment no determined reversal of policies has become noticeable. The other is that while at the present moment interest in the issue of "full employment" seems to have receded, it is safe to assume that this situation is only a respite, which will end the moment there is a flagging of the present boom.

It is, in fact, all too probable that "full employment"—always in that special sense as it is understood by the Post-Keynesian school—will soon again become the center of discussion of economic and financial policies, even if there is no imminent prospect of a major economic recession in the West. Indeed, at this moment it is not difficult to detect the influence of "full employment" concepts and ideologies on present plans for the development of "under-developed countries"—plans whose ambitious scale and optimistic assumptions are out of proportion to the sober facts.

THE U. N. REPORT

Nowhere has the doctrine of "full employment" been more simply and succinctly stated than in a Report made in December 1949 to the United Nations on "National and International Measures for Full Employment." [1] This Report outlines the theory of "full employment" on which a number of European countries, and the United States to a limited extent, have proceeded during the past two years with resultant increasing socialism and inflation.

In view of the fact that in this Report there is contained much of the philosophy that will actuate future policies of the United Nations, and in view of the subsequent developments throughout the Western World since the Report was issued, it is highly important that there be a clear understanding of the "full employment" doctrine expressed in this Report, both as to its theory and practice. It is equally important that there be a clear understanding of its fallacies and inevitable consequences. The purpose of this study, therefore, is to submit the Report to critical analysis, with the object of evaluating these extreme views and their potentially disastrous consequences, in the hope that the issue can be turned from one of passionate dispute into a joint effort of moderation, reasoned analysis and practical common sense.

---

[1] *National and International Measures for Full Employment* (Report by a group of experts appointed by the Secretary-General). United Nations, Department of Economic Affairs, Lake Success, New York, December 1949. Hereinafter referred to as *U.N. Full Employment Report.*

The Report claims the double authority of being both an official document of the U. N. Secretariat and a statement worked out and "unanimously" agreed upon by five economists of repute.[2] It must be pointed out, however, that the choice of experts made the panel one highly weighted in favor of Post-Keynesian orthodoxy, with the notable exception of Professor J. M. Clark of Columbia University. He entered a separate statement. This marred the appearances of unanimity. It also has great significance in that it draws attention to a fact which is of capital importance and which goes a long way toward upsetting the whole theory of "full employment," namely—that the height of wages may have something to do with the level of employment.

The Fundamental Ideas of the U. N. Report

While the U. N. Report recognizes that unemployment may have quite different causes—lack of capital, frictions and maladjustments, etc.,—the major cause as seen in the report is a "deficiency of effective demand." [3] This is the point on which everything else hinges and which, as we shall see later, vitiates this whole philosophy of "full employment." The Report leaves the term "effective demand" undefined. But it is clear that what is meant is the sum total of purchasing power used for buying commodities or services, no matter whether this purchasing power is based on previous production or created by monetary expansion.

After having made their amazingly simple statement and after having admitted that a reasonable definition of "full employment" must include the allowance of a residual unemployment of 2 to 4 percent (which is not only normal and necessary, giving the "play" needed for the labor market as for any other market, but also socially bearable and manageable) the authors

2 The group was composed of the following: John Maurice Clark, Professor of Economics, Columbia University; Arthur Smithies, Professor of Economics, Harvard University; Nicholas Kaldor, Fellow of King's College, Cambridge; Pierre Uri, Economic and Financial Adviser to the *Commissariat général du Plan*, Paris; E. Ronald Walker, Economic Adviser to the Australian Department of External Affairs.

3 *U.N. Full Employment Report*, p. 13. "Under normal conditions, any unemployment exceeding the amount which is due to the frictional and seasonal factors to which we have referred above is a clear indication of a deficiency in effective demand."

of the Report go on to explain the process by which the "deficiency of effective demand" is created in our economic system.[4]

What we find here is an outline of the mechanics of the Keynesian "full employment engineering," which has now become rather familiar. But the exposition is so simplified as to read sometimes like a parody. Once more we are told that maintenance of full employment requires that savings and investments, current revenue and expenditure of the government, and exports and imports of a country must be in balance. And if one of these three pairs of factors shows an excess of one over the other, full utilization of resources demands that this excess be offset by an opposite imbalance of another pair of factors e.g., an excess of savings over investments must be offset by an excess of exports over imports, or of government expenditure over revenue, to the same extent.

It should be noted, and it is most significant, that the authors of the Report only speak of an imbalance causing a *deflationary under*employment. They entirely leave out of account the possibility of an opposite imbalance causing an *inflationary over*employment. Thus they do not seem to see that this is exactly the situation in which the West has found itself ever since the second World War. Anticipating some of our later criticism, it should also be noted that there is no hint whatever, in the Report, that this simple "full employment" mathematics approaches the meaningless in that the several pairs of factors which must be in balance may act upon each other in a way which is wholly unpredictable. That is, deficit spending of the government, meant to offset an excess of savings over investments, may actually discourage private investment still further, as happened in the United States under the "pump-priming" policy of the 1930's.

Such, then, is the chain of reasoning of the Report: Unemployment is almost always and everywhere the result of a "de-

[4] *Ibid.*, p. 21 "If balance is achieved at less than full employment, a full employment policy requires an unbalanced movement which expands aggregate effective demand, and continues to expand it until full employment is reached, when a balance must again be established between the several factors, in order to maintain employment at the full employment level. The condition necessary for balance is that the sum of factors having a plus effect on expenditure—private investment, government expenditures and exports—shall equal the sum of the minus factors—savings decisions, taxes and imports."

ficiency of effective demand"; this "deficiency" is the result of some essential "global" entity or entities not being in balance; to ensure "full employment" we must ensure their being always in balance. To this end, it is of capital importance to maintain a high level of investments. Since, however, there is no force automatically bringing about and maintaining the required balance, attainment of full employment and its maintenance require sustained actions on the part of the government.[5] Implicit in this line of reasoning is the assumption that the government at all times will have omnipotent wisdom in the sense that its actions will always produce the desired and planned for result.

THE RECOMMENDATIONS OF THE REPORT

Just as the underlying philosophy of the Report, as described above, is familiar to students of the Post-Keynesian school, so the action recommended by the authors of the Report follows, on the whole, along well known lines.

In private enterprise economics, the authors point out, stability in the level of private investment can only be promoted by what they call indirect control. Apart from monetary and credit measures—particularly variations of the interest rate—two ways are recommended by the Report: one is the use of special tax incentives for influencing private investments; the other is the policy of offsetting fluctuations in private investments by countervailing fluctuations in public investment.

Such measures of stabilizing the level of investment, however, may not be sufficient, the Report argues, to bring total demand up to the level which is necessary to ensure full employment. In that event these procedures must be supplemented by measures raising consumer demand to the desired level, preferably by revenue and expenditure programs of the government, thus making it a real virtue to enlarge the normal share of governmental expenditure as much as possible. Fears of the state running increasingly into debt are waived aside with the insou-

[5] *U.N. Full Employment Report* p. 21. "There is no reason to assume that the full employment level will be reached automatically or that, if it is reached, it will be maintained at that level. The attainment of full employment and its maintenance may therefore require sustained action, purposively directed to that end; and while numerous agencies may cooperate, the central role must be assumed by governments."

ciance and flimsy arguments characteristic of this whole school.

To summarize the program outlined in the Report, the following passages are presented for the convenience of the reader.

On the question of fiscal policy:

The adaptation of the fiscal policy of the state to the needs of full employment will undoubtedly be one of the principal vehicles for stabilizing effective demand at the full-employment level in private-enterprise economies. The means for such an adaptation consist of changes in the level and kinds of expenditure, changes in the level and kinds of taxation, as well as changes in the relations between these two; and finally, in the adaptation of both taxation and expenditure to increase their flexibility in response to fluctuations in effective demand.[6]

On the control of the volume of private investment:

Governments can provide special credit facilities or give guarantees or special tax inducements to private investors when it is desired to promote the expansion of investment in the private sector of the economy. . . . It may also be feasible for governments to co-operate with the private industries concerned in the establishment of long-range investment programmes in well-established industries.[7]

On the planning of public investment:

In those cases in which the public sector of the economy includes certain basic industries such as mining, steel production and public utilities, and a substantial part of transport, housing and industrial construction . . . the level of investment could largely be stabilized as a result of a co-ordinated public investment programme. The stabilization of the total volume of investment could further be ensured by timing the execution of postponable public investment projects so as to dovetail with the fluctuations in private investment.[8]

And finally, all these measures being considered insufficient in the advanced industrial countries, the Report proposes:

For the maintenance of an adequate level of effective demand, such countries would therefore place their main reliance upon the expansion of consumer demand. In many countries a long-term pro-

6 *U.N. Full Employment Report* pp. 76-77.
7 *Ibid.*, p. 78.
8 *Ibid.*, pp. 78-79.

gramme for the expansion of consumption could be carried out by employing the instruments of fiscal policy discussed above . . . Furthermore, the control of monopoly prices may serve the purpose of increasing consumer demand through the reduction of profit margins. Some countries may wish to extend this principle further and use price control more generally in order to effect a more equitable distribution of income.[9]

The authors conclude with a proposal which illustrates well the fact that the policy of "full employment" is as mechanical as the underlying theory namely, that the fiscal machinery of keeping up the level of effective demand should be brought into operation automatically whenever the actual level of unemployment exceeds for three successive months a pre-announced level by a stated percentage. Under the heading "Automatic Compensatory Measures in the Event of Unemployment" the Report states the proposition as follows:

> We believe that the adoption by each country of a system of automatic compensatory measures which would come into operation in clearly defined circumstances announced beforehand is a most important element in a successful full-employment policy. . . . We suggest that the automatic counter-measures should be so constructed as to produce an expansion of effective demand whenever unemployment exceeds the range defined in the full-employment target by some pre-determined amount for three consecutive months. The increase in the unemployment percentage necessary to bring the automatic measures into operation may vary with the circumstances of different countries, but in each country it should be no higher than is necessary to give a clear indication of deflationary tendencies in the economy; and it should be high enough to make it possible for measures for expanding effective demand to be undertaken on a scale sufficiently large to make an immediate and substantial impact on the employment situation.[10]

Economic policy would thus, indeed, attain the dignity of engineering, without regard to the fact that society can never be made into a machine nor can statistics succeed morality as a guide to behavior and policy.

[9] *Ibid.*, pp. 79-80.
[10] *U.N. Full Employment Report* p. 81.

II

THE FUNDAMENTAL FALLACIES

It should be stated very emphatically at the outset that the conflict of opinions in this field do not arise because some people desire maximum employment and others do not. In common with many other catchwords of our time—so it is with this phrase, of which the present author wrote about ten years ago: "The term 'full employment' has a dangerous quality that is calculated to disarm criticism from the start. Everyone advocates full employment in a reasonable sense, because no one considers involuntary mass unemployment for more than a short period as anything but a national disaster." [11] But the basic issue considered in the Report is not whether we should aim at the general and obviously desirable objective of achieving and maintaining a maximum level of utilization of all productive forces. On the contrary, the program projected in the Report is concerned only with a special theory of maximum employment, and with an equally special policy to sustain the theory.

This *special theory* of the Report explains under-employment as a disturbance in the general flow of money and income, which is said to find its expression in a lack of "effective demand." According to this theory, there is a danger of continuous pressure towards deflation. To this corresponds the *special policy* proposed by the Report which consists in monetary expansion equipping people with the "deficient effective demand." Against the alleged danger of continuous deflationary pressure the authors of the Report would set continuous monetary counterpressure. Even if there is unemployment not *caused* by a general contraction of demand, so goes the theory, it can be *cured* by monetary expansion. That is the teaching of the present school of "full employment" of which the U. N. Report is such a remarkable representative. Its monotonous answer to the problem of unemployment is: monetary expansion. It does not seriously look for other remedies which are less convenient, less spectacular, less sweeping and less spurious.

Can such a bold policy be carried through without serious

11 Wilhelm Röpke, *"The Social Crisis of Our Time,"* p. 170.

prejudice to the most elementary values of our society, which are to be ranked higher than some degree of temporary unemployment or the inconvenience of other measures against unemployment? Or does it lead us into inflation, permanent fiscal disorder, loss of elementary liberties and civic rights, destruction of the free economy, the spread of socialist controls, inefficiency, material waste, national isolation and international disintegration? And if even this frightening price is paid, can the goal of full employment be reached in this way and indefinitely maintained? That is the real issue.

A reasonably balanced stand in this issue can be summarized under two main points:

(1) It is true that a situation may arise when mass unemployment ensues as the result of general disturbance in the flow of money and income principally due to a prolonged paralysis of investment activities, as occurred during the depression of the early 1930's. And it is further true that, in such a case, one remedy among several possibilities may be a policy of general monetary expansion. Also, it is true that in order to bring about such a general monetary expansion, a judicious combination of drastic monetary and fiscal measures may be less dangerous than a policy of letting things drift. But such a situation —the "secondary depression" as the present author called it during the Great Depression in the early thirties [12]—is altogether exceptional. And even then the greatest circumspection is called for if any "pump-priming" policy is to be a real success.

The evident failure of such a policy under the Roosevelt administration—which in fact did not succeed in bringing about a self-sustaining prosperity until the armament boom of the second World War set in—illustrates particularly well the necessity of relying less on reckless "deficit spending," and more on measures apt to encourage entrepreneurial confidence and initiative, instead of radical state intervention that is only too likely to kill these energizing forces. But whatever may be the right policy in this exceptional case of the "secondary depression," this surely is not the situation which has prevailed in the West since 1940, nor is likely to prevail in the foreseeable fu-

[12] For the term and meaning of "secondary depression" see the author's contribution to the symposium *Economic Essays in Honour of Gustav Cassel,* London 1933 pp. 553-568.

ture. As we shall see, the economic condition of most countries today is in fact the exact opposite of that which the "full-employment" school supposes.

(2) If we admit the occasional possibility of general economic standstill, and of monetary expansion being a recommendable policy, we must state all the more clearly that to generalize on this abnormal eventuality constitutes the fatal error of the "full-employment" school. For it is emphatically untrue to contend that, normally and on the average, unemployment is caused by a general disturbance of money circulation (deflation) and is therefore capable of being cured by a policy of continuously filling the gap of "effective demand" without inflation and all the other disastrous consequences which we shall consider more closely.

Indeed, it should be obvious that there are as many causes of unemployment as there are causes of economic maladjustment. Many of these have nothing to do with the money flow—such as: people doing wrong things or working at wrong places or with wrong methods; changes of demand; dislocations of markets, nationally or internationally; lack of capital; shortages of raw materials and other complementary products; changes of governmental policies; flooding of the labor market by migration or natural population increase; and particularly, excessive wage demands, by which "labor prices itself out of the market."

Any one or any combination of such causes may bring about at any time a considerable amount of unemployment or "unused capacity" of production. But it would, of course, be quite wrong to suppose that this makes it safe to expand "effective demand" without the immediate danger of inflation. Once such a policy is admitted there is no degree of maladjustment, inefficiency, dislocation, slackness, immobility, stickiness of costs or wage demands which can not be used as a justification for a monetary expansion large enough to fill the gap of "effective demand."

When the U. N. Report speaks of deficiency of "effective demand" it leaves the term undefined, as we have already observed. But more often than not, the Report seems to use it in the meaningless sense of the loss of income and employment, which is the natural consequence of any sort of maladjustment.

And it presumes the possibility of safely filling this gap by a corresponding infusion of money. Now there is no doubt that, at least for a while, almost any kind and amount of unemployment can be made to disappear by monetary expansion. This is why, during the war, there was no unemployment. To this fact the authors of the Report point with a sort of strange nostalgia. But to pursue the policy of "full employment" regardless of the causes of unemployment means nothing else than to drown all economic maladjustments in a flood of money. As new causes of maladjustment arise a new dose of inflation will have to be applied, in order to keep up "full employment."

A policy, therefore, which sees unemployment of whatever kind, and due to whatever cause, as sufficient reason for increasing "effective demand" is necessarily tantamount to a *policy of constant inflationary pressure.* But that is precisely the policy which today goes under the name of "full employment" and which the U. N. Report now wants to persuade all nations to accept as an international obligation.

Very much the same result follows when we analyze what happens when a government applies the same principle of "full employment through thick and thin" in order to perpetuate general boom conditions. There is fairly universal agreement today that it is part of a reasonable policy of economic stabilization to cope with the problem of a general depression, as it occurs in the ups and downs of the business cycle, by a policy of credit expansion. The error of the "full employment" school, however, is to believe that it is safe to continue such a policy as long as there still exists some amount of unemployment or other form of "idle capacity."

Long before general full employment is reached there will appear at certain "strategic" points of the economy shortages of important kinds of labor and other productive resources. These will create more and more tensions and higher costs, the more the general expansion is continued, under the pretext that full employment is not yet universal, even though it has been attained in the "bottleneck" areas of the economy. Rather early, let us say, bricklayers, skilled metal workers, or steel or some other strategic raw material will become scarce, while in other branches there are still unemployed. When this critical mark has been reached monetary expansion will lead to higher prices and costs rather than to more employment. It follows, therefore, that by this policy of increasing "effective demand" full employment will be reached only at the cost of inflation and the maladjustments characteristic of every major boom. The social evil of partial unemployment will then be combatted by the even greater social evil of general inflation.

To perpetuate this highly unbalanced condition of boom full employment (which, in reality, means "overemployment") calls for an ever higher dose of inflation. This is precisely the way by which the "full employment" policy of the Third Reich in Germany went after a few years--around 1936—from the phase of "compensatory credit" expansion to the phase of "inflationary" expansion, which was one of the main reasons of the collectivist system of the Nazi regime. We would do well to remember that the "full employment" of the Third Reich is so far the only example of such a policy carried through in peacetime, with some measure of temporary success. And we should also remember the tragic price that had to be paid for this spurious success. It is strange and startling to find that the U. N. Report makes no reference to this experience.

III

EUROPEAN AND AMERICAN EXPERIENCES

The members of the modern school of "full employment," including the authors of the U. N. Report, persist, with imperturbable determination, in regarding every type of unemployment whatsoever—whether it be due to lasting structural changes or to temporary economic causes, of short-term or long-term character, partial or total—as the expression of a "lack of effective demand."

Their sole remedy for the trouble is to increase the volume of money and credit whenever and wherever some unemployment becomes visible. That is the form in which the theory is nowadays put into effect in a number of European countries, particularly in Great Britain, the Scandinavian countries, and the Netherlands. The result is, as was to be expected, a constant inflationary pressure. Since the Korean crisis it has taken on alarming dimensions in all those countries and can no longer be controlled except by a determined but politically difficult reversal of the whole policy of "full employment."

It is almost unnecessary to add that the constant inflationary pressure in these countries, which results from "full employment" policies, is inextricably mixed up with a more or less elaborate system of collectivist controls which prevent prices, interest rates, and exchanges from truly expressing the real inflation. And all of this is at the cost of the destruction of the price mechanism, of the choking of the economic processes, of disorder and of international disintegration, together with the loss of free enterprise and liberal democracy.

While these above mentioned countries illustrate the actual consequence of "full employment" policies as recommended by the U. N. Report, there are in Europe other countries like Germany and Italy which evidence particularly well the fact that the actual economic situation of almost all European countries is the exact opposite of that assumed by Keynes. In these two countries it is particularly obvious that it would be disastrous to give way to the pressure brought to bear by the "full employment" school, including American representatives, in spite of the existence of a still considerable amount of unemployment. For whereas the "full employment" school works with the idea of a deficiency of investments relative to savings as the principal cause of unemployment, here we have the exact contrary case—an almost unlimited willingness by business to use capital, even at high interest rates, which cannot be satisfied because of a shortage of capital. Here the problem is not how to find investments as an outlet for savings but how to find savings as a non-inflationary basis for investments.

The U. N. Report occasionally admits that unemployment may be due to lack of capital instead of "deficiency of effective demand," but its authors think that this is only important in "underdeveloped countries." A more careful study of present conditions in Europe, however, would have convinced them that they have been guilty of grossly underestimating the importance of this factor. It is the case in almost all Europe today.

A country like Germany, moreover, provides a particularly interesting and extreme example of the fallacy of the "full-employment" theory. This theory conceives the labor market of a country as a homogeneous fluid mass. Whereas it is a fact that full or over-full employment for a country as a whole may be concomitant with underemployment in particular trades, branches, or regions, without any prompt adjustment. For example, unemployment in Germany today is confined to certain groups of unskilled workers and to the millions of refugees —whereas even before the Korean crisis the general business conditions were already rather those of prosperity, with shortages of skilled workers, and a steady increase of the total number of employed.

Even prior to the international rearmament boom Germany presented, like many other countries, a state of affairs which has been called "prosperity unemployment," a phenomenon which, at the same time, seems to have been produced in the United States by excessive wage demands. To apply to such a situation the patent-medicine of "full employment" is to create inflationary pressure, with its well known domestic consequences, to say nothing of a deficit in the international balance of payments.

That is why the German government and the German Central Bank were right in the summer of 1950 in resisting the campaign of the "full-employment" school, as represented by certain German groups and American experts in Germany, and why the Government and Bank were correct in warning that such a course would lead immediately to inflationary conditions and a strain of the balance of payments. When finally, considerable concessions had to be made to this vociferous campaign of the "full-employment" enthusiasts, the subsequent serious crisis of the German balance of payments nearly upset the newly created machinery of the European Payments Union, thus proving how justified resistance to this pressure had been. Nevertheless, this development did not prevent bitter criticism of the German authorities from those who, a few months earlier, had criticized them just as bitterly for their reluctance to plunge into "full employment" policies.

While developments in Italy show striking parallels with those in Germany, the United States seems to offer an altogether different picture. And yet the case of the United States provides further illustration of some fundamental fallacies of the "full-employment" school.

In the case of the United States, it may be conceded that

rather soon after the war the question arose whether private investments would be forthcoming in a steady amount sufficient to ensure the desired economic equilibrium. There was concern over possible unemployment, such as had arisen in the 1930's, when the generally unsuccessful efforts of the New Deal to bring about a stable and natural equilibrium had been rationalized as necessary because of an alleged "mature economy." But now, as then, the truth of the matter seems to be that no understanding of the problem of deficient investment activities is possible without full regard to other characteristics of economic policy—such as the tendency of massive and comprehensive state interference—which may discourage private investment and diminish the demand for labor. For these policies, while meeting with the hearty approval of the members of the "full-employment" school, are likely to discourage investment decisions. Such decisions, being directed to the uncertain future, always require the highest degree of courage, optimism and confidence. Stiff taxation of investment profits, ruthless exploitation of labor monopolies, cynical disregard of firm principles in economic and financial policy, threats of socialization, currency manipulation, reckless budget deficits and ever higher public debts, contempt for private property nationally and internationally, arbitrariness and insecurity everywhere—all these may be regarded as highly progressive. But one must not be surprised if, when such conditions prevail, the amount of investment is less than it might and should be.

The conclusion is that, for maximum employment to be assured by a high level of investments, the right course is not a policy which frightens people away from such hazardous activity. Rather the opposite policy, which will encourage such activity and stimulate investment in an orderly manner, is the correct one. If a country like the United States should prefer, instead of the last-named policy, the course of "full employment" it would be following the dangerous road which seeks to compensate continuously the unbalancing factors of economic life by *monetary expansion*. Of particular moment here might be the action of powerful trade unions, which tend continuously to push wages upward beyond the point where all workers can be employed at current wages. Monopolistic wage rates, therefore, are likely to cause unemployment even under general conditions of prosperity. If the government, committed to the principle of "full employment," combats by credit expansion this "prosperity unemployment," which has been created by excessive wages, and which outdistances increases in industrial productivity, the government is necessarily caught in a vicious circle whose outcome is again constant inflationary pressure.

The entire economic policy of a country under such circumstances threatens more and more to develop into a permanent race between a wage policy that, by imposing excessive wages, creates unemployment, and a credit policy that tries to compensate this effect of wage policies by monetary expansion. As the race develops the combination of full employment and of inflationary pressure makes possible and gives rise to higher and higher wage claims; these in turn induce a further credit expansion; thus is the wage spiral kept in perpetual motion.

IV

THE CONSEQUENCES

Theoretical analysis as well as international experience seem to lead inevitably to the conclusion that policies of "full employment," as understood today, involve consequences which should prompt the members of the "full employment" school to think twice before they shoulder the formidable responsibility of continuing their campaign.

We have seen that there is enough reason to fear that one of the most serious effects of "full employment" as a continuous policy will be an equally continuous pressure of inflation. There is further good reason to suppose that, in modern post-Hitlerian and post-Schachtian times, this pressure of inflation will prompt governments to turn it into "repressed inflation," namely, to combat the natural effects of inflation by collectivist measures. Thus the policy of "full employment" is likely to end, via inflation, in the destruction of the market economy and free enterprise by a system of collectivist controls. In this way, we get that curious type of national economic order which—and it is difficult to say precisely what is cause and what is effect—is characterized by a combination of "full employment," collectivism, and inflationary pressure. It is this type of "national collectivism" that we find in various degrees and varieties in many European countries today.

Nobody can be unaware of what all these consequences named so far mean to liberty, civic rights and constitutional government. To this list of consequences we have to add another very serious one. It is the probable effect of "full employment" on industrial productivity, economic development, and labor efficiency. Anybody passably familiar with the waste, the sluggishness, loss of incentives and the rigidity of the labor market that result from "full employment" and "repressed inflation" will understand why, from this point of view also, "full employment" must be viewed with pronounced pessimism.

That "full employment" may even retard the whole general economic development of a country in a very serious way can be seen in the following strong words of an otherwise rather charitable reviewer of the U. N. Report.

Even economic growth—in the stock of capital, productivity, efficiency, innovation—is likely to suffer in the end from the consequences of extreme full employment, in the long run probably more than in the short. The chief points of conflict here are diminishing flexibility and incentives, the probable strait-jacketing of foreign trade, and particularly the stimulation of consumption in lieu of investment—a procedure defended with such logic in the report.[13]

Now the disquieting thing is not that the U. N. Report takes little or no cognizance of these real dangers of "full employment." Its authors are indeed not entirely unaware of them. But what is alarming is the lightheartedness with which they stick to their program in spite of their knowledge and the insouciance with which they belittle the inevitable consequences and trust in pseudo-solutions—if not in the magic effects of simple words. Their general line is (1) to argue away the danger of inflation, or (2) to belittle its consequences, or (3) if neither the one nor the other seems possible any more, to have recourse to its "repression" by collectivist controls. If, finally, driven into a corner, they take cover behind a verbal smokescreen—that is, when compelled to face the very real danger of

[13] Henry C. Wallich, *United Nations Report on Full Employment, American Economic Review,* December 1950, p. 883.

excessive wage increases—their answer simply amounts to the suggestion that something or other should be done about it.

Summing up the attitude of the authors we may say that they cannot deny the immense danger of "full employment" leading to inflation but that, when any other argument fails—which is more often the case then they would admit—they simply prefer inflation to anything less than "full" employment. Indeed, they state their preference, even though they say it in a most involved way: "Our task here is . . . to urge that it would be inappropriate for any country to pursue policies having the effect of raising unemployment above the level resulting from seasonal and frictional causes, merely in order to restrain upward pressures on prices." [14]

The explanation of this strange attitude of the authors of the Report may lie in two errors which seem to have led them astray.

The first of these is the tacit assumption that a milder inflation may be a not unreasonable price for avoiding any degree of the major evil of "unemployment." On this point they convey the impression that we must choose between some measure of inflation and a social catastrophe called "unemployment." This impression is, however, dangerously misleading, because the cost (of inflation) must in reality be balanced not only against the various kinds and degrees of unemployment but also against ways of combatting unemployment other than this quite special way of so-called "full employment." In short, unemployment is not always a social catastrophe, and there are other and better ways to deal with it.

The second error which seems to account for the inflationary bias of the Report is the confidence of its authors in the efficacy and virtues of "repressed inflation." That they do not like this outspoken term is understandable, but it is the policy which they recommend again and again, though in somewhat subtler phrases. It is almost fantastic to assume that they should not have been aware of what modern economists have to say on the nature and the consequences of "repressed inflation" and of the lessons taught by the ample experiences which many countries have had with this particularly pernicious economic disease. Furthermore, it is difficult to believe that the authors did not

[14] *U.N. Full Employment Report* p. 45.

realize that to recommend "repressed inflation" is to admit that the policy of "full employment," as one of compensating any flagging of employment by monetary expansion, is incompatible with the system of free enterprise whose preservation the authors nevertheless feel able to promise.

Yet one must not forget that to admit the real extent of the danger of inflation involved in "full employment" policies, and to recognize the truth about repressed inflation, would indeed be equivalent to acknowledging frankly the fundamental fallacies of the whole idea of "full employment." It is human nature to resist such retreat. But it is a case where retreat is more creditable than desperate resistance.

V

THE INTERNATIONAL IMPLICATIONS

The international implications of the policies of "full employment" as outlined in the U. N. Report, constitute one of its most important aspects. As the Report has particularly interesting things to say on this problem we have earmarked it for special analysis. The subject is so vast and involved that we can only indicate some of the salient points.

There has always been some degree of conflict between autonomous national policies of stabilization and free multilateral world trade, and to find some compromise between these conflicting aims has always been a serious problem. "Full employment," always as understood in the special sense explained several times, is bound to turn this conflict into a head-on clash and to become one of the main sources of international economic disintegration. Here again, the experience of the Third Reich has served as the model by producing all these external consequences which have now become familiar in all countries pursuing this course—disequilibrium of balance of payments, "dollar shortage," exchange control, bilateralism, severe quantitative trade restrictions, an elaborate system of ever-changing import and export regulations, national economic isolation, and grave disturbances in the whole system of international payments and international trade relations.

One must realize, in fact, that one of the most indispensable parts of a system of sustained "full employment," with its inflationary pressure and its machinery of collectivist repression, must be exchange control—which may be defined as a policy of defending a "wrong" exchange rate by police force. Exchange control is the veritable keystone of this system of "national collectivism" into which any policy of sustained "full employment" is most likely to develop. Exchange control, however, means inconvertibility of currencies, and this destroys the multilateral network of international trade. And the destruction of free multilateralism is the synonym for international economic disintegration.

The authors of the U. N. Report are not unaware of these things. In fact, they present a penetrating analysis of the international implications of their program. They most certainly know that its cost is the dislocation and disintegration of international trade—indeed, the very international economic disorder as we have it today and which most persons would agree we can no longer afford.

Confronted with this situation, there are three possible courses. We may accept the formidable cost of "full employment"—namely, international economic disintegration. Or we try to find some workable solution of the problem by constructing some sort of international machinery of constant planned adjustment. Or we may admit that neither the one nor the other is feasible, which means that "full employment" is not feasible either.

The authors consider the first course, and though they characteristically prefer the fulfillment of their program of "full employment" to the ideal of international integration, they evidently do not like this course. So they give all their attention to the second course. In this connection they devise a highly elaborate machinery of international adjustment and of reciprocal financial help. The aim is to assure a steady flow of long-term international investments, mostly for the benefit of the "under-developed countries." The method is to organize, by international agreement, "procedures whereby the international propagation of deflationary pressures and the consequent tendency towards a cumulative contraction of world trade may

be effectively prevented." [15] Under this scheme each partic-
ipating government commits itself to replenish

... the monetary reserves of other countries concurrently with, and
to the extent of, the depletion of those reserves which results from
an increase in its own reserves induced by a fall in its demand for
imported goods and services, in so far as this fall is caused by a
general decline in effective demand within its own country.[16]

In other words, any country which fails to live up to the
authors' program of continuously keeping up what they call
(though do not precisely define) "effective demand,"—and
which adjusts its balance of payments by restrictive credit policies in order to correct an inflationary pressure, would have to
put the equivalent of this adjustment in its own currency at
the disposal of those countries who want to go on with "full
employment," undisturbed by inflationary pressure and its awkward effects on their balance of payments. This means that the
more extravagant the economic policy of a country is, the more
it will be entitled to refill its depleted reserves at the expense
of the more responsible countries.

The scheme is ingenious but unwise and unworkable. First
of all, the technical difficulties are so numerous and so great
that one finds it impossible to see how they could be overcome.
Secondly, we have to consider that under this plan, the countries
which are not yet convinced of the unqualified wisdom of "full
employment," or which simply fall behind in the general course
of inflation, would be compelled to subsidize and relieve the
others of some important part of the cost of their "full employment" program. In other words, the authors of the Report
have actually succeeded in providing that any disbelief in their
program shall be penalized. Perhaps they have not sufficiently
taken it into account that governments might be somewhat
unwilling to submit themselves beforehand to such a system of
sanctions for non-conformity to modern economic orthodoxy.

Most important, however, is a third point. What the whole
ingenious scheme amounts to is to contrive the adjustment of
international trade by a complex machinery of collectivist international planning which does the work done before by the

15 *U.N. Full Employment Report* p. 94.
16 *Ibid.,* p. 96.

free functioning of international markets and price movements. Only in this way would the necessary coordination of national trade and investment plans be possible. Behind the whole project is the more or less clear recognition that national economic planning ("national collectivism") has ended in an impasse, and that the way out is to supersede it by international planning.

But if we accept the stubborn fact that replacement of the market economy with collectivist planning means substituting the free functioning of price mechanism by orders and sanctions of government administration, then international collectivist planning becomes either an illusion or a nightmare. The reasons are clear.

This sort of international collective planning cannot be brought about by the free cooperation of democratic nations, since international planning presupposes an international state able to give and enforce its orders like a national state. Such an international state is utterly utopian and impractical. For, in order that the plan may work, it is necessary that it be a collectivist international state, whose inevitable centralism cannot tolerate any kind of international federalism. Yet everyone, including the socialists, agree that an international federation is the only way in which, at best, we could hope for an international state in our life-time. So much for the illusion.

International planning thus becomes possible only under the kind of international dictatorship which Hitler called "Grossraum." Then, however, it would be a nightmare, and surely for the authors of the U. N. Report no less than for all of us.

It would, therefore, appear that not only the present plan but also any other attempt, however ingeniously contrived, to get out of the impasse of national "full employment" by the machinery of planned international adjustment, is a snare and delusion. There is left only one course:—to admit that "full employment," in the extreme sense of the Report, is not feasible and to be satisfied with a less ambitious, more reasonable and better balanced program of economic stabilization.

Conclusion

This is not the occasion to give a detailed idea of an alternative program. There are admittedly a few ideas of the U. N.

Report which could be worked into an alternative program, but most of them have been vitiated by the fallacious dogmatism of "full employment." And any alternative program must be free of this obsessive idea of "effective demand" which blocks the way to the realities of the economic process. Instead of being a policy based upon the continuous filling of "gaps" a practical alternative must be inspired by the concept of a free, natural, and real equilibrium, compatible with national flexibility and a free international economic system.

There is today a prevailing view which makes free multilateral trade responsible for a large part of economic instability. It has become almost an axiom that it is incompatible with national policies of maximum employment. It is high time to correct such views. Although the possibility of serious conflicts cannot be gainsaid, we should not forget that a free multilateral world economy with stable and free exchange relations has in the past and would still be today one of the most powerful factors promoting high and relatively stable national levels of employment. It was not such an international system of economic freedom and stability which brought about the crisis of 1931 and its aftermath. For the fluctuations of employment under universal convertibility of currencies and free multilateralism of international trade, made possible by the gold standard, on the whole were mild. On the contrary, what wrecked the world were the same political and unmoral forces which undermined the liberal international order itself.

Those who are working for the reconstruction of free multilateral trade are working for and not against economic stability. Here, however, is a tragical irony. The present policies of "full employment" are one of the main obstacles to such reconstruction. While employment conditions are thereby being made all the more unstable, demand for further "full employment" is being pushed forward all the more vigorously. It is of the utmost necessity that this vicious circle be broken. The first step to this end is to combat current fallacies on "full employment" and to present convincingly the case for stable high employment, by free, natural, and genuine equilibrium, both nationally and internationally.

XIX

W. H. Hutt was born in London in 1899. He attended the London School of Economics and after graduation took employment in business. In 1928 he was appointed professor of commerce at the University of Capetown, South Africa, where he is now dean of the Faculty of Commerce. His works include: *The Theory of Collective Bargaining,* 1930; *Economists and the Public,* 1936; *The Theory of Idle Resources,* 1939; and *Plan for Reconstruction,* 1943.

Professor Hutt's *Theory of Collective Bargaining* was a penetrating "history, analysis and criticism of the principal theories" by which economists from Adam Smith down have attempted to prove that unions and "collective bargaining" had raised or could raise the average real level of market wages for the whole body of the workers without causing unemployment. His book, *Keynesianism—Retrospect and Prospect,* published in 1963, is a thorough, comprehensive, and brilliant refutation of the whole literature of Keynesianism. The following article appeared in *The South African Journal of Economics* for March, 1954, pages 40-51.

THE SIGNIFICANCE OF PRICE FLEXIBILITY

W. H. HUTT

The period 1932-1953 has witnessed a revolution and counter-revolution in thought on the function and consequences of price flexibility.

In considering this remarkable phase in the history of theory, it is useful to begin by referring to a related field of hardly disturbed agreement. There has been no controversy during the period of our survey among serious economists about the desirability of a system which tends to ensure that different kinds of prices shall stand in a certain optimum relation to one another, or about the desirability, in a changing world, of continuous *relative* price adjustment in order to bring about some conformance to the ideal relation. From the so-called "socialist economists" of the Lange-Lerner type to the so-called "individualist economists" of the Mises-Röpke type, there has been agreement that the price system has important equilibrating and co-ordinative functions. Moreover, until the appearance of Keynes's *General Theory*, in 1936, the measure of agreement about the *aims* of institutional reform for the better working of the price system seemed to be slowly but definitely growing.

There was not the same marked tendency towards agreement about *methods*. Some thought that improved pricing could be achieved through a greater centralisation or sectionalisation of economic power, with the final voice to decide both preferences (choice of ends) and productive policy (choice of means) entrusted to elected representatives or syndicates. Others thought that the required reforms involved exactly the reverse— the breaking up and diffusion of economic authority so that the final voice about ends rested with the people as consumers, whilst the final voice about the choice of means rested with those who stood to gain or lose according to the success with which they allocated scarce resources in accordance with consumer-determined ends. But in spite of this apparently basic clash, as soon as explicit plans for the devising of a workable economic system were attempted, even the divergence of opinion about methods appeared to be narrowing. The so-called "socialist economists" were clearly attempting to restore *the market* and the *power of substitution*. So much was this so, that I believed the result of their labours would ultimately be the re-building of *laissez-faire* institutions, in elaborate disguises of name and superficial form, the result being regarded as the perfect socialist pricing system.[1]

---

[1] In a discussion with A. P. Lerner about 1933, I pointed out to him that, however opposed our approaches might seem superficially to be, the institu-

This interesting trend towards unanimity of opinion in several fields was overlapped by and rudely disturbed by Keynes's *General Theory*. Since 1936, the economists have become sharply divided about the nature of the price changes which ought, in the interests of "full employment," to take place in any given situation.[2] Consider trade union or State enforced wage-rates. At one extreme, we have the Keynesians who argue that, in maintaining wage-rates, we are maintaining consumer demand, creating a justification for new investment, and so preventing the emergence of depression. At the other extreme, we have those who argue that each successive increase of wage-rates so brought about renders essential a further element of inflation in order to maintain "full employment"—a development which tends permanently to dilute the money unit.

The Keynesian theory on this point proved enormously attractive. The idea as such was not novel; but before *The General Theory* it had enjoyed a negligible following in respectable economic circles. After 1936, it gave many economists what they seemed to have been waiting for, a non-casuistic argument for the tolerance of the collective enforcement or State fixation of minimum wage-rates.

Curiously enough, Keynes's challenge was based on a sort of admission of the evils of current collective bargaining and a further admission (by no means explicit, but an inevitable inference [3]), that labour in general was unable to benefit in real terms at the expense of other parties to production, by forcing a rise in the price of labour. Gains achieved by individual groups of organised workers were paid out of the pockets of other workers. At the same time, Keynes's new teachings seemed to support strongly those who cried, "Hands off the

---

tions which we were seeking would, in the end, turn out to be exactly the same things. He refers to this conversation in the Preface to his *Economics of Control.*

[2] J. Viner, *The Role of Costs in a System of Economic Liberalism,* in *Wage Determination and the Economics of Liberalism* (Chamb. of Com. of U.S.), p. 31; To-day, different groups of economists "give diametrically opposite advice as to policy when unemployment prevails or is anticipated."

[3] Compare A. Smithies's statement of the implications of *The General Theory,* in his article, "Effective Demand and Employment," in Harris, *The New Economics,* page 561—". . . concerted action by the whole labour movement to increase money wages will leave real wages unchanged. Real wage gains by a single union are won at the expense of real wages elsewhere."

unions!" Although his thesis was accompanied by the charge—not wholly without foundation—that orthodox economists had closed their eyes to the consequences of the wage rigidity caused by trade union action, he always seemed to range himself on the side of the unions in their resistance to wage-rate adjustments. The reasons for his views on this question were two-fold.

Firstly, he argued that the price of labour had to be regarded as *inevitably* rigid. This empirical judgment about economic reality is, of course, not confined to the Keynesians. Where Keynes was original was in the subsidiary and supporting assumption that what other economists have called "the money illusion" was a basic cause of the rigidity.

Secondly, he argued that, in any case, wage-rate flexibility downwards, even if other prices were flexible, would aggravate and not alleviate depression. For even under perfect wage-rate flexibility and perfect flexibility generally, an equilibrium with unemployment could exist.[4] As I have previously argued,[5] Keynes would have preferred to rely wholly upon the second argument. But he kept the first, as Schumpeter has put it, "on reserve." In this survey I shall be dealing only with this second argument.

The contention is that wage-rate cuts must in any case be ineffective, as a means of restoring employment in labour, because it is possible to cut money rates only and not real wage-rates. Reduced money rates, Keynes explained, would mean reduced wages in the aggregate and lead to reduced demand. Hence the wage-rate rigidity, which former economists had been inclined to criticise ought, in his opinion, to be regarded as a virtue in times of depression.

At two points, Keynes appeared to have some misgivings about this thesis. He admitted firstly that if the price of labour *could* be flexible, things would be different, i.e., "if it were always open to labour to reduce its real wage by accepting a reduction in its money wage . . . . " This condition assumed, he said, " . . . . free competition among employers and no restric-

---

[4] These two propositions were very much confused in Keynes's exposition and it is usually difficult to know, at any point, on which proposition he was relying. The exceptions are in passages which are rather puzzling, when related to the rest of his argument, as on pages 191 and 267 of *The General Theory.*

[5] In this *Journal,* March, 1952, p. 53.

tive combinations among workers." [6] And he explicitly admitted later that, if there were competition between unemployed workers, "there might be no position of stable equilibrium except in conditions consistent with full employment . . . ." [7] But he did not attempt to reconcile these passages with apparently contradictory passages.

We are left, then, with the principal contention, namely, that changes in wage-rates are "double-edged," affecting both individual outputs and general demand. As this infectious doctrine has been developed by Keynes's disciples, costs as a whole are no longer regarded as merely *limiting* output, but as *calling forth* output through demand.

The objection to regarding costs as a source of demand can be simply stated. The only cost adjustments which defenders of price flexibility advocate are those which must always increase real income, and hence always increase money income under any system in which the value of the money unit remains constant. If we concentrate attention upon wages, it can be said that, on the reasonable assumption that the growth of real income will not mean a re-distribution against the *absolute* advantage of the wage-earners, the effect of the wage-rate reductions which are advocated must always mean an increase and not a decrease in aggregate wages received, and hence an increased demand for wage-goods. (The possibility of hoarding being induced is discussed later.)

In part, the Keynesian attempt to handle the problem in terms of the crude concept of "the price of labour" has confused the issue. We are concerned with the prices of different kinds of labour, whilst the index number concept of "the wage level" screens off from scrutiny all the issues which seem to me to be important.[8] Throughout Chapter 19 of *The General Theory* Keynes talked simply of "reduction of money wages." And he discussed the orthodox view of the desirability of price

[6] *General Theory*, page 11.
[7] *Ibid.*, p. 253.
[8] Compare criticisms of "the wage level" concept by R. A. Gordon (A.E.R. Proceedings, May, 1948, page 354) who refers to ". . . the concentration of attention upon aggregates and upon distressingly broad and vaguely defined index number concepts—with insufficient attention being paid to those inter-relationships among components which may throw light upon the behaviour of those aggregates . . ."

adjustments as though it was based on a "demand schedule for labour in industry as a whole relating the quantity of employment to different levels of wages." [9]

Through thus thinking rather uncritically about aggregates, the Keynesians appear to have *assumed* that wage-rate reductions imply reduction of aggregate earnings,[10] irrespective of whether the labour price which is cut is that of workers in an exclusive, well-paid trade, or that of workers doing poorly paid work because they are excluded from well-paid opportunities. When the Keynesians do think of adjustments in individual wage-rates, they think of blanket changes. At one point Keynes objected to price flexibility as a remedy for idleness in labour on the grounds that "there is, as a rule, no means of securing a simultaneous and equal reduction of money wages in all industries." [11] But it is not *uniform* reductions which are wanted, it is selective reductions, the appropriate selection of which can be entrusted to markets when non-market *minima* have been adjusted.[12]

But even if equi-proportional wage-cuts were enacted, in a régime in which there was much unemployment, aggregate and average earnings might still tend to increase,[13] owing to the redistribution of workers over the different wage-rate groups. It would become profitable to employ more in the higher-paid types of work, whilst in the lower-paid types there would have to be rationing.[14] Keynes's static, short-term methods exclude consideration of these reactions.[15] Clarity will not be gained

[9] *The General Theory*, p. 259.

[10] It is an interesting commentary on the uncritical nature of current assumptions that Professor Viner has felt it necessary to remind economists that it does not necessarily follow, "and I think that many economists have taken that step without further argument," that an increase of wage-rates at a time of unemployment will increase the pay-off. "An increase of wage-rates may quite conceivably reduce the pay-roll." (Viner, *op. cit.*, page 32).

[11] *The General Theory*, page 264. It was partly this which led him to argue that wage-rate adjustment would be possible only in a Communist or Fascist State. (*Ibid*, page 269).

[12] Actually, Professor Pigou has shown that equi-proportional wage-cuts, even under Keynes's other assumptions, must mean increased employment of labour if the reaction is a reduction of the rate of interest. Professor Pigou suggests that this reaction is "fairly likely." "Money Wages and Unemployment," *Economic Journal*, March, 1938, p. 137.

[13] As measured by money units of unchanging value.

[14] For simplicity, I am assuming that *maxima* are enacted.

[15] The possibilities of transfers of workers from low-paid to high-paid work

whilst we try to think in terms of "wage levels." We have to think in terms of changing frequency distributions. This is important enough for the consideration of employment in individual industries, but still more important in relation to employment as a whole.

The Keynesian argument is that it is no use cutting the wage-rates of say, carpenters, if there is unemployment among them because, even if *their* employment fully recovers, their incomes and expenditure will fall and so cause the demand for the labour of other workers to fall.[16] But the case for price flexibility by no means assumes that a moderate fall in carpenters' wage-rates, together with a corresponding fall in the price of the product will, in itself, greatly increase the employment of *carpenters*. Such a reaction, although *possible,* is most unlikely.[17]

The correct proposition can be put this way. *Increased employment among carpenters can be most easily induced as the result of wage-rate and price reductions on the part of those persons who ultimately buy the carpenters' services.* The assumption is that the reductions result in the release of withheld capacity in the industries which do not compete with carpenters, whilst the increasing flow of products becomes demand through being priced to permit its full sale. This is the argument which the Keynesians should answer.

In his *Prosperity and Depression,* Haberler expressed doubts about this type of argument. He stated the case for it briefly, in a footnote,[18] but added that it assumed MV to be constant. I shall try to show that whatever MV may be, the value adjustments needed to secure the consumption or use of all goods and services may still be brought about. Haberler argues also that we cannot infer the truth of the proposition from facts which appear to support it. During the depression, outputs and em-

---

are magnified in the long run, because it will be possible to train for the well-paid employment opportunities which are brought within reach of income.

[16] Professor K. Boulding has used this actual example and argument in his *Economics of Peace,* pp. 141-2.

[17] Moreover, whilst wage-rate and price adjustments are required to dissolve withheld capacity among carpenters, to adopt that remedy *in individual trades* and on a small scale would bring severe distributive injustices in its train. Indeed, the aggregate wage receipts of the larger number employed in any trade might be smaller than before the increased employment.

[18] Haberler, *Prosperity and Depression,* p. 493.

ployment were maintained in the agricultural field, in which the fall of prices *could not be* effectively resisted, but shrank in industry, in which prices *could be* effectively maintained. It would seem, then, that full employment and outputs could have been maintained. It would seem, then, that full employment and outputs could have been maintained in industry also, had price competition been effective. That, says Haberler, "has not yet been rigorously proven." [19] But is it not self-evident that, given any monetary policy, *selective* reduction of the prices of industrial goods would, in general, have made smaller reductions of agricultural prices necessary (in order to secure full employment in that field), whilst the maintenance of outputs as a whole would have eased the task of financing full production without diluting the money unit? [20] And is it not equally obvious that, had the price of agricultural products been maintained, so that these products absorbed a greater proportion of the total power to purchase, industrial unemployment would have been still more serious?

The relation between wage-rates and the aggregate pay-roll cannot, I suggest, be effectively considered, except in relation to the price system as a whole. But the Keynesians appear to take the co-ordinative effects of the value mechanism for granted and concentrate upon what they regard as the motive power behind it, namely, money income. They do not continuously envisage and consider the *synchronising function* of prices, the fact that the prices attaching to individual commodities or services determine the *rate of flow* at which these commodities or services move into consumption or into the next stage of production. The co-ordination of the rates of flow of materials, services, etc., is brought about through the raising or lowering of prices. *Ceteris paribus,* a rise in price causes a falling off in the rate of flow, and a fall in price causes a rise in the rate of flow of anything through the stage of production at which it is priced. If certain prices cannot change, other prices

[19] *Ibid.,* p. 243.
[20] I feel that Haberler would now admit this argument, in view of his unequivocal rejection, in 1951, of Keynesian teaching about unemployment equilibrium under price flexibility. "Welfare and Freer Trade," *Economic Journal,* Dec., 1951, pp. 779-80. See also his article in *The New Economics,* pp. 166 *et seq.*

(i.e., other rates of flow) must adjust themselves accordingly if the economy is to be synchronised in any sense.[21]

"Full employment" is secured when all services and products are so priced that they are (i) brought within the reach of people's pockets (i.e., so that they are purchasable by existing money incomes) or (ii) brought into such a relation to predicted prices, that no postponement of expenditure on them is induced. For instance, the products and services used in the manufacture of investment goods, must be so priced that anticipated future money incomes will be able to buy the services and depreciation of new equipment or replacements.

Admittedly, the view that co-ordinative reductions or increases of wage-rates must always tend to increase real income (and probably real wages in the aggregate also) does not imply that money income (and money wages) will *also* increase, except on certain assumptions about the nature of the monetary system which exists. Perhaps the pre-Keynesian economists could be criticised for having made tacit instead of explicit assumptions on this point. But orthodox economics (as I understand it) did not overlook what is now called "the income effect." The tacit assumption [22] was that the monetary system was of such a nature that the increased real income due to the release of productive power in individual trades (through the acceptance of lower wage rates) would not result in a reduction of money income. No-one suggested that the monetary system *had* necessarily to be like that; but from the actual working of the credit system, it seemed to be unnecessary to consider the case in which an expansion of production would not be accompanied by an increase in money income induced by this expansion. The assumption on which Keynes built, namely, that the number of money units is fixed, would have seemed absurd to most pre-Keynesian economists, unless they were considering the economics of a community so primitive that a fixed number of

21 What is commonly expressed as changes in cost-price ratios, i.e., in the price of output in relation to the price of labour, I think of in terms of divergencies from, or conformance with, synchronizing prices at various stages of production. (The last stage is, of course, sale for consumption.)

22 Some economists in the pre-Keynesian era, in attempting to deal with the relations of employment and wage-rates, made *explicit,* highly simplified assumptions consistent with the assumption as I have worded it, for purposes of abstract analysis. But I do not know of any economist who has stated the fundamental assumption as I have done. Quite possibly the point was made.

tokens (shells, for instance) served as the sole medium of exchange, whilst no lending or credit of any kind existed.

In a credit economy, there could never be any difficulty, due to the mere fact that outputs had increased, about purchasing the full flow of production at ruling prices. That is, expanding real income could not have, in itself, any price depressing tendencies. Only monetary policy was believed to be able to explain that. But given any monetary policy, they believed that unemployment of any type of labour was due to wage-rates being wrongly related to the "amount of money" existing at any time.[23] It followed that downward adjustments of minimum wage-rates and prices could never *aggravate*—on the contrary would always *mitigate*—the consequences of any deflationary tendency caused by monetary policy.

Ought we not now to recognise that it is unnecessary to modify this pre-Keynesian view? Under *any* monetary system, the price situation which permits ideal co-ordination, in the sense which I have explained, must maximise the source of real demand—real income. Whilst this may be clear enough in the case in which monetary policy precipitates *primary* deflation, it may be less obvious when *secondary* deflation is induced. But postponements of demand, with their self-perpetuating consequences, arise when current costs or prices are higher than anticipated costs or prices.[24]

In more general terms, expected changes in costs or prices, unaccompanied by immediate cost and price co-ordination to meet expectations, lead to "secondary" reactions. A *cut in costs* does not induce demand postponement; nor, indeed, do *falling costs* have this effect. Postponements arise because it is judged that a cut in costs (or other prices) is less than will eventually have to take place, or because the rate of fall of costs (or other prices) is insufficiently rapid. It follows that "secondary" deflations are attributable to the unstable rigidities which prevent continuous co-ordination of prices. Confusion arises because secondary deflation can be brought to an end, not by true co-ordination, but at the expense of a prospective permanent sac-

---

[23] Compare F. Modigliani, "Liquidity Preference and the Theory of Interest and Money," *Econometrica,* January, 1944, and this symposium, pp. 132-184.

[24] My article in the issue of this *Journal* for December, 1953, is an attempt to deal rigorously with this situation.

rifice of real income, i.e., through the imposition of cost and price rigidities (in the form of minima) which are expected to continue indefinitely.[25]

Now if, for any reason, a change in the value of the money unit becomes the declared object of policy, or the expected consequence of policy, *the whole price system is immediately thrown out of co-ordination.* Thus, if the value of the money unit is expected to rise, then until the necessary adjustments have all taken place, "willingness to buy" must necessarily fall off—most seriously where values of services and materials in the investment goods industries do not at once respond.[26]

We turn finally to explicit criticisms of the reasoning on which Keynes based his suggestion of unemployment equilibrium under wage-rate flexibility or, as his disciples were later forced to argue, under price flexibility.

Through the attempts of disciples [27] like Lange, Smithies, Tobin, Samuelson, Modigliani and Patinkin to defend or strengthen the new creed, successive refinements have gradually paved the way for the ultimate abandonment, by would-be Keynesians, of the view that wage-rate and price adjustments are powerless to secure full employment. The contributions of these very friendly critics, said Schumpeter, "might have been turned into very serious criticisms" if they had been "less in sympathy with the spirit of Keynesian economics." [28] He added that this is particularly true of Modigliani's contribution. He could have made the same remark about that of Patinkin, which appeared two years later. But the criticisms of these writers *were* very serious in any case. Their apparent reluctance to

[25] Imposed cost and price rigidities *in the form of maxima* (i.e., ceilings) may similarly prevent secondary inflation, but in this case, *the effect is the opposite.* In so far as the maxima force down monopoly prices nearer to marginal cost, there is a mitigating co-ordinative and deflationary action which creates an incentive to increased outputs (i.e., increased real income).

[26] It should be stressed, however, that this is no conclusive argument against policies seeking to increase the value of the money unit, as tardy rectifications of the distributive injustices of inflations. Nor is it a good argument against rectifying price disharmonies which have been allowed to develop and strain the ability to honour a convertibility obligation.

[27] I do not include Haberler, whose criticisms have been damaging, as a Keynesian. It is difficult to pick out the other non-Keynesian economists who have been most influential on the point at issue; but Marget, Knight, Viner and Simons must take much of the credit.

[28] Schumpeter, in *The New Economics*, p. 92.

tainty" and "adverse expectations" be explained, unless in relation to unstable price rigidities? And the same tacit assumption of rigidity is present in his statement of what he terms, "the Keynesian position, closest to the 'classics.' " In this position, he says, although price flexibility would eventually "generate" full employment, "the length of time that might be necessary for the adjustment makes the policy impractical." [43] He tells us that this statement (like that in the previous quotation) is *not* "dependent upon the assumption of wage rigidities." [44] But what "adjustments" other than tardy cuts in rigid wage-rates has he in mind? He must be thinking of unstable price rigidities *somewhere* in the system.

A critic writes that this argument seems to overlook *inevitable* rigidities. In practice, contracts cannot be varied constantly, so that costs tend to follow prices with some interval. Thus, copper miners' wages can hardly change every time the price of copper changes. But for Patinkin's argument to hold, it would be essential for the wage-rates of the miners to be maintained when actual or expected copper prices had fallen to such an extent that formerly marginal seams became unworkable at current costs. The most complete measure of price flexibility practically attainable involves discontinuities at both the cost and the final product ends. [45] But periodic adjustments through recontract (as idleness threatens) can meet that situation. [46]

In short, the kind of price flexibility for which we can reasonably hope is one in which the price inconsistencies which must exist at any point of time *are never in process of material or cumulative worsening.* That need not mean unemployment. Contract covers the short run. And inconsistencies need not accumulate: they can be in process of rectification at about the same rate as that at which they arise.

Hence, "the dynamic approach" does not, as Patinkin maintains, obviate the necessity for the assumption of rigidities and revalidate the Keynesian fallacies. On the contrary, it was largely Keynes's neglect of the dynamic co-ordinative consequences of price adjustment which led him into the error that

[43] *Op. cit.,* p. 282.
[44] *Op. cit.,* p. 282.
[45] That is not, *in itself,* likely to mean discontinuity in movements of the scale of prices (i.e., in a price index).
[46] Sliding scales can render the need for recontract less frequent.

wage-rate and price adjustments are no remedy for unemployment.[47]

What are the implications? In my judgment, the abandonment of the theory of unemployment equilibrium under price flexibility means that the Say Law stands once again inviolate as the basic economic reality in the light of which all economic thinking is illuminated. But I do not think that all the critics of Keynes on the point at issue will immediately accept this inference. Indeed, Haberler adheres to a rejection of the Law at the very stage at which his own reasoning seems to be prompting him to recognise it.[48]

Yet even so extreme a Keynesian as Sweezy has been rash enough (and right enough) to admit, in his obituary article on Keynes, that the arguments of *The General Theory* "all fall to the ground if the validity of the Say Law is assumed." [49] If my own view is right, then the apparent revolution wrought by Keynes after 1936 has been reversed by a bloodless counter-revolution conducted unwittingly by higher critics who tried very hard to be faithful. Whether some permanent benefit to our science will have made up for the destruction which the revolution left in its train, is a question which economic historians of the future will have to answer.

We are now forced back to the stark truth that the elimination of wasteful idleness in productive capacity is attainable only through the continuous adjustment of prices or the continuous dilution of the money unit. But the latter is a tragically evil method of attempting to rectify disco-ordination due to inertias or sectionalism. For the harmful repercussions of inflation become the more serious (and force an accelerated inflation) the more successfully entrepreneurs and consumers, in

[47] The confusion in this field ultimately stems, I feel, from a failure to achieve conceptual clarity, and particularly owing to the absence of a sufficiently rigorous definition of price flexibility.

[48] Haberler, in Harris, *op. cit.*, pp. 173-176. The acceptance of the Say Law does not imply, as Haberler suggests, the absurd assumption that the phenomena of hoarding or dishoarding cannot exist. It merely accords to money assets and the services which they provide the same economic status and significance as all other assets and the services which they provide. Nor does the existence of depression or idle resources (under unstable price rigidity) prove that this law does not hold, any more than balloons and aeroplanes invalidate the law of gravity.

[49] In *Science and Society,* 1946, p. 400.

the free sectors of the economy, correctly forecast monetary policy. But the new Keynesians, like the old, appear to believe that monetary or fiscal policy, through the control of spending, can act as a universal solvent of all price disharmonies and, like an invisible hand, make unnecessary, or less necessary, the difficult task of overhauling the institutions which make up the price system.

We must remember that the attack on wage-rate adjustment as a policy of securing full employment in labour is an attack on a policy which has never been experimentally tested. For whilst there is a great deal of evidence of wage-rate adjustments forced by depression being followed by recovery, no deliberate attempt to increase income (including the flow of wages) by reducing all prices which appear to be above the natural scarcity level (including wage-rates) so that all prices and wage-rates below the natural scarcity level may rise, has ever been purposely pursued. Actual policies have, for decades, been based precisely upon the politically attractive rule, justified by Keynesian teaching, that disharmony in the wage-rate structure must not be tackled but offset; whilst the current tendency is to assume dogmatically with no examination of the institutional and sociological factors involved, that to advocate wage and price adjustments is to recommend the conquest of the moon.

XX

Arthur F. Burns was born in Austria in 1904. He studied at Columbia University, took his doctor's degree there in 1934, and became professor of economics there in 1944. He has been director of research at the National Bureau of Economic Research since 1930, and is now president of that organization. From 1953 to 1956 he was a chairman of the President's Council of Economic Advisers. In 1946 he collaborated with the late Wesley C. Mitchell in the study *Measuring Business Cycles*. The following is an excerpt from the article "Economic Research and the Keynesian Thinking of Our Times" which appears in a collection of sixteen of Dr. Burns's essays published by Princeton University Press for the National Bureau of Economic Research in 1954 under the title: *The Frontiers of Economic Knowledge*.

KEYNES' THEORY OF
UNDEREMPLOYMENT EQUILIBRIUM

ARTHUR F. BURNS

I have said enough to set the theme of my report, which is to relate the work of the National Bureau to the Keynesian thinking of our times. The opinion is widespread that Keynes has explained what determines the volume of employment at any given time, and that our knowledge of the causes of variations in employment is now sufficient to enable government to maintain a stable and high level of national income and employment within the framework of our traditional economic organization. If this opinion is valid, the solution of the basic problem of democratic societies is in sight, and the National Bureau would do well to reconsider its research program. Unhappily, this opinion reflects a pleasant but dangerous illusion.

The basis for the Keynesians' confidence is Keynes' theory of underemployment equilibrium, which attempts to show that a free enterprise economy, unless stimulated by governmental policies, may sink into a condition of permanent mass unemployment. The crux of this theory is that the volume of investment and the "propensity to consume" determine between them a unique level of income and employment. The theory can be put simply without misrepresenting its essence. Assume that business firms in the aggregate decide to add during a given period $2 billion worth of goods to their stockpiles, using this convenient term to include new plant and equipment as well as inventories. This then is the planned investment. Assume, next, that business firms do not plan to retain any part of their income;[1] so that if they pay out, say, $18 billion to the public, they expect to recover $16 billion through the sale of consumer goods, the difference being paid out on account of the expected addition to their stockpiles. Assume, finally, that the "consumption function" has a certain definite shape; that if income payments are, say, $18 billion, the public will spend $17 billion on consumer goods and save $1 billion, and that one-half of every additional billion dollars of income will be devoted to consumption and one-half to savings. Under these conditions, the national income per "period" should settle at a level of $20 billion.

The reason is as follows. If income payments were $18 billion, the public would spend $17 billion on consumer goods. But the firms that made these payments expected to sell $16 billion worth to the public and to add $2 billion worth to their stockpiles; the actual expenditure of $17 billion on consumer goods would therefore exceed sellers' expectations by $1 billion, and stimulate expansion in the consumer goods trades. On the

[1] This assumption is not essential to the Keynesian system; I make it here in order to simplify the exposition. The figures used throughout are merely illustrative. Further, the exposition is restricted to the proximate determinants of employment in Keynes' system; this simplification does not affect the argument that follows.

other hand, if income payments were $22 billion, the public would spend $19 billion on consumer goods; this would fall short of sellers' expectations by $1 billion, and set off a contraction in the output of consumer goods. In general, if income payments fell below $20 billion, the sales expectations of business firms would be exceeded; while if income payments rose above $20 billion, the expectations of business firms would be disappointed. In either case, forces would be released that would push the system in the direction of the $20 billion mark. Hence, in the given circumstances, $20 billion is the equilibrium income, and it may be concluded that the basic data—that is, the volume of investment and the consumption function—determine a national income of unique size. If we assume, now, a unique correlation between income and employment, it follows that the basic data determine also a unique volume of employment—which may turn out to be well below "full" employment.

This is the theoretical skeleton that underlies the Keynesian system. The theory implies that when unemployment exists, an increase in consumer spending out of a given income will expand employment; so too will an increase in private home investment or in exports, and so again will governmental loan expenditure, its effect on employment being in a sense similar to that of private investment expenditure. The theory implies also that the magnitude of the expansion in employment by any of these routes is a precisely calculable quantity, since the determinants of employment are alleged to have been isolated. To get more out of the theory, more specific assumptions must be made.

At this vital juncture the Keynesians differ somewhat among themselves, but two institutional assumptions dominate the thinking of the school. The first is that consumer outlay is linked fairly rigidly to national income and is unlikely to expand unless income expands; in other words, there is little reason to expect, at least in the short run, that a condition of unemployment will be corrected through a reduction in individual savings. The second assumption is that investment opportunities are limited in a "mature" economy such as our own; consequently, private investment may continue, year in and year out, at a level that falls considerably short of what the community would save if "full employment" existed. If neither an upward shift in the consumption function, nor an expansion of private investment at home, nor an increase in net exports can be confidently counted on, it follows that our lot may be persistent mass unemployment. We may escape the fate of secular stagnation, however, if the effective demand for employment is supplemented by governmental spending. Furthermore, this remedy for secular stagnation is also the remedy for business cycles, since the most that can be expected of private investment is that it may rise sufficiently to generate "full employment" during a fleeting boom.

Of late this theory has been refined and elaborated, so that "deficit financing" need no longer be the key instrument for coping with unemployment, and I shall refer to one of these refinements at a later point. But the practical significance of the modifications of the theory is problematical, and in any event the theory as I have sketched it still dominates the thinking of the Keynesians when they look beyond the transition from war to peace. The similarity of this theory to the Ricardian model is unmistakable. The most important proposition in Ricardian economics is that the production function in agriculture has a certain shape, that is, the marginal product diminishes as the input of labor increases. The most important proposition in Keynesian economics is that the consumption function has a certain shape, that is, consumer outlay increases with national income but by less than the increment of income. The Ricardians treated the production function as fixed, and deduced the effects on income distribution of an increase or decrease in population, or of a tax or bounty on the production of corn. The Keynesians treat the consumption function as fixed, and deduce the effects on the size of the national income of an increase or decrease in private investment, or of an increase or decrease in governmental loan expenditure. The Ricardians believed that population was the key dynamic variable, and they drew a gloomy picture of the course of events if that exuberant variable was not counteracted. The Keynesians believe that investment is the key dynamic variable, and they draw a gloomy picture of the course of events if that timid variable is not fortified by governmental loan expenditure. To be sure, the Ricardians recognized that the production function in agriculture was subject to change, and they frequently inserted qualifications to their main conclusions. The Keynesians likewise recognize that the consumption function is not absolutely rigid, and they frequently insert qualifications to their main conclusions. But I have formed the definite impression that the Keynesians—except when they discuss changes in personal taxation—attach even less importance to their qualifications than did the Ricardians; all of which may merely reflect the fact that the Ricardians were concerned largely with secular changes, while the Keynesians are mainly concerned, despite their anxiety over secular stagnation, with comparatively short-run changes.

There is, of course, nothing unscientific about Ricardianism as such. But *ceteris paribus* is a slippery tool, and may lead to serious error if the premises accepted for purposes of reasoning are contrary to fact, or if the impounded data are correlated in experience with factors that the theorist allows to vary, or if the very process of adjustment induces changes in the impounded data. Let us go back to the theoretical skeleton of the Keynesian system and examine it more carefully. Suppose that the volume of intended investment is $2 billion, income payments $20 billion, and consumers' outlay at this level of income $18 billion. On the basis of these data, the economic system is alleged to be in equilibrium. But the equilibrium is aggregative, and this is a mere arithmetic fiction. Business firms do not have a common pocketbook. True, they receive in the aggregate precisely the sum they had expected, but that need not mean that even a single firm receives precisely what it had expected. Since windfall profits and losses are virtually bound to be dispersed through the system, each firm will adjust to its own sales experience, and within a firm the adjustment will vary from one product to another. Under the circumstances the intended investment cannot—quite apart from "autonomous" changes—very well remain at $2 billion, and the propensity to consume is also likely to change. Our data therefore do not determine a unique size of national income; what they rather determine is a movement away from a unique figure. Of course, we cannot tell the direction or magnitude of the movement, but that is because the basic data on which the

Keynesian analysis rests are not sufficiently detailed for the purpose.

I have imagined that Keynes' aggregative equilibrium is realized from the start. But suppose that this does not happen; suppose that, in the initial period, the intended investment is $2 billion, income payments $16 billion, and that savings at this level of income are zero. Will income now gravitate towards the $20 billion mark, as the theory claims it should? There is little reason to expect this will happen. In the first place, windfall profits will be unevenly distributed, and the adjustment of individual firms to their widely varying sales experiences will induce a change in the aggregate of their intended investment. In the second place, unemployed resources will exercise some pressure on the prices of the factors of production, and here and there tend to stimulate investment. In the third place, if an expansion in the output of consumer goods does get under way, it will induce additions to inventories for purely technical reasons; further, the change in the business outlook is apt to stimulate the formation of new firms, and to induce existing firms to embark on investment undertakings of a type that have no close relation to recent sales experience. In the fourth place, as income expands, its distribution is practically certain to be modified; this will affect the propensity to consume, as will also the emergence of capital gains, the willingness of consumers to increase purchases on credit, and the difficulty faced by consumers in adjusting many of their expenditures to increasing incomes in the short run. These reactions, and I have listed only the more obvious ones, are essential parts of the adjustment mechanism of a free enterprise economy. Under their impact the data with which we started—namely, the amount of intended investment and the consumption function—are bound to change, perhaps slightly, perhaps enormously. It is wrong, therefore, to conclude that these data imply or determine, even in the sense of a rough approximation, a unique level at which the income and employment of a nation will tend to settle. In strict logic, the data determine, if anything, some complex cumulative movement, not a movement towards some fixed position.

If this analysis is sound, the imposing schemes for governmental action that are being bottomed on Keynes' equilibrium theory must be viewed with skepticism. It does not follow, of course, that these schemes could not be convincingly defended on other grounds. But it does follow that the Keynesians lack a clear analytic foundation for judging how a given fiscal policy will affect the size of the national income or the volume of employment. Fiscal policy is now the fashion among economists, and three fiscal paths to "full employment" have recently been delineated. The first is to increase expenditure but not taxes. The second is to increase taxes as much as expenditure. The third is to reduce taxes but leave expenditure unchanged. The first of these methods—that is, loan expenditure—avoids, we are told, the excessively large expenditures of the second method, and the excessive deficits of the third. This is a highly suggestive conclusion, and may have much to recommend it on practical grounds. But to accept it as an approximation to scientific truth we must be willing to make assumptions of the following type: (1) the consumption function is so shaped that the dollar volume of savings increases as income increases, (2) the consumption function is practically invariant except in response to personal taxation, (3) an increase in taxes will lower the consumption function considerably but by less than the addition to taxes, (4) a reduction in taxes will raise the consumption function but by considerably less than the tax reduction, (5) the planned savings of business enterprises are correlated simply and uniquely with income payments, (6) monopolistic practices of business firms can safely be neglected, (7) private investment will not be influenced appreciably by the character of the fiscal policy pursued by government. Although assumptions such as these may be extremely helpful at a stage in our thinking about an exceedingly complicated problem, it seems plain that the inferences to which they lead cannot be regarded as a scientific guide to governmental policies.

XXI

MELCHIOR PALYI was born in Hungary and educated in Switzerland and Germany. He has combined business activities in Continental countries, Great Britain, and the United States with academic work in leading universities both here and abroad. Since 1933 Dr. Palyi has lived in America, where he has been active as a research economist and as visiting professor at the Universities of Chicago, Northwestern, Wisconsin, and Southern California. The following short excerpt is from pages 28-30 of his book, *The Dollar Dilemma: Perpetual Aid to Europe?* published by Henry Regnery Company in 1954.

THE KEYNESIAN MYTHOLOGY

MELCHIOR PALYI

Lord Keynes taught, and "put over" on both sides of the Atlantic, the age-old doctrine of money cranks that the chief objective of public policy is to combat depressions in order to maintain a perpetual boom, now called Full Employment. It breaks, he claimed, when people do not keep up their spending; in other words, whatever things are being produced, however large the output and high its cost, consumers ought to buy them *at given prices* and like them. Otherwise, unemployment raises its ugly head and snowballs into a depression. Which is what happens: as people's incomes rise, consumer spending grows, but at a declining rate. A growing percentage of incomes is being saved, and less and less of the liquid savings turned into investments.

411

Savers are the villains in the Keynesian economic mythology; the desire to hold liquidity is the great curse on humanity. The problem is, therefore, to make people either buy consumer goods or spend on investments in plants and equipment. The solution is, in academic language, "a controlled allocation of income to consumption and investment, together with an increasing proportion of socialized investment." Every trick will do to incite more spending of one kind or another: artificially low interest rates—eternal Cheap Money is the prime law of Keynesianism—to punish the *rentier,* that rascal who lives on collecting interest on bonds and savings accounts; ample credit fostered by government guarantees; outright devaluing of the currency (raising the price of gold); public works which run the national budget into the red and inflate the money volume. Coincidentally, foreign competition should be kept out, the home market protected against foreign depressions; domestic competition in depressed industries should be regulated by compulsory cartels.

Full employment is always the objective. Its spokesmen ignore elementary economics: that full employment of a durable nature can be arrived at only if prices and costs adjust themselves to the market. That may take temporary unemployment; but the mere threat of such adjustments evokes near-hysterical expressions of anguish from the Keynesian bosoms. Keynes himself assumed naively that real wages would not rise under full employment; labor does not mind, he argued, if its real income declines, provided the jobs are secure. If that were true, prices could be inflated without raising costs. Before he died, he had to learn a lesson in fundamentals.

Stripped of crypto-scientific semantics, the Keynesians' medicine is Inflation—to cure the last depression and to avoid the next. This is their over-riding problem; what the future consequences may be, is no worry to them. "In the long run we all are dead," was the motto of their Master. Short-term-minded as he was, and opportunistic like the proverbial politician, Keynes changed his theories without hesitation, usually in the direction of greatest popular *éclat.* As one of his innumerable English admirers phrased it: "You never could be sure . . . whether Keynes' utterances expressed deep convictions or extemporized combinations of a fertile fancy. . . ." The Great

Depression upset his brilliant but unstable mind. It inspired his prompting of public spending and nationalistic isolation for the sake of full employment. He turned from "classical" economics to unrestrained intervention and nationalistic isolation. "The decadent international but individualistic capitalism," he stated in 1933,

. . . is not a success. It is not intelligent, it is not beautiful, it is not just, it is not virtuous—and it doesn't deliver the goods. In short, we dislike it, and we are beginning to despise it. . . . It is my central contention that there is no prospect for the next generation of a uniformity of economic system throughout the world, such as existed, broadly speaking, during the nineteenth century; that we all need to be as free as possible of interference from economic changes elsewhere, in order to make our favorite experiments towards the ideal social republic of the future; and that a deliberate movement towards greater national self-sufficiency and economic isolation will make our task easier. . . .

By 1945, he tried to back out of his own spiritual mousetrap by admitting that American mobility, venturesomeness and resilience must be emulated; that the proper line of policy is to "marry the use of necessary expedients to the wholesome (classical) long run doctrine." But it was too late and too little. His revolutionary doctrines of the 1930's had met with an instantaneous and tremendous acceptance—thanks to their affinity to Marxism. In Europe, they were combined with big slices of the panacea imported from Moscow: public ownership of the essential means of production, social security "from womb to tomb," vital consumer services to be provided at nominal cost or none at all.

XXII

David McCord Wright was born in Savannah, Georgia, in 1909. He studied at Harvard University and took his doctor's degree there in 1940. In 1953 he was Fulbright lecturer at Oxford University. Since 1955 he has been William Dow professor of economics and political science at McGill University, Montreal. His books include: *The Economics of Disturbance,* 1947; *Capitalism,* 1951, and *A Key to Modern Economics,* 1954. He also edited, in 1951, *The Impact of the Labor Union,* a round-table discussion by eight prominent economists. The following article appeared in *Science* for November 21, 1958, pages 1258-1262. Dr. Wright is engaged on a full-length study to be published under the title: *The Keynesian System.*

MR. KEYNES AND THE "DAY OF JUDGMENT"

DAVID McCORD WRIGHT

If consistency is the bane of little minds, Lord Keynes had certainly a great one. No one who studies the work of John Maynard Keynes can fail to be impressed by the frequent brilliance of his insights and the usefulness of many of his tools of analysis. But he lacked that sober quality which causes a man to sit down and carefully consider the consistency of his various successive theories and pronouncements. Keynes at various

414

times approved, in writing, the essentials of a number of different restatements of his system, including one written by me.[1] But when we compare the different models, thus approved, we find them to vary widely among themselves. The trouble lies in the fact that his basic model was founded on extremely narrow assumptions, and that he did not bother always to make clear to what extent he felt these assumptions applicable at a given time, and how much, in any case, he was willing to relax them.[2]

Keynes' successors and disciples therefore differ widely among themselves in their interpretations. Also, it is difficult to separate one part of Keynes' analysis from the rest. However, since selection is necessary, I have picked out for explanation and criticism that interpretation of Keynes which has, unfortunately, become most widely connected with his name.

Few aspects of Keynes' system influence modern thought more than what one of his early reviewers has called "Mr. Keynes' vision of the day of judgment"—that oft expected crisis when unregulated capitalist expansion shall be brought to an end by overinvestment or underconsumption. So deeply has this picture affected the minds of a whole generation of econ-

[1] A word is in order concerning my relationship to Keynes. I had published an article in the *Economic Journal*, of which he was editor, and sent him a copy of my first book, *The Creation of Purchasing Power* (Harvard Univ. Press, Cambridge, Mass., 1942). Shortly thereafter, I received a letter from Keynes commenting upon it at length. This began a correspondence which lasted down to his death; indeed, the last letter which I received from him reached me after I had read of his death in the newspapers. Thus, although I never met him personally, I do feel that I have some knowledge of one side, at least, of his outlook. My interpretation of Keynes' system, which Keynes himself approved in general and in writing, is given in my article "The future of Keynesian economics," *Am. Econ. Rev.* (June 1945). A good, brief explanation of the more mechanical approach to Keynes' work will be found in Joan Robinson, *Introduction to the Theory of Employment* (Macmillan, New York, 1937). Extensive bibliography and biographical data, as well as technical essays, are to be found in S. E. Harris, *The New Economics* (Knopf, New York, 1947). See also R. F. Harrod, *The Life of John Maynard Keynes* (Macmillan, New York, 1951). My reservations concerning the general line of interpretation followed in these titles will be found in my review article "The Life of John Maynard Keynes," *J. Public Law* (Emery University, Ga.) (Spring, 1952).

[2] How far Keynes himself was from a merely mechanical application of his model will be seen by the fact that he wrote me that he agreed with me that we would not be likely to have unemployment and saturation after World War II "for some time to come," but rather inflation. This was at the time when most of his American disciples were predicting an unemployment crisis practically immediately upon the conclusion of peace.

omists that whenever—as in the last few months—the employment index falters, it requires unusual courage and balance for
an economist to resist the cry that here at last is the predicted
collapse.

Yet it is not easy to dig out of Keynes' *General Theory of
Employment, Interest and Money* the reasoning which underlies his frequently gloomy views.[3] The book is an unusually
difficult and disorderly one. In essence it consists of three separate and distinct threads of analysis which Keynes himself and
many of his disciples often confuse: (i) a very precise mathematical model based upon factual assumptions which are frequently
inapplicable, (ii) a set of tautological definitions which *sound*
as if they conveyed meaning but which, as one acute critic puts
it, "achieve a magnificent generality by being about nothing
at all," and (iii) a number of practical policy suggestions, some
of which are extremely valuable and some quite the reverse.
Space is lacking here to review the complicated but arid field
of Keynesian terminology. What I shall do in this article is,
first, to outline Keynes' basic mathematical model on which
his "day of judgment" ideas are based, second, to show how
limited it is, and third, to show, from a study of these limitations, wherein scientific truth requires that his conclusions and
many of his policy suggestions must be seriously modified.

How the Basic Model Works

Characteristically, Keynes deferred a statement of the basic
assumptions of his fundamental model until the *eighteenth*
chapter of his book, where they are often overlooked. Yet everything in his model depends upon these assumptions, and I am
sure that if their limited nature were more widely recognized,
Keynes' conclusion would have far less prestige. The crucial
passage runs as follows:

> We take as *given* the existing skill and quantity of available
> labour, the existing quality and quantity of available equipment,
> the existing technique, the degree of competition, the tastes and
> habits of the consumer . . . the social structure including the forces
> . . . which determine the distribution of the national income. This
> does not mean that we assume these factors to be constant; but
> merely that, *in this place and context, we are not considering or*

taking into account the effects and consequences of changes in them" (italics supplied).[3]

This passage (some of the more technical sentences are omitted) assumes in effect that (i) there is no technical change or invention, (ii) there is no change in taste, (iii) there is no change in population or resources, and (iv) there are no changes in the preferences of the population between work and goods, on the one hand, and leisure, on the other. These assumptions, it will be seen, in effect "freeze" the system, and practically every dynamic element of capitalist civilization is removed. Of course, as he explains, Keynes did not mean that these forces were always lacking in reality. But what he did mean, and the point cannot be too often stressed, is that *in the basic model* on which his system rests, virtually *all the dynamic social forces are omitted.*

Let us, however, proceed. By a combination of intuition and mathematics, most, but by no means all, economists assume that *granted* such a frozen system, three absolutely vital conclusions can be drawn. These are: (i) Investment depends upon consumption. Nobody will build a new factory unless demand for its product is increasing. (ii) There is a fixed mechanical ratio, called by R. F. Harrod of Oxford "the relation," between the flow of consumer goods and the amount of "capital" or equipment needed to produce them. (iii) Finally, and most important, it is possible under these fixed conditions to assume an ultimate condition of "full investment" or saturation. At this saturation point, a society has (i) accumulated as much equipment as it can usefully employ and (ii) is producing a maximum output of consumer goods. This does *not* mean that everybody has all he wants. It only means that given the existing state of knowledge and resources, and the given preferences between leisure and goods, expansion has reached a limit. People *could* make and enjoy more goods, but they would rather take a vacation.

Let us now proceed to the working of Keynes' basic model, presenting it, however, in simple language, and not employing his special terms. An economic system, we may suppose, is beginning to expand from a state of unemployment. Or else a

[3] J. M. Keynes, *The General Theory of Employment, Interest and Money* (Harcourt Brace, New York, 1936).

given set of new techniques is being introduced in some undeveloped country. What will happen? Keynes has two models. The first depends upon what he calls the "normal law of consumer's behavior." This means that, as output rises, consumption also rises, but not as fast. People get richer but do not increase their consumption expenditure as fast as their income is rising. Such a difference in production and consumption trends spells, he thought, inevitable crisis. For consider: *under our assumptions,* investment depends on consumption. Factories are not built unless their products are being demanded. Now, if more and more factories (proportionately) are being built, and less and less increase (proportionately) in consumption is taking place, there soon must come a point beyond which more equipment cannot profitably be built. Yet people are not spending their full income. The unspent money piles up in the banks, which cannot find solvent borrowers for it. Men are unemployed. There is a crash.

Keynes' second version is more sudden. People, we may suppose, keep consuming the additional output of consumer goods right along. But finally the "condition of full investment" or saturation point is reached. There is no need for further construction of houses, factories, and equipment. Only replacement is needed. But society has gotten itself into the habit of saving more money than is needed for mere replacement. This habit, it is said, will persist though no longer needed. Again money will go unspent. Funds will pile up. There will again, but more suddenly, be a crash. The capitalist urge to accumulate survives its usefulness and produces unemployment. This is the Keynesian vision of the day of judgment.[4]

THE HERETICS VERSUS THE ORTHODOX ECONOMISTS

Curiously enough, once we scrape all the verbiage off Keynes' model, as has been done in the preceding section, and omit his special analytical constructs, it will be seen that the model is not particularly original. Much the same line of reasoning can be found in the work of the "heretics"—Marx and Veblen, for

[4] There is a special possible exception to this theory of collapse. It could be that about the time further *net* accumulation ceased to be necessary, the replacement demand to maintain the (hitherto) growing stock of capital would increase. Thus the gross demand for newly produced equipment and capital goods would not drop, though demand for a *net* increment had fallen to zero.

example. Still more remarkable, many of the same assumptions, but with quite different conclusions, appear in the work of the "orthodox" economists, notably David Ricardo (*circa* 1810) and John Stuart Mill (*circa* 1848).[5] Ricardo and Mill both often used models that were just as "frozen." They both assumed a "saturation" point was possible. They both often felt that investment depended on consumption. Yet they came out at quite a different place. How was this possible?

The difference lies in the fact that Ricardo and Mill switch the argument over from how much investment is needed to why people save. They considered motives, and by considering motives got very different consequences. "Why," Ricardo asked, "did a man build a new factory?" "Why, because he expected to make a profit from it," was the answer. "Why," he asked further, "did a man save money?" "Well, because he wanted to get interest on his savings" was Ricardo's answer. "Suppose I expect to make a considerable profit from a new factory," said Ricardo, "but I don't have enough money to build it. What will I do?" The answer seemed obvious: "Use part of your expected profit to pay interest on a loan from someone else."

From these ideas it was possible to deduce a complete theory of adjustment. If, as at the beginning of an expansion, there are many prospects of profit, profit expectations will be high. Many people will be wanting to borrow money to build new factories to take advantage of them. Competing against each other for a limited supply of savings, they will force up the price of loans—the rate of interest. But on the other hand, thought Ricardo, if interest rose, more people would want to save. Thus his argument was as follows: A need for new construction will produce high profit prospects. High profit prospects will increase borrowing for investment and force up the rate of inter-

---

[5] See J. S. Mill, *Principles of Political Economy*, ed. 6, book IV, chap. IV, sect. 4 "Such a country . . . is habitually within as it were a hand's breadth of the minimum and the country therefore on the verge of the stationary state." Ricardo's views, which I here paraphrase and summarize, will be found scattered through his various books, pamphlets, letters and notes, all set forth in *The Works and Correspondence of David Ricardo* (10 vol.) edited by Piero Sraffa with the assistance of M. H. Dobb (Cambridge Univ. Press, London, 1951). A typical quotation from Ricardo's works (vol. 2, p. 438) is as follows: "no mistake can be greater than to suppose any evils whatever can result from an accumulation of capital. The sole consequence might be an indisposition to accumulate further from the fall of profits."

est. But higher rates of interest will increase saving. This will make it possible to expand even faster.

Still more important, the argument can be put into reverse. As society approached a saturation point, profit prospects, Ricardo thought, would fall. Fewer people would want to borrow. In consequence, the rate of interest would fall. But if interest rates fell, fewer people would want to save. Thus, as the need for saving declined, the urge to save would drop with it. People saved for the same reason, say, that they grew potatoes. If the price of potatoes is high, more potatoes will tend to be grown; if lower, fewer. So it was also, Ricardo thought, with saving and the rate of interest. While at one point there might be high interest and high saving and investment, and at another low interest and low saving and investment, there would, it is true, be adjustments back and forth, but never serious unemployment. Ricardo's theory was followed by Mill. And with much refinement and elaboration this remained the accepted, orthodox theory of interest, saving, and employment until the publication of Keynes' *General Theory* in 1936.

Wherein, again scraping off special verbiage, does Keynes spoil this pretty picture? He does it in two ways. First of all, Keynes points out, people do not save money merely to get interest. In the short run they may have quite other motives—to provide for old age, for instance. Thus a drop in the rate of interest, because of a drop in expected profit, need not stop people from trying to save, or start them spending. On the contrary, they may, for quite a while, not react at all. But the situation is even worse. For, said Keynes, people do not merely save money to lend at interest. They can also merely *hold* money, or accumulate stocks of it. And a man may be unwilling to let go his stock of money unless he is paid for doing so. Thus Keynes said that the rate of interest was the price "paid for parting with liquidity." Men want at the very least to be sure of getting their principal back. And when there are many risks they must be paid a premium to compensate for bearing them.[6]

[6] The special risk, which Keynes particularly elaborated, is that of a capital loss if prosperity returns and the rate of interest *rises*. A perpetual income of a dollar a year at 2 per cent has a capital value of $50. At 4 per cent its capital value is only $25. Because of this special danger of capital loss, men may hold money rather than invest it at low interest rates. Keynes called this

An elaborate and complicated analysis has been built around these questions. All that we need to remember here, however, is that the rate of interest is determined not merely by the profit prospects of the borrower interacting with the desire of people to save, but also by the "liquidity preference" or caution of lenders. The repercussions upon the optimistic interest and employment theories of Ricardo and Mill are most severe. For not only does consumption not necessarily rise as the rate of interest falls, but also, even though society is thought to be experiencing a glut and hence profit prospects are low, the rate of interest may not fall at all, since "liquidity preference" may have risen in an offsetting manner. There are thus not two but three possibilities: continual smooth growth, Ricardian adjustment to saturation, and unemployment crisis.

It is from this analysis that most pessimistic "day of judgment" theories take their beginning. Forgetting the limited nature of the basic model upon which their ideas depend, many modern economists assume: (i) investment depends on consumption; (ii) a glut of equipment or "condition of full investment" is possible; (iii) when profit prospects rise or fall the rate of interest need not move with them because liquidity preference may be shifting independently; (iv) consumption does not necessarily shift with changes in the rate of interest. Add all these assumptions together and the possibility of devastating and even permanent crisis arises. But a scientific economist cannot stop at this point, for we have not yet considered the validity of the basic assumptions. Our job next, therefore, is to carry the argument back to its base and to show wherein its ultimate foundations are inadequate.

VALIDITY OF THE UNDERLYING ASSUMPTIONS

Does investment necessarily depend upon consumption? I mean, is it true that investment in the real world will be made only on a rising demand? To show how mistaken the idea is, when stated as a universal principle, let us ask ourselves under

---

the "speculative motive" of "liquidity preference." The subject has become much tangled in elaborate verbiage. Increasingly, however, it is being realized that Keynes' theory can be treated as supplementary to, rather than contradictory of, "orthodox" theory. See my "The future of Keynesian economics" (*1*) for a technical discussion.

what circumstances a brewer, say, might build a new brewery even though the volume of total beer sales or the price of beer, or both, were falling.

There are three cases: the better beer, the cheaper beer, and what I have called the "bullheaded brewer." [7] If a man invents a new kind of beer which he thinks is going to attract sales from other brands, it may pay him to build a new brewery even though general beer sales are falling. And the shot in the arm given by his new construction *could* raise not only general beer sales but employment in other lines as well. Next, if a man gets hold of a new and much cheaper method of brewing, it may pay to build the new brewery even though beer sales and prices are falling. For though prices are declining, say 2 percent, if costs are reduced 20 percent, a substantial profit margin remains. Finally, a business man may simply feel that he is smarter than the market and he (the "bullheaded brewer") may go ahead and build though things are still depressed. And it is again undeniable that his courage and the stimulus of the construction he is carrying through may start the economy once more expanding.

One final case must be mentioned in which investment does not depend upon present consumption. That is the case of investment made on a basis of long-run trends, say of population growth, and not on the basis of present demand. Among such projects are tunnels, highways, subways, and railroads. Such projects are actually stimulated by depression. For in depression, interest rates are often low, and costs low, and since it is the long-run trend that is the motivating force, and not present consumption, the immediate drop in demand will not be important. Thus, as one well-known writer has put it, "the system can be dragged out of depression by that section of construction which belongs to the future."

One does not get the full impact of what we have been saying until one realizes that the economic system is not just a two-story affair of machines and consumer goods. Rather, it is set up in many layers, like a cake. There are the machines that

[7] An elaborate explanation of this problem, in simple language, will be found in D. M. Wright, *A Key to Modern Economics* (Macmillan, New York, 1954), chap. IX, sect. 2. The reader is referred to this book for general elaboration of the points set forth in this article.

make consumer goods, and the machines that make machines, to say nothing of the machines that make machines that make machines, and so on ad infinitum. The problem is further complicated by many loops and whirlpools in the input-output flow. Now *anywhere,* and at *any time* or point in the flow, the cheaper and the "better" product may be being introduced, or some businessman may think he can outguess the market, or investment of a very long-term nature may be stimulated. Thus, while department store sales, let us say, have dropped 5 percent, this does not necessarily mean a drop in investment. New inventions may at the very same time be *boosting* investment demand by 10 percent. The economic system in a capitalist economy (and in most socialist ones) is not, practically speaking, a single, tidily articulated mechanical flow. All sorts of spontaneously occurring changes up and down the stages of production may completely nullify the effects of either a drop or an increase in consumer purchases.

Businessmen, who, to succeed, have to be good practical economists, usually know the leeway there is in the system for unexpected change. Consequently, a businessman is much more interested in his expectations regarding his immediate market than in fluctuations in demand for more remote industries. Consumption is therefore only one factor in the situation, and not necessarily a controlling one. Furthermore, even consumption does not behave with the mechanical simplicity postulated by Keynes. Many consumers have cash or can obtain credit. So far from always lagging during expansion, consumption can sometimes rise faster than general expansion. This would reduce inventories and stimulate the economy still further. The statistical record is clear that, in the real world, we must be prepared for highly erratic, unpredictable shifts in the general level of consumption.[8]

So much for the vagueness of the relation between consump-

---

[8] I have given an elaborate theoretical analysis of the interrelations (and lack of interrelation) between markets in "What *is* the economic system?" *Quart. J. Econ.* (May 1958). The egregious failure of most Keynesian forecasts after World War II was very largely due to an unexpected upward jump of the consumption level. Similarly, in 1953 and again in 1958 the Keynesian models of mechanical interrelationships between investment and consumption did not work out. Of course this does not prove that his model cannot sometimes be useful. It only proves that it is not universal or reliable.

tion and investment. What about the point of general saturation, or "full investment"? Here, too, precision vanishes as we
approach reality. For, again, the statistical record is clear that
in the real world human wants do not stay put. As output rises
wants, on average, tend to rise with it. Luxuries become necessities and erstwhile necessities drop out altogether. Even a
monastery of contemplative monks can generally use a larger
library! And Lewis Mumford lists among the *necessities* of life
"Poetry, drama, and idle play," all of which, if one knows anything of comparative civilizations, can absorb immense amounts
of capital.

The problem, then, is not so much a lack of general desire,
as an inability, in the short run, of the directors of production
perfectly to foresee the shifts of consumers' desires and to adjust
the pattern of production to them. Were businessmen or socialist
bureaucrats equipped with x-ray eyes which would enable them
to read off the wants of the consumer six months *before he knew
he had them,* and able to make quick and perfectly accurate
adjustment to these wants, there would never be a glut. But the
expanding society (any expanding society) is always advancing
into what I have called a "fog of futurity." There are bound to
be mistakes. Such advantages as socialism possesses in the matter of stability lie largely in the ability of socialist bureaucrats
to refuse to gratify the known wants of consumers and to slow
down the whole process of growth-change to a slow enough pace
(frequently very slow) for them to handle.[9]

The problem in fact is best visualized in terms of *flows of
demand* of various sorts, plus *rates of change* of those flows. We
can think of a certain proportion of the output of society being
used to produce, say, wheat, so much used to produce cloth, and
so forth. We can think also of such and so many men being employed in technical change, so many in simple expansion, so
many in replacement. The essence of the problem is that all
these rates of flow are, in an expanding society, constantly shift-

[9] For an analysis of some of these problems of speed which the socialist
planner encounters, see D. M. Wright, *The Economics of Disturbance* (Macmillan, New York, 1947), chapters III and VI. This book was written during the
war and its analysis was worked out entirely from *ad hoc* logic, given a few
premises which I believed to be true. It has, therefore, been extremely interesting to watch the subsequent accumulation of an immense mass of data
illustrating the practical occurrence of the dilemmas therein predicted.

ing. We get full employment when all of these shifting relationships add up to full employment. We get pressure toward
inflation when they exceed that amount, and deflation when
they fall below it. But the movements of these flows do not
conform to the simple rules of the Keynesian model. In practical experience, the Keynesian forecasters have quite a poor
record.[10] On a purely pragmatic basis, therefore, we have excellent grounds for questioning the adequacy of the Keynesian
models.

What determines the rates of change? Here the mathematical
economist must call in the sociologist and many other social
scientists, besides the accountant. Advertising, the anthropo-
logical culture concepts of a people, even their religion and
politics, will deeply affect the rate and direction of their shifting patterns of wants.

Yet, confining the question to the purely economic calculus,
I have already demonstrated enough in this article to call in
question much of Keynesian thought. While Keynes himself
knew better (and often remembered to say so), the general trend
of his argument, and the normal reaction of most of his disciples
is: In the face of a drop in output and employment, just stimulate demand.[11] Put in more money, it will be said, say by increasing the national debt through bank credit, or discourage
saving by "soaking the rich."

Now so far as I am concerned, it cannot be denied that circumstances could arise in which it would be desirable to inject
more money, rather than risk a general collapse. But I hold
that Keynes' one-eyed concentration upon consumption, and

[10] Examples of failure of the postulated Keynesian relationships are mentioned in (8).

[11] Keynes' views on wages have been particularly often misunderstood and
misstated. How many people, for example, remember that Keynes wrote the
following: "When we enter on a period of weakening effective demand a sudden large reduction of money wages to a point so low that no one believes in its
indefinite continuance would be the event most favorable to a strengthening
of effective demand" (3, p. 265). Or, "a general reduction [of money wages]
may also produce an optimistic tone in the minds of entrepreneurs, which may
break through a vicious circle of unduly pessimistic estimates . . . and set
things moving again on a more normal basis of expectation" (3, p. 264).
Finally, in his *Essays in Persuasion* [(Harcourt Brace, New York, 1932), p. 341]
he refers to the labor unions as "once the oppressed, now the tyrants, whose
selfish and sectional pretensions need to be bravely opposed." The truth is that,
scientifically, Keynes was a highly schizoid character.

the "soak the rich" policies often deduced from it, constitute very often an important barrier to real understanding of the problem. In other words, his remedies are sometimes not merely useless but actually harmful. For they keep us from thinking about the main problem.

A Practical Example

A practical example will be helpful, and it is ironic that the one most easily cited is the crisis from which Keynes wrote his book: the English unemployment crisis of the 1920's. There, the real trouble lay in a lag in the relative technical productivity of British industry which placed British goods at a disadvantage relative to those of Britain's competitors in export trade. Because the United Kingdom's industry was lagging technologically, her prices were high and sales low. Because her prices were high, investment prospects were unprofitable. Because investment prospects were unprofitable there was unemployment. The real need was thus for modernization. Keynes, however, picking up the argument in the middle, talked about increasing consumption, or tinkering with exchange rates. These remedies were in the nature of treating a fever with aspirin. They could at best be short run.

But not only in the case of countries like the United Kingdom which depend on export trade, is Keynes often misleading, but in general analysis as well. The real motive power of industry as it advances into the future is not just consumption, but what might be called the perspective of profit, seen over several years, between expected price trends and expected cost trends.[12] It is true that business does not take advantage of every immediate profit. It takes a long view, often foregoing short-run advantage for the surer gains of prolonged "good will." It is true that some investment is made in which profit considerations have no part. But there is a critical margin in which they are enormously relevant.

Now the real cause of a depression can sometimes be not a lack of consumption but a maladjustment of cost and prices. Wages can be rising faster than productivity, and hence the prospect of profit is reduced. Or taxes may be so heavy as to

---

[12] Concerning the "perspective" of profit, see D. M. Wright, "What *is* the economic system?" (*8*).

have the same effect and leave little incentive. Under these circumstances, just putting in more money will not help the basic problem. And there is one further problem that can never be forgotten. The extra money put in during depression to stimulate the economy may not *at first* cause inflation, but that money will not just die. As after World War II in the United States, the piled up accumulations of years of deficits may later on suddenly explode, plunging the nation into severe inflation.

abandon standpoints which their own logic was urging them to reject, clouded their exposition; but it did not weaken the implications of their reasoning.

Modigliani (whose 1944 article [29] quietly caused more harm to the Keynesian thesis than any other single contribution) seems, almost unintentionally, to reduce to the absurd the notion of the co-existence of idle resources and price flexibility. He does this by showing that its validity is limited to the position which exists when there is an *infinitely elastic* demand for money units ("the Keynesian case"). Modigliani does not regard this extreme case as absurd and, indeed, declares that interest in such a possibility is "not purely theoretical." [30] Yet Keynes himself, in dealing explicitly with this case, described it as a "possibility" of which he knew of no example, but which "might become practically important in future," [31] although there are many passages in *The General Theory* which (as Haberler has pointed out [32]) rely upon the assumption of an infinitely elastic demand. "The New Keynesians" appear to be trying to substitute this "special theory" (Hicks's description) for the "general theory" which they admit must be abandoned.

It is my present view that any attempt to envisage the "special theory" operating in the concrete realities of the world we know —even under depression conditions—must bring out its inherent absurdity.[33] But let us keep the discussion to the theoretical

[29] "Liquidity Preference and the Theory of Interest and Money," *Econometrica*, January, 1944. Reprinted in this symposium, pp. 132-184.

[30] Pigou regards the contemplation of this possibility as "an academic exercise." He describes the situation envisaged (although he is not criticising Modigliani) as extremely improbable, and he adds, "Thus the puzzles we have been considering . . . are academic exercises, of some slight use perhaps for clarifying thought, but with very little chance of ever being posed on the chequer board of actual life." "Economic Progress in a Stable Environment," *Economica*, 1947, pp. 187-8.

[31] *General Theory*, p. 207.

[32] *Op. cit.*, p. 221.

[33] No condition which even distantly resembles infinite elasticity of demand for money assets has even been recognized, I believe, because general expectations have always envisaged either (a) the attainment in the not too distant future of some definite scale of prices, or (b) so gradual a decline of prices that no cumulative postponement of expenditure has seemed profitable. General expectations appear to have rejected the possibility of a scale of prices which sags without limit, because of such things as convertibility obligations, or the necessity to maintain exchanges. or the political inexpediency of permitting prices to continue to fall.

plane. If one can seriously imagine a situation in which heavy net saving persists in spite of its being judged unprofitable to acquire non-money assets, with the aggregate real value of money assets being inflated, and prices being driven down catastrophically, then one may equally legitimately (and equally extravagantly) imagine continuous price co-ordination accompanying the emergence of such a position. We can conceive, that is, of prices falling rapidly, keeping pace with expectations of price changes, but never reaching zero, with full utilisation of resources persisting all the way.[34] We do not really need the answer which first Haberler, and then Pigou, gave on this point, namely, that the increase in the real value of cash balances is inversely related to the extent to which the individual (or for that matter the business firm) prefers to save, whilst the rate of saving is a diminishing function of the accumulation of assets which the individual holds.[35]

I have argued above that the weakness of Keynes's case rests on his static assumptions; and that once we bring dynamic repercussions into the reckoning (*via* the co-ordination or disco-ordination of the economic system) his arguments for unemployment equilibrium under price flexibility fall away. Strangely enough the new Keynesians have themselves transferred the fight to the dynamic field. The position they now seem to assume is that, whilst Keynes's own analysis (essentially static) cannot be defended, his propositions survive if they are explained through dynamic analysis. But in their attempt to retain Keynes's conclusions, they have abandoned the very roots of his own reasoning.

Thus, Patinkin [36] is equally specific in rejecting the original Keynesian arguments concerning unemployment equilibrium. He says, "it should now be definitely recognised that this is an indefensible position." [37] Even so, Keynes's errors on this point, and the similar errors of his manifold enthusiastic supporters

---

[34] See below, and compare Pigou, *op. cit.*, pp. 183-184; Haberler, *Prosperity and Depression*, pp. 499-500.

[35] In any case, this argument is no answer to the case in which the nature of saving is speculative hoarding. For this reason Haberler claims only that there is "a strong probability" and no "absolute certainty" of there being a lower limit to MV so caused. (*Op. cit.*, p. 390.)

[36] Patinkin, "Price Flexibility and Full Employment" (*A.E.R.*, 1948). Quotations are from the revised version in the A.E.A. *Readings in Monetary Theory*.

[37] *Ibid.*, p. 279.

over the period 1936-1946, are represented by Patinkin as quite unimportant. The truth which the early critics of *The General Theory* fought so hard to establish (against stubborn opposition at almost every point [38]), namely, that price flexibility is inconsistent with unemployment, he describes as "uninteresting, unimportant and uninformative about the real problems of economic policy." [39] In spite of the mistakes which led Keynes to his conclusions, he did stumble upon the truth.

Let us consider, then, the conclusions concerning price flexibility of what Patinkin continues to describe as "Keynesian economics" (meaning by that an economics which rejects the logic but retains the conclusions of *The General Theory*). This version of "the New Keynesianism" contends—again in Patinkin's words—"that the economic system may be in a position of under-employment *dis*equilibrium (in the sense that wages, prices, and the amount of unemployment are continuously changing over time) for long or even indefinite, periods of time" [40] (Patinkin's italics). "In a dynamic world of uncertainty and adverse anticipations, even if we were to allow an infinite adjustment period, there is no certainty that full employment will be generated. I.e., we may remain indefinitely in a position of under-employment dis-equilibrium." [41]

This sounds like pure orthodoxy. Indeed, the use of the word *"dis*equilibrium" implies that some Keynesians have now completely retreated. And the reference to "uncertainty and adverse anticipations" seems to refer to hypothetical situations which, using my own terminology, can be described as follows:

Given price rigidities regarded as unstable, deflation will cause the emergence of withheld capacity. Three cases arise: (a) general expectations (i.e., typical or average expectations) envisage a fall of prices towards a definite ultimate scale which is regarded as most probable; or (b) general expectations are constantly changing so that the generally expected ultimate scale of prices becomes continuously lower; or (c)

38 For an example of the stubbornness, see Keynes's reply to criticisms in his "Relative Movements of Real Wages and Output," *Economic Journal*, March, 1939.

39 Patinkin, *op. cit.*, p. 279.

40 *Ibid.*, p. 280.

41 *Ibid.*, p. 281.

general expectations envisage a certain rate of decline of the
scale of prices in perpetuity.

In case (a), the withholding of capacity will last over a
period which will be longer the more slowly the predicted
price adjustments come about. In cases (b) and (c), the withholding of capacity will last over an indefinite period, *unless
downward price adjustments take place as rapidly as or more
rapidly than (i) the changes in expectations, or (ii) the generally expected rate of decline,* in which case full employment
will persist throughout. In short, when the scale of prices is
moving or is expected to move in any direction, the notion
of perfect price flexibility must envisage current prices being
adjusted sufficiently rapidly in the same direction, if the full
utilisation of all productive capacity is sought.

In admitting that Keynes cannot be said "to have demonstrated the co-existence of unemployment equilibrium and
flexible prices," Patinkin explains that this is because "flexibility means that the money wage falls with excess supply, and
rises with excess demand; and equilibrium means that the system can continue through time without change. Hence, *by
definition,* a system with price flexibility cannot be in equilibrium if there is unemployment." [42] Now if by "excess supply"
is meant more than can be sold at current prices, and by "excess
demand" more than can be bought at current prices, *it remains
true, equally "by definition," that price flexibility so conceived
is inconsistent with wasteful idleness, even when we take into
account the full dynamic reactions which are theoretically conceivable under a condition of falling or rising prices.* For price
flexibility then requires that all prices shall be continuously
adjusted so as to bring the spot and future values of the money
unit into consistency; in other words, to establish harmony between current and expected prices. Under such adjustments,
even unemployment *dis*-equilibrium is ruled out.

Do not the words "adjustment period" in the passage quoted
above show that Patinkin, in using the term *"disequilibrium,"*
is in fact still envisaging some price rigidity? What other adjustments, apart from changes in prices and effective exchange
values can he be envisaging? How else can the terms "uncer-

[42] *Ibid.,* p. 279.